# Just Passing Through:
## A Memoir

by Phyllis Evans Long

Published by Snag Mountain Cottage Press
Washougal, WA

Editing by Leanne Sype
Interior Formatting by Wendy C. Garfinkle
Cover design by Aaron Smith

*To my grandchildren and great-grandchildren.*
*This is for you.*

# ACKNOWLEDGEMENTS

A special thanks to all my brothers and sisters who made my journey with me: Dorothy Evans Hyle, Adren Evans, Dale Evans, Norma Jean Evans Horst, Betty Evans Patterson, Dwight Evans, Richard Evans, Philip Evans, Charles Evans and Sharon Elaine Evans. Thanks for sharing your memories and your faith that I would finish this. We had a good time. I was the most blessed with supportive, loving brothers and sisters when I needed them the most.

Gratitude and thanksgiving to my loving husband and partner, Kenny, who shared our dreams and adventures together as we trusted in a loving God.

And love and thanks to all my children; Chip Long, Phillip Long, Amber Long Theobald, Grace Long Trask, Drew Long, Tim Long, Eric Long, and Sarah Long Paea, who thrived and survived the adventure.

Life is an adventure and a gift. The one who gives is the one who loves. Thank you to all of my family, living and yet to be born, for being our heritage from God. God is good!

# PREFACE

**HOW IS A FAMILY HISTORY** put together? I have started with parents and grandparents and family history that influenced and shaped my life. Who I am today started with my grandparents and parents. Research on this book took me back to Indian Territory in 1877, that later became the state of Oklahoma, where my Grandma Lucas was born, and involved many visits, emails and phone calls to my six living brothers and sisters. I'm spending this year to bring back to mind and record the life and events of an unusually large and colorful family so the present generation of grandchildren will know from where they have come. This is a gift from one generation to another generation.

Recording and reliving through a century of life, the times of 1901 – 2001, will be in memory and honor of my parents, Adren and Amber Evans, and the one hundred-year anniversary since my mother's birth. My parents left us no estate, but a legacy. Their faith and obedience and trust in God are my legacy. Within this legacy I have found my inheritance and estate – a place with God. This is the year for this book. I have found it to be a journey in self-discovery. I have found out what is important in my life and why.

It has been said that all you can do is give what life is about from your point of view, and that is what I intend to do. I often thought as a child that what I believed and thought was different; not more important, but different. My birth came more than halfway through the long line of eleven children born to my parents, and my viewpoint won't be that of others in my family, but it will be uniquely mine. And my experiences were just a small part of the whole picture.

# Table of Contents

# Chapter 1: Heritage

MY FATHER, ADREN C. EVANS, was born in Crane, Missouri, June 6, 1893. He came from an Evans family that two generations before came to America from Wales in the 1800s during a potato famine. Calvin Evans, my father's great-grandfather, served as a ship's master mechanic on a journey from Wales to America in 1844. In Illinois Calvin Evans found work, then married and raised his family. He became an American citizen and was grateful for his new life. In farming the land, he found opportunities in this country that were absent in Wales. He looked back on his decision to come to America and his long journey on the ship from Wales, pressed by circumstances, as the best decision for his life. But he never forgot his family in Cardiff, Wales.

Calvin Evans had two sons, William and Zebulon. His youngest son, born in 1844, was my great-grandfather. After moving to Kansas, Zebulon and his brother William enlisted and served in Company B of the 12th Regiment of the Kansas Infantry Volunteers in the Civil War from 1862 to 1865. Zebulon also served as an Indian Scout. Zebulon became sick in 1864 with measles, then pneumonia and lung disease. He was also diagnosed with rheumatism. Zebulon was sent to the General Hospital in Little Rock, Arkansas and was later released from the service with a disability.

After leaving the service, Zebulon met and married his wife Martha in 1867, and they raised a family of eight children in Washington, Missouri. After farming for many years he died in 1889 in Crane, Missouri at the early age of forty-five years from complications from his illness during the Civil War. Martha received forty dollars per month as a widow of a Civil War disabled veteran.

Robert, the oldest son of Martha and Zebulon's eight children, and my grandfather, met and married his wife Sarah in Flat Creek, Missouri where they raised their family. My father, Adren, was Robert and Sarah's second son, born in Flatcreek within a large family of three brothers — Sidney, Dewey, and Lawrence — and four sisters — Pearl, Audrey, Martha and Amelia. After many years my Grandfather Robert moved his family to Miami, Oklahoma and bought farming land. My father was a third-generation immigrant from Wales and I am a fourth generation.

Exploring this family connection many years later while visiting England in 1981, I confirmed these roots with a trip to Cardiff, Wales with my two youngest children, Eric and Sarah, and Kenny's mother Grace Long. Although I didn't have the records on Calvin Evans at this time, I knew that the Evans family emigrated from Wales to America. Visiting there we saw the Evans name displayed on many businesses and on posters in the Cardiff Historical Museum. One poster from the 1800s reported with a picture, "Miss Evans would be preaching tonight." My spiritual roots came from many sources.

I felt very much at home in the Welsh countryside as we munched our tomato and cheese sandwiches and rode the fast train from London, whisking us along the tracks through the rolling green hills dotted with black and white Holstein cows. The scenes looked quite familiar to our Kansas farms. The hospitality and friendliness of the people was heart-warming. We ended our visit there celebrating Eric's eleventh birthday with dinner at the much-weathered, centuries-old gray stone Cardiff Castle. That was a birthday party to remember. He thought that was really great.

## The Miami Indian Tribe of Oklahoma

My mother, Amber Lucas, was born in 1901 in Indian Territory that later became Oklahoma. Her mother was Silver Dollar Lucas, my grandmother. My grandmother's mother, Mary Addiline Bourie, a Miami Indian, had run off from the reservation to marry Winchel Theodore Dollar, my great-grandfather and a white man. Silver Dollar Lucas was born in 1877, and received her name because she was born on the day the Miami Indians received their government allotment, paid in silver dollars. My Grandmother married Otho Richard Lucas in 1900, and my mother Amber was born April 20, 1901. She was named after my grandpa's sister, Amber. We have a black and white family picture that has captured Grandpa, who had the nickname of "Doc," and Grandma with sober and intense looks on their faces holding my mother at about two years age and her younger sister Marie on their laps. Oklahoma did not become a state in the Union until August 1907.

The Miami Indians, like all Indians, were treated as foreigners at that time although they were the real Native Americans. I have felt compassion for foreigners who come to America. My grandmother Silver Dollar had a Mohican chief called "The Turtle" as one of her ancestors, and a grandmother who was descended from his daughter, Tacumwah, whose brother was the great Chief of the Miami Indian Tribe called "Little Turtle." The history of the Miami Indian Tribe includes some colorful pictures in the history books. One photo is of Little Turtle at the signing of the Greenville Treaty in 1795, tall, proud, feathered, distinguished and regal looking as the Chief of The Miami Indian Tribe. Whether the picture is realistic or not, he looked pretty distinguished.

Little Turtle represented the many tribes whose land was bought by the U.S. government with the signing of this peace treaty on August 1795 near Fort Wayne, Indiana. At least ten other treaties were signed with the Miami in The Century of Destruction written about in many history books when the Indians were displaced from their tribal lands. Another painting of the Miami Indian Tribe described their forced leave of their homelands when they were shipped down the river. This picture poignantly tells the story of their dispersion. Little Turtle, as leader of an alliance between Miami, Delaware, Shawnee, Chippewa, Potawatomi, and Ottawa Nations, handed General St. Clair one of the worst defeats in U.S. history. In 1787 Congress had passed an ordinance to assure the Indians that: "The utmost good faith shall always be observed towards the Indians. Their lands and property shall never be taken from them without their consent; and in their property, rights and liberty they never shall be invaded or disturbed, unless in just and lawful wars authorized by Congress."

But William Henry Harrison, the governor of Indiana and then later president, one history book reads, obtained the signatures of Indians to treaties through bribery, treachery, and fraud. The total payments made to tribes for this vast territory of Ohio, Illinois, Indiana, Michigan, and Wisconsin that belonged to the tribes, amounted to only about one cent per acre. The Miami Indians with Chief Little Turtle in the picture are Blue Jacket, The Crane, Black Hoof, Leather Lips, Bad Bird, White Pigeon, The Sun and Buckongehles. The government representatives included General Anthony Wayne, William Henry Harrison, William Clark, and Meriweather Lewis, of the famed Lewis and Clark Expedition. Chief Little Turtle was well known for his negotiating skills. Many of my family have this picture hanging in our homes. With Indian names like Nah-We-Lanh-Quah, Ma-Cat-A-Chin-Quah, Lan-A-Pin-Chah and So Ne-Lan-Gish-Eah and Won-Sop-E-Ah in our family line up, we knew that our Grandma Lucas was pretty unique.

A background history shows that:

The Miami Indians, an Algonquian tribe, were first found in the Green Bay, Wisconsin area in the mid-17th century, and shortly after that, migrated to the region around the southern end of Lake Michigan. They had a well-organized political structure, based on the clan system. Each person inherited the clan of his father and was forbidden to marry within his own clan. Each village had a council made up of the chiefs of the various clans. The council elected one of their number as village chief. Delegates were sent from each village council to the band council, which in turn sent delegates to the tribal council. Clan, village, band and tribal chiefs were all chosen on the basis of merit and enjoyed a great deal of respect and authority. Along with other Algonquian tribes in the region, the Miami had a Midewiwin or Grand Medicine Society made up of priests who had special magical powers for curing. Lesser shamans also cured with the aid of medicinal roots and herbs. The sun was the supreme deity and "master of life" for the Miami, although lesser spirits or manito were also important.

Miami were befriended by both the English and French and fought with the English in the American War for Independence and the American War of 1812. There was intermarrying with the French. By 1827, most of their lands had been taken from them and some of the Miami began moving to Kansas. After the Civil War the various bands in Kansas moved to the Quapaw Reservation in Indian Territory (now Oklahoma). Grandmother Silver Dollar is on the Western Miami Indian Roll of 1891 that I have a copy of, at the age of twelve years. My mother is on my copy of the Official Miami Indian Roll of 1938, and she made sure that each one of her children were also enrolled in the tribe as they joined our family. We were often told that someday this would be to our advantage because the government had taken our land from us. And I believed it.

I was proud of my Indian heritage, although it was unpopular, and I believed our mother, even though relatives often joked and said that we would never get a dime from the government. I grew up thinking that the Indians had really owned the country and had been treated shamefully, but the government now owned it. My mother was proved right when in 1966 this was validated and all the grandchildren and great-grandchildren of Silver Dollar Lucas born at this time, descended from Chief Little Turtle, received their share of a government settlement. There were more judgments awarded in 1969 and 1977. This was put in a trust for minors, and my children used this Indian inheritance for college. In the late 1970s, more than 1,200 Miami descendants were registered on Tribal Rolls in Oklahoma.

Included in this tribal roll were the ten living children of my mother, twenty-five grandchildren and eight great-grandchildren in our family. The present numbered descendants are 2,387 and those from my mother on the Miami Tribal Roll has doubled. The Oklahoma Miami had been in the past and continues to be represented by an active tribal organization. I attended some of these tribal meetings, and I have passed on to my children my knowledge of their Indian heritage. Our teenage daughter, Amber, named after her Grandmother Amber, served as Tribal Princess at one of our yearly meetings in Miami, Oklahoma. She sewed a traditional Miami Indian Tribal Dress, decorated with Indian silver and turquoise jewelry, to perform the Lord's Prayer in Indian sign language.

The Second Miami Nation Pow Wow was in June 2001. The Miami Tribe has a newspaper published quarterly and encourages tribal members to become educated on tribal matters. College scholarships are awarded to tribal members and special consideration given to those who attend Miami University in Oxford, Ohio, which is named after the Miamis and located in the area of the original Miami Indian Tribal Lands.

Before 1854, Kansas was known as Indian land. My mother and father met as teenagers on their family farms near Miami, Oklahoma. My father's family, the Robert Evans family, and my mother's family, the Otho Lucas family were farmers and neighbors. My Aunt Mary Mae tells of my father coming home from the fields each day past the Lucas family home, and seeing the six girls out on their front porch. His remark was, "I am going to marry that girl someday" as he looked at my mother. I don't know what kind of looks my mother gave him, but my father's determination and optimism carried through to his yet unborn children. We have a picture of my father working on a sawmill as a young man.

In 1917, when my father joined the other two hundred-fifty thousand men in the U.S. Regular army to serve in the Army Infantry in World War I, he was sent to Camp Travis, Texas, and my mother and he wrote to each other. My father wrote on a postcard that he was "fine and dandy." We have a family portrait of him taken at that time sitting tall and straight and handsome in his full uniform. His vocation was listed as farming on his discharge papers in March 1919 when he was discharged as a sergeant. Later in college at Kansas State University I used a copy of these discharge papers of Pop's to obtain a Laverne-Noyes Scholarship, available for descendants of World War I veterans. This paid my tuition cost each semester until I graduated from college. I was always grateful for that privilege.

# Chapter 2: A Taste of Home

MY FATHER RETURNED HOME from the war, and since he had grown up as a farmer he continued to farm. He also married that beautiful girl on the neighbor's front porch that he greatly admired. Adren C. Evans and Amber Lucas were joined in matrimony on August 21, 1919, and they were both from Miami, Oklahoma. Mom was eighteen years and Pop was twenty-six years old. Eighty years later in researching family history, my niece Brooke Eastburn obtained the original copy of their marriage license and certificate from the courthouse in Miami, Oklahoma because they had forgotten to pick it up. After all, it was just a piece of paper and I guess they had more important things on their minds.

Their wedding picture vividly captures their happiness as they stand side by side in front of a white frame house. Mom is wearing a long dress leaning to one side laughing. Pop, a broad-shouldered man of six-feet plus a few inches, is beaming beside his bride wearing a bow tie and showing the white brow of his suntanned face where jaunty brimmed hat usually rested upon his forehead.

They started out their married life doing what was familiar to them, what they already knew to do. While farming in Oklahoma, they had Dorothy in 1920 when mom was nineteen years old, and then Adren was born in 1922 in Miami, Oklahoma. They had their third child, Dale, in 1924 in Chetopa, Kansas. Mom and Pop moved to Hilltop, Kansas from Chetopa around 1924 –1925 to try farming there.

Having a young family and wanting to try something different, they struck out on their own and drove to Madison, Kansas about 1925 to work for the Empire Oil Company, which later became the Cities Service Oil Company. By 1925 Kansas was producing an average of

32,733,000 barrels of crude oil per year of the nation's total of 647,961,000 barrels. Crude petroleum was selling for about $1.50 a barrel; one barrel contained 42 gallons of oil. Pop was a pumper and operated the powerhouse that ran the oil wells.

Mom and Pop drove to Madison, Kansas in a single-seat, shiny black Ford in 1925 with three small children and all their worldly goods. I have often thought of their optimism, sense of hope and adventure, and confidence in their future they must have had as they left their families. I am reminded of the quote by Helen Keller, "Life is either a daring adventure or nothing." Although Pop grew up a farmer and tried farming, he decided the oilfields were where the action was. Oil had been discovered in Kansas in the late 1800s, but commercial production started in 1900. They arrived in Madison in a 1925 Model T Ford with Pop driving and my mother in the only passenger seat. My oldest sister Dorothy, about five years old, sat on a wooden box at my mother's feet. My oldest brother Adren, three years old, sat between the seats, and Baby Dale sat on Mom's lap. There were 3,871,000 passenger cars sold that year in the entire country. In Kansas there were 457,000 motor vehicle registrations in 1925.

Living in Madison for a short while on Dutch Hollow Road, they eventually rented a house out of town on the Kipfer Lease. The house was down a deeply rutted oil road through the pasture and across a cattle guard. Their house was called a "shotgun" style home because the rooms were in a straight line and you could see right through it. The house had one bedroom with a living, dining room, front porch, and screened in porch off the kitchen, and was right next to an oil well in 1926. This would be their home for the longest time in their marriage, over ten years, and was the birthplace for many more children.

The house was versatile and portable. It was even picked up and moved to a new location while we were living in it. The house was situated next to the power station that moved the oil wells up and down where Pop was in charge. The oil well right beside our house blew black rain down upon the house when the oil came in. My parents and siblings left the house and stood looking down from a hilltop as the oil shot up and rained down, spattering the house and everything else with black rain. This incident surprised them all, and the house had to be cleaned and washed off. Before school age my sister also remembers playing in the dirt beside the house with her brother near the gas pipe that came off of the well. One day she was overcome with gas and woke up lying on her back on the ground with a crowd of people surrounding her. My parents decided the house was too close to the well and moved the house to another location.

My oldest sister has the most vivid memories of those days, since she was six years old and had started first grade in Madison, their first year living there. She remembers her little brother, Adren, two years younger, visiting her at school and feeling proud to introduce him to her class. They carried their lunch in lard buckets to school each day.

The Verdigris River ran close by with swinging bridges. These bridges provided a thrill and adventure to cross the river for us children. I remember crossing these bridges when I was older and living in Zaire, Africa now called the Congo again. Sarah my youngest daughter and I were crossing a raging river on a swinging rope bridge near the Uganda border, and the swinging bridges of the Verdigris River came to my mind. The Verdigris River also provided motivation and opportunities for my oldest brother Adren to attempt boat making out of corrugated tin and blocks of wood at the age of eight years old. His older

sister was skeptical about his efforts but later attempts at
building boats were better and some even floated.

In 1942 Adren joined the Navy and served on a
Destroyer, the *US S Woodward* in the South Pacific in World
War II, which must have satisfied his attempts at being on a
ship. Instead of cruising the Verdigris River, he traveled the
Panama Canal, Okinawa, Guam, Hawaii, Philippine Islands,
Formosa, Kuadalin, Palau, and Ulithi territory. During that
time submarine nets were strung from island to island, and
two Japanese midget submarines were caught and sunk
while he was in port. He ended up in Tokyo Bay after the
Japanese surrendered, and where the Peace Treaty with
Japan was signed on the Battleship Missouri. It has been
found that there are a disproportionate number of men from
Kansas in the Navy; they like to see the horizon as they did
in Kansas. Childhood fantasies and pastimes often give a
window into adult choices later in life.

The older boys spent much of their time on the banks
of the Verdigris River fishing for catfish, swinging on ropes
over the river, and jumping in to swim. One afternoon
fishing trip ended unexpectedly when my oldest brother
Adren caught the earlobe of his younger brother Dale
instead of a catfish. They both walked half a mile hooked up
like this until they could reach home and have Pop remove
the hook from Dale's ear. My older sister Betty said a
favorite pastime was to play near the pumping wells and
stand on the low rod lines that moved back and forth to see
if they could keep their balance. The high rod lines provided
opportunities for all kinds of swinging and tricks. There was
a sludge pond behind the barn that the cows sometimes
wandered into and had to be pulled out. Dale's Billy goat
climbed on cars and ate the clothes on the clothesline, so
Dale had to walk him back to the previous owner. There
was burgeoning plant, insect and wildlife for the children to
explore. Sheep shire plants, gooseberry bushes with bitter-

sour small light green berries, and wild strawberry plants; paw-paw trees with fruit similar to a mango and with black seeds, provided a wealth of different tastes to a child's curiosity and imagination. My enterprising sister Betty said that she looked for spider holes in the ground and enjoyed filling them with water and watching the spiders float up to the top and out. Left to devices of their own for entertainment the children became very creative.

Pop often shot squirrels to add to the family food supply and the children helped in cleaning the squirrels. In 1926 milk was fourteen cents a quart delivered to your door in the city and coffee was fifty cents a pound. The U.S. census population was 119,682,000 in 1928 and 1,862,000 in Kansas. My oldest brother got his first Remington Rifle for Christmas in 1933 and turned from fishing to hunting in the winter shooting squirrel and rabbit for Mom to fry.

Norma Jean, Dwight, Betty, Richard, and Philip and I were born at our house on the Kipfer Lease. When I asked which house had Philip and I had been born in, I got three different answers from older brothers and sisters. This was narrowed down to a vote of two for the same house that was the birthplace of four of our siblings. The question was whether we were born before or after a move to a different house. As these births were all in our home, the older children were sent to the house of our nearby Aunt Pearl who ran a boarding house the men who worked on the pipelines, also known as pipeliners. Pop readied the house for the arriving doctor. My sister Norma Jean arrived in 1926, my sister Betty in 1928, my brother Dwight in 1931 and my brother Richard in 1933. Three girls and four boys had made their way into our family.

Not only did the oil well produce abundantly but our family was also very productive. January seemed to be the most popular month in our family since all four of my older brothers — Adren, Dale, Dwight, and Richard — had

January birthdays also. It was Monday, January 28, 1935, when the birth of twins was signaled by one high-pitched cry and a second cry that was lower-pitched. I had a head start by a few minutes on my twin brother Philip, which I reminded my brother when we were teenagers. The news of two births was suddenly upon the family. Twins were unexpected, and my oldest sister Dorothy remembered echoing "twins!" when they first received the news over the telephone.

One of the 17,000,000 telephones in the Bell system in the U.S. at this time was placed prominently on the wall of our home, and our birth was announced on this telephone to all relatives and friends. More country people had telephones than those who lived in towns. We were the eighth and ninth children born to this eleven-member Evans family and our birth did nothing to change the balance of the sexes. Born female twenty-five years before the 1960s, I did not buy into the commonly accepted culture of "it's a man's world" and considered myself equal to all those born before and after me in "my world." As a twin I reasoned that I must have had to fight for my space in my mother's womb as a matter of survival. Biologically I was born a survivor. My oldest brother Adren was just hoping for one baby, being very experienced by now in birthing times and had noticed added size to the girth of his Mom. He was beginning to add up the numbers. We were both a good seven pounds. I was blond and Philip had black hair. When Mom woke up the next day on January 29, 1935, I wonder what she was thinking when she had two hungry newborns instead of one at her breast. I think I can pretty well guess her sentiments.

In later years I heard my relatives complaining about the depression back then, but I never heard my parents complain about getting twins in 1935 instead of one baby. During the depression milk had gone down to eleven cents a quart, and coffee to twenty-five cents a pound. Pop was earning around twenty-eight dollars a week in 1935, supporting our family of nine children by working in the production of crude petroleum for Cities Service Oil Company.

My twin brother Philip and I shared a large iron-rail baby bed that was painted white in Mom and Pop's bedroom. I don't ever remember sleeping alone until I was a teenager. My brother Richard, two years older, remembers Mom holding both of us in her arms at this house. Although we both looked chubby, Philip gained a few pounds on me in size. He showed distinct broad shoulders in our six-month-old picture, wearing pretty white dresses with matching crocheted booties sitting on a fancy velvet chair at the photographer's studio. My straight blond hair was curled on top and Philip's black hair sported a neatly straight right-side part. As fraternal twins coming from separate eggs we just looked like brothers and sisters.

By one year of age I had developed a problem with a possible thyroid condition needing surgery, and Mom and I spent a few days in the nearest hospital in Emporia, Kansas, where my oldest sister, Dorothy would later attend college. Since food was a high priority in our family, my father told my mother to teach Dorothy how to make biscuits before we left for the hospital, since Mom would be absent due to my surgery. I came home from the hospital with a drainage tube in my neck, which left a small scar. Life was too busy to talk about an illness, and no one really knew what kind of surgery I had and it was never recorded in my health history. I also had scarlet fever as an infant and was told that I was very sick. My mother nursed her family of nine children, later to become eleven, through measles, mumps, rheumatic fever, scarlet fever, sore throats, ear infections and childhood accidents, with the technology and medicines of the 1920s and 1930s, which would have rivaled Florence

Nightingale at her best. I grew up active and healthy, but skinny with a smaller frame than Philip. I was happy with this body I had inherited and competed with Philip in everything.

Our parents never owned land, never owned a house, but accepted what they had and found their joy in life and in their growing family. Our parents worked hard, but they also knew how to enjoy life. Dorothy remembered exciting times with square dances being held on Saturday nights at our house. The chairs would be pushed back and rugs rolled up to make room for lots of dancing; Pop would play on his harmonica while his friend played the fiddle.

More oil wells were drilled and produced in Kansas. By 1937 there were 21,850 producing wells in Kansas, and in 1938, 1,108 more oil wells were drilled. Later when I was in grade school, I asked Pop to help me on a school report that I wrote on the beginning of oil production in Kansas. After supper one night when he had finished reading the paper, I perched on the arm of his special old brown overstuffed chair in the living room where he always sat to read. While he put on his glasses I found the K through L of our dark green-bound World Book Encyclopedias with gold letters, and we looked up and read about oil production in Kansas. I was pretty special to have this time with Pop when I knew that he always read the paper and listened to the news on the radio each night. I thought he enjoyed learning things that he had never known. Since he had worked in the production of oil for a long time, he seemed interested.

Pop was never out of work during the depression and even had a younger brother Uncle Lawrence visit and stay with us for a short while. We grew up with a sense of security and knowledge of being loved and provided for within a large and extended family of grandparents, uncles, aunts and cousins. When there were discussions on whether the oldest would take violin lessons at school, Pop said we did not take anything we couldn't pay for. However it was settled, Mom prevailed about lessons and we had a beginning eighth grade violinist in the family.

My mother Amber was the oldest of six girls in the Lucas family, and we had visits from her younger sisters. Mom wrote her family names in her Bible, Amber, Marie, Katharine, Lucille, Mary Mae and Edna. A young infant brother Joseph had died in 1905. A picture of my mother and three of her Indian-looking young sisters now sits on my bedroom bureau.

The same year Joseph died was also the year that my Grandma Silver Dollar Lucas signed a petition on behalf of the Miami Indians requesting Congress to lift the restrictions on their two-hundred-acre allotments of land that they had received in 1889 in an act approved by the U.S. Congress. They were asking: "that all restrictions upon our allotted lands to be removed, to the end that we may sell, exchange, mortgage or devise our said lands with the same freedom allowed to other people." The tribe felt that these restrictions were a great injustice to them as citizens of the United States. The Miami Tribe stated in this petition: "they had lived among civilized people for more than half a century and believed that they were fully competent to manage their own affairs. They wanted to be treated as other citizens of the United States and to enjoy the same liberties and freedom guaranteed to and enjoyed by its citizens under its Constitution." This is a part of the injustices of history.

I remember visits in my aunts' homes as a child and playing with cousins at family reunions. We picked blackberries at Aunt Kate's and had to keep our arms and legs covered to avoid getting scratches. And we checked each other's hair for ticks when we finished. Uncle Tom, Aunt Kate's husband, had lost a leg in a mine accident as a young man of nineteen years old. In attempting to set the dynamite down in the mine to loosen the ground, it blew up and badly damaged both legs and his eyes; one leg was removed. It was a tragic accident since he had used a jackhammer without knowing that someone had already put in the dynamite. He had a wooden leg up to his hip and was left blind. Aunt Kate married Tom after the accident and they ran a dairy farm. Later he was sent to the Mayo Clinic for a possible eye transplant, but he never got one. I had never seen a wooden leg before, and I was very curious but too shy to ask him about it. He managed very well although he couldn't do heavy work.

Dorothy remembers being the oldest grandchild of the Lucas family and a pretty crocheted yoke on a dress that an aunt in the Evans family had made for her. She still has that crocheted dress. Mom's youngest sister was close to the same age as her first child. One summer two Lucas aunts stayed in our home and everyone played softball games. These aunts all laughed and talked just as my sisters and I do now when we get together.

During the depression there were times when a dime for the movies and a new dress for school were not available. There was a lack of everything for most families. That's just the way things were. Since our parents were good managers, we did not suffer as others who felt deprived or poor and learned how to work.

Pop owned a succession of cars since transportation for work and school was a high priority. There was a Ford, Studebaker, Pontiac and then a brand new 1937 Chevrolet bought for $600 cash with his bonus money from serving in the infantry in World War I. The published reports for passenger car factory sales in the U.S. were up to 4,000,000 in 1937, and there were 570,000 motor vehicle registrations in Kansas that year. A family of nine children driving a new 1937 Chevrolet and Pop paying for it with $600 cash was astounding for people who knew us.

The memories of our living on the Kipfer Lease reach until probably 1936. Then we moved to the Kellison Place, one and a half miles west of Madison on the main gravel road. The children rode the school bus to school and some cousins lived close by. My oldest brother remembered carrying Pops' lunch to the power station at noon. We lived here for only a short while before moving on to the Boles Place. An inside bathroom distinguished this house. There was no inside toilet, but we had our first tub and bathroom sink. The outhouse was a standard fixture for most farm homes.

This home was larger for our growing family and all the family remembers it as a very nice wooden white painted modern house. Betty remembers having measles and staying in her dark room here with the window shades drawn, the standard treatment for measles at this time. And it was summer time. Mom asked Betty what she wanted to eat and Betty chose strawberry shortcake, her favorite. Dorothy, the oldest of all nine of us siblings, had a room of her own, and she also learned to drive our Studebaker car while we lived in the Kellison Place.

We lived one-quarter mile from a country schoolhouse that was adjacent to a cemetery. The combination of schoolhouse and cemetery provided the children with many good jokes and scary stories. My sister Betty, who was six years older than me, and Dwight, who was four years older, started first grade here at District 8 School. The community held a little event called Box Suppers. These were social occasions where the neighborhood met together and the girls made suppers put into a cardboard box and auctioned off at the evening event. Whoever bought your box was your date for the evening as you sat and ate supper together. No one was left alone and the best cooks got to shine. This custom was a matchmaker's invention of that time.

In 1937 we moved to another pretty, white, and modern house call the Freeman Place. This home had a full bathroom. This was the year that Pop bought our first brand new buffalo-brown Chevrolet. This car served as our family's main means of transportation and suffered through a number of us children's efforts to learn how to drive. This car accumulated many fender benders, dents and scrapes during the next eleven years. It even had its doors knocked off and reattached many times. My oldest brother learned to drive on Grandpa Evans' Model T Ford pickup, but the rest of us learned to drive on the brown 1937 Chevrolet.

There was a shortage of gasoline during the war, but oil field workers collected casinhead, which was the drip from the oil wells in the winter when the water would freeze. Casinhead was a high-octane gasoline before it was refined. There was a ready supply for those who collected this off the wells for their own use. We always had our own gas storage tank to fill up as needed and kept it in the garage or barn.

Dorothy as the oldest child and a teenager was the children's chauffeur since Mom never learned to drive. She drove our car on illegal gas and with no drivers' license, often with five or six children in the back seat. Backing into the garage, she knocked off the two back doors of the new 1937 Chevrolet. My sister Betty says that we were told to keep the kittens out of the driveway because Dorothy reduced our cat population while learning to drive. My oldest brother Adren also remembers knocking the doors off the same car. But I think Dale must have won the prize knocking off the most doors of the brown Chevrolet. While driving into the garage he knocked off the two front doors that were open, and then, realizing his mistake, he put it into reverse to knock off the two back doors.

My brother Charlie, two years younger than Philip and me, was born at the end of 1937 while we lived in the

Freeman Place. I was beginning to be hemmed in on all sides with boys. There was Richard two years older, Philip my womb mate, and now Charlie two years younger. I learned early that you had to be heard in order to be recognized. My twin brother Philip remembers catching fish in the river, but I don't have any memories here.

My brother Dwight brought back our black, white and tan mixed-breed, long- haired family dog that we named Fritz from a neighbor's house. Fritz stayed with us for thirteen years. He went everywhere with us and was much loved by us all, another member of the family. He got cranky in his old age and killed some of my favorite kittens. Pop punished Fritz by kicking him, and I once threatened to run away from because I felt so sorry for the cats . . . or the dog, I don't remember which one.

This year had its joys and sorrows when Dwight lost the tip of his finger in a windmill that pumped water for the cattle. That was enough excitement for the whole family to remember. We all have our own versions of the story, but Dwight got the prize for the worst accident to date. Although average in childhood accidents with a family of ten children, this was the first accident with permanent damage. He had no nail on that finger and we often asked him to tell us about it. Later Dwight lost some hearing in one ear from mastoiditis, an ear infection involving the mastoid bone.

Other accidents we had included my brother Dale who cut his hand with a knife while carving a willow tree to make a whistle. It left a deep scar on one hand. Another time, Dale rode a neighbor's racehorse and fell off. All the children carried him back to the house, one leg and one arm each, but he no broken bones.

My Granddad Robert Evans also came to live with us in the Freeman house. That put the three oldest girls in one room, while Granddad Evans had a room of his own.

He taught my oldest brother how to make rabbit traps. Granddad Evans visited all his children in the area and later became very ill. He had traveled from his home in Hollywood, California where he lived with his second wife, Cora, after his first wife, Sarah Evans, had died. While he was very ill his daughters kept him in Madison where he died, and he was buried in Crane, Missouri next to his first wife Sarah and the mother of his children. This was a family decision, and he never returned to California alive or dead.

Many of Pop's sisters and brothers had followed him to Kansas and lived in the area. During this time Madison was a thriving town of 3,000 people. Pop and some uncles gathered to butcher hogs in our garage, cutting their throats, stringing up the carcass to drain the blood, and watching the entrails pour into a metal wash tub. I hated seeing all the blood and couldn't understand how they could laugh and kill those pigs. Cracklins were baked in the oven from the hog skin, and Mom even cooked the pigs' brains.

The Verdigris River ran close by, and a railroad track nearby led to the small town of Madison, where we attended school and church. My older brother Adren remembers walking down that train track to get home from track and football practice after high school. All the high school kids were on the honor roll. Dorothy set a high standard for grades in school that her younger brother said made it tough to follow. Dorothy also sang solo in operettas.

She had started dating Bud Hyle in Madison during high school and Bud often drove out to our house to see her in his black Model T Ford. Norma Jean and Betty used to sit at the top of the stairs to spy on their conversations and dancing in the living room. Bud would later say that he had to marry Dorothy to get her alone. Everywhere she went she was surrounded with brothers and sisters. They graduated from high school in Madison, went off to different colleges, and met again during the war to marry in 1944. They were in different branches of the service, so they had to live separately until after the war.

Living in the country with so much personal freedom and few scheduled events, we all made up our own entertainment, roamed the countryside, picked wild strawberries, read books, fished and swam in the rivers or tried to build boats or rode horses. The dark side of having all these children making up their own entertainment was when one decided to chase his brother around the barnyard with a pitchfork, or a brother that enjoyed chasing his little sister around the house just to hear her cry. There were limits and everyone felt free to complain. When justice was needed our parents administered it swiftly. Our parents had a positive and cheerful outlook on life and did not complain about the hardships. I think that they had learned to practice "an attitude of gratitude" in their Christian lives. That was evident in the way that they lived. I don't ever remember them complaining much about anything except the way we kids would often argue and fight with one another to entertain ourselves. Our negotiating and competition got very loud and vocal. We made what was to be our last move as a family in 1939 to the Sheets Place near Madison.

My youngest sister Sharon and the eleventh child in our family, born in 1939 when Mom was thirty-eight years old, was born in Emporia, Kansas at the Newman Hospital. Dorothy had started her freshman year at Emporia State College that year and walked twelve blocks to the hospital to visit Mom and her new sister. My father had stopped by her dormitory to leave a note and asked her to go visit her mother. He was busy with his job and the children at home. Philip and I were four years old when we moved to the Sheets Place southwest of Madison.

Our closest older brother Richard started grade school here and Philip and I followed him two years later. Richard said that he wore overalls to school but always had a new pair of shoes to start school. My sister Betty sang in operettas and said that they performed in the Madison theatre. She remembers one performance of Alexander's Ragtime Band. She also ran track in school and was quick in the fifty-yard dash. My brother Dale played the clarinet in the band and orchestra.

My first childhood memories were of walking around the Sheets Place with Pop and Philip. We found a black umbrella that was broken and I was fascinated by how it opened and closed. I remember asking to keep it and thinking what an interesting place this was and what adventures must be ahead for us. We had one-hundred-sixty-acres here with our house, barn, smokehouse, chicken house, outhouse and red shed, where we farmed and explored. Most of my childhood memories are here. My youngest sister remembers growing up in this house and thought it was beautiful. The old pictures show an attractive two-story, white farmhouse with a front porch and large yard surrounded by cedar trees and white flowering spirea bushes. We had a gravel driveway at the side of the house that was lined with cedar trees, many iris, and other flowers on both sides.

Our Indian heritage was reinforced each summer with visits to Chetopa, Kansas with our Grandma Lucas to see our cousins. These relatives all looked more like Indians. We had fish fries on the river; the "eat all you want" freshly caught and cleaned fish, cooked right there by the river, was tender, sweet and delicious, probably similar to the fish fries of our Indian ancestors of long ago. Chetopa was very small, and staying with Grandma Lucas in town was a treat for country kids as we got to walk around Chetopa. The drinking water didn't taste good. It had a metal taste of iron and left a brownish tint on everyone's teeth that lived there. I did not know at the time it was the water staining people's teeth; I just thought those relatives were born that way.

I was always amazed to think of Mom as having once been a child, and I noticed all the laughing and good times she had with her mother. This made me feel happy and secure. I loved to come here and looked forward to it each year. Grandma Lucas even told Mom what to do as they prepared our meals together. Grandma Lucas was definitely in charge. There was happiness here, and I could see how much my mother enjoyed it. We went to Grandma's church that was very lively and had a lot of action during the service. I took it all in and enjoyed the enthusiasm of the singing. Money was not talked about and problems were minimized as they just enjoyed being together. I began to see my mother in a different way, as a person before I knew her. My world was enlarged.

When my youngest sister was about three years old, we had our first and only family picture taken at a studio in Emporia, Kansas. Philip and I were seven years old. This was about a thirty-minute drive from our house near Madison. Maybe this was in 1942, before all the older kids departed for the war. I remember that it was very late at night and it was difficult getting all thirteen members of our family all together in one place. But it happened and everyone was awake. The results were really a miracle. Mom and Pop look like the proud parents of eleven handsome children.

My youngest sister wore a red and white and black checked dress. I wore a light blue sailor dress that Mom had made for me. All the boys were dressed in suits or sport coats and white shirts. I was chewing gum and the photographer told me to take the gum out of my mouth. I did and held it in my hand, switching the gum back and forth from hand to sweaty hand until it eventually got stuck to the front of my dress during that long time of trying unsuccessfully to get everyone to smile and look in the right direction. It was my favorite dress, and I was pretty upset about getting gum stuck to the front. This picture has been hanging in all our families' homes, children and grandchildren, reminding me of that long night of torture. It was a solemn occasion so not many of us are smiling. I wanted to go to sleep very much. But even so, this photo attested to the fact that we were a happy family together and this one time we were all together in one place to record it for posterity.

There was also Evans family reunions at our home or at the homes of other aunts and uncles in Madison, and sometimes at parks where all the cousins gathered around big shiny metal wash tubs with ice and pop for the kids. We drank soda pop to our hearts' content and had so many different choices. Strawberry, orange, grape and root beer; it was really hard to make a decision. And we were always told how much we had grown from the last year. I had very few girl cousins and so many boy cousins I never kept track. The adults played horseshoes, tossed balls, played croquet and just laughed and visited with each other, everyone so glad to see each other. It was fun to get lost in the crowd of so many cousins.

At one of these gatherings I stood too close behind an older boy cousin and received a blow on the head with the flat back of an ax while he was chopping wood. It was not enough of a blow to cause much damage, but I still have the dent in my skull. There was no blood and it didn't knock me out, but it caused a little concern.

We felt a lot of freedom to just be children and play. We also chipped the blocks of ice, ate it and threw it at each other. We ran and played so hard that I always fell asleep in the car on the way home. My brother Richard remembers "there was homemade ice cream made with lots of cream you could scrape the butterfat off the roof of your mouth it was so good."

Growing up in the country we had simple and questionable pleasures. The boys went on coyote roundups with the men and learned to hunt and trap. They also worked in neighbors' fields shocking milo for fifty cents a day. We usually fed it to the chickens. They tried smoking the corn silk. We tried popping the dark brown corn kernels, and they would pop tiny white puffs of popped corn to eat. We also chewed the raw wheat stored in the feed barrels in the barn and made our own gum from it. It stayed together in a sticky gray lump in our mouths and we pretended it was wheat gum. I hate to think how many rats also enjoyed eating from those barrels.

My favorite time was Saturday night when Mom cooked hamburgers for supper and we went to the movies in Madison. There was the least amount of dishes to wash for us, and we could get an early start to town for the show. We quickly got the evening chores done and dressed in our favorite clothes anticipating the evening. Saturday night supper was a happy event and twenty hamburgers were probably the least Mom ever cooked. She made her own bread and hamburger buns and cooked the beef from our own steers. Mom canned many jars of delicious, light green salty dill pickles with a twig of pickling spice, and she always had small bright green sweet pickles on the table. I think I was addicted to sweet pickles. Ketchup, mustard, mayonnaise, pickles, lettuce, tomatoes, cheese, onions, all made the perfect hamburger. Our family's Saturday night hamburgers made today's McDonald's burgers look like a pale substitute. A homemade burger was a burger at its finest, and it has always been my favorite food. Today when I really get hungry, especially while living in many different parts of the world, I think about a good hamburger and remember those Saturday nights.

Mom also made delicious cinnamon rolls that we all loved. My youngest sister remembers getting the raw dough from the ends of the cinnamon rolls before they were cooked. She'd sit at the kitchen table waiting and watching for this special treat. Mom sliced the long rolls of dough sprinkled on the inside with lots of butter and cinnamon and sugar. I often got to help her put the rolls on greased pans to rise and bake later. We all loved the raised doughnuts that she also often made. I got to use a thimble dipped in flour to cut out the centers. And I sometimes ate the raw dough. The smell of these doughnuts cooking brought everyone into the kitchen wherever they were. My sisters dipped them in the sugar glaze after they were cooked which made these doughnuts mouthwatering.

Each of us had our favorite foods that Mom made. My sister Betty said her favorite dinner was navy or brown beans cooked with our own cured ham, fried potatoes and cornbread. Her favorite food was corn, on or off the cob, and peaches, fresh or canned. She also adored Mom's biscuits left in the oven after it had been turned off and they became crispy. My brother Richard's favorite meal was mashed potatoes, chicken and roasting ears.

We all remember the leftover ground roast mixed with cold cooked oatmeal, mayonnaise, and sweet pickles that we took on our sandwiches with lettuce from the garden for school lunches. Mom called it mock chicken. I remember grinding it in the iron hand grinder attached to the kitchen table and eating it as I ground away. My brother Dale told a story of trading his steak sandwich with a friend at school for a bologna sandwich since bologna was bought at the store and seemed such a treat. Steak was always available.

We had a huge kitchen table and everyone usually sat in the same place. It needed to accommodate at least ten to thirteen people, and was usually covered with a colorful but worn oilcloth tablecloth. Our table was also used to roll out pie crust and to hold the work of canning. I'm sure that we had a motley assortment of kitchen chairs, mine being painted white. And if I sat in it long enough, I usually managed to peel off some white paint. I remember sitting to Mom's left at one end. I was her kitchen helper and could get up and get anything that was needed after the meal was started.

We preceded each meal with a prayer of grace and thanksgiving. Eating was serious business, and Pop did not tolerate any messing around. One evening, though, he must have been finished and left the table because we molded small balls of mashed potatoes in our hands and threw them at each other. We never went hungry for sure. My youngest sister said that there was so much talking going on that she never got to talk.

We had soft-green crockery bowl that was a standard fixture for every meal on our kitchen table. It held mashed potatoes or potato salad when Mom took food to our church suppers or family reunions. We knew to look for the soft-green crockery bowl to find Mom's potato salad among the assortment of strange food dishes on the tables. We just assumed the other dishes at the potlucks were inferior to our mother's creations. Her creativity on behalf of her brood knew no bounds; she decorated her potato salad with a little beet juice for color and daisies arranged on top made from hard-boiled eggs with the yellow centers and white petals. We knew that whatever was in the soft-green crockery bowl was a taste of home. This bowl lasted through the years and now adorns the table of one of my daughters. Since the bowl is still around after lasting through thirteen members of our family, my older sister's family, ten members of my own family and now serves nine more members of my daughter's family, it is one of those childhood memories that brings back our family dinners. If a crockery bowl could talk what a family history it could tell!

The kitchen pantry was another story. It was a small room off the kitchen with the door kept closed, and our food was stored on shelves or bushel baskets or in large earthenware jars. The pantry is where bushel baskets of fruit for our school lunches were stored, and the large cloth-covered containers of bright-green sweet pickles and salty, dull-green dill pickles brewed in the lime until they were ready to eat. It was so hard to keep my fingers out of the sweet pickles! There were one-hundred-pound sacks of flour or sugar that we bought at the Farmers Co-op. There were stacks of cardboard egg cartons that we filled as we gathered eggs every morning. I especially remember trying to get the small feathers off the eggs before putting them into the cartons. We also stored large, glass gallon-jars of milk with smaller blue glass quart-jars of cream to keep cool until we took them to Madison to sell.

The pantry was a jumble of mysterious containers that I never learned to decipher. The shelves had all the spices and flavorings, baking soda, cornstarch, baking powder and salt. I learned at an early age that baking chocolate was very bitter to eat, but the grated coconut was delicious. Mom used coconut in her coconut sweet rolls that were so good and a family favorite. She always made tapioca from what looked to me like a box of white pearls on the shelf. It always felt cool inside the pantry and the mice loved it. We always had several mice traps set, and when one was caught, I could never empty it.

Mom raised chickens and sold eggs so that we could have an allowance of twenty-five cents each, which was given out as a quarter every Saturday night. This was the big event of the week. Everyone had their choice of spending their quarter at the movies. A movie was ten cents and popcorn and ice cream was a nickel. Our Sunday school offering also came out of this quarter. While we kids attended the local movie theatre, Mom and Pop stocked up on groceries at the Farmers Co-op. Then they sat in or on their cars, depending on the weather, to visit with all their farmer friends who came to town on Saturday night with their families. Everyone caught up on all the gossip and events in this small town, and we would have new things to talk about at the supper table until next Saturday night.

On Saturday nights no one stayed at home from the movies because it was our family night out. But as the high school kids got older, they enjoyed staying home to listen to "The Hit Parade" on the radio and pop popcorn. The radio was a large floor-standing Philco that had push-button dials, and it sat in the center of our living room near Pop's chair. Having the house to themselves was a rare occasion.

The Farmers Co-op was a huge room with open shelves and everything a farmer would need from mayonnaise, sugar, and flour to work gloves, fly swatters, worm medicine and mouse traps. We also had a compartment in the walk-in cold storage freezer where we kept our slaughtered and packaged meat. It was always so cold in there, and I would never go in by myself, thinking the door would close on me and I would end up as frozen as the meat.

Pop always paid his Farmers Co-op bill once a month, and it was a treat to go to town with him. He usually just took one or two kids at a time and treated us to a bottle of orange soda pop. The bill was usually $80 - $100 for anything that we didn't grow on the farm, and he got a sack of candy for the children when he paid his bill. Once when I was around five years old, I hid on the floor in the back seat of the car so I could go to town with Pop when he paid the monthly Co-op bill. He must have seen me but pretended not to and enjoyed the game.

When he parked in front of the store and my head bounced up, he acted knowingly surprised. I thought I was very clever in making the trip to town and relished my bottle of orange soda pop all alone in the store with Pop. And I was entrusted with the sack of candy to hand out to everyone. For a five-year-old this was a big deal. Times alone with Pop were rare, and I guess I thought I needed some special time with him.

# Chapter 3: Timeless Images

We learned at an early age how to work the family system. My youngest sister, Sherry, once wanted a doll for her birthday, but Charlie, who was two years older than her, conned her into asking Pop for a little red wagon. She did and got one, and both Sherry and Charlie enjoyed that little red wagon. Being so close in age, they were close companions, and Charlie pulled her around in that little red wagon much of the time.

Sherry was a lovable, gregarious, very pretty little girl who kissed her first boyfriend in first grade. On Sundays we all got to sit with our friends at church, and Sherry sat with her boyfriends, one on each side. As the youngest of eleven children, Sherry says that Mom or Pop never spanked her, but I can hardly believe that. I guess they ran out of steam with her. I do remember quite a few spankings. And the worst part was when I had to go find the switch from the nearest tree for the spanking. That prolonged the torture.

One time I left Sherry at the neighbor's in town after riding her there on my bike, she had to ride home about a half mile over the bumpy gravel road by herself crying the entire way, while I went off with a friend. I felt a little guilty about that, but not enough to miss out on being with a girlfriend. After all, sisters were always around and you didn't always get to be with girlfriends. She complained a lot about my betrayal and thoughtlessness. She told me about this while I was writing this book, so I sent her flowers. Only fifty years late!

Charlie was quiet and shy and didn't say much. He liked to fit in with our plans and just go along with whatever we decided to do. We usually played together around the house. He loved holding the kittens and playing with them as much as I did. Daisy Mae, our family calico cat, kept us in kittens most of the time. She was our oldest and most respected cat.

We all loved to read comic books, and we had a huge family collection kept in a large cardboard box on the porch that we read over and over again. The comic books became tattered and torn over time, and many were missing covers so you had to read a few pages to find out what it was. My favorite was Wonder Woman. I liked her bright red, white and blue outfit with the stars on it and readily identified with her daring acts of bravery and rescue. We traded comics with many neighborhood kids who would often come to our house to visit and read comics. An older mentally disabled boy, the brother of one of my sister's friends, often joined in the fun. He was readily accepted and we shared our comics with him. The comics accumulated each year. Batman and Robin, Superman, Archie, Bugs Bunny, Pluto, Porky Pig, Dagwood and Blondie, Roy Rogers, The Masked Man and Tonto, and Tarzan were all favorites. I remember having a dollar to buy all my Christmas gifts, and I spent ten cents a comic for all my brothers and sisters. I wrapped them and put them under our decorated cedar tree taken from our pasture. That was a big task. We always counted the gifts and there was usually a hundred. It was so much fun to have something for everyone.

I remember playing many card games at the kitchen table with my brothers, like slap jack and spoons. We wore out many decks of cards especially on rainy days. You needed to be pretty quick to avoid having a smashed hand. Many years later while working in Russia, I astounded the school kids with my fancy ability to shuffle cards the way I had learned on those rainy days.

My parents played Pitch, a card game with friends and relatives who came out to our house. My youngest sister remembers this happening on one of Mom's birthdays. Sherry and I and my younger brother Charlie had pooled our resources to buy Mom a special birthday present. We gave her a pink hairbrush, which she received with much gratitude. Pop just smiled. We usually didn't have birthday parties as kids, but we did choose a special cake on our day. My favorite birthday cake was a sponge cake, which I always requested and Mom always made for me. We ate birthday cake the whole month of January.

We listened to the news of World War II and mystery programs on our large Philco radio. "The Squeaking Door" and "The Shadow" were my favorites. I could never have listened to these scary programs in my bedroom by myself, but sprawled on the living room floor with others around me felt safe. Those voices sounded so real and scary reaching into our living room from the radio-speakers.

When I was six years old, there was a time of great sadness and quietness in our home. It was December 11, 1942. The heaviness in our house was unusual, and it was the only time this had happened. At first I thought my Aunt Pearl had died, Pop's sister. But then I found out there was a place in the South Pacific that had been bombed called Pearl Harbor and this attack would change everyone's life. A fear had been introduced into our peaceful family life that I had not known before.

My sister Dorothy soon quit college and went into the Women's Coast Guard called the SPARS in 1942. My brother Adren enlisted in the Navy in 1942 and went to the South Pacific on a Destroyer. My brother Dale enlisted in the Army in 1942 served as a medic in Italy and North Africa. Dale even got his picture on the front page of the Army newspaper, *The Stars and Stripes,* as he took a vacation on the Italian Riviera. He was photographed at the tender age of nineteen years in his swimming trunks lounging on a beach chair as the caption noted, "U.S. Servicemen with Mussolini's Beauties." Dorothy and Bud Hyle were married during the War in 1944 while Bud served in Europe with the Army Infantry.

We knew we had to be very quiet or suffer the wrath of our father when the news came on the radio at night. Pop had served in WWI and was not ignorant of the sacrifices of war. I wonder now what Pop thought as he followed the progress of the war knowing that two of his sons and a son-in-law were in the thick of it. Dorothy was stationed in Washington and didn't go overseas until after the war. When President Roosevelt spoke there was complete silence. We all prayed every day for their safety.

I remember sitting with Mom on the couch in the evenings after supper while she wrote letters to the three older children in the service. I also wrote letters to my siblings and stuck them in the same envelope with Mom's. As I folded the transparent paper just right and put it into the red, white and blue air mail envelope, I felt so important. I loved to lick the stamp and put it on my letter, knowing that it was going to far-off places that I read about. And I imagined that Mom's letters were longed-for and received with anticipation and joy when they arrived in those far-off places. I learned early in my life to record the events of the family through these letters that I wrote to my brothers and sister.

It was a great occasion when we stopped by the Madison Post Office after school and checked our mailbox. We could always recognize those familiar red, white and blue airmail letters as we looked through the tiny glass window of our mailbox and knew that those were very important letters from overseas. Sometimes I got to carry these proudly into the house to Mom and experienced the satisfaction of being a link in the line of communication. She was always extremely happy when she received them. Pop would sit in his old brown chair in the living room after supper and read those letters over and over again.

I received a box of assorted sized seashells in the mail from my sister when she was stationed with the Coast Guard in Long Beach, California. As a little girl living in Kansas with beaches very distant, I treasured these shells. I guarded these treasures and kept them in a large matchbox upstairs in my bedroom. I loved their smell and feeling the smooth or ridged surfaces and enjoyed playing with them. I imagined them lying on far-off white, sandy beaches under beautiful green palm trees, and it brought me closer to a reality that I would experience when I got older. Every time I saw a picture of an ocean beach, I thought proudly of my seashells. I retained a fascination for seashells still gathering them from many beaches around the world.

All my brothers received white cotton sailor hats from their oldest brother in the Navy. They wore those with pride. These things still connected us as a family even though we knew the distance and dangers that separated us.

Playing in the hayloft of the barn was a great pastime. I was convinced that haylofts were created especially for children, they were always available. Swinging down on ropes and jumping from high distances into the soft piled-up hay seemed pretty exciting. We jumped together and piled up on top of each other and tumbled in the familiar softness. I had no jeans to wear and suffered thousands of scratches on my feet and legs from the hay after I sailed into the air and landed. There was no blood, but these tiny scratches were the source of stinging hurts when I washed up for bed. Still a small price to pay for all that excitement.

The corncob fights we had between us were our version of fighting a war. We chose sides, gathered and stacked our piles of ammunition and then shouted, "Go!" We threw these at each other until we were bored or too tired to continue the battle. The corn cobs rarely hurt anyone and we never ran out of ammunition. Sometimes we used rotten eggs, which were not hard to find and the fights were always pretty smelly. We also played King of the Mountain on high-stacked piles of dried, dark brown cow manure. Everyone charged the person on top to try to topple him and become the new King for a few seconds. As the only girl playing, I had no problem with becoming King; I had not heard of the word "gender." This game went on as long as anyone accepted the challenge.

We collected old scrap metal from around the cluttered-up barnyard for the war effort to sell and earn money. Dwight as the oldest boy at home assumed the role of the Captain in charge and would give out the orders. Then he would haul the scraps in a trailer to town to sell and give us our share of the money. We played Army ourselves and became soldiers marching around the house with rubber guns.

These were actually wooden guns and rifles intricately sawn out from boards with a coping saw. We attached a clothespin as a trigger at the handle, cutting out rubber strips from old bicycle tires to use as ammunition. The two ends of the rubber were held in the clothespin and then stretched over the end of the barrel, shooting enough distance for us to hit one another as we released the spring of the clothespin.

I begged Richard or Philip to craft my guns for me. Since we made new ones all the time, there were always old ones lying around. Using my mother's sewing scissors was forbidden, but I think they were the only ones around and often got requisitioned when we were desperate for ammunition. Everyone competed to see how far his rubber "shot" would go. We had full-scale battles with those guns.

We also made sling shots from a green peeled elm tree branch cut at the Y of an intersecting branch. The leather for the pouch that held the stone was usually taken from the tongue of an old shoe and connected to the sling shot with strong twine. Pigeons and birds were often hit with practice. We used the tree branches with childhood abandon as we also made bows and arrows from green branches and became Indians and let out war whoops as we did target practice.

On rainy days, we would compete to see who could get the most mud on themselves by swinging on a rope and sliding into the slippery mud in the ditch along the driveway. I don't ever remember being told to stay clean. My mother must have made her peace with dirt. We had the outside pump to wash all the dirt off ourselves before coming into the house. I also liked just sitting in the gravel of the driveway picking out pretty rocks from the river rock. The variety of shapes and colors always got my interest and I always had a rock in the pocket of my dress. There were far to many treasures in my ordinary days to leave behind, so I always insisted on pockets when my Mom sewed my dresses. Mom sewed my dresses on her faithful Singer treadle sewing machine, and she made them out of the pretty prints from the prints of the feed and flour sacks we bought at the Farmers Co-op.

We had a dirt basketball court and a hoop where the boys spent hours shooting and playing. I joined them whenever I could make a basket. Playing capture the flag in the front yard provided hours of entertainment in the summers after dinner until it got dark and we could no longer see each other or the flag. The flag was usually one of our old socks. We spent more time rescuing captured prisoners on-demand than getting the flag, which is probably not much different than the real thing.

We had a pond for ice-skating in the winter, but few ice skates, which we passed around and shared. In winter we made snow forts in the front yard with captains chosen and plans made. We spent a lot of time designing and making those forts out of packed snow like igloos. Our snowball battles raged with complicated strategies until forts were destroyed and we were all frozen and had to come into the house to thaw out by the big pot-bellied stove in the living room. We often used old socks for gloves.

The smell of wet clothes sizzling on the hot stove with the steam all around us reminds me of how cold our bedrooms were because they were unheated. We had two bedrooms upstairs; one for the boys with two double beds and one for the girls with one double bed. In the winter, we always came down to the living room with our clothes to get dressed by the pot-bellied stove.

Sometimes my rambunctious behavior at home with my brothers transferred to my relationships at school. The first time was in first grade at recess on the school playground on the merry-go-round. I knocked one girl off and her front tooth came out. I apologized and was very sorry when I saw her bloody mouth. I hadn't lost a tooth yet, so I thought that this was very serious. I really didn't think that I had hit her hard, but loose teeth in the first grade were common, and I was very embarrassed when the story got back to my mother. She didn't think I should be so rough. My brothers just thought it amusing. Philip and I were in the same class so my mother heard it all.

Embarrassment came in a different form in second grade when a girlfriend brought a chocolate Easter bunny to school, the first one I had ever seen. I begged and pleaded with her until she was so annoyed that she gave it to me. I had just confronted the green-eyed demon of jealousy big time and lost. It didn't even taste that good. I was shocked when I realized later how determined I was to have that chocolate Easter bunny for my own. I felt like I had stolen it.

My favorite teacher was in third grade and she was Philip's favorite also. I remember her by one name, and

Philip remembers her by another because she got married that year. We had many spelling bee challenges which I never did remember winning. But I usually had to stop and go to the bathroom before it finished and lost my place in line. The tension and excitement was more than I could deal with.

School was fun, and I am from a long line of brothers and sisters who were expected to do well. All the teachers asked me about my siblings, and I felt important that I had so many and could tell them wherever they happened to be. I liked math and in fourth grade my teacher just let me go as fast as I could through the entire math book at my own pace. It was fun, and I tried to finish it before anyone else. You could just do so much with numbers.

I wanted to be alone, my favorite pastime was climbing trees, which were always available and seemed to be beckoning me when I wanted solitude. My twin brother Philip said he doesn't ever remember being alone. There was always someone around. I probably followed him around when he was away from his brothers. While climbing many different types of trees I enjoyed the views hidden inside the branches and leaves, or on the top, getting as high as I could. I was in my own little world up in the tops of the trees. I liked the atmosphere and the solitude. I couldn't see why anyone would prefer to be on the ground. Having such a variety of perspectives on life seemed essential to me. I never ran out of trees that offered a challenge to my barefoot skills. And I always judged a tree by whether I could climb it.

I took off my shoes as soon as spring came and never put them back on until fall when school started, except for trips to church on Sundays and the movies on Saturday night. The soles of my feet were like well-worn leather by the end of the summer and thorns and sharp rocks were no more than a slight nuisance. I ran over the gravel roads just to show how tough my feet were. I laughed at the soft white tender feet of my brothers. We had an outside pump at the well between the back porch door and the cellar where I could wash and remove the stickers from my feet each evening before going to bed. Sometimes this took quite a while using a needle and Mom to help. I found out the hard way that it was no fun limping around with a painful infected sticker in my foot that had turned swollen and red.

Every September when school started I spent a month having nightmares that I had arrived at school having forgotten my shoes with everyone laughing at me. One year in seventh grade, Mom ordered me a pair of red leather sandals from the Sears & Roebuck Catalogue. It was my favorite book with shiny pages filled with everything anyone would need. I spent many rainy days just looking and reading it. I wonder how many farm kids learned to read that catalogue before they started school. I got to pick out a new pair of red sandals.

When my new red sandals arrived in the mail, they were the prettiest shoes that I had ever seen with shiny gold buckles. I felt very special. I loved showing them off on the first day of school, and I must have made twenty-five trips from my desk to the pencil sharpener. I spent more time at my desk looking at my new red sandals than my books for a few days. I felt so lucky to have them. They made a lovely clapping sound as the fresh new leather soles hit the clean waxed classroom floor when I walked. Next to being barefoot, this was the best.

I had a special place under a large mulberry tree in our pasture where I often took a box of saltine crackers and sat alone in the shade. I ate the dark purple ripe mulberries with the crispy crackers thinking what a grand life I had. I felt like the luckiest person in the world as I listened to the birds singing while they gorged themselves and the wind softly whispering in the leaves of the tree and contemplated my life. The Kansas sky was a penetratingly blue on a spring day when the rain and wind had driven the dust away. My dirty bare feet and grubby stained hands were familiar colors. Later as an adult I learned how many bugs I had consumed in those mulberries. But they tasted delicious to me. My black and purple stained lips were a small price to pay, and I relished the freedom to pick all I wanted. It was not a good climbing tree but one of my favorites.

Our cows often congregated under this same mulberry tree to get shade from its thick, dense, dark, green shiny leaves and broad branches. Although I didn't begrudge them their shade, I chose one side where the cow pies were not so fresh and smelly. Barefoot, I sometimes found out too late after I stepped on them. The cow pies were crusty and brown on the outside and looked dry, but slimy yellow-green on the inside that turned your feet yellow when your foot sunk into the middle.

While on a missionary trip to India much later in my life, I saw the village women of Madras, India using the cow dung for a totally different purpose. They took their brown hands and mixed the abundant and available fresh cow dung with mud and smeared the mixture on the walls of their houses. I watched this process with amazement. I had tried so hard to keep my feet out of them as a child and I was astounded to see the women working in this slimy green stuff with their hands. But this was a centuries-old tradition here and they didn't waste anything. It served a very useful purpose when it dried smooth on the outside of their houses.

We fished in the pond with our homemade cane poles, tried to build boats from scrap lumber, caught the fast-moving crawdads trying to hide under the rocks in the streams and swam in a shady swimming hole. The boys swam naked and enjoyed their special tricks if they thought I was watching. Their stark white skin was contrasted with the brown river water. I did not tell Mom about these. I was always outnumbered as the only girl and had to make my peace with that.

It was also in seventh grade that a girlfriend of mine, Patsy Crumpacker, lost her mother with cancer. I remember looking at this girl with awe not understanding how she could go on with life and school. I guess I expected to see some visible sign painted on her forehead, yet she looked so normal. I felt so grieved for her, knowing how close I was to my own mother and thinking that I just could not live if that happened to me. Just for a moment I had thoughts of near-hysteria of what it would be like to be an orphan, but the thought was too terrifying. This prompted bad dreams later. With no sex education classes and hearing only vague information from my older sisters about the menstrual period, I remember burning the trash at home and finding the used pads and thinking that my mother was dying of cancer. I never mentioned this to anyone but knew that I wanted her to always be with me. I eventually forgot about this fear since she never seemed to be sick and was always so cheerful.

We had a horse named Black Beauty that everyone took a chance at riding. She was all black with a white star on her forehead. Dale was a good horseback rider and my youngest sister remembers him take her on Beauty and galloping down our dirt road in front of our house when she was three years old. She was pretty scared. My twin brother, Philip, had a lot of experience riding Beauty because he was usually the one who rode her in the pasture after the cows to bring them in at milking time. The cows often wandered and grazed in the pastures and found the wild onions that made our milk and cream taste like onions. This was not good when we sold our milk to the neighbors. I thought riding our horse Black Beauty with Phillip was rather scary too. Philip held the reins, and I was just a passenger bouncing around on the rear end of Beauty. I held on to Philip's waist and never knew when he would go off in a gallop with me yelling, "Stop!" Beauty was a little sensitive and skittish to blowing paper in the ditch, and as we started down the dirt road, Philip and I would often fall off when she suddenly shied and took a different direction. He usually didn't use the saddle when he rode by himself, but with me behind him he knew that I could also hang on to the saddle. I landed upside-down in the dirt many times, but got on again and forgave her. It seemed only reasonable that horses would have fears too.

I had a well-known family nickname of Sissy Jean that Philip called me, as did most of my other brothers. But I was embarrassed by this name at school when Philip used it, and I insisted on his calling me Phyllis. When he wanted to tease me or make me mad, he called me Sissy Jean.

We picked and ate the sweet wild strawberries wherever we found them and carried tin-lard-buckets when we went to work with Pop in the summertime to pick strawberries all day in the pastures. We had eaten so many during the day that the buckets were rarely full when we got home. And after we got tired of picking them, I think we tried to smear them all over each other to see if the strawberry juice would color our skin.

Wildflower picking in the fields was a wonderful way to spend an afternoon. Sometimes Sherry went with me but her interest dwindled quickly. All the variety of colors, shapes, textures and flavors occupied me for long hours. I also enjoyed finding pretty rocks, a variety of interesting insects, especially big fat green grasshoppers and beautiful black and orange soft, furry caterpillars so timid, always changing directions, rabbits, and toads and occasionally snakes. We called the black spit from the grasshopper "tobacco juice" because it stained our hands. Pinks, reds, blues, oranges, yellows, whites, and sunflowers made up my flower bouquets. I learned to blow on a blade of grass stretched between two thumbs, which emitted a high squeaky reedy squawk.

I doubt wild strawberries were the reason for our being with Pop at work in the summer. Mom tried to get a nap in the afternoons. In the summertime Philip said that he sometimes went to work to spend the day with Pop and just followed him around. Pop drove a black Model A Ford with a rumble seat to work each day. Pop kept two twenty-five gallon drums in the rumble seat of his Model A Ford, in which he put the casinhead from the wells to store in our barn. He had his own brown mixed-breed bulldog named Butch that went to work with him. Butch usually slept under the boys' bed in their room at night.

We played hide-and-go-seek at night in the front yard, with many trees to hide behind and ditches where we could lie flat on our stomachs. It was always fun to wait and hear the "All out in free" and try to beat everyone to the home base tree. I was an extremely skinny kid and could hide behind a telephone pole for a long time.

Mom gave my sister, Betty, money to take me to the drugstore at school over lunchtime for a milkshake hoping that I would gain some weight. I remember weighing seventy pounds in seventh grade. We both were skinny and didn't drink milk but loved the milkshakes. This was probably from our Indian heritage for lactose intolerance.

Betty had a bad case of mumps in the eighth grade and missed a lot of school. She said that she never caught up with her math. I was the only one allowed in her room during that time to take her meals. All the children were quarantined at home, and Philip says that we both had mumps in the fourth grade. I think we sat out the quarantine and were ready to go back to school, but then I got the mumps.

When the dark black thunderclouds came rolling in we gathered on the front porch to watch the show. Kansas has great flashy first-class rainstorms and we would run around outside the house in the pouring rain in our swimsuits, as long as there was no lightning. That was my shower for the week. Otherwise it was our Saturday night bath in a large round metal wash tub in front of the kitchen stove before we went to the movies. The water had to be heated in the dishpan on the stove and poured into the washtub. Severe thunderstorms with flashing lightning and high winds drove us often to hiding from tornadoes in the dark and damp window-less cellar filled with spider webs. Although tornadoes never hit our farm or houses, we were brought up with the danger and reality of the possibility. I remember often swinging in the porch swing on the front porch with Mom and Sherry on warm summer nights during high winds and watching the stars and singing. We always identified the big and little-dippers and the Milky Way.

I worked hard with a hammer building stilts made of blocks of wood nailed to the sides of a two-by-four, long enough to lift me two or three feet off the ground. I adjusted them and held them like crutches to fit under my arms. It was a whole different world for a little girl suddenly elevated two feet taller. I was quite adept at running, jumping, knocking others off their stilts, and even tried to play basketball on them since it put me at a favorable advantage. Later at thirteen years and on crutches for real with a broken leg, it didn't take me long to learn to play baseball on crutches. After hitting the ball in a backyard neighbor game, I often threw away my crutches and just hopped around.

One of my favorite types of evening entertainment in the summer was climbing trees to catch locusts when they came out at dusk. I became an expert at catching them and would share my catch. Their dark, shiny bug eyes on their green and black bodies and W mark on their backs with their silvery wings was fascinating to me. Such detail and so intriguing. Since they couldn't see you coming up on them they were pretty easy to catch by just following their croaking. Catching locusts and tying a piece of thread around their heads and putting a loop on my finger and letting them fly like a pet, was my own invention. They had enough string to just hover above my head but go no further. I could have as many flying pets as I wanted and usually offered them to others. At the end of the evening I would untie the thread and let them go to wherever locusts go at night. I probably caught the same ones over and over.

Catching lightning bugs in the summer after dark every night was standard routine and we never ran out of them. We always got our glass jars with a lid to put them in with nail holes in the top and carried them around like lanterns. I don't ever remember being bored as a child. There was always something to do and places to go around the farm. Now that I look back on my childhood, trees played an important and significant part. I loved them. I looked for action or solitude in the trees. Swimming in the creek, catching crawdads in the streams after a rain when we went wading, chasing the turkeys, and gathering eggs added variety and adventure. You never knew when the sitting hens would peck you or the turkeys would jump on you with their loud gobble and flapping red goatee.

Many uncles gathered at our house around October to help Pop and my older brothers butcher one steer and one pig for our yearly supply of meat. Mom and the girls were in charge of chopping up the large white globs of fat after the skin was removed and cooking and storing the lard. And the fried pork rinds were a tasty snack. Hams were hung up in the smokehouse to cure along with the bacon. The slaughtered meat was put in packages in our freezer at Farmers CO-OP in Madison.

Mom washed clothes on Monday with our old Maytag ringer washer located on the back porch off the kitchen. Our dirty clothes hamper was a large, empty soap barrel that Pop had probably retrieved from Aunt Pearl's restaurant in Madison. We had this large barrel on the landing at the bottom of the stairs leading up to the second floor bedrooms. Everyone could toss their dirty clothes into this and it kept Mom from looking for them. If it wasn't tossed into the barrel, it wasn't washed. After the hot water had been heated on the kitchen stove in large pots it was poured into the Maytag washer.

I helped with this chore and stirred the dirty clothes in the washer with a long handled wooden stick worn smooth. I also stirred the beans and ham that cooked on the large gas stove in the kitchen for supper, but not with the same stick as the laundry! I was very careful putting the clean smelling rinsed clothes through the double ringer because Mom had told me many stories of kids getting their hands or arms pulled into the ringer. That seemed pretty gruesome, and I didn't want that to happen to me. I'm sure I had nightmares more than once about having flattened out hands and arms. I had a vivid imagination. It took all day to wash and hang up clothes on the clothesline out by the chicken coop for our large family. The lines were full of jeans and boys' work clothes. I had the job of getting them off the line. The clothes froze in the winter and the stack of jeans were like boards, stacked higher than me. Although I had this considerable close contact with jeans, I never had any of my own to wear, which I considered grossly unfair.

The door to the back porch from the kitchen was closed in the winter months to keep the kitchen warm. A shotgun stood by that back door leaning against the wall. We had a hole in the ceiling of the kitchen where it had gone off when my brother, Dwight, said that he had just walked by. I never heard the whole story but wondered why the shotgun went off when he just walked by. It was removed from the kitchen and kept on the porch after that and the hole in the ceiling repaired.

We had a stainless steel milk separator in the red shed where we separated the cream from the milk. Mom sold jars of cream to the creamery in town, and we used the separated milk to feed the many kittens we always had, compliments of our calico cat, Daisy Mae. I liked turning the separator because it wasn't my job, but I hated washing up the many parts in the kitchen, which was my job every morning. The dishwater looked like milk when I finished.

Another one of my jobs was churning the butter in a large thick, square, bluish glass, gallon-jar with a round lid. A crank screwed on the top that had wooden paddles reaching down into the cream. I cranked and cranked until the soft golden-yellow butter formed on the wooden paddles and separated from the cream leaving transparent bluish milk. I usually sat at the kitchen table while I did this and asked for help from anyone who walked by. The paddles got harder and harder to turn as the golden-yellow butter formed; my arms were always very tired when I finished.

Peeling apples for Mom to make the apple butter we always had canned in jars was also a job I often had. I tried to peel the whole apple with one curling red peel. The white paraffin sealing wax, melted and put on the top, was always good to chew later like gum. I liked eating the apple-peelings and really loved the dark brown sweet apple butter spread on top of our fresh baked bread with butter. This was a favorite after-school snack.

I absolutely loved black walnuts and spent many hours in the sun cracking and eating black walnuts on the long narrow concrete sidewalk running from the house to the barn. This long sidewalk served many useful purposes. Although it had many cracks, I learned to roller skate on this sidewalk with shoes on. My bare feet were always yellow and brown stained from the husks of the walnuts from our trees. We had big mounds of nuts stacked around with the green husks partially removed from running the wheels of the car over them. They were left to dry in the sun, and then we used our shoes and feet to get off the dried brown shells, letting them dry in the sun again before putting the walnuts in bushel baskets in the red shed. I never remember running out of walnuts to crack. That was one of the certainties of my life. When there was nothing else to do I could always crack and eat walnuts or put the cracked walnuts in a wooden bowl to take in the house to pick out later. After picking out the nutmeats, we kept them in glass jars in the pantry for Mom to use in cooking. I became an authority on greens ones, rotten ones and those just right. A hammer was a real treat to have and when I couldn't find one, a brick or rock had to suffice.

My brothers Richard and Philip remember getting up very early with Pop and Dwight to hand-milk cows before going to school; sometimes as many as twenty to twenty-five cows. They also baled hay in the summers and stacked it in the hayloft and sometimes put in loose hay on slings filling up the hayloft. As the winter came to a close, the distance you dropped from the ropes tied to the rafters down to the hay got farther and farther until the floor was bare in the spring.

We had an inside hand pump with a sink in the washroom off the kitchen where we did all our washing up. My sister, Betty, who was obsessed with cleanliness in our family, sewed ten separate slots on a pretty floral piece of vinyl tablecloth with all our names written on each separate slot for our toothbrushes. She woke up one morning to find that her toothbrush had already been used by an unknown brother or sister. I suppose that someone could not read yet. You had to fight to maintain an individual identity in our family. I remember washing my hair with rainwater from the rain barrels outside kept under the rain spouts by the side of the house. Water was not taken for granted since our well would sometimes go dry in the summer and drinking water had to be hauled from another well.

I had the normal childhood fears, but the dark outside cellar was one of my worst trials. I was afraid to go down in the dark cellar alone to get canned jars of peaches, pears, cherries and vegetables from our garden, and pickled pig's feet. I couldn't reach the light and used matches to see my way around in the damp and dark cellar with no windows. I had to stand on the wooden boards in the cellar as they floated in the water on the floor and I was usually barefoot and afraid of snakes. I always asked one of the boys to go with me, usually Charlie. There was such comfort in a companion at a time like this. My bedroom upstairs had a window close to the branches of a tree. When the wind blew in the night, the branches scratched up against the screen of the open window in the summer, and I just knew that some animal was coming in to get me. And going out to the outhouse after dark was always scary.

Corn was my favorite food reflecting my Indian heritage, and I liked it in any shape or form. We picked and shucked and ate bushels of corn from the corn patch for supper. It was the right time to pick when the tawny-golden corn silk had turned brown on the ears of corn. Removing any fat green worms that had found their way in was a special job. We picked corn about an hour before the meal and cooked it as soon as it was shucked. I thought that God created corn especially for me, but my brother Richard said that roasting ears was his favorite food also. How did all those kernels know to line up in so many straight lines on every cob? It was a miracle to me, and my teeth just fit for a delicious bite each time. We usually had a competition to see who could end up with the most corncobs on their plate. I think I ate the most because that's all I ate.

Watermelon from our patch was sweet, red, delicious, and warm, right off the vine. Mom and Pop sure knew how to grow gardens and ours seemed to be always the best. I liked the small pear-shaped yellow and golden tomatoes. Food was never lacking at our house. We all did the hoeing and pulling weeds in the garden, especially the boys and often ate the vegetables and strawberries while we were working. Eating raw potatoes was a special treat. I must have eaten more than my share of dirt. We had to keep the gate closed so the turkeys, chickens and pigs couldn't get in the garden, and it was a serious offense if anyone left the wooden gate open. There were just some things that had to be severely dealt with.

I didn't mind feeding the chickens or gathering the eggs while risking the brooding hens. I had developed the skill of catching them by one leg with a wire coat hanger straightened out with the hook on the end. But I hated helping kill the chickens to cook for Sunday dinner. The boys would put a board over the neck and pull the heads off or chop their heads off on a block of wood. I left this massacre scene trying to keep the blood from the flopping chickens off my bare feet and legs. I went away feeling guilty for my part in the whole mess. It grieved me that we had to go through this ritual every Sunday to have such good tasting fried chicken. I was happy taking care of the babies when they first arrived in the boxes from the post office in the spring. The newborns, having been hatched in the box en route to the post office, had fluffy, soft, yellow down, and with their cheep-cheep they were so much fun to play with. I was very much aware of the chickens' short life cycle. And like a neighbor once said to my children when they were raising chickens for a 4-H project, "It's hard to have a relationship with a chicken."

Since corn was my favorite food and it was always so sweet, I usually saved it until the last on my plate as sort of a desert. We all had our unique favorite foods or habits. Ketchup was one thing I didn't like, even on my hamburgers. My brother Richard loved it so much that he put it on his fried eggs in the morning and stirred it up with the yolk of the egg. It almost made me ill just to watch him, and I thought this was a ghastly habit. I thought he was crazy and he usually sat right beside me. He made sure that I was watching when he did it and stirred like crazy just smiling at me. I was emotionally unable to eat pickled pigs feet, cows' tongue or fried brains either.

At some age I decided to try my hand at writing poetry. Blank pages of paper were in short supply at our house, and I decided that my attempts would only warrant the best. I tore out the fly leaves from a couple of books on our living room bookshelves and climbed and sat in a tree and wrote. I don't know why I decided to do this, but I felt that I just needed to put some words on paper. The blank pages represented to me infinite possibilities, and I felt like those blank pages. My attempts at poetry were very disappointing; I would not be a poet.

Our telephone was a wooden box attached to the wall, and we cranked it with a black metal handle on the right side when we made a call and talked into the black mouthpiece coming out of the lower center at the front of the box. The receiver was removed from the left side to put to the ear to listen. As I was talking to a friend, my older brother, Dwight, decided that I had talked long enough and it was his turn. As he walked around the kitchen table and passed me on the phone, he knocked my mouth into the mouthpiece. I ended up with a bloody lip. I made sure that I kept my eye on him if he was anywhere near me while I used the phone again. Later with a broken leg in a cast and when I needed to be carried from the car to school, Dwight redeemed himself and never dropped me or slipped on the ice as he carried me with my heavy cast.

Church and Sunday school class were an important part of my life, and I enjoyed helping Mom with her class. We memorized the books of the Old and New Testament, the Ten Commandments, Beatitudes, John 3:16 and many Bible verses. We were rewarded with savings stamps to put in $10 or $25 stamp books during the war.

Helping Mom with her class, I found out that she was losing her sight in one eye. She would ask me to read the Bible for her. I remember church dinners, playing outside the church, singing, youth group at night, Pops' baptism, my baptism at Easter, new Easter dresses, hats and shoes, praying at the table before we ate, and saving a dime from my allowance for collection. I accepted all this to be the center of our family life and what my parents considered important. I lost so many of my nickels and dimes and pennies down the window slot of the brown Chevy car door as we drove to church. It was like a magnet as it swallowed them right out of my hand. I knew that the car door held a lot of my money and wondered how much. I don't know if anyone ever got it all out.

Mom and Pop often lingered after church visiting with many friends, and we children just ran and played. It was another regular social time in our week. We children were all baptized, immersed into water, at an appropriate age. I was baptized at Easter of my thirteenth year, but my youngest sister was baptized at eight years old. Our parents knew that life was serious and religion was not a game. We were given the example of thanking God for his kindness and mercy and love each day. It was what gave our lives meaning and purpose. We listened to and believed the Bible; I knew God was real and He lived in our house.

We were shown the example of generosity and kindness towards the poor. Mom found a warm coat to give to a young girl in our church who needed one. Pop paid for a friend of Philips' to join us on a trip to the circus who couldn't have gone otherwise. The fact that he was taking five or six children of his own didn't matter. There was always room for one more. Friends, neighbors and relatives were always welcome at our house. Growing up in this atmosphere of authentic Christian living and hospitality was a great personal influence to me.

Our parents were well known for their hospitality, hard work and integrity. My mother was known for her boundless energy and cheerfulness, and my father for his honesty and good business management. The day of their funeral in Madison in October of 1948, all businesses closed. Many of us remember the neighbors who came to buy eggs, milk or strawberries and they would stand to talk with Mom on the porch. We had our kerosene refrigerator here and she set up the ironing board to iron there in the summer. She laughed a lot and could visit and iron at the same time. I don't think everyone could always pay for the eggs or milk. I remember her talking to Aunt Mary on the telephone, laughing and having a good time.

We often visited uncles and their families, brothers and sisters of Pop. Uncle Lawrence in Burden owned a movie theatre and it was really a treat visiting his family and watching movies in town. I wore a sundress to one movie and air conditioning had just come out. I practically froze to death during the movie, but never would have left. I could never have found my way to their house by myself. Aunt Audry and Uncle Jim lived in Madison, and we loved to go for visits to their house so we could just walk around town. Aunt Mary always played her piano when we came to her house, and I loved to sing with her. I received special treatment since she had five boys and no girls. She said that

I would have to be her girl too. I didn't mind receiving all that special attention, and would often help her in the kitchen.

I joined Girl Scouts and had meetings and summer camp when I was thirteen years old near Topeka, Kansas. This was my first trip with strangers. In the small community of Madison everyone knew the details of our lives. Coming from such a large family, it was the first time that I was aware of seeing myself as an individual with no brothers or sisters around. When we were sitting around the campfire one night, and I was asked to describe my family, I didn't know where to start. It took me longer to name everyone than anyone else. It was quite an adventure. My older sister Norma Jean gave me the money to pay for camp since she was working at Kansas Power & Light Electric Company in Madison.

Norma Jean brought home movie magazines, which she gave me to keep when she was finished reading them. I cut out all the pictures of the movie stars and mixed up my white flour and water paste, putting them in a special scrapbook by category. They all looked so glamorous. After graduating from high school in Madison, Norma Jean attended a Teletype School in Nebraska. Then she worked in Washington D.C. and lived with our sister Dorothy who was the personal secretary to the head of the Coast Guard. Later Norma Jean moved back to Madison and started working for Kansas Power & Light. She met and later married Adam Horst in Madison.

There was a school carnival in Madison in my eighth grade year, and I was selected as the eighth grade queen candidate and won. Our class had sold the most tickets to the carnival so I was crowned queen. I borrowed a lovely soft lemon-yellow formal dress with lots of lace and net trimming for the dance from a friend. My picture was taken and put in the Madison newspaper; I was seated with my crown on my head and all the other candidates surrounding me. On the day they took my picture, I had gone to school with my hair in pigtails, but I decided I wanted some curls for the picture because I had never heard of a Carnival Queen in pigtails. I took out the pigtails and borrowed some bobby pins to set curls in my hair in time for the picture after school. The photo turned out very nicely, and I thought I looked a little older.

I watched my brothers play basketball at school, and I was involved in all the school activities. I watched a lot of basketball games as Dwight, Richard and Philip all played. Philip was pitcher on our eighth grade boys' softball team, and I was pitcher on our eighth grade girls' softball team. We traveled to surrounding towns to compete and sometimes Mom would go to see us play.

Inviting friends to our house and going to friends' houses to spend the night was the highlight of a weekend. Mom planned Philip and my thirteenth-birthday-party in a hall in town — a taffy pull — and Mom made everything. We got to invite all of our mutual eighth grade friends. I finally got jeans, and I received a red and blue plaid cotton flannel shirt like Philip's because I always wore his. I felt very grown-up and was allowed to wear nylon stockings on my very skinny legs for the first time that Easter.

As a teenager I helped Mom more around the house as the oldest girl at home. I picked strawberries for people to buy from the garden. I started out drying dishes for Betty whenever she could catch me, and then washing dishes and fixing the school lunches. I was her reluctant kitchen-helper. Betty has to chase me around the kitchen table and flipped me with a dish towel until I consented. If the dish towel was wet, it made more of an impression on me as it hit my legs.

I loved making and eating fudge, learning to sew on the old Singer treadle sewing machine, popping corn, and making after school snacks. I sewed an apron with Mom's help as my first sewing project. The Singer sat in front of a kitchen window on one side of the kitchen facing the porch. Mom was always making clothes for herself and us. I began asking Mom more questions about her family and learned some cooking while helping her in the kitchen.

We bought a new 1948 Studebaker at the end of 1947. It was maroon and sleek with wrap-around back windows. We felt pretty classy driving to town on Saturday nights or Sunday mornings. It was not easy to purchase a car after WWII. People wanting to buy new cars had to put their names on a list and wait. I remember a man from town coming out to talk to Pop about it. When he arrived at our house Mom sent me to the barn to get Pop and I ran as fast as I could. They talked this over as they sat at the kitchen table and it was exciting to hear them talk about buying a new car. Along with the excitement, I was beginning to be interested in how Mom and Pop operated. They made this decision together and the money seemed like more than I had ever heard. I sensed that it was a big decision and an important occasion.

New styling marked the Studebaker's return to production after the war. Studebaker advertising touted that while all pre-war manufacturers resumed production with warmed-over pre-war models, Studebaker introduced its new styling for the 1947 model year, highlighted with the wrap around rear-windowed Starlight Coupe. Philip said that Pop paid cash for the car, about $2000 at that time. Our family transportation had just turned spiffy and modern.

Later, Dwight managed to tear off a car door while backing out of the garage in the barn that was promptly repaired. When Adren came home for a visit and arrived at the train station, Pop had picked him up in the new car and let Adren drive it home. While they were driving the car home from Emporia, another car sideswiped them. Pop had him stop the car and they caught the other driver when he was stopped at a railroad track. Pop had heated words with the man, a painter, and he agreed to paint our barn.

On Saturday nights we saw Tom Mix, Roy Rogers, Hopalong Cassidy, Gene Autry movies, Lone Ranger and Tonto. We also watched *The Three Stooges*, and *The Abbot and Costello Show*. I was mesmerized with the musical shows and dancers. I did not know feet could move so fast. Fred Astair and Ginger Rogers, Gene Kelley and Doris Day were dancers who seemed to move like magic to me. Inspired by what I was watching and my movie star scrapbook collection, I made up my mind that I would be a dancer.

We also saw the gruesome newsreels of the war — Hitler and the surrender of Germany, concentration camps, end-of-war atomic bombing, and the Japanese surrender. We watched a lot of world-altering dramatic history taking place on Saturday nights at the movies, and we knew that we had two brothers and a sister involved in it. When the war was over and the newsreels showed the liberation of concentration camps in Europe, it was too horrible to watch. I could not understand the horror of the pictures.

We received a telegram from the War Department with news that Dale had been wounded in action, for which he received Purple Heart war medal. I remember Mom holding and reading the yellow pages of the letter to us. When Dale came home we got to hold the Purple Heart and admire it. He also received the Bronze Star for rescuing many wounded soldiers. We were very proud of him. Dale told us of how he worked as a medic during the war. It seemed very dangerous.

Dorothy, Adren, and Dale came home for visits during the war. We knew they were in danger and that it was a dangerous world. We had large eight-by-ten portraits of them in their uniforms sitting on top of the piano in our living room. It was my job to keep the pictures and piano dusted. We were very proud of them all.

Dale was the musician in the family and played our piano. He had played clarinet in the band and orchestra in high school, and he was a good dancer. I remember one of his special pieces, "Deep Purple," that he played all the time. I inherited his clarinet and played in the high school band for a few years before I lost it on a school bus later in Columbus, Georgia.

I learned to drive the old brown Chevrolet barefoot with Philip as my driving instructor; we were thirteen years old. We drove up the gravel road to townsite, and I felt pretty confident, but I didn't listen to Philip nor did he have much instruction. When we arrived at the water pump, I ran into it and broke it off because I didn't know how to put on the brakes. I just wasn't sure which pedal was the clutch and which one was the brake. Driving was more complicated than I had thought. We were hauling water, and I had to tell Pop what I had done. I think Philip and I both shared the blame on that. I never drove again at home. When I could get a ride to town, I went roller skating in Madison on Sunday afternoons with friends where the sidewalks led to more interesting places than our barn. I Dwight or Betty would drive me to school.

When we got ready for church on Sundays, I brushed and combed my mother's hair. She sat at the vanity table in her bedroom with a large mirror in front of her, and I stood behind her stroking through her soft, fine, dark black and gray hair that went down her back. It was very long and turning gray. I sensed our time together was something that Mom enjoyed. As I brushed and then twisted her long hair into a bun on the back of her head secured with black metal bobby pins, I saw our reflection in the vanity mirror. It was an image I'll never forget. Maybe this was one of those timeless images that are common of mothers and daughters everywhere. Although I didn't know it, this was a special moment. Maybe it crossed my mind that I would not always be thirteen years old and my mother was growing older and would not always be here.

Norma Jean and Adam Horst were married at the First Christian Church in Madison. The whole family came except for Dorothy and Bud because they were living in France. Betty and Pat drove to our house to visit us at the farm when they started dating in Wichita. They were married in June of 1948 in Wichita at the Broadway Christian Church, and Norma Jean, who was a few months pregnant, was the Maid of Honor. Sherry and I got new white shoes and pink dresses. We kept the guest book at the church and felt very important.

Life was good. None of our family had been killed in the war. We were all back together within close range. Pop had just received a twenty-eight dollar a month raise at his work. My brother Dale had quit college and was working in Kansas City as an accountant for General Mills. Norma Jean and Adam Horst married and were expecting their first baby in December. We had all gone to their house in town for dinner, and Mom and Norma Jean did her laundry together. Norma Jean was looking forward to getting a new washing machine in a couple of weeks.

Bud and Dorothy had lived a year in France since Bud was in the Regular Army and part of the reconstruction of Europe under the Marshall Plan after WWII. They returned from France and lived in Columbus, Georgia. Adren, who was working at Boeing Aircraft, and his wife, Sally, had my parents' first grandchild, Steven Patrick. I don't think I even realized that I was an aunt now. Betty and Pat Patterson had just married and were living and working in Wichita.

Our parents had gone through many hard times, two World Wars and the Depression, and they were on the home stretch with their last six children at home. Dwight was about to graduate from high school, and my youngest sister

Sherry was nine years old. Our parents had lived an extraordinary life of hard work and faith in God as they married and raised their large family through a difficult period of history.

Mom learned from an appointment at the Kansas University Medical Center that she had lost the vision in one eye and might lose the vision in her other one. Dorothy drove her and Pop to the appointment in Kansas City, and they later told some friends and relatives. Mom was diagnosed with glaucoma and there was nerve damage in her eye and no treatment available. She never talked about it at home.

She accomplished more with one eye than most people could do with two. She sewed for Sherry, me, and herself, and did everything else she had done for her family for the last thirty years. October was a busy month with our family. Norma Jean visited the Horsts' farm and fell over the barnyard gate, but she was ok. Mom went shopping with Norma Jean in Emporia and bought material. She made Norma Jean some baby things and sewed herself a new gray skirt to wear to a Cities Service Christmas Banquet at the First Christian Church in Madison. She had just made me some new skirts since I had outgrown most of my others and passed them on to my younger sister Sherry. I remember a gray skirt with green and brown checked pattern for school. Mom wrote Dorothy that she wanted to go to her mother's in Chetopa for Thanksgiving. But Pop decided that it would be better for him to stay in Madison and work that holiday for the extra pay since it would be double his daily wage. He earned about $271 a month. October was already getting cold enough to snow.

Mom wrote all the older children and received letters from them all. Adren and Sally visited us the first of October. Mom wrote Dale in Kansas City to come to Madison if he wanted to ride with them to Wichita on

October 23rd. Pop cleaned out the flu of the house and got it ready for winter. The outside had gone dry and we hauled water for drinking and cleaning. This was their last trip of the autumn.

They drove to Wichita in our new Studebaker for the weekend and had dinner with Betty and Pat, then visited with Adren and Sally and saw their new grandson. Betty made an appointment at a studio to have their pictures taken. Norma Jean rode with us remarking that it was her last trip to see her sister before the baby was born. My brothers Dwight, Richard and Philip stayed at the farm, milking the cows and feeding all the animals for the weekend while we were gone. Charlie, Sherry and I went with our parents to Wichita. I wore my newest clothes for the trip to Wichita, excited about the weekend.

# Chapter 4: The Accident

**THE DARKNESS WAS PITCH BLACK,** and I couldn't see anything. Where was I? I drifted in and out of consciousness. What could have happened? I was all scrunched up in a very small dark place and unable to move anything but my head. I thought I must be in a dream. I could not think or remember anything. I was confused and dazed. Who was I and where had I been before this? There was complete darkness and nothing. Then, consciousness, and I woke again. I knew who I was and where I was. The last thing I remembered was that we were all in our car. Now I seemed to be on the floor behind the front seat of the car, but why? This was a crazy place to be and what was I doing here? Pop was driving and I just talked to him. They must be with me, but I could see no one. But where is everyone? I was not alone, but with my family here in this dark place. That was comforting to me.

We needed to get home. We had started driving back to Madison from Wichita Sunday evening in late October, 1948, after we had been visiting my sister and her husband as well as my older brother and his wife and baby. We had to get home to my three brothers who had been holding down the farm while we had all been away. I felt my clothes with one hand and remembered that I was wearing my new, light blue plaid wool skirt that Mom had just made me, with a new light blue wool pullover sweater. This was my finest and favorite. I hurt in many places but didn't know why. My head and right eye hurt. My right arm hurt. But the biggest pain was in my right leg, and I clutched it to my chest hoping that it would stop hurting. I just could not figure out what was going on. Then the darkness got darker and my memory faded. The next time I woke up I wanted to find out where I was.

I looked at the back of the front seat and decided that I really was scrunched up on the floor clutching my right leg. I turned my head and saw Sherry, nine years old with her eyes closed, lying on the back seat and breathing heavily. Last I remembered she had been sitting on a small cosmetic case on the back seat behind Pop and asleep. I remember thinking she seemed ok just sleeping. But where was everyone else? I could only move my head, so that was all I could see in the darkness.

Pop and Mom and Norma Jean, eight months pregnant, were all in the front seat, but I couldn't see over the seat or stand up. Pop had been driving and Norma Jean was sitting by the door with Mom in the middle. Everyone but Pop and I had been asleep. I still couldn't figure out what had happened. It was so dark. I couldn't understand why I couldn't move.

After a long time I heard voices outside the car, but I couldn't understand what they were saying. I don't remember saying anything. I don't remember seeing the car or seeing any people. More time passed, and when I woke up again, I found myself in the back of an ambulance riding over rough roads with someone telling me that we would soon be at the hospital. But all I could think about was the pain. Everything hurt so badly. I gritted my teeth and clutched my right leg and closed my eyes. I was very confused. What had happened? This was a different world that I knew nothing about.

The next thing I knew I was in a hospital bed and everyone was telling me that I had been in a car accident; I had a compound fracture of the right leg and a broken right arm and tremendous back pain. My broken limbs were set in casts, and I would be alright, but I slept a lot. I finally asked about Mom and Pop and Norma Jean. Were they ok? Yes, I was told, they were ok. I looked around to see where I was and my eleven-year-old brother Charlie said 'Hi' from the hospital bed across the room. After everyone had left the room and we were alone, he said Mom and Pop were not ok, but dead. He said this as a matter of fact. I remember thinking how could he talk about such terrible things! He said that he was thrown out of the car in the accident and saw them. He'd also seen our sister Norma Jean.

I could not take all this in and just cried and cried from the pain and the news from Charlie. I felt he must have been wrong. Why would he tell such lies? They had told me that everyone was ok. But why would they lie to me? I argued with him. This was just too much for my thirteen-year-old brain to handle, and I was unable to think clearly. Charlie looked ok and seemed to be alright. He just kept looking at me. My face must have looked pretty bad, but he didn't say anything. I asked him what had happened, and he said that we were in a car accident. He had been thrown outside and had a severed kneecap, which was reattached with many stitches. Otherwise he was okay. Sherry, our youngest sister, was in a coma with a concussion. I went back to sleep but I was very upset and angry, not wanting to believe him. And my head, leg and arm still hurt badly.

I had this terrible sinking feeling that everything was wrong. That maybe Charlie was right. But how could this be? I didn't want to believe that anything had changed. But of course in a fraction of a second my whole secure and wonderful world had changed drastically. Mom, Pop, and Norma Jean were gone. Our family had been reduced from thirteen members to ten. Life would never be the same for any of us, and we all coped in our own way. I cried and cried, not wanting to believe the truth of what had happened.

Was it a heart attack that caused my fifty-six-year-old father to hit the concrete culvert in our new 1948 maroon Studebaker? No one knows because there was no autopsy, but probably. Even though the speedometer on the

Studebaker was broken at eighty miles per hour when emergency workers found the car, my father never drove fast. There was talk that maybe my father had a heart problem, and Mom had at times suggested that Pop go see a doctor. He always refused because he said he had to work. I remember some days Pop would come home from work and have to lie down to rest.

Before the accident, he and I were the only two in the car who were awake, and he had asked me if there was a car coming around the long curve of the converging gravel side road. I had answered no. It was getting towards dusk, and he had the car lights on. I did not hear him say anything else before it was all darkness. There was no warning, and I didn't remember the sound of the crash.

I remembered that I had argued with Norma Jean about sitting in the front seat of the car instead of her. I remembered what a wonderful time we had in Wichita and how Mom and Pop had their pictures taken at a studio there. There were abundant memories of a happy childhood that flooded through my mind.

All of our relatives were notified of the accident, and all my older brothers and sisters came to the Eureka Hospital. Adren and Sally and Betty and Pat came from Wichita. Aunt Audry, Pop's sister, and Uncle Jim from Madison arrived at the hospital late Sunday night, and they brought my brothers Dwight, Richard and Philip with them. When my aunt and uncle had received the news of the accident in Madison, they went out to our farm to tell my brothers and to bring them to the hospital. Pop's oldest brother, Sidney, also arrived. My brother Dale came in early the next morning from Kansas City where he was working. Sherry, with the brain concussion, was in the operating room when he arrived. Dorothy and Bud flew in from Columbus, Georgia on Monday. Mom's family arrived a few days after the accident.

The funeral took place at Madison Christian Church while Sherry, Charlie, and I were in the hospital. A friend from the church stayed in the hospital with us during the funeral. The three caskets were opened in the funeral home before the funeral, and relatives and friends came to pay their respects. During the funeral, my older brother Richard felt overwhelmed seeing the three closed caskets in the front of the church. Not only did friends and relatives come to pay their respects, but all the businesses in Madison were closed for the funeral service. There had never been a tragedy of this proportion before in this small town. The entire town showed their support and concern for our loss. My grandmother and my mother's sisters were getting ready at our house for the funeral, and they were reminiscing on the happy lives of my family before the accident. They were all happy to see each other and laughing, yet the family was very solemn and still in shock.

The Indian side of my family celebrated the life of my Mom, Pop, and Norma Jean. They even laughed at happy memories instead of being overcome with grief at the present tragedy. But other family, not understanding and consumed with grief thought, "What a way to behave." Our parents were buried with Norma Jean at Blakely Cemetery in Madison, Kansas.

This accident was just too horrible and unthinkable to be a part of the life that I had known. In my own thirteen-year-old mind I coped with this tragedy and shock by believing for a long time that my parents were somewhere else and not really dead. I had not attended the funeral and had no closure of this event. I had not seen the three caskets at the front of the church or the many grieving relatives and friends of our family. It did not seem real to me. But my family was part of the statistics of motor vehicle fatalities in 1948 in Kansas.

After a few days in the hospital, I was able to go home in a wheelchair. I went back to school in Madison in a wheelchair, and Philip and my friends pushed me around helped take care of me. The plaster cast on my right leg went from the top of my leg to my toes with just enough breathing room for my toes to stick out. At first my toes were purple and would swell up each day; they were uncomfortable in the cast. As my right leg healed, it itched terribly under the cast; I devised a straightened coat hanger to insert from the top of the cast to scratch my leg. There was an unpleasant smell coming from my toes.

Sherry was still unconscious in the hospital. Family and friends took turns sitting by Sherry's bedside in case she came out of her coma. She was totally unresponsive and had brain surgery by a young surgeon, Dr. Bacon from Wichita. He drilled holes on either side of her skull to relieve the swelling in her brain, which hastened her recovery. She stayed in the hospital for another month and was tube-fed, though she looked as though she was wasting away. It was a thirty-mile drive from our farm to the hospital and the car was kept busy going back and forth. My oldest sister Dorothy brought Sherry a chocolate milkshake to add to her nutrition and Sherry started to eat. Although in a coma, my nine-year-old-sister could hear and the family was cautioned to be very positive about her recovery in her presence.

This was a very difficult time, both emotionally and physically draining for brothers and sisters who were trying to keep our home together and running while providing care for Sherry at the hospital. We just dealt with the present not discussing the past or speculating on the future. We were all just trying to survive. Every time we went into Madison people asked, "Has your sister woke up yet?" The whole town was concerned and anxious to hear any good news.

Sherry gradually became responsive, opened her eyes and spoke after one month. She was unable to use her left leg and right arm for a long time. She had to learn to sit up, walk and talk and eat all over again. When she came home from the hospital she slept in a hospital bed in Mom and Pops' bedroom. Before she learned to walk, Dale carried her into the car and into the theatre to see a movie in town. Sherry was taken to school to visit her fourth grade class, and her classmates gave her presents. But Sherry never returned to attend fourth grade in Madison.

Sherry didn't remember a lot. Betty told her that Mom and Pop and Norma Jean were not here, but in heaven. She asked me at the dinner table one evening where Mom and Pop were. Through tears I told her about the accident, but she only remembered waking up with tubes coming out of her nose in the hospital. Sherry was terrified, feeling so alone and abandoned as she missed our parents.

It was the hardest time of everyone's life. Very kind neighbors and friends in Madison paid the hospital bills. Women from the church and community brought in food every day. Dorothy continued to stay at the farm to supervise the older children: Dwight, seventeen years old; Richard, fifteen years old; and Philip, my twin brother thirteen years old. They took care of the farm animals and the chores. My sister Betty and sister-in-law Sally arrived to help cook. My brother Dale was working in Kansas City, but he came home on weekends to help with the work. Norma Jean's husband, Adam Horst, suffering the loss of his wife and unborn child, often came out in the evenings to visit. He played cards with me to keep me entertained until I went back to school. He looked very sad and lost.

The question of what to do with our family dog, Fritz, was settled by Dorothy who decided he should be put to sleep at the veterinarian's office since he was fourteen years old. The boys drove the brown Chevrolet with Fritz to the vet in Emporia. Before the vet could give him a shot, Fritz bit him on the hand and escaped. The boys left the vet and tried to find him on their way driving home to Madison, but without any luck. They came home telling the sad story, secretly glad that Fritz was alive and free. They knew that he could survive on his own and would find another home. Later the vet drove to Madison and asked many people in town where the Evans family lived. In this small town of Madison, we were the only family by that name. There was a conspiracy of silence and no one told him where we lived.

Our last Christmas together as a family was December of 1948, and then we had to move from our farm. We had an auction to sell the furniture, cars, farm equipment, and livestock. Leaving our family farm was painful. It was a sad and tearful goodbye for us all, and I don't know how we all got through it. (None of us could know that a year after we had moved and another family had moved into the house, that it would be entirely destroyed by fire in the middle of the night while that family was absent.)

We all had our own thoughts. Mom and Pop had never complained about much in life, but accepted what they had with gratitude. Their integrity and faith while raising a large family was known throughout the community. Stepping into their shoes was a hard act to follow under the circumstances.

There were offers from relatives and friends to adopt some of us younger children, and an uncle who had no boys wanted to adopt my youngest brother. Mr. Chase, the attorney handling our situation, just needed to make sure that all the children were provided for. The older children all decided to stick together as a family because my parents were very proud of their family. My oldest brother, Adren, was designated the legal guardian for the six of us siblings who were eighteen years old and younger for distribution of social security funds.

Then began the years of shuffling us younger children around to the best home for our age and the circumstances of the older ones. It was not easy for anyone, but we were determined to stick together as a family. Philip and I left for Wichita to live with Adren and his wife, Sally. Sally took us to enroll in school. My sister Sherry went to Columbus, Georgia to live with Dorothy and her husband Bud. My older brother Richard, and younger brother Charlie planned to live with Betty and her husband Pat. My brother Dwight, who was seventeen, stayed in Madison and finished his senior year of high school, living with Aunt Audry and Uncle Jim, Pop's sister's family. In 1949, my older brother Dale met and married Rachel Ivorene Hardin who had been one of my sister's roommates, and they also helped out to take care of us.

I don't believe any of us could comprehend what was happening because we were in shock. Leaving the farm, including the house, barn, sheds, ponds, pastures, animals, and all the special places that made up the sum of happy memories from many happy years, was a great loss for us all, but especially for the school children with their unfinished childhood lives. And the security of our parents was now gone. The happy memories of our parents, our neighbors, relatives, church, school and friends, were all that I had ever known.

My world had been small, but rich with family, relatives and friends, happiness and security. I had sure knowledge of a loving and caring God who took care of us all, and I did not feel that I had lacked anything. When I visited other friends and relatives and their families in Madison, I knew that I had the best with my family. Although I didn't know this at the time, the first fourteen years of my life with the stability, security and love from my parents were the most impressionable years of my life. I was the person that I would be as an adult because of this time with my parents. I learned what life was and what it could be from their example, and I accepted their values and standards as my own. I thought I was leaving happiness behind and that I would never be happy again.

After I moved to Wichita with Adren and Sally, Dorothy came over and Sherry begged me to move to Georgia with her. Only nine years old, she was still recovering, unsure in her walking and suffering memory loss. She was understandably frightened and I was her closest sister. She was afraid to be without any brothers or sisters and really didn't know her oldest sister Dorothy very well.  I wanted to stay with my twin brother Philip in Wichita, but with a sense of family loyalty and knowing what my parents would have wanted, I knew that I should move to Georgia with Sherry. I know that I would have wanted the same thing if I were in her shoes. Philip and I had shared everything: a crib when we were little, food, clothes, friends, and a special friendship as twins. The decision to leave my brother was one I didn't want to make, but no one would make it for me. It was probably the hardest decision that I ever had to make. We were a close family and I knew I would miss all my brothers and sisters, and Georgia was an unknown place very far away. After I left my brother's house, my youngest brother Charlie moved in with Philip at Adren and Sally's home.

Bud, Dorothy, Sherry and I packed up and left for Columbus, Georgia, where they were stationed in the Army at Fort Benning. We had a drive of two days, pulling in a trailer some things from our farm. I often got sick on car trips to Grandma Lucas' in the summer to Chetopa, and this trip was no different.

Sherry and I slept on a daybed in the living room of their apartment in an old southern colonial home in

Columbus, Georgia. Bud went to Fort Benning each day and was in school, and Dorothy had quit a civil service job as secretary to stay home and take care of Sherry. Sherry was not yet able to return to fourth grade, but I enrolled in Columbus High School in January 1949 to finish eighth grade and to start a new adventure in my life.

An x-ray revealed that my right leg had not healed properly with the bones evenly matched, and the surgeon at Fort Benning recommended breaking the leg again and resetting it, but I declined the offer and settled for the leg I had for the rest of my life. I had been through enough trauma for one lifetime.

* * *

"Blessed are those who mourn, for they shall be comforted." Mathew 5:4

"Every great loss demands that we choose life again. We need to grieve in order to do this. The pain we have not grieved over will always stand between life and us. Grieving is not about forgetting. Grieving allows us to heal, to remember with love rather than pain. It is a sorting process. One by one let go of the things that are gone and you mourn for them. One by one take hold of the things that have become a part of who you are and build again." ~ Dr. Rachel Remen, M.D.

# Chapter 5: Culture Shocked

THE LONG DRIVE TO COLUMBUS, Georgia after Christmas brought gradual changes that felt sudden in my life. Columbus was an old southern colonial town one hundred miles south of the capital city of Atlanta, Georgia. It was a town under 100,000 people that felt like a million to me, directly across the Chattahoochee River from Phoenix City, Alabama. It looked like a foreign country to me. I had never been in the south before and didn't even know there were so many colorful people in the world. Our small, all-white town of Madison, Kansas was on the opposite end of the color spectrum. The larger town of Emporia near Madison, where we went to a swimming pool in the summers while Mom shopped, had integration of all people, and the pool was my first opportunity to see this practiced. Although only a few people of color were there, all were treated the same. I remember going to the swimming pool and was very curious about the different color of skin. When I asked Mom, she just said that people were all the same.

My new home also radically confused my view on the color of dirt. There was a big difference between the black dirt of Kansas and the red dirt of Georgia. I just didn't know that dirt came in different colors. My chief concern was how corn was going to grow in red dirt. We traveled from miles upon miles of what had been summer cornfields and winter wheat fields covered with snow, to fields of cotton, all fluffy white in brown pods. There was no snow and the air was warmer. I had read stories of cotton growing in fields and here it was. Reading is not always believing, but seeing is. I was amazed. Growing something that you couldn't eat or feed your animals seemed foreign to my way of life on the farm.

I was struck by the pathetically long lines of impoverished shacks strung out for miles along the sides of the highways where poor people of colored lived. They worked in the fields, bent over picking cotton in their bare feet. Where were their shoes? I had known some poor neighbors near us in Madison, but I didn't know people could live in such places. Our barn at our farm had been infinitely much nicer than these sad shacks.

The streets were lined with all kinds of beautiful flowers. Dogwood, camellias, gardenias and azaleas were abundant as soon as spring came. They smelled delicious. Picking wildflowers had been a favorite past time in the fields near our farm in Kansas. We had a lot of irises and other flowers around our house, so I especially noticed and appreciated the new flowers in Columbus, Georgia. The large blossoms, vibrant smells and extravagant colors were strange and exciting. I sure could like anyplace with such beautiful flowers and trees. Even if these trees didn't look familiar to the ones I knew or weren't especially good for climbing. With a broken leg in a cast I wasn't thinking of climbing trees anyway. I was definitely in transition and asked many questions on that trip from Madison, Kansas to Columbus, Georgia.

I was both curious and apprehensive about the events unfolding in my life. Curiosity won over. My familiar warm and loving home with my parents and family was no longer my compass. If adventure was now my fate, I had better learn all I could. Beyond my grief I was thinking of my basic instinct to survive.

My first day in my new school was filled with unexpected events. It was a challenge for a sheltered thirteen-year-old kid from a small town school. Going on crutches with my right leg in cast was a handicap; I just wanted to blend in and not be noticed. Fat chance I had to go unnoticed in this crowd of one thousand teenagers at the all-white segregated Columbus High School. It did not even sound like they spoke the same language as me. My ears were assaulted and confused with different slurred sounds, slang and intonations. Some words were familiar, but they had softer sounds and intonations to them. I wasn't quite sure what was being said and was slow in reacting, but my senses were alert. I had never been timid, but this was going to take all the guts I could muster. Even the odors were new and different. Along with a certain amount of fear, I had a feeling of curiosity about how this was all going to work out. Would these kids accept me? My right arm had healed and was working ok, so I could handle my crutches up and down the three flights of stairs for classes, albeit slowly. I just concentrated on getting to where I needed to be. Since I didn't really know where I was going, it gave me a lot of time to look around. As I started up the stairs some kids offered to take my books for me. I felt woefully inadequate with just two hands and all this stuff to carry, so their offer helped a lot and I was encouraged to keep going. But, when I asked directions I couldn't understand those given to me to follow. I felt so stupid. I made it through a very strenuous and long morning, and I was very grateful for lunch break. I needed time to rest and recover from all the strange surroundings and happenings.

I had my lunch money and slowly shuffled through the cafeteria lunch line, pushing my tray slower still, and managing my crutches. This was the first time I had ever seen so many kids together in one place in my life. When I had picked out a sandwich that looked familiar, potato chips and a strange looking candy bar that I had never seen before, I picked up a bottle of Royal Crown Cola that I never knew existed. The soft drinks I had drunk at the Farmers Co-op were not there. I had led a very sheltered life. I arrived with my lunch tray at the end of the line.

The cashier smiled and waited for my money to pay as I fumbled with my change, a quarter and a dime. After paying for my lunch, the reality of my situation hit me and I must have started to panic. The distance to the first table looked farther than a football field, more than I could possibly manage. Time stood still for what seemed like an eternity. I just stood there paralyzed with indecision, not knowing what to do. Kids behind me took their trays and walked around me to their tables and I still didn't know what to do. How would I manage two crutches and a lunch tray all at the same time and walk – impossible! This was definitely my greatest challenge since I had left the Madison School where I had plenty of friends volunteering their help. Oh, for a friend now in all these strangers!

A small girl on crutches with both legs in metal braces came to my rescue and asked if she could carry my tray for me. I said yes and was much relieved as I followed her to her table on my crutches. She leaned her crutches up against the lunch table. Feeling very clumsy and sorry for myself, I thanked her and struggled into a chair. She asked me what had happened and I told her that my leg had been broken in a car accident. She just looked at me and smiled and said, "You are so lucky. Your leg is just broken." The truth of my situation struck me and came through like a bolt of lightning. As I looked at her paralyzed and withered, non-functional legs encased in the braces, a victim of polio, I knew that she was right. She would never walk without crutches. She offered me compassion, but no pity, and hope as only those who have suffered can. I had learned the most important lesson of my life right there in that moment.

She was my first friend and had reached out to help me when I needed it so desperately and was swimming in self-pity. I learned that self-pity is a deep hole that destroys us and saps all our energy. If she could reach out to me with hope knowing that she would be spending the rest of her life on crutches, then I could handle these crutches for now. She never knew what an angel she was and how much she gave me. Hope was wrapped up as a gift for me in her lovely smile and courage. She was there for me because she had experienced the same need. I learned that there is enormous healing power in the simplest of human relationships. Kindness is a beautiful gift to give to another human being. I went to bed that night exhausted from my first long day at school and three flights of stairs on crutches, but warmed with the knowledge that I had made a friend in this strange land. Tomorrow was another day.

Before my cast was off I often joined in a backyard softball game in our neighborhood, throwing my crutches down after I hit the ball, and running and hopping around the bases on my cast. I did not plan to let my broken leg slow me down too much. With the warm winter weather in Georgia, I felt like it was spring in Kansas.

Bud and Dorothy bought me a bicycle and I rode it to school for a short time, then got my cast off and was able to get back to a more active life. I got my cast off at the Post Medical Clinic at Fort Benning. They used a little buzz saw to cut off the cast, but it sounded like a chainsaw to me; I dreaded looking at my leg, thinking that my leg would be cut too. My cast had been signed by all my family and friends in Madison before I left, and it was attached to me like a familiar friend. Could I really walk without it? I had depended upon this cast for six weeks, and I doubted the ability of my own leg to function without it. My first glimpse of my right leg was not a pretty sight. My leg was covered with long black hair and the cast had rubbed an oozing sore on my ankle, which looked pretty gross. Since I hadn't seen my leg for so long, it seemed very strange, like it didn't really belong to me. I desperately hoped that it would return to its normal function and look like it used to before the accident. I cautiously welcomed my leg back to my body again and got used to it.

Since Columbus High was a large school with three floors and a basement, I think that I was pretty well lost for the first year. I was constantly asking for directions and using a school locker was beyond my comprehension. I usually carried all my books with me. My dreams at night were mostly about being lost at school. I was afraid of missing classes and arrived late many times. I was just never very good with directions even in Madison. I knew that I was the same person but I felt different. Life was not the same and I missed Mom and Pop and the farm. I joined clubs at school and made friends and enjoyed the many new choices I now had.

When we rode the city buses, I didn't know that the people of color had to sit in the back section. But I wondered about that, since the front of the bus often had empty seats and some people still went and stood in the back. I noticed this many times and didn't understand it. I thought it was pretty stupid and asked Dorothy why people didn't sit down when there were seats available. She told me the traditions of the south and a little about the Civil War. I was shocked and it was my first look at discrimination; I knew that it was wrong. I felt very ashamed and sorry for these elderly people who couldn't even sit down when there were empty seats available. My sense of justice for them was violated. We had poor and dirty neighbors near our farm on the road to school in Madison, and Mom said that they were just as good as anyone, but just didn't know how to take care of themselves. And we often took them food or clothes.

Then I began to notice other things in my new environment. With learning the new word in my vocabulary, discrimination had sharpened my awareness. There were restrooms for "Colored" and "White," and water fountains marked the same way. Separate waiting rooms at the bus station, restaurants with "Whites Only" signs above the doors, and public buildings with separate entrances for "Coloreds" were everywhere in town. Because I now lived in Georgia, I realized that here they see some people in a different way than other people. I knew I couldn't do that. And there were many poor people on the streets, many without shoes and begging. While I stared, nobody else seemed to notice. When I asked someone at school about this, they replied, "that's the way they want to be", or "that is just the way things are, you'll get used to it." I never did, but decided when I had my chance, that I would do something about it.

I joined the high school band and played the same clarinet I brought from Madison that my older brother Dale had played in the orchestra. The Columbus High Band was a large group and we marched for football games and took a summer band trip to Orlando, Florida to play and go to the beach. The trip to Orlando was my first trip to the ocean and I was amazed. I never got tired of just walking along the beach and staring out at all the water. I collected seashells. I could tell that my love for trees now had a rival. Playing in the band gave me a smaller group of friends, especially the clarinet section.

I also joined the Latin Club and took two years of Latin, which I liked and helped me in my language studies later in life. I was always called a Yankee because I did not talk like everyone else and came from "up north." I really didn't know where "up north" was, but accepted my new status in life. I enjoyed pitching again on a softball team and playing basketball. I ran fast and could steal bases like a pro, most of the time making it into score if I got a base hit. We didn't have a track team.

I was enjoying new experiences in 1949 while also grieving the loss of my parents and sister along with the separation from the rest of my family in Kansas. I was also adapting to an entirely new culture. I didn't know then that life was preparing me to adapt to many new cultures for the rest of my life. The challenge of this first experience sparked a curiosity that would last a lifetime.

Dorothy and Bud bought their first home on Seventh Avenue in Columbus, and I rode the city bus to school. Sherry and I shared a bedroom and had twin beds. We often went to the movies and to Fort Benning to swim at the pool at the Officers Club. Dorothy was pregnant with their first child and was due in the spring of 1950. She had a colored lady who came in to clean the house each week named Alberta. I used to sit and talk with Alberta as she did the housework and asked her about her family and how they lived. I was curious. We often gave her extra food to take home and some of our clothes along with her pay. She was very thin and had a lot of missing front teeth. She was always cheerful and happy and wore a handkerchief tied around her head. I enjoyed talking with her.

We had a backyard full of pine trees and a tool shed that Sherry said I locked her in at one time. Sherry's hair had grown out long again and her physical abilities returned. There was a Pit Barbecue Restaurant and Carry Out just at the end of our street, and I was often sent down to get a bag full of smoked barbecue sandwiches for a special treat. They were delicious and reminded me of Mom's cooking. When I was sixteen, I decided that I would quit band and sell my clarinet at the end of the school year. I had it appraised for one-hundred-dollars at a music shop and began planning how I would redecorate my room and spend the money. The last day of band that year, I brought it home on the bus. Later at home, I started looking for it in my room. I couldn't find it anywhere and knew that I had left it on my seat on the bus and called the bus station, but never found it. Many of my umbrellas had been left on the bus, but I was so disappointed about this loss. I learned a big lesson, not to spend money before you get it.

Adrienne, my niece, was born in April of 1950, part of the Baby Boom after World War II. Sherry and I rode the bus to Kansas that summer when I was fifteen and she was eleven. I visited with my twin brother Philip in Wichita and all my family. We had both changed a lot, and I got to meet some of his high school friends. It seemed strange, like we were no longer a part of the same family as we had been. Sherry then stayed with Betty and Pat in Wichita, and I rode the bus back to Georgia by myself.

I now had a room to myself and I did a lot of babysitting that year. I discovered the post library and read all the next summer. Then we moved to post housing at Fort Benning. We had large quarters and I had my own room. I got acquainted with all the kids on the post and we rode the school bus to Columbus High School.

Children in the military were called Army Brats, so we were known as the Benning Brats at the high school in Columbus. Living on a military post had its advantages. We were close to the Officers Club pool and tennis courts. I tried to swim and play tennis as much as possible and walked there frequently to hang out with friends. West Point, the U.S. Army Military Academy, arranged for cadets to visit the Army bases and would contact all the local high schools for dates for them. I went to many dances and parties to entertain the cadets at the Officers Club, and sewed all my dresses on Dorothy's portable Singer sewing machine. I remember one particular date that had the engaging name of Lt. Theodore E. Bear, which I promptly shortened to Ted E. Bear. He wore the military dress white uniform for the dances; he was tall with dark hair, friendly and good dancer. The other kids taught me how to jitterbug and I loved those dances.

The high school kids would meet at the local bowling alley on post to plan our Sunday afternoon fun. We would take sack lunches and all pile in one or two cars and decide on a destination. We often went to Stone Mountain, Georgia and the mock villages on the base that were constructed to look like European villages, empty and used for training soldiers. We made night visits to the jump towers where soldiers were trained as paratroopers. The soldiers were taken to the tops in a parachute and harness, and released to practice their landings. These were definitely "off limits" places, but they drew the high school crowd like magnets. The daring kids would climb the towers in the dark and walk out on the catwalks at hundreds of feet above the ground. Fortunately there were no accidents.

I often used the sewing machine for making my clothes and enjoyed staying up late at night to finish something that I could wear the next day. I babysat for my niece and many of my sister's friends' children throughout high school. I joined a sorority of girls on post during my junior year. I saw my first television in 1950 at a friend's house at Fort Benning. Bud took me out and taught me to drive their car during our time at Fort Benning, but I had very little opportunity to drive.

I spent four years in Columbus, Georgia and my time there gave me a much broader view of the world. I was accepted and made many friends and learned how to fit into the southern culture and military life. I observed injustice every day in the way the folks of color were mistreated. I'm sure this influenced my decision later in life to work as a missionary in the countries of Haiti and Zaire, Africa.

The summer after my junior year of high school, we moved to Manhattan, Kansas, while Bud, my sister's husband, went to Korea for a year. Adrienne was two years and Dorothy was pregnant with their second child. I started my senior year of high school in Manhattan. I was not happy about the move and did not want to leave Georgia. I wanted to finish high school in Columbus with my friends and moved to Manhattan reluctantly.

We located to a small house on Humboldt Street, just a couple of blocks from Manhattan High School and from the city park. Arriving in Manhattan in the summer, I got my first job as a cashier at the city swimming pool. It was here that I met Kenny Long, a smiling, handsome, tanned, college student home for the summer from a football scholarship at the College of Emporia. He had played for two years at the college and was on the Little All American College Football Team. I had picked up a southern drawl with my four years in Georgia, but I didn't know it was quite so obvious. Georgia peaches were well-known fruits in Kansas, and my new nickname became "the Georgia Peach"; Kenny enjoyed teasing me. Going from "Yankee" to "Georgia Peach" seemed ridiculous to me, and I didn't think this was fair. I couldn't believe that I could be made fun of for just the way I spoke. Since no teenager wants to be too different, this reminded me that I didn't talk like everyone else again.

My sister said that I could not date college boys until I had graduated from high school, so Kenny and I just enjoyed visiting at the pool when he would come to swim. I tried to read a book at slow times and he tried to sneak in the pool without paying when he saw me reading. He flirted and I read my book and told him to fork over the change. He also played on a baseball team, and I managed to go many evenings to the city park to watch him play. I couldn't decide if he looked more handsome in a swimsuit or a baseball uniform and baseball cap, but the athletic body and smile was the same. It was a fun summer that took my mind off my friends in Georgia and allowed me to make friends before my senior year in Manhattan High School. New friends invited me to join Sub Debs, a girl's club before school started.

I became a cheerleader and starred in school plays. This was my first drama opportunity and I found that I enjoyed acting. Little Orphan Annie was our main production and I got the leading role, feeling very much the part. I also had a class in Stage Craft where we made the props for the plays. Kenny had been a star athlete at Manhattan High School and his picture was in all the athletic teams at school. I turned eighteen years old in January of my senior year.

My senior prom date was Bill, the twin brother of one of my best friends, but he got a bad case of mumps and was at home in bed the night of the prom. Two of his friends took me in his place, so I had two dates and plenty of opportunities to dance. And they got to share the expenses of one date. We visited Bill in his room before going to the prom and he didn't look very happy; I felt sorry for him.

I worked in the lingerie department at JCPenney after school in downtown Manhattan on Thursday nights until 9:00 p.m. I considered attending college at Kansas University in Lawrence during that year, but my sights were set on Kansas State College. Many of my friends were also going to Kansas State. My sister had a miscarriage during this time at the hospital at Fort Riley, and we were all grieving the loss of their second child, a boy, with Bud still in Korea. We made it through this difficult time together.

Bud returned from his year-long tour with the Army in Korea, and they moved to Fort Leavenworth, Kansas for the Command and General Staff College. I moved with them, but soon returned to Manhattan to start my freshman year at Kansas State. Although I had hated to leave Georgia my senior year of high school, I had a good senior year in Manhattan and made friends. I had a job to start college and was ready to be on my own. I had received some Veterans

Administration Funds as a benefit from my father serving in World War I, which was put into a bank account for my college expenses. This would be used for my room and board at the dormitory. I applied for and received a scholarship for all my tuition that could be renewed each year.

After graduation in May 1953, I got a job working twenty hours per week at the Kansas State College library for the summer, which earned me enough for clothes and other expenses, and I planned on moving into a dormitory in the fall. I started dating Kenny, and we enjoyed being together after baseball games, and going to the movies and parties that summer. I also dated a couple of his friends on his baseball team. It was then that I found out that he would be transferring to Kansas State College in the fall on a football scholarship.

I had no idea what my major in college would be, though chemistry was one of my favorite subjects. My brother Dwight was in the Navy and serving in Korea. My brother Richard had enlisted in the Air Force. Most of my family was still around Wichita, Kansas. My twin brother Philip planned to go into the Army after his graduation from high school.

# Chapter 6: "Pinned"

**I WAS EXCITED ABOUT MY NEW JOB** and starting my freshman year of college. I moved into a freshman dormitory to start my first year at Kansas State in August 1953. Dorm life was new and interesting. I had two roommates and lived on the third floor of Southeast Hall on campus. There were so many new things to learn. I found my way around campus and made many new friends. Kenny and I dated often. We both loved to dance and would often go to a steakhouse outside of town where they had a dance floor. We also attended many of the school dances together.

My freshman year kept me running with work at the campus library, classes, activities, and dating. I joined a freshman pep club and took on responsibility in the freshman dorm. I had a scholarship for tuition, but had to remember to maintain a certain grade point average. With good college-prep classes my senior year of high school, my freshman year was not difficult. After my freshman year, Kenny worked in Manhattan and played football while we dated. I lived in the freshman dormitory and took summer school classes. In August after summer school, I went to Fort Leavenworth and stayed. I spent this break before fall semester taking a correspondence course, working as a waitress at the Officers Club and sewing clothes for school.

Kenny was studying for a business degree while he played football for Kansas State. Our football conference was called the Big Eight. I traveled to many out-of-town games with his parents or friends to see him play. Sometimes we went to his parent's house on Sunday evenings to eat. He had a younger brother, about four years old, and two older sisters. His parents were very proud that he was attending college and would be the first in their family to graduate from college.

Dorothy and Bud came from Leavenworth with friends to see Kenny play football games. He played right halfback and really enjoyed football. The team did well and almost made it to the Orange Bowl in Miami, Florida. We began selling oranges on campus with high expectations and much excitement. Kenny and I became "pinned" my second year at Kansas State when Kenny had joined a fraternity. I wore his fraternity pin and we considered ourselves engaged. It had tiny pearls and diamonds on it and was very pretty.

I also joined a sorority my second year of college and moved off campus to the sorority house, where I had a job as treasurer to help with the payment of my room and board. Keeping the books helped my financial situation, but I was way over my head in accounting. I had to call on Kenny many times to rescue me and do the books. I was in tears one night when I called and told him that my books had to balance by the next day and I had no idea how to do it. I needed the job. I calculated my finances and knew that I just had enough for three years of college using my savings and my salary from my library job, where I had started at sixty-five cents an hour. I decided that needed to go to summer school and take the full amount of hours possible in order to get my degree in just three years instead of the normal four years. I knew that this would be possible and a challenge. I needed one hundred and twenty hours for a degree in home economics with a major in family and child development. I took four semesters of French as an elective and enjoyed the challenge of a new language. My high school Latin class in Columbus helped. Summer school was relaxed and I could work more hours at the library.

The second summer of college, I lived with some friends in a girl's boarding house off-campus near the sorority. I played in the college band and took the hours I needed for my degree. I entered a Miss Manhattan/K State Beauty Pageant along with the other girls at the boarding house and won runner up at the Manhattan City Pool ceremonies. Kenny was in ROTC and had to go to boot camp training in Colorado with the Army that summer. We wrote letters often and expressed our thoughts on marriage, but did not make any plans. We just knew that we would probably marry some day in the future; I wanted to wait until after I had graduated. He wrote me about a freak accident where someone in the top bunk came crashing down on him in the middle of the night, bunk and all. He came home with a dent on the bridge of his nose where the frame of the springs had landed.

Home Economics Days was a special week where high school seniors visited the campus from all over Kansas. We presented our best displays, and the Department of Family and Child Development had an open house. As a senior student, I was in charge of the event and borrowed mannequins from the clothing store where Kenny worked in Aggieville for our real-life clothing displays. I had taken on a lot of responsibility and was very grateful for his help. I joined an Orchesis Modern Dance Club on campus and we gave performances, and I also played on our sorority basketball team.

Sometime in the second year of our dating, I had second thoughts about getting married and decided to apply for a job with the airlines as a stewardess. I interviewed with TWA in Kansas City and was accepted, so I thought that I would take a job and fly for a year before finishing college. Kenny decided this was the time to make his move and proposed marriage with a beautiful diamond ring. I was very surprised and it was very romantic. I knew this was the time for a decision for a career or marriage.

Kenny did not want to wait for me to work a year with the airlines, and I knew that he would be leaving college after graduation and going into the Army. Was I really serious about a career before I married and had a family? I knew Kenny was my choice and that was the most important. I said yes and turned down the job with TWA. I had no plans for working and raising a family at the same time.

We had talked about children after we were married. Since there were eleven children in my family and four in Kenny's family, we compromised with six as a good number. After our engagement, on one of my visits with his parents, I mentioned that we wanted to have six children. His mother replied, "I think you might change your mind after you are married."

Our last year after we were engaged, Kenny joined one of my classes in the Family and Child Development Department called Family Relations. As the only male in the class, the professor considered him the male authority and asked his opinion on most everything. She was charmed with his smile and delighted to have him in her class. It was an easy A for him, and he enjoyed being in my class. My plan for the future was to go into some kind of work with children, and I would be certified for teaching kindergarten. But I didn't know how this would work with Kenny in the Army and our moving so often. In Kenny's senior year of college, and my third year, we both worked at jobs and tried to finish up all our requirements for graduation. It was his fifth year, so he chose a second degree in accounting instead of a Master's in Business.

Kenny worked two jobs and made excellent grades since he wasn't playing football. One job was at a men's clothing store in Aggieville and the other evening job was cleaning the kitchen at the Wareham Hotel in downtown Manhattan. He couldn't start this job until late, and usually finished about two in the morning. He liked to cook a steak for himself before he cleaned everything, which was what he liked most about his job. My room in the sorority house was on the second floor at the end near the street. Kenny said he would come by on his way home after work and throw rocks at my window to wake me up. He asked if I would come down to the back door and give him a kiss. Many times I woke up to noises at my window and would run down the stairs half-asleep. We had a hurried kiss and embrace when I opened the door. He didn't have early morning classes as I did the next day.

Our goal was to graduate in June, and planned our wedding a week after graduation. He would receive his commission in the U.S. Army as a second lieutenant upon getting both his degrees. We were both very busy that year and it went very fast. We were running in the fast lane all year long working as many hours as we could. Sleep was not a priority. I remember driving to Wichita, Kansas with Kenny to introduce him to my family before we were married. He enjoyed meeting them all and went fishing with my brother Adren while we were there.

In April at Easter Break, I went to Fort Leavenworth and made my wedding dress. Dorothy and I went to Kansas City and I picked out a white embroidered organza material. I had the dress finished by the time I went back to K State. Dorothy helped me with all the wedding plans. While I was in college, Sherry had moved back to Fort Leavenworth with Dorothy and Bud, and she planned to be my maid of honor in our wedding. There were often times before the wedding that I thought how wonderful it would have been to have Mom and Pop there. During my last year of college, my brother Dwight came to Manhattan to visit me and brought his new wife Marge from California. She was expecting their first baby and they seemed very happy. It was the first time that I had met her. During this year my older brother Richard who had joined the Air Force was in a terrible automobile accident in California and had a ruptured spleen. I received a copy of the telegram saying he was in critical condition. The whole family was very concerned for him, and I had hoped that he could come to the wedding. My twin brother Philip was in the Army in Maryland and would not be able to come.

The week before our wedding I lost my diamond ring somewhere in our house in Fort Leavenworth. I think I found it in the paper bag with my wedding veil that I had bought. As I tried my veil on one morning, my ring caught on the net and was pulled off, landing in the bottom of the bag. I was so worried that I would not find it and was so relieved when I did. June 10th, 1956, and one week after our graduation, Kenny and I were married at the old historic and picturesque Post Chapel in Fort Leavenworth, Kansas, at about 4:00 in the afternoon. The reception was at the Officers Club. I didn't know it at the time, but this was also his parent's wedding date many years before. Everything went as planned and it was a very beautiful and happy occasion. We were both pretty exhausted after the hectic school year and graduation activities the week before. Dale and his wife Ivy came as did others from Wichita; even my brother Richard made it to the wedding looking very thin and pal. My bridesmaids were high school and college friends, and Sherry was my maid of honor. My niece, Adrienne, and her girlfriend were my flower girls.

Many of Kenny's relatives and friends came from Manhattan. Kenny had planned our honeymoon and kept it a secret. We drove to Kansas City for the first night after the wedding, then on to Lake Geneva, Wisconsin for our honeymoon. We had reservations in a lovely hotel on the lake and special tickets to a Louis Armstrong Band Performance. We loved Jazz, and we had danced to so many of his songs throughout college. We spent two weeks in the area, enjoying all the restaurants on the lake and stopping in Chicago to see the musical *Oklahoma* on the way back to Manhattan to our new apartment. We were ready to get on with married life. Kenny stayed at his job at the clothing store in Aggieville until he received his orders for active duty in the U.S. Army. I was not working for the first time in a while and was attempting to cook, with limited success, and sewing new clothes for myself. It was a very hot July in Kansas without fans in our second floor apartment. Fortunately we were only there a month before we moved out for Kenny's orders of active duty.

# Chapter 7: Remember Paris

**IT WAS EXCITING WHEN KENNY** got his orders for active duty in the Army Signal Corps at Fort Monmouth, New Jersey. It was August 1956, right after our graduation from Kansas State and our wedding the following week. We were not used to waiting for things to happen and had been living in anticipation for a month while eagerly awaiting these orders since we had arrived back from our honeymoon. It was completely different to be suddenly waiting after going at such a fast pace for all our college years. We had accomplished our goals and were ready to launch new careers. I was cooking pork chops for dinner in our hot second floor apartment in Manhattan, Kansas trying to impress him with my culinary abilities as a new bride. He came home from work and gave me the good news. I was ready for some action.

We packed and left Manhattan driving a 1954 light green two-door Ford sedan, and we pulled a trailer with all of our wedding gifts and clothes. The two-day drive to New Jersey began our military odyssey that would take us back and forth across the country many times in the next eleven years. We were both ready to get on with life and felt that we were starting a new adventure. Young, healthy, hopeful, and optimistic, we thought that together, anything was possible. After Kenny reported in at Fort Monmouth, we found a furnished second-floor apartment one block from the Atlantic beach in West Long Branch and moved in.

We enjoyed long walks along the beach in the evenings and picnics on the weekends. Our first home away from our families in Kansas made us realize that this was what we wanted. Neither of us had been to the East Coast and we liked to drive in the surrounding area exploring shops and small towns. Kenny's ROTC had prepared him for military life, and I was familiar with military posts as a teenager living at Fort Benning, Georgia, and then Fort Leavenworth, Kansas.

When Kenny reported for duty, I located the post library and decided that now was my opportunity to read for pleasure while Kenny was at work. All my hours in college had been carefully planned for study or work, and I had kept a tight schedule for the last three years. It was wonderful to have no job or classes, and I only had to decide what to fix for dinner. I was a lady of leisure and loved it. I often read all morning and then cleaned our small apartment and started dinner. We had not met any other military couples yet, and we were enjoying our time together as newlyweds in a new city. I checked out the Officers Club and joined a conversational French group in the Women's Club on post. I also took golf lessons. Kenny and I played golf together, and I lost many balls in the pond in front of the ninth hole. I had a psychological problem with hitting over water and like a magnet, the water drew all my balls right into the pond. Kenny thought it was pretty funny. As a beginner golfer I had a lot to learn.

By the time Kenny finished his four-month Basic Training Course and received his next orders for Fort Huachuca, Arizona, I was three months pregnant with our first child. We had talked about a family of six children while we were engaged, and this was an early start. We played bridge with another couple in their home and they asked us to listen to a salesman selling baby furniture after bridge one night. We fell for his sales pitch hook, line and sinker, as we used to say in Kansas. We bought that baby furniture, a sturdy chrome and vinyl combination set of highchair, stroller, buggy, and car bed that night for one hundred and fifty dollars. I guess that you would say when it came to our first baby we were impulsive buyers, since I was only three months pregnant! This was more than half of

Kenny's paycheck. The literature looked good and why not get the best? It was guaranteed to last through six children, although we were just concerned with the first one at that time, but we considered it a good investment for the future. We were high on optimism and confident of our ability to provide for our first child.

We met other newly married couples in Kenny's basic course at Fort Monmouth and went out dancing together. Some couples were from New York City, and they knew many good places to go in the area. The Officers Club had dances every Saturday night and we never missed one. We both loved to jitterbug and had plenty of practice together through college. Kenny was an excellent dancer, extremely quick and agile as an athlete, and I could follow any of his innovations on the dance floor. We rarely sat out a dance and loved the music, fast or slow.

At our Christmas vacation we drove cross-country to Kansas to visit both our families on our way to Fort Huachuca, Arizona. We arrived in Fort Leavenworth for Christmas with Dorothy and Bud and Adrienne. Since we were expecting a baby, we both thought we needed a pet, and Kenny surprised me with a registered, eight-weeks-old blond cocker puppy for my Christmas gift. I was delighted! We named her Carmen, and I took her for walks and loved having a puppy for company.

After the Christmas holidays, we headed for the Southwest and Arizona with our new puppy. Fort Huachuca was an Army post near the small town of Sierra Vista and across the border from Nogales, Mexico. Compared to Kansas, it was really hot here. When we arrived, we drove all over the countryside and up in the mountains and found nothing to rent. We met other army couples living in the country on ranches and little bungalows but could find nothing available. We had hoped to find a cabin in the mountains. We finally had to move into a small motel in Sierra Vista for a couple of months until we could move into in post housing at Fort Huachuca. After moving into a small efficiency apartment in the pink adobe Sierra Vista Motel, Kenny reported for duty at Fort Huachuca.

What a treat to be in a swimming suit out in the warm sun in the middle of January! My blood had been conditioned to the cold winters in Kansas for the past few years and didn't know how to react. Kenny enjoyed playing golf on his days off where the greens were sand at Fort Huachuca. I played once, but enjoyed the swimming pool more. We adapted quickly and learned to love Arizona in the five months that we were there. It was so different from the Midwest, and we decided that we would come back here to live another time in the future, if not before, maybe retirement. We often drove to Nogales for Mexican food and shopping. We bought colorful serapes and used them for blankets and in the car for picnics. One of the Mexican border custom officials recognized me from my job at the Kansas State College library when he had been a student at K State. This was beginning to be an extremely small world.

I assisted with a Brownie Scout Troop and prepared to have our first baby. I hand-sewed bright orange denim curtains for our kitchen and bedroom. I made maternity clothes by hand when I needed something new to wear and needed extra space in my five-months-pregnant waistline. But with very little extra money, I usually made my clothes from something else rather than buying new material. Wanting a new dress for a party, the bright orange denim curtains looked perfect, so I made a lovely maternity party dress. We were invited to a formal dance and dinner at the Officers' Club, and I really had to stretch my imagination in deciding what to wear. Going through all my clothes, my eye caught my wedding dress and I knew that all that lovely white embroidered silk organza skirt would make a beautiful formal maternity dress. And it was beautiful! A wedding dress converted to a maternity dress seemed natural. I was not sentimental and considered the material in the dress in a practical way as useful for weddings and babies. I had picked out the silk organza and fashioned it into a wedding dress, so I felt I could fashion it again into what was needed. I felt very stylish in such a unique and lovely dress, and I needed the confidence boost that I would not be permanently pregnant. I sewed a pink and white cotton checked flannel layette for our expected baby, convinced that it was a girl and picked out the name Tamara from a Russian novel that I had just read.

We moved into a duplex on Fort Huachuca in March, and Kenny applied for Flight School. We hoped we didn't have to leave Fort Huachuca, but we knew that we would have to if he was accepted for Flight School. We loved the warm, dry climate of Arizona, golf and swimming. Kenny received orders for Flight School in Texas in April and we celebrated. To fly airplanes was his dream. Now all I needed to do was have this baby. I was two weeks late, our time growing short, and I hoped to go into labor soon. We just had ten days left before moving to Texas, and I went into labor with our first baby. While walking the floors at home and timing my labor pains, Kenny asked me if I wanted something to eat before we left for the hospital. I replied that I would really like a fried egg sandwich and he fixed me one. Then we left for the post hospital. Kenneth Darrell Long, Jr. was born on May 1, 1957, at Fort Huachuca in Cochise County, Arizona. We were deeply happy to have a handsome, healthy, blue-eyed son and named him after Kenny. With two men in the Long family already named Kenny, his Dad and Granddad, we started calling our first son Chip.

With my family and child development studies in college, I had read many books on childbirth and thought I was prepared, but I think no one is really prepared for their first baby. There are just some experiences that are not describable and this was one. I thought of my mother during my labor and decided that she must have been crazy to go through this ten times! No sane person would choose to do this. I was not prepared for the acutely strong emotions that I experienced. All I knew was that I would never go through that again! A neighbor with seven children helped me cope with my new role as a mother because I felt totally inadequate for the job.

Ten days later carrying our new baby boy, I cleaned the house and we moved out and traveled to Camp Gary, Texas for Kenny's Army Fixed-Wing Flight School. As we packed everything into our trailer, I swept out our duplex. Carmen, our cocker spaniel had moved once by now, and was acting very insecure, curled up in an empty box, hoping that she was going also. I was told that inspection of military quarters was carried out with a white glove to determine if everything was clean before they let you clear quarters, so I worked my tail off to get it sparkling clean. We passed! Traveling cross-country with a ten-day-old baby was to be our first of many challenges traveling with children around the world over the next many years. Chip was a happy baby to care for, and he seemed to be content with the basic essentials. And that was all I was prepared to offer in this stage of motherhood.

We found a brick duplex on Blue Bonnet Drive near the base in San Marcos, Texas and moved in. We celebrated our first anniversary on June 10, 1957, with a six-week-old son. The post nursery had an age limit for babies, and Chip slipped under the wire. We celebrated with dinner and dancing at the Officers Club; we recognized how fortunate we were to have a healthy baby boy and that Kenny had selected for flight training.

Kenny's family came to visit from Kansas to see their first grandson that summer of 1957. It was a very dry climate in Texas, and I found a coral snake hiding in our backyard and scorpions nesting in our shoes in the house. It was quite unsettling! Our puppy Carmen sniffed the baseboards in the house every morning to locate the scorpions for us. I was sure glad to have her take on that responsibility because I was frightened to have them around Chip. We enjoyed all the friends we made during our time in San Marcos and Flight School was a sink or swim situation. Many washed out. Our duplex neighbor was an instructor pilot from England. He and his wife had no children, but they had a large yellow lab that they taught to open the kitchen drawer and get his own ball. Chip was just a few months old and hadn't learned too many tricks yet, so we were called on to applaud their dog. Our puppy Carmen was not as tall or so talented and we felt that we had neglected her training.

A Britannica World Book salesman arrived on Blue Bonnet Drive one day and convinced me that our new six-weeks-old son needed a set of reference books for college. Wanting to provide the best for our children, I signed the contract for monthly payments. When Kenny came home from flying that night he was amazed. He couldn't believe that I fell for that sales pitch again. It was many years before Chip started using his Britannica World Books, and eighteen years later all the children were still using them.

Not all the men who started the flying program finished. A large percentage of the pilots were unable to fly solo. It was hard to see friends wash out of the program and leave. It was a time of much stress and we were both worried at times, but flying was Kenny's choice in the Army and he loved it. He had much confidence, and I had confidence in him too. He learned to fly the L-19 and the L-20 single-engine Army aircraft while we were there. In a photo taken while we lived there, he has a huge smile on his face, dressed in his flight suit with his parachute on his back and leaning nonchalantly on the plane. Here was a man who had found his dream. The L-20s, sometimes flying as low as fifty to sixty feet, had been used by the Army in aerial reconnaissance missions during WWII in Europe.

We celebrated again at his graduation from Flight School and moved to the Peanut Capital in Enterprise, Alabama for more Flight Training at Fort Rucker. We first rented a small trailer and then moved into a small house with gas heat. That was the year the Alabama Gas Company ran out of gas. Water froze in the shower and we had to keep Chip in bed between us to keep him from freezing. Holes in the floorboards of the house let mice into our kitchen, and I never knew how many mice I would face in the mornings. As a child on our farm I had hated mice. When I got up in the morning in our very cold house, I usually stomped on the wooden floors and sang to alert them of my coming so I could put the coffee pot on the stove with no company in the kitchen. I kept our kitchen silverware in a plastic divided container in the oven, thinking it was safer from the mice. One day I forgot about the silverware when I turned on the over and melted it all.

We bought our first black and white television set and my new portable Singer sewing machine while living in Fort Rucker. I was confident that I could now make anything that was required for our family. That included my own clothes, shirts and a bathrobe for Kenny, clothes for Chip, curtains, bedspreads and even a gun case for Kenny's shotgun. Our Saturday night treat was to buy a large bag of hot roasted peanuts from the sidewalk vendors in downtown Enterprise and snuggle on our couch together, watching *Gunsmoke* on our small, black and white television set.

We bred our dog Carmen with a blond, registered cocker show dog that came from long pedigree of blue ribbon winners in the family. Unfortunately while we were living a short while in the trailer home before we moved into our house, she was also bred "accidentally" with a black stray dog when I took her outside one evening. So her first litter of puppies was a mix of four blond and five black puppies. We were terribly disappointed. Unable to think of how to explain it, I told my friends that Carmen had been raped. We could not register them. I learned early the woes of dog breeding.

Upon completion of Kenny's training at Fort Rucker, Alabama, we moved to Fort Sam Houston, Texas near San Antonio where he flew with the 178th Signal Corp Battalion. Our brick duplex on Forbush Avenue on Fort Sam Houston was near the golf course and we started playing golf frequently on his days off. I got my first set of women's golf clubs as a gift on our second wedding anniversary in June. Kenny brought them home to surprise me, and I was absolutely astonished. I was beginning to get serious about this game, and his confidence in my potential ability with this investment was what I needed. Kenny played baseball on the Battalion Team and Chip was the mascot. I made Chip a t-shirt with the 178th logo in bright red, and we went to all the games. We made many good friends here and started going to church. Kenny often had night flying and wouldn't get home until late. I was lonely when he was gone, and I tried to keep busy. We started adding some furniture to our home, and Kenny made a couch and some end tables for our living room. I picked out a burnt-orange overstuffed chair for his Father's Day present.

With very little money to buy furniture, I soon learned the skill of painting and decorating old Army footlockers, stenciled with Kenny's name, rank and serial number on the top. We shipped our personal and household goods in these lockers from post to post across the country. It was an art. Military wives were creative.

I would use a three-foot by eighteen-inch rectangular container, twelve inches high, and use my imagination. Black, brown, blue, maroon, bright green, red, white; there was no end to the combinations of colors. The reinforced metal corners and edges, handles, and lock plate provided different planes for painting interesting contrasting colors. I even put a brushed gold paint on these edges to give an antique and elegant look. Bright bamboo woven mats from Mexico, or tile, or contact paper created a designer's touch on top. Footlockers were our main piece of household furniture before we had any furniture. We used them over the years in the Army for a multitude of purposes; they served as: Coffee tables, end tables, bedside tables, cushioned seats, room dividers, cedar chest, toy chests, step stool, tool chest, sewing cabinet, book chest, locked gun cabinet, sports equipment chest, liquor cabinet, magazine storage, and anything that required its own space.

Kenny built Chip a fort with a picket fence around it in our backyard and we added a small plastic swimming pool since it was very hot in San Antonio. I crocheted a round rag rug like my mother had made to put in the playhouse. Children's television programs were just beginning to take off and I interviewed at the local television station in San Antonio to be the teacher of a new preschool show. It sounded like a fun opportunity and thought this would be a perfect use of my Child Development degree; plus it was just a one-day a week job. My Midwestern accent was an advantage instead of a Texas drawl. I had to do a commercial which I thought was fun. I was called back for the final selection and then asked how soon I could start. I had to admit to being eight months pregnant and would need a short break for the imminent birth of our second child. The producer looked at me and was completely surprised. He didn't know that I was pregnant with the tent style dress that I was wearing. The style was in vogue and hid a lot, so I had sewn all my maternity clothes to fit the latest fashion. I did not get the job. Kenny offered his condolences, as he had encouraged me, and knew that I was especially excited about getting the job. My television career would have to wait.

My obstetrician at Brooke Army Medical Center at Fort Sam Houston was a graduate of the Kansas University Medical Center in Lawrence, Kansas. We discussed our rival football and basketball teams at our Kansas Universities and sang our school fight-songs during my labor. I think a glass of champagne to celebrate the coming birth relaxed me considerably. Phillip, our second son, was born at Brooke Army Medical Center in San Antonio on October 23, 1958. He was a dark-haired handsome boy with dark-brown eyes. We were perfectly happy with another healthy boy, and I put my pink and white checked layette away for another day.

I was in an open hospital ward and had a bed in a row of beds for the new mothers and babies. I found a deck of cards and was not always in my own bed when the doctor made rounds, but playing cards with another mother. After our postpartum exams before discharge, which were conducted with no privacy, and on his way out the door, the doctor turned around to face us and made a general official announcement. "Remember ladies, no sex or intercourse for six weeks."

With an integrated ward consisting of women from many countries, an African American mother replied, "You mean with my husband?" The comment was meant to elicit some humor in our recovery from the trauma of childbirth. Sex was the last thing anyone was thinking about three days after childbirth.

The doctor instantly replied "I mean with anyone," as the women all laughed and he exited.

The woman in the bed on my right had lost a baby at birth, and I felt deeply sad for her, and realized that not everyone was happy. It must have been acutely difficult for her to be on a ward with so many happy new mothers. Space was at a minimum or medical knowledge totally ignorant for her to be in the same ward with us. Kenny and I were especially grateful to have two healthy boys.

I told Chip that a baby brother was the best gift that we could give him. Only eighteen months old, he wasn't impressed. When Phillip was only three weeks old and lying on his back in his crib, Chip climbed up on the crib rail and leaned over to feed Phillip Chocolate Coco Puffs cereal. Luckily I walked into the bedroom at the right time to see Phillip gagging and choking. I learned quickly that you couldn't trust a one-and-a half-year-old around a new baby.

Kenny enjoyed cooking out on our backyard grill almost every night, and we enjoyed the warm climate of Texas. As we enjoyed our family of four, Chip and Phillip were getting to know each other. They were eighteen months apart, and Chip gladly assumed the role of the older brother. He got a tricycle on his second birthday and joined the neighborhood kids on their wheels. Our parenting skills were copied after our own parents and not from the books from my courses at college. We took the boys to the San Antonio Zoo to ride elephants and had many picnics and fun family times together. The boys played in their backyard fort and swimming pool.

Our neighbor in the other half of our duplex watched the boys, and I managed to play golf during my next pregnancy with our third baby, Amber. I came home from playing golf one afternoon and Chip, at about two years old, was sitting on the dining-room table beside a bowl of apples looking totally guilty. He had taken one bite out of every apple in the bowl, putting all ten back very neatly. I thought that was quite interesting for a two-year-old. Child development in progress is always interesting and surprising.

Chip, Phillip and I spent three months in Tuscaloosa, Alabama with Dorothy and Bud where they were assigned with the military, while Kenny left for another three-month flying assignment in South Carolina. He called us often. Adrienne had a sandbox that they loved to play in together. Bud and Dorothy took us out to dinner for fried chicken at a nice restaurant. Phillip sat happily in his highchair and threw his chicken bone across the room when he finished eating; we hadn't had a lot of experience eating out with the children. Before Amber's birth we returned again to Fort Sam Houston, Texas. Chip got measles right before I went to the hospital to have Amber, and I noticed Phillip looked strange when they came with Kenny to pick me up from the hospital after Amber was born. I looked closely at Phillip, now eighteen months old, and recognized the rash as measles. That was a warm welcome for our new baby that had me a little worried.

We now had our beautiful little girl, born on April 22, 1960, named after my mother Amber. Amber was brown-eyed with brown hair and a welcome change of sex; I finally got to use the pink and white checked layette. My sewing machine literally flew over those frilly little girl dresses. With Kenny and me as producers, we were quickly forming our own preschool television show. Kenny received orders for helicopter training at Fort Rucker, Alabama and we moved there for a few months. He learned to fly the glass bubble Bell Helicopter. My thoughtful husband bought me a portable dishwasher because I couldn't keep up with the dishes, and that was not in his job description as a pilot. I was delighted and the daily sink-full of dirty dishes disappeared. Our time at Fort Rucker finished, we returned to Fort Sam Houston again for a short period before we had orders for Stuttgart, Germany. We were excited about the possibilities of living in Europe.

Before moving to Germany for a three-year tour of duty in July of 1960, I flew with the children to visit our families in Kansas. Kenny joined us after putting our Ford station wagon car and Carmen on the ship. My older brother Richard had married Carol Barnard from Madison in 1959. Richard had graduated from Kansas State College in electrical engineering and we saw them before we left for Germany. My flight with the three children was made more difficult when I had to change planes at midnight in Dallas to go to Wichita. Fortunately Phillip at eighteen months was walking well and could carry box of diapers, and Chip led him by the hand while I carried Amber. It is never easy travelling with three small children; a mother needs more than two hands.

After our visit with our families in Kansas we all flew on Pan American Airlines to Newfoundland for refueling, then on to Frankfort, Germany in July 1960. We had eighteen pieces of luggage. Chip was three years, Phillip one and a half years, and Amber three months old. Our family was growing and travelling became more complicated. I dressed all the children in their pajamas on the plane and after a short layover in Newfoundland in the middle of the night, we landed in Frankfurt, Germany. It was an eighteen-hour flight. On arrival, I remember thinking how drab and gray everything looked in Germany but very neat. It was fifteen years after the end of WWII and they were still rebuilding. I don't think that I had ever heard German spoken before, but I was familiar with French. I did not recognize a word.

We took a train from Frankfurt to Stuttgart, Germany and lived on the fourth floor of a German hotel for six weeks after arriving. I started adding to my German vocabulary word by word since all my time was spent taking care of the children. It was an especially difficult time. Like many times in the Military, it was a test of endurance.

Kenny joined the 34th Signal Battalion and only spent a few days with us. He was sent out on field maneuvers while the children and I with Carmen, our dog, stayed in our fourth floor suite. It was an especially long six weeks. We ate lots of cold cereal and peanut butter and jelly sandwiches. For a change we went out for dinner in the evening, which would be the highlight of our day. Chip had the job of walking Carmen down four flights of stairs and taking her outside. He enjoyed doing this as he slowly descended the stairs holding the handrail with one hand and the leash on the other. Carmen was in a hurry and Chip was an especially responsible three-year-old.

It was a welcome relief when Kenny returned and we were finally able to move into an apartment in a small German village near a park. The weather was still nice and I took the children and Carmen out each day for walks. We had picnics in our backyard and the park, and I often took the children to another larger and beautiful park with a swimming pool. The park was meticulously clean with not a scrap of paper or trash. You could not walk on the grass, but had to keep to the paths. That was a little hard to explain to the children, but they learned. German families were all out enjoying a beautiful day. It was easy to feel at home in a park with all the children, including ours, running and playing.

We lived in a second floor apartment and I lowered the boys' snacks and drinks to them into one of our straw Mexican baskets off the balcony using a rope; this way I didn't have to leave Amber alone. They thought this was great fun and often asked for snacks. We were there for Halloween, so Kenny and I took turns dressing up as trick or treaters and knocking on the front door to ask the boys for candy. Not recognizing us, they looked at us wide-eyed and gave us a treat. We dressed them in costumes too. We didn't think the Germans would understand and we didn't want the kids to miss this holiday that we had enjoyed so much ourselves. Improvising, we quickly adapted to the celebration of traditions in two cultures.

After two months, we moved again to post housing at Kelley Barracks, a housing area where we stayed for the rest of our three-year tour in Germany. It was not a barracks but a large, three-bedroom, first-floor flat furnished with heavy, dark wood, German furniture. It was much easier to have no stairs to climb when taking the children out each day to the playground. I was often asked how I could stand all the noise from the outside street living on the first floor. There was so much more noise with the children inside the house, that I never noticed any outside noises.

We drove in the German countryside and saw all the farms and small villages. We were amazed at how green and neat and clean the countryscape was. We enjoyed eating out at the gasthauses (restaurants), and always took the children with us. The Germans were amazed at how well behaved our children were and often watched us. On one occasion as we exited the gasthause after dinner, the Germans applauded us and said "Bravo." We were so surprised and just said "Dankashurn." They didn't usually bring their children to the restaurants, but they often had their small Dachshund dogs on leashes tied to their chairs.

I played golf and then became pregnant with our fourth child. My golf partner in the Women's Club asked me, "Phyllis, when are you going to stop having children and get serious about golf? I was serious about golf, just not as serious as she had already raised her family.

We had our blond cocker spaniel dog Carmen bred again and she had her first litter of registered cockers, ten and all blond. I sent Kenny a message to his field location to let him know. "Carmen and ten babies are doing well." When this message was relayed to Kenny, all the men wanted to know who Carmen was. We kept the puppies in our large kitchen separated by a temporary plywood two-foot high wall and the children all enjoyed playing with them. Chip and Phillip took turns leading Carmen on a leash outside with ten puppies following. It was a hilarious sight! It was good advertising and they were so sweet and easy to sell before they were six weeks old. After six weeks we were more than ready to give them to their owners. Every morning I faked being asleep, pulling the covers over my head so Kenny would have to go into the kitchen first to make his coffee and clean up the newspapers off the floor in our make-shift puppy kennel. What a smell with ten puppies! There was a lot of cleaning up to do.

In the spring of 1961 Kenny and I took a trip through France, Belgium, and Luxembourg, staying in a small fishing village on the North Sea in Holland. We also visited Rotterdam and Amsterdam, Holland. This was the first of many trips that we took throughout Western Europe during our stay there. We visited the military cemeteries in France and Belgium, which were beautifully kept and acutely sobering. Hundreds of white crosses were lined up covering the entire cemetery with names of men who had died in the battles of World War II, reminding us of why we were in Germany and the cost of our freedom. The enormous fields of tulips in Holland were gorgeous, reflecting every possible color; we would always remember the beauty of that country. Our B&B hosts insisted that we try the local dish, electric eel. I liked fish in general, but this was peculiarly different from catfish that I knew in Kansas. I did not develop a taste for eel while we were there. We went shopping in the villages that had ancient windmills and bought all the children colorfully painted wooden shoes.

They enjoyed wearing these until they outgrew them and especially loved the clacking noises they made on our hardwood oak floors. They sounded like a train coming down the track. We had a wonderful time and said that it was our second honeymoon.

Then we had our second beautiful blond and blue-eyed daughter, Grace Gene, born at the Stuttgart Hospital on June 23, 1961. The hospital was very bare and impersonal. The German nurses did not seem too friendly and treated our requests as bothersome. Grace was the smallest baby of our four children at six pounds and ten ounces, but she was healthy. We were particularly happy to have another girl. Her first name was after Kenny's mother Grace. Our sexes were even now and the children were learning to play well together. I decided to give up golf and put my clubs away for another day in the future. I didn't like being gone for such long hours from the children, and they were my first job.

My sewing machine was going frequently as I made furnishings for the house and clothes for the children and myself. I tried out a series of live-in German maids, but finally gave up. I went into the boys' room one day and it was a mess with toys scattered everywhere. I told Chip, who was five years old, that he should pick up his toys. He replied, "Oh, I think that I will let the maid do it." I didn't like the way that sounded and what it implied. He ended up picking up his toys. During this time I became acutely ill with strep throat while Kenny was gone on field maneuvers and he had to be called home. Neighbors took me to the hospital and the doctors put me on antibiotics. Later I also had three wisdom teeth pulled and spent a day or two recovering.

I took German language lessons, but didn't get very far beyond the basics. My French did not help me at all. I could shop, ask directions, and find my way around the countryside and city with the little German that I knew. But I got lost quickly in a conversation. We enjoyed German Oktoberfest with all the great food, lots of beer, and outside dancing in the streets. It was a carnival atmosphere with the last days of nice weather before winter. It was fun sitting at the long tables, rubbing elbows with the local Germans and singing.

The winters were unusually long with snow covering the ground from November to April. We lived across the street from the Black Forest and took the children into the woods for hikes. Kenny bought a wooden German sled with wooden runners and took the kids on sled rides all around our street. They loved it. I also started piano lessons and started shopping for antique German furniture and clocks with a close friend, Marilyn Rademacher, who also had four children. We put our eight children in her station wagon or mine, and shopped at second hand furniture shops on Saturdays in downtown Stuttgart. One shop was opened only on Tuesdays called the Two o'clock shop. My limit was five dollars. I found two beautiful oak wood round dining room tables that we cut down to use as living room coffee tables. They were great for toddlers who were learning to walk and had no sharp corners. We enjoyed using these in our family rooms and living rooms for many years. The Germans were dumping their traditional heavy wood furniture with marble tops and getting all the new modern furniture that they could find. And the Americans were looking for antique heavy wooden furniture with marble tops for their modern houses.

We kept Leon and Marilyn Rademacher's four children when they went on trips and they kept our four when we went to Paris for another second honeymoon. Kenny and I enjoyed a week in Paris and had a wonderful time. It was a romantic week of seeing all that we could of the sights of Paris and enjoying the French cuisine. We had been told by friends to take the Nightclub Tour and we did. I fell asleep at our table at one show about two in the morning and Kenny had to practically carry me back to our hotel. I didn't like all the naked ladies. We took a midnight dinner boat ride and discovered the magic of the Seine River, seeing Paris at night. It was breathtakingly beautiful! The flood lights on Notre Dame added to the spectacular Parisian night. After we had been to the Eiffel Tower we bought some beautiful engraved prints near Montmartre where we had lunch in a small restaurant. I planned to have these lovely prints framed back in Stuttgart for our living room. We browsed the Louvre and Notre Dame cathedral and walked the streets along the canals. We gathered at the Arc de Triomphe to watch the eternal flame with other tourists. We had a tour of the Palace of Versailles and our picture taken in front. It was more gold and wealth than we could ever imagine. Kenny bought a black beret at the Paris Flea Market downtown, wearing it jauntily cocked to one side on his head. We ate the French onion soup that was our favorite. Later in our marriage when we had difficult limes, we would say "Remember Paris." It brought smiles and happy memories to our marriage.

Another vacation we rented a German camping trailer and took Chip and Phillip on a camping trip to Barcelona, Spain and camped on the Mediterranean Beach. We went to restaurants and saw flamenco dancers and at one restaurant, Kenny got up and joined the dancers. Chip and Phillip loved the bullfights. We took popcorn like we were going to a football game. I think the boys were too young to really know what was happening, but I did and I didn't want to watch. A framed bull-fighting poster with the matador and his red cape and the date was on our living room wall for many years to remind us of that day. Years later when we arrived in Manhattan and drove past the football stadium where Kenny used to play football, Phillip said, "Oh good, there are bullfights here." He saw something familiar from his perspective of five years.

Our friends, Leon and Marilyn, were in our battalion and we visited and spent many good times together. Leon was from San Diego, California and Marilyn from Oceanport, New Jersey. They were devoted Catholics, and they loved children and to entertain and to dance. They also had a great sense of humor. Marilyn made her spicy hot chicken-wings recipe for our cocktail parties forty years before party wings became the rage. Kenny and Leon worked together in Seventh Corps Headquarters, and Marilyn and I had much in common. The four of us often went out to dinner together on the weekends to the Balkan Grill at the Stuttgart Train Station during our three years in Germany. We enjoyed the good food, wine and music. Marilyn and I shopped and often had tea in the mornings together. We both sewed clothes for our children and decorated our homes with German antiques.

Leon and Marilyn were a few years older than us and were in the military many more years. Leon was going on eighteen years as an enlisted man. He was now a Captain and Kenny a First Lieutenant. While marriages in the military were strained from so many separations and drinking problems, we shared our problems together with these friends and drew closer to our families. With four older children, they had already met many of our challenges with raising a family and turned to church and faith in God. We formed a bond of friendship during these three years and our paths came together at other times in both the military and civilian life.

The Cuban Missile Crisis in October of 1962 took place during our time in Germany. The crisis was making the headlines in the States and we were alerted for possible evacuation. Everyone talked about it. We had always been on alert and we were living in a high-risk situation, but if Russia decided to send the missiles flying, Berlin and our military base at Stuttgart were strategic targets. For two weeks we were on high alert and it was an acutely tense time when we needed to be prepared to evacuate on a moment's notice. There had been dry runs preparing for evacuation of dependents into France going through the Gilder Gap in North Germany. The troops would go first and the dependents would go alone by car. We were told that we would have to shoot our dogs. It all had to do with security. I was awfully upset about that since by then Carmen was a permanent part of our family, and I don't think I realized how dangerous the climate was. But the crises progressed to a standoff and we did not have to evacuate. Many years later, in 1990, and living in Zaire, Africa I was always on alert status as a missionary; I decided whether military or missionary, the danger was about the same.

We sold all Carmen's puppies, and Kenny and I were able to finance another trip, this time on a German train to Vienna to celebrate New Year's in 1962. We stayed in a beautiful hotel near St. Stephen's Cathedral. Vienna was an unusually exciting city at the crossroads of Eastern and Western Europe, but Americans weren't welcome in certain parts. We spent a lovely New Year's Eve in Vienna having dinner at a restaurant. I found a beautiful pair of hand-made, tall black leather boots in a boot shop. I wore those boots for many years. We had to go home a day early in order to pay for them, plus we were missing the children by now even though Vienna was an exciting place to be. Budapest was just kilometers away, but off limits for us and we could not go there.

Chip had started kindergarten while we lived in Kelley Barracks. He walked just a few blocks with a neighbor boy and was learning a little German. It was a good experience for him in his first year of school. He made friends with other kindergarten children in the neighborhood. Our three-bedroom apartment on the first floor of an eight-apartment complex was comfortably furnished. We had shipped a television set, but it sat in one corner of the living room blank, reminding us that it did exist in other parts of the world. The children often asked what it was for and it served as a nice counter to display pictures.

Kenny walked to work at 7th Corp Headquarters where he worked in Intelligence. It was very convenient for him to come home and rescue me on one occasion when the front door slammed shut and locked me out, leaving me stranded in the hallway in my bathrobe and four children inside with the youngest in her highchair. The handles and locks on the German doors were difficult for the children to open, so I went to a neighbor's apartment to call Kenny at work and have him bring home a key. It was extremely cold out, and I couldn't walk in my bathrobe and slippers to his office or leave the children alone. I talked to Chip through the locked door and gave him instructions.

Living on base was convenient for many reasons. The commissary was within walking distance as was the post chapel. Everyone lived in a very close area. I could walk to a neighbor with the children anytime. U.S. military wives sat together at picnic tables in the yard when the weather was nice, and we watched the children play in the sandbox. We were pleased with how well they played together. Taking care of the children was our full time job while our husbands frequently went to the field. I often called my friend Marilyn and asked her to meet me at the picnic table with a pot of tea, and I made the banana bread. When our husbands were in the field the wives were all especially supportive of each other.

I had hoped to take a train trip on the Siberian
Railway to St. Petersburg, Russia, but the CIA came to our
home to warn me of the dangers. Kenny had a top-secret
clearance for his work, and the wife of an Army Lieutenant
working in the intelligence sector was too big of a target for
kidnapping and blackmail. Kenny never said that I couldn't
go, he just sent the CIA to let me know the dangers.
Although I had wanted to go, I saw the wisdom in
canceling my trip. I loved my family too much to risk that
danger.

Later I took the train through the Berlin Corridor to
West Berlin on a trip with two friends, Marilyn
Rademacher and Sue Leister, officers' wives in our
Company. We each had four children. This was one month
after the Berlin Wall had been built to divide the city. Our
train was often stopped and searched by Russian soldiers
armed with machine guns and German shepherd guard
dogs. We wondered if we would ever make it to Berlin. We
visualized being snatched off the train and landing in
Siberia. Our husbands had warned us to never give up our
passports before we left, having not been able to persuade
us from going.

We took a bus through Checkpoint Charlie, the
security dividing point between West and East Berlin.
When we arrived at the entrance they asked for our
passports to get on the bus, so we all made a quick decision
to risk it. We had gotten this far and wanted to go on into
East Berlin and that was the only way. We prayed that we
would get our passports back again and not be detained. I
asked some questions of the East Berlin tour guide on the
bus and Marilyn and Sue told me to be quiet. We were
followed and watched closely everywhere we went by
their intelligence. Sitting at an outside café for dinner felt
like being on display in a show window; we looked so

different in our clothes and shoes that it was obvious we were from the West.

We had military friends that we knew from Huachuca, Arizona who were now stationed in West Berlin, and when we contacted them by phone, they assured us that it was an acutely tense and trying time in American-Soviet relations. East Berlin was still devastated from World War II and nothing had been rebuilt as it had been in West Berlin. There was a sharp contrast in East Berlin from the West, completely dismal, with the people terribly gloomy and oppressed. We took a city bus tour around to all the War Memorials and National Monuments. It was awfully sad. We were all glad to get our passports back and return safely to West Berlin. Taking the train back through the Berlin Corridor, Marilyn, Sue and I were deeply happy to be back safely to our homes. It had been a stressful trip, but we were all glad that we had gone. We knew that we would never go again. Our husbands and twelve children were thoroughly glad to see us. Living in a dangerous part of the world anyway, the degrees of danger didn't always feel relevant.

Kenny went on many field maneuvers six months out of the year and flew helicopters. While I was loading up our station wagon with a playpen, our dog, and four children, a neighbor and friend came out to ask me where I was going. I told her that I was going to have dinner with my husband. I drove on the autobahn four hours in a snowstorm, from Stuttgart to Heilbronne in Northern Germany to meet Kenny near his field campsite. He flew his helicopter to our lodging to join us at night so that we could have some time together as a family. With Kenny gone often on maneuvers, we tried to take advantage of all opportunities to be together as a family. It was a special treat for us to be near his field maneuvers and have him join us for dinner and stay with us. We ate out at German gasthauses in the evening. The children were absolutely excited to see him fly off in his helicopter in the mornings to go back to work. After he got into the cockpit, we all stood around waving in the wind of the rotors while he flew away. The boys stood looking at the helicopter a long time on the last morning. It was a long drive home to Stuttgart, but a happy time for us all.

We took a family skiing vacation to Berchtesgaden in Southern Germany in the Bavarian Alps and Chip learned how to ski for the first time. The snow-covered mountains were just spectacular. It was a lovely vacation spot for both German and American families with many things for the children to do. We also took the children in an open cable car up to the top of the highest mountain in Germany, the Zugspitz. Two nuns with us were praying for our all of our safety with their rosaries as the open cable car swung back and forth and the blowing snow came in through the window and covered us. It was an unusually scary time while we clutched the hands of the children. We were relieved to get down safely. Kenny and I later took another ski trip to France alone and stayed in a small village up in the French Alps and skied. I enjoyed all our trips together, but felt an inner discontent and restlessness that had nothing to do with Kenny that I didn't understand, there was something missing in my life.

* * *

After the death of my parents I was no longer on speaking terms with God. I never prayed or read my Bible; rarely went to church and never admitted a need for religion or God. I was in an all-out rebellion against any kind of spiritual need in my life. I became emotionally bankrupt trying to live alone on my own resources, but God came looking for me and found me a thoroughly confused, mixed up and angry, miserable and lost sinner in desperate need of His grace and mercy. In spite of a wonderful, loving husband and four beautiful children, and a happy home, I knew this wasn't LIFE. I cried out for help to the God of my childhood faith and He answered. He was with me. I had just not paid any attention to Him in my anger and rebellion.

I read the book by William Shirer, *The Rise and Fall of the Third Reich,* and saw the terrible darkness and depravity humans can reach without God. Humanly speaking, life looked so hopeless. I started reading my Bible and asking questions. I found the answers. It was a personal relationship with Christ that I needed. I read another book by Billy Graham, *Peace With God,* and I was ready to make mine. I woke up one Easter morning and knew why Christ had died on the cross for me. I got up and went to church services and started attending post chapel services with the children regularly. My life changed. Peace and contentment came into my heart. I knew that this was Life. I was so excited and filled with joy that I knew the meaning and purpose for my life— fellowship with God! I became active in and President of the Protestant Women of the Chapel. I could not be separated from my Bible as I tried to make up for years of neglect. I had been starving for the bread and water of Life and didn't know it. I attended Christian retreats and conferences, and I visited the women's groups in the German Lutheran Churches in Stuttgart.

A love and peace that I had not known since living with my parents filled my heart. I did not know that there could be such happiness in life. I no longer felt alone. I talked to others about my newly found happiness. I knew this was real. I prayed with the children each night as l put them to bed, and we started praying as a family at meals. I visited the Kinderheims, German orphanages in the area, and took gifts to the children. The German children were all organized by houses into families, instead age groups. It was the first time that I had seen this. I looked into adoption procedures and had two teenage girls come to our house for dinner on Sundays. I remembered so well when I had first been orphaned and my loneliness for my parents. God was giving me a chance to help others who felt abandoned as I had. I was a deeply spiritually thirsty child of God.

Kenny and I went out for dinner to a German gasthaus one night and met a group of Canadian girls backpacking through Germany. They were looking for a place to stay, so we brought them home with us and they camped out on our living room floor. They stayed with us a couple of days, doing laundry, getting more peanut butter and replenishing their supplies from our kitchen cupboards. It felt like such a wonderful adventure to offer hospitality to these strangers in need. Our lives began to take on a concern for others and their needs. We found fellow officers and their families who were Christian. God was doing wonderful things in our lives.

We took family camping trips to Lake Geneva, Switzerland and throughout Italy with the Chip, Phillip, Amber and Grace. Lake Geneva had beautiful white swans on the lake where we camped. The children had not seen swans before and they were really impressed. We visited Zurich and many small villages. We enjoyed the fondue and the children liked cooking their own meat on skewers in the fondue pot in the center of the table. Later we bought a fondue pot and started a family tradition. We took a family trip to Italy which included Venice, Florence and Pisa, where the children loved the gondola and horse and carriage rides and Italian food. We celebrated Grace's second birthday at an Italian hotel and they baked a cake for her.

We decided that we needed to climb the Leaning Tower of Pisa. Kenny and I took two children each, and we made it slowly to the top at the children's pace. But the open stairs and the height were a little more than I wanted. Our time, patience and money ran out before we made it to Rome.

We were saved from a disastrous camping site when Leon and Marilyn Rademacher preceding us, told us of their beach campsite that almost got blown away in the strong winds off the Adriatic Sea. They warned us of the dangers and we quickly found another campground.

In Summer of 1963, we had orders for Fort Monmouth, New Jersey, and I was three months pregnant with our fifth child. Kenny had orders to attend a four-month Advanced Training Course as a Captain. We started getting ready for our trip back to the States, and it was exciting to think about seeing family again after three years of separation. We had grown as a family in number and spiritually with Christ as the center of our family. God had blessed us abundantly. We decided to travel back to the States by U.S. Military Transport Ship called the *Darby* for eight days instead of flying. We thought that this would be a good experience for the children, and we had never been on a large ship.

Leaving from Bremerhaven, Germany, we docked in Brooklyn, New York eight days later. It was an experience that I'll never forget with four small children in a small cabin room and rough seas. The fire drills with our life-jackets on the open deck, with the high waves crashing around us within a few feet of the rail, and trying to hold on to two small hands on either side of us, was dangerous and especially scary. I couldn't believe that two college-educated, intelligent parents chose to do this. I doubted my sanity in our decision. Kenny checked on our cocker spaniel Carmen and took her for walks on the lower deck. I looked at the slow progress of the ship plotted on the map each morning and sat the children in front of the porthole in our small cabin and told them to watch television — the crashing waves! The Kids Club showed cartoons and Chip, Phillip and Amber went to a special area to watch. Phillip remembers getting lost on the wrong deck going into a wrong cabin right above us. He quickly retreated and found ours. Another morning I heard a shrieking cry that sounded like Amber, and ran down the ship corridor to find someone carrying her to the hospital emergency room. She had fallen off the back of a seat and cut her lip, needing stitches. Amber remembers the bright lights and stitching in the emergency room.

By this time, three months pregnant and nauseous, I found it hard to enjoy anything and just wanted to be OFF the ship. The food was wonderful, but it was hard to get all the meat cut for four children, cut your own and let everyone eat in the allotted time before the dinner bell rang and announced time for the next group to eat. It was not fast food, but we had to eat faster. I should have just dumped it all in a bag and taken it to our room to eat at the leisurely pace more suited for our two-, three-, five-, and six-year-olds.

We arrived in Brooklyn Harbor on the eighth day, and the Statue of Liberty was an exciting and welcome sight. I couldn't believe that we were soon to be on American land again. Three years had been a long time without seeing any family. After much red tape Kenny reclaimed our green Ford Station wagon and Carmen and we started on our road trip to Kansas for a vacation. We had used checks on our bank account in Kansas while we were living in Germany on base, but no New Yorker would cash them anywhere. We ran out of cash and had a Texaco gas credit card, so we just kept filling up with gas, and drove all day and night until we hit Kansas and could cash our Kansas checks. We noticed the trash and debris on the streets was a complete contrast to the neatness of Germany.

It was awfully good to be back to the States. We hadn't realized how much we had missed. My brothers and sisters and their families all met at a park in Wichita, Kansas in July for a family reunion. There were many new babies for us all to share. Everyone came and this was the first time we had all been together since the accident and funeral of our parents many years ago in Madison in 1948. We were still a family. My brother Charles had married Glenda Moore from Manhattan, Kansas in 1961. He attended Kansas State College for a while and then dropped out and they lived in Manhattan. My sister, Sherry, went by her middle name Elaine, and had attended Kansas State for a year and was now working in Wichita. There were thirty-six members of our family together. It was a great time getting to know one another again and meeting all the new grandchildren.

We visited with all of Kenny's relatives in Manhattan for two weeks then drove to New Jersey. This was our second drive from Kansas to New Jersey, but this time with four children. We found a nice house to rent near Redbank, close to an elementary school where Chip started first grade. I attended a Baptist Church and Bible study and Kenny drove to Fort Monmouth each morning to attend the Advanced Officers Training Course and studied hard to graduate.

President Kennedy was assassinated in November while we lived in New Jersey. It was a terrible time for the whole country. My emotions during pregnancies were unusually volatile and I remember crying a lot. It seemed like an impossible thing to have happened. Everyone was in shock and mourning. I attended a Bible study with other military couples and this helped me through the hard times. I really enjoyed it. The leader's wife had twin two-year-old boys, and no left arm because it had been removed due to cancer. She was a beautiful woman, and I was in awe at how she managed their twins and cared for her family. I knew what hard work it was. I had taken so much for granted. She was cheerful with no signs of self-pity. I knew that was the kind of Christian that I wanted to be. I read my Bible constantly and learned Christian hymns. One night I fell asleep in bed with my Bible open and a hymn that I had copied stuck out from the pages. It was "A Mighty Fortress Is Our God" by Martin Luther, one of my favorites that I had learned and sang a lot. Kenny asked me if I had written it. He noticed a definite change in me. The words definitely described my sentiments.

Dorothy and Bud lived in Arlington, Virginia where Bud, as a full Colonel, was stationed at the Pentagon. Dorothy came in January to help after Andrew's birth at the hospital at Fort Monmouth, New Jersey. Andrew was born on January 3, 1964. What a blessing! Another handsome boy with brown eyes and brown hair and very healthy. Dorothy stayed a week with us and took care of the children and let me get some rest. It was a great blessing to be close to family and have her help. After she left, Kenny always fixed a plate of sandwiches and put them in the refrigerator for us before he left for his classes. It was a great help and I appreciated his thoughtfulness. Andrew was four months old when Kenny graduated and we had orders for Fort Riley, Kansas near Manhattan. We were excited and extremely happy.

# Chapter 8: Don't they Look Lonely

IN APRIL 1964, WE PACKED UP and the movers came for our furniture. With the car loaded and Chip, Phillip, Amber, Grace and Andrew, and our dog Carmen in the back, we prayed that God would find us the house we needed for our family in Kansas, and left New Jersey. After living three years in such close quarters in Germany and no private yard, we prayed for a five-bedroom home on one acre of land, and then took off on our two-day drive to Manhattan, Kansas. We were able to stay with Kenny's parents while we searched for a house, but it looked like we were going to have to settle for less than our dreams. The last day when we needed to make a decision on where to live, a five-bedroom farmhouse on an acre, halfway between Manhattan and Fort Riley became available. We had hoped to buy it but it was only available to rent. It was just what we had prayed for and so we took it and moved in. Our farmhouse was over one hundred years old, but newly wallpapered on the inside, lovingly well kept, and had the same family in it for all that time. The elderly couple had tears in their eyes when they moved out, but I think they were glad to know that a young family with five children would be enjoying the house and appreciating all the love that they had shared there. We knew that God had answered our prayers. It was just perfect for the children and for Kenny's drive to Fort Riley for work. And I was glad to be out in the country again with our children. I was looking forward to the children enjoying the same things that I had as a child. I knew these things were important in their lives.

Our two-story farmhouse had pink siding with a blue-gray roof and trim, and an enormous grassy front yard. There was plenty of room for the children to run play. The children's rooms were all on the second floor with a front and back stairs, which were quite steep with no carpeting. Amber and Grace's room had many large, low windows, and after we moved the girls into their bedroom, they came down the stairs bringing their clothes to dress. I asked them why they didn't get dressed in their rooms and Amber, at four years replied, "We can't get dressed. The birds are watching us." Beautiful large robins sitting on the low bedroom window-sills looked at them with their beady eyes, quite large to a three- and four-year-old. We even had a second bathroom (an outhouse), that I decorated with pictures on the inside. We used this bathroom often, especially when we had my family come to visit. There were many unexpected hooks, nooks and crannies that the children enjoyed hiding in and an old potato bin in the kitchen. It was a perfect house for five children. We thanked God for such abundance. We started calling it "The Pink Palace."

We were barely moved in when Kenny received orders to report to Fort Rucker, Alabama on temporary duty to learn to fly the Mohawk, a new Army turbo-prop aircraft. He hated to leave us so soon, and I really hated for him to go, but we knew this was temporary and that the children and I should stay in Manhattan. After so many moves of lock-stock-and-barrel, it was time to stay. But if I had known that a longer separation was right ahead of us, we would have gone. Kenny barely got the washing machine hooked up and all our furniture moved in before he left for Alabama. He bought an old green pick-up truck to drive and we kept our green Ford station wagon in Manhattan.

Chip started back to school and finished his first grade year in Manhattan. Andrew had a visit with the pediatrician at Fort Riley at four months old, and the visit revealed a diagnosis that had Andrew with casts on his legs for two months. Later he would need to wear shoes on a brace for a few months to slightly straighten his feet before he learned to walk. Andrew was a happy and contented baby and this did not bother or limit him at all. He became extremely clever at crawling everywhere with the brace on his shoes. By one year Andrew was walking fine and really fast. He had been thinking about all the places he wanted to go when he could run. Phillip started kindergarten at Theodore Roosevelt that year and both boys rode the school bus to school. The children and I enjoyed our large acre of land and met all the neighbors who were especially friendly.

All of Kenny's family lived in Manhattan and came out to visit us often. The children and I started attending Crestview Christian Church in Manhattan, and Kenny attended a Baptist Church in Dothan, Alabama. Although living apart for the next four months, we were still continuing to grow as a Christian family, and Kenny called often to talk to the children. He sent devotional tapes of Bible readings for the children to hear each morning. The summer went quickly and Kenny came back in August to be with us again. The children waited eagerly at the mailbox at the end of our drive to see his green pick-up truck arrive. They had missed him so much.

Kenny now flew with a Mohawk Battalion at Fort Riley at Marshall Airfield. When he arrived home in the evenings in his gray nylon aviation flight suit, all the children loved the many intriguing zippers on his flight suit. When he picked up one of the smaller ones, they started zipping away at any they could reach, expecting to find gum, candy, pencils, or keys to play with. The zipper on his leg pockets were always a magnet for the children. I can imagine that the children thought their daddy was pretty important with so many zippered pockets.

We joined the church and became reacquainted with many old college friends in Manhattan. One called and said that he was a Catholic priest of the Catholic Church in town and had been notified that we were a new Catholic family who had just moved to town with many children. I knew it was a joke and replied "No, we are not Catholic, just passionate Protestants," and we both had a good laugh.

My brother Charlie and his wife Glenda lived in Manhattan and visited us often. Later Glenda became concerned about Charlie's paranoia and jealousy and came to our house to talk to me. She said that he became unusually angry when she tried to talk to him about it. They were going to the Baptist church, and I suggested Glenda get counseling with her minister. Then we prayed together about the situation. Glenda did, but Charlie would not go to counseling. Glenda wanted help, but Charlie said there was no problem. Later she asked for a divorce.

Charlie dropped out of engineering school at Kansas State University because he told me they could not teach him anything. Later when he had moved to Wichita, he was picked up by the police for strange behavior while driving his car. My two older brothers living there went to his apartment and decided that he definitely needed help. Charlie told them that his "voices" were telling him what to do. They also found that Charlie had an abnormally large collection of empty, clean glass jars and bottles in his apartment that he was saving for something. He also had engineering plans drawn for a new Ford Model car that he was designing. He told me that he had submitted his plans to the Ford Motor Company and that they were using them, but the company had not given him any compensation. I knew this was strange, but Charlie was always drawing plans.

The psychiatrists diagnosed Charlie with schizophrenia and recommended shock treatments. None of us knew anything about schizophrenia at the time and really didn't know how to help Charlie. No one in our family, as far as we knew, had ever had this disease. He was committed to the state hospital for treatment. This was in the early sixties. We were at a loss in knowing how to help Charlie, and we left his treatment plan up to the psychiatrists who had diagnosed him and my older brother who signed the papers. I had felt prayer was what could help him the most, and I'm sure that it did. Without the medical knowledge to offer a cure, prayer helped him endure his treatment and illness. Dorothy and I visited him often, and he said our visits were the only thing that got him through his treatment and hospitalization. He said, "I couldn't have made it through this if it weren't for you girls." Dorothy and I felt so helpless. She was comforting and reassuring, and I was confrontational and questioning. He probably needed both from his sisters. I was the closest in age to Charlie while we were growing up and thought that I knew him best.

I was now pregnant with Timothy and due in September of 1965. I planned to have the birth at Irwin Army Hospital at Fort Riley. In New Jersey, I had used a diaper service that picked up and laundered my diapers and returned them weekly. We wondered why Manhattan didn't have one and decided to launch a business of our own. Kenny did all the purchasing and business plans and we launched the Lullaby Diaper Service with one delivery van. He employed his father to help him run it. I looked forward to exchanging the dirty and urine soaked diapers for the nice, clean-smelling and sanitized diapers arriving on my doorstep each week. Only a new mother with a newborn can appreciate the blessing of this service. Lullaby Diaper Service had a contract with Irwin Army

Hospital at Fort Riley to do the laundry for the hospital nursery.

Kenny often called from work and told the children to go outside to watch for his plane. Then he flew over the house and tipped his wings at them. He enjoyed flying this new aircraft, the Mohawk. I don't know what they thought about that, but the boys liked to ask him questions. Kenny and I enjoyed our unique one hundred year-old-farmhouse and felt completely at home in the country. Many of our military friends drove out into the country from Fort Riley to visit us. We hosted Bible studies with the Officers Christian Union, which we attended at Fort Riley, called OCIL and had many family dinners at the Pink Palace.

It was 1965, which was the year of many of the Civil Rights demonstrations in the southern states. I identified with this movement, knowing what terrible and unjust conditions the people of color in Georgia had to deal with when I lived there as a teenager. I felt that this was a time that I should do something. Many people from northern states were taking buses, called Freedom Riders, in support of the peaceful sit-ins in Alabama and Mississippi. I talked this over with Kenny and he advised me not to go as I was pregnant and almost due with our sixth child. My emotions were deeply strong about this movement and my pregnancy just made them stronger. I knew that I shouldn't go, but it was hard to stay home. I wanted to provide some moral support for the people who were able to go. So we prayed in our Bible study group for the Freedom Riders' safety and that the necessary laws were passed to end segregation. It was a violent and bloody outcome and many people were killed.

Before we got really far along with our diaper service, Kenny received orders for Vietnam and his battalion had to leave before Tim was born. I was awfully upset about this and wanted Kenny home for the birth. He asked for a six-weeks-delay after the birth and got it, so he was able to be with me. I had some problems with this pregnancy and had to rest in bed for a couple of weeks. Tim was born at Fort Riley Hospital on September 17, 1965. He was a very handsome, healthy, blue eyed, dark haired baby boy, and we were especially blessed and happy. The nurses told me that he had unusually healthy lungs. We had a family picture taken right before Kenny left for Vietnam. We looked like an unusually sober but happy family of eight, innocent of the suffering of war that lay right ahead of us.

We drove to Wichita to visit my family on a weekend, and it was really hot with no air conditioning in our car. With five children in the back seat complaining of the heat, and nursing a baby in the front seat, I felt thoroughly tired and uncomfortable, sweaty and ragged. I was looking forward to getting home from this trip. A Cadillac cruised by us with all the windows rolled up; the couple inside looked perfectly cool and comfortable in their expensive air-conditioned car, as they stared back at us with pity. Kenny turned to me and smiled and said, "Don't they look lonely?" He had read my thoughts, and I had to smile in our hot, muggy car with six tired, thirsty and hot children. We definitely weren't lonely. Kenny always had a great sense of humor just when I needed it. We were very much blessed.

Amber turned five years old in the spring and started kindergarten at Theodore Roosevelt in the fall. She was really excited and had a friend in her class. She rode the big yellow school bus with the boys. Kenny departed for Vietnam at the end of October when Tim was six weeks old, and I will never forget that day. I dyed all his underclothes jungle green in the washing machine with thoughts of what this meant as he prepared to go for a year. Pilots were shot down over the jungle, and I didn't want to think about that. As his day of departure came closer, I was dreading our good-byes. I just didn't know how I would make it, but we had trust and faith in God to get us through. When I took him to the Manhattan airport to see him off for the coming year, I did not think that I would ever see him again. I was thirty years old and he was thirty-two. We had talked about him getting out of the Army when he returned from Vietnam. When he first committed to twenty years in the regular Army we didn't have six children, and he felt that God gave him the responsibility to raise them. He wanted to serve with his battalion in Vietnam and then submit his resignation papers when he came home.

When I came home from the airport crying after seeing Kenny off for a year, I just wanted to dig a hole and crawl into it. This seemed just to be too much for my raw emotions and weak body to handle. I looked at the children and noticed that four of them had red spots all over their faces. I looked closer and realized it was chicken pox. For the next two months someone had chicken pox all the time until all six were infected, including Tim as an infant of six weeks. It was all I could do to just keep up with the six sick children and the house. I did not have time to worry about anything but getting out of bed each morning. I quickly learned what it was to be the only parent on duty twenty-four hours a day. The church was especially helpful and supportive. Kenny's family came out to visit from Manhattan and offered help. My family living near all came for visits to encourage us and let us know that they cared. The neighbors were particularly helpful and kind. Christmas was the hardest. I almost didn't make it through.

Kenny and I learned a lot about suffering and God's comfort that year. How do you explain war to six

young children who miss and need their Daddy? How do
you explain war to the mother of six young children who
misses and needs the help and support of her husband?
How did Kenny get through the suffering he saw all
around him each day? You can't, but the promises of God
were our only hope. God became more of a living reality
every day. The Army called this a 'hardship tour' for
Kenny. There were no words to describe what it was for
me and the children. We waited. Kenny and I wrote each
other every day, and the letters were what kept us sane.
Our joy was in knowing that he was alive each day as we
received and read his letters. We grew in dependence on
God for everything.

Kenny went to Danang, an airbase in the south of
Vietnam and they all lived near the jungle in tents. He
flew extremely dangerous low-level night-reconnaissance
missions in his Mohawk, as did all the crews. The
Mohawk was equipped with heat-seeking radar to locate
enemy camps, which they then radioed the location to the
Air Force. He was also Operations Officer for his
battalion. I met with a weekly Bible Study from Fort Riley
with other officers and their wives and we prayed for
them. The Flight Surgeon and his family at Fort Riley
were good friends of ours. One young pilot from our Bible
study was shot down and lost in the first few months. It
was a deeply tense and agonizing time for us all.

Kenny and I had plans to meet together in Hong
Kong after he had been in Vietnam for six months and
was given rest and recuperation leave. I got my passport
ready and made arrangements for a family from the
church to keep the children. But Kenny called from Hong
Kong and said that he had to take his leave early and had
to leave Hong Kong before I could arrive. He was so
sorry, and I was deeply disappointed, as I had been
looking forward to this time to be together since he had

gone. The anticipation of our visit was what kept me going.

The Vietnam War was on the nightly television news, but I never turned the television on. I did not want to know what Dan Rather had to say. My mornings started about 5:00 a.m., and the day ended early when the children were all put to bed. There were people building a house near us named the Delmezes. They worked hard all day on their house, and I took banana bread when I went over to meet them. As they built their house themselves it was fun to watch their progress. They were an older couple and this was to be their retirement home. They also planted many flower bulbs and planned to have a nursery. With no other close neighbors, they were our first. They were kind and asked about Kenny. Watching our children was a lot of entertainment for them. They had grandchildren of their own and often invited them when they finished their house and our children played together.

Tim at six months became acutely sick and dehydrated. He was always so active and became quiet and would just lie in his crib. I took him to the Emergency Room at Fort Riley and sat and waited to see a doctor. When I took Tim into the examining room, the doctor asked about his symptoms. Then he started asking me how I felt. I was exhausted and cried from the worry about taking care of all the children. The doctor thought Tim would do fine with more liquid supplements and suggested that I get help with the children and more rest. I was thoroughly relieved to find that Tim was not seriously ill. I think a sympathetic ear was what I needed most, and we both recovered. There were some times that were harder than other times. Usually on the weekends I didn't get as much rest.

We had a tornado in Manhattan in the spring and lost our outhouse, a boat and ten trees around the house. We had many broken glass windows but we were safe. We had spent the time in the cellar singing during the tornado. The dirt floors and darkness of the cellar were scary for the children, but a wonderful haven from the tornado. The neighbors came to clean up all the trees and repair all the windows. The city of Manhattan had sustained some damage, but there were no deaths.

Kenny called from Vietnam when he read about the tornado in the Stars & Stripes, the military newspaper. He got to talk to all the children and find out that we were ok. He called by radio from Vietnam to Fort Riley and to us. His time was up and the operator said that he needed to say goodbye. Kenny asked for permission to tell each of his children good-bye and she said yes. For the next ten minutes he spoke to each child again. I'm sure the operator never realized how long it would take. It was wonderful to hear his voice.

Kenny was sent to Saigon for his last six months in Vietnam. He met many of his pilot friends that he had served with in Germany or had been with in helicopter training. Bud, my sister's husband, was in Vietnam also and they met at the Rex Hotel in Saigon. Dorothy called often to find out how we were. This was Bud's second tour in Vietnam and she had been able to meet him in Hawaii, so she had been through it before.

My friend, Sue, who had gone on that adventurous trip to East Berlin on the train with me was now living with her mother in Oklahoma. Sue's husband was also in Saigon and called to see if she could come for a visit with me in Manhattan. We had a wonderful time just catching up on all our news. We were both suffering and waiting together with six children each while our husbands were flying in Vietnam. Camaraderie of fellow sufferers is a blessing. When I was with civilian couples, I wondered why they were nit picking, complaining, or annoying each other when they could be together. Oh, how I would have loved to be with Kenny and would not have complained about anything.

Andrew was two years old and usually went to the mailbox each morning with me to pick up the daily mail. Kenny often sent Andrew a pack of gum in his letter to me for Andrew to share with his brothers and sisters. Little did I know that a two-year-old would think that the mailman was his dad leaving him gum. He thought it was great that his dad was so generous with him sending gum in the mail, and of course it was teaching him how to give and share.

In the summer we planted a garden and kept telling Kenny in our letters what we had planted and how it was growing. We decided to send him some radishes in a box, hoping they would survive. We sent the radishes in popped corn for packing. They arrived in good shape and he sent us a picture with him and his friends cutting and enjoying the radishes grown in our Kansas garden. I know that meant a lot to them all. Home was a reality and they were able to taste it. Tim at one year had just learned to walk and was especially strong. He enjoyed carrying the bathroom scales around into different rooms. One day he dropped the heavy scales on his big toe. He eventually lost the toenail, and I sent it to Kenny in a letter. I also included the girls' hair when I cut it. I sent him a few locks of Amber's brown hair and Grace's blond hair.

Kenny often sent Chip, who was eight years old, a twenty-dollar bill to take us all out for hamburgers or Dairy Queen after church. Chip felt happily important as the oldest male in the family with his dad gone and enjoyed the occasion. In fact, the whole family had gone to a movie called *Old Yeller* before Kenny left for Vietnam.

The father in this movie told the oldest boy of about eight years old to take care of the family while he was gone. Kenny sent us many gifts from Bangkok, Thailand, Hong Kong, and Saigon, Vietnam. We have pictures of the girls in straw hats and silk pajamas, and the boys wearing jackets with Saigon embroidered on the backs. Water buffalo horns, pictures, brass vases, hand-made cotton blouses and purses were just a few of the gifts that Kenny sent and reminded us that he was thinking of his family.

The children and I built a wooden patio onto the house by the hand pump near the back door. This was a big project and a fun time for us and we painted it red and blue. We put old furniture out on it and sat out in the evenings. Since I lacked carpenter skills, it looked very primitive. During that summer I remember a timeless moment that shall always stick in my mind during that long year. 1 was sitting out on the concrete front steps of the Pink Palace after supper, holding Tim and watching the other five children, Chip, Phillip, Amber, Grace and Andrew, playing games in our large front yard. One game after another, Red Rover, Capture the Flag, Tag, and Hide-and Seek, kept them going all evening. Seeing the children on the wide sweep of grass, running, shouting, tumbling, and playing full speed in the evening after supper, squeezing every last second out of the daylight and evening hours before dark for their enjoyment, they were living life in the Big Now to the fullest. This is what children do. I knew that this was childhood as I remembered it myself. Time seemed to stand still and I was aware that we were all one with God and the universe. I could experience the same feelings that they were, like tomorrow might never come. God was in control and I was at peace. My worry, frustration and anxiety just melted away as the sun set.

In October 1966, we began planning Kenny's homecoming. A year had been a long time. The Martin family, good friends from the church, offered to keep the children while I flew to San Francisco to meet Kenny and spend a few days together. It was just unbelievable that he would be home soon. The excitement was almost too good to bear. Many days before I left, I could think of nothing else. I flew to San Francisco, and Kenny and I met at a hotel. Being together again was all we had dreamed it would be. I never wanted to let go of him. We just kept touching each other to see if we were real; we held hands and just clung to each other most of the time. We were both much thinner and had changed during our year of separation. He had a dark tan and looked more handsome than I ever remembered. I saw suffering in his eyes. I sure don't remember San Francisco.

He had put in his paperwork for a military discharge. It did not take long for us to go through the red tape and turn in our military ID cards. We walked out of the building as civilians, and we were out of the Army. I tried not to run, but I was afraid they would call him back again and he would be snatched out of my hands. It was wonderful to be civilians and know that he didn't need to return to Vietnam. We were both so deliriously happy and relieved. It was like we had our life to start all over again. His homecoming gift to me was a beautiful mink stole that he had bought for me in Hong Kong since I couldn't join him there. I wore it that night when we went out for dinner and dancing. I had brought some of his civilian clothes with me from his closet at home for him to wear. I was awesomely grateful to have a husband again, and I can't imagine how grateful Kenny was to be alive and coming back to his family. What a gift God had given us! We knew that we were the fortunate ones. Many of his friends did not come home. We had four days to celebrate and get to know each other again, and then we flew back to Manhattan, Kansas and our six children.

We drove to the Pink Palace and the children were in Manhattan with our friends. The doors were locked and we had no key so we crawled through the kitchen window and called the children to let them know that we were home. When the children arrived, Kenny grabbed each one and hugged and kissed them all with tears in his eyes. It was quite a reunion! Everyone stayed home from school to be with Daddy. Chip and Phillip and Amber had lots of questions. Grace, Andrew and Timothy were shy around Kenny at first. Timmy hadn't known him at all. But it didn't take long for him to warm up and want to be right in the middle of everything. He liked this new guy in the family. We were ecstatic and grateful to be a family again and it only took a little while to get used to being whole again. The children all wanted to be around Kenny constantly. I heard "Daddy" a hundred times or more for many days. What a sweet word for Kenny to hear! I am sure that there were times during the past year that he thought he would never hear it again. It must have been music to his ears.

The first night Kenny was home I remember telling him that it was so good to be off night duty, and I slept like a rock. Kenny began by putting a wagon together for Andrew; he had plenty to do for all his children, and He could hardly believe how they had grown. I loved to say to the children 'ask your Daddy' many times a day. It was so wonderful to share parenthood. He planned to be home for a month before he made any decision about a job. Kenny said that he had learned not to sweat the small stuff and everything was small stuff. I had learned complete dependence on God for everything this past year of our separation. He often had bad dreams and didn't want to talk much about the fighting in Vietnam.

One of Kenny's first decisions, after making the big one to get out of the Army, was whether he wanted to continue his flying career. He had his Senior Army Aviator Badge, Vietnam Campaign and Service Medals, National Defense Service Medal, and the Basic Air Medal with First and Second Oak Leaf Cluster. He had flown the Army fixed wing aircraft, the L-19 and L-20, the Bell helicopter and the Mohawk. He had loved to fly but mentioned "when they're shooting at you, it takes a lot of the fun out of it." We had done much travelling and moving in our married life with many separations that it just felt good not to be going anywhere.

In 1966, Pan American Airlines and United Airlines were at the top of the commercial carriers. Kenny received an offer from United Airlines to start as co-pilot. This would involve moving every six months to their training facilities and more short-term separations. We knew that this was an excellent career opportunity for him with good pay and benefits. We talked about what our priorities were as a family. It was to be together as a family and mine was to raise the children in the country. He needed to make a decision on the airlines before his 34th birthday in February. We talked about this for a few months and knew that being together as a family was what we both wanted. He decided not to go with the airlines although it meant leaving his flying career and much more money than we had been earning in the Army. We had learned what was important to us as a family and to trust in God to provide. Kenny supervised running the Lullaby Diaper Service, but he looked for a business that would provide better support for the family. There were times of searching and trusting in the Lord to lead us. He was offered a position as salesman with a Volkswagen dealership that an old friend had started.

We hosted Bible studies, school picnics, family reunions, and many church potluck dinners and functions at our home. We were expecting a large group from our church to come for dinner one night, and I had Chip turning a freezer of ice cream. After realizing how long this was going to take, Chip asked if he had to make the ice cream for the whole church. He was assured when I told him that others were also bringing ice cream.

Kenny's father found two ponies to buy for Chip and Phillip. Phillip was six years old and Chip eight years. They named them Star and Frisky. Kenny built a corral and small shed in the back yard for them. The ponies were great entertainment for the children and they all learned to ride. He also got chickens for the children to raise and made a chicken house. We decided that we would stay in the Pink Palace until we found land to buy and build our own home. While flying at Fort Riley Kenny had seen and knew much of the geography around Manhattan. He had been looking for ten to twenty acres of land to buy for us to build a home. I was content to rent, but he had always wanted to build a home of his own.

We had a dead-end gravel road next to the apple orchard by the Pink Palace that ended at the runway of the Manhattan Airport. The children liked to walk there and take picnics and play under the bridge. It was exciting for the older boys to go there and see the planes landing and taking off. What I didn't know was that they sometimes they would lie in the grass at the end of the runway, and sometimes inch their way onto the tarmac with the planes landing over their heads.

Grace had started school, and we now had four children at Theodore Roosevelt Elementary School in Manhattan. During one of these years Roosevelt Elementary School started a day with special Field & Track events, awarding ribbons for the best in each event.

Chip, Phillip, Amber and Grace did a lot of running and enjoyed Field Day. They looked forward to competing. I was unable to go the first year to watch them, but they all brought their ribbons home that they had earned. They jumped off the school bus and came running into the house waving their ribbons in the air, excited to show me all their ribbons that they had won. On the porch off the kitchen that we used for our dining room, they laid out all their ribbons on the table to show me. There were twenty blue ribbons; each of the four children had won five. I was amazed and asked if blue was the only color that they gave out. They all excitedly replied it was first place, and that they had all won first place in all their events! I found this hard to believe and kept questioning them about the other colors of ribbons and places. Since I hadn't been able to attend the Field Day, I didn't know that there were different heats in their events, and they had been placed in the fastest heats. But I knew that we had some very fast runners in the family and they had monopolized the blue ribbons. I was especially proud of them all after they convinced me that they had all won them.

In 1967, we took a trip to Yellowstone National Park with all six children, a nephew Mitch Knight, our dog Carmen and pulled a boat behind our station wagon. Tim was the youngest and one year old. We camped in the Black Hills of South Dakota first, and Kenny enjoyed boating and fishing with the children. After a few nights of camping and looking at our map, we decided that Yellowstone National Park wasn't that much farther so we drove on. We stayed in a cabin at Old Faithful in Yellowstone and the children had a wonderful time. We stopped at Betty and Pat's in Colorado Springs on our way back home where we stayed one night and picked up a kitten. They had seventeen kittens and were trying to find homes for them. We decided that we wouldn't take such a long trip again with so many small children.

A couple from our church in need of a place to stay came out and stayed for two weeks. Ginny Smith was blind and it was a challenge to watch over her while her husband was at work at Fort Riley. She wanted to learn to ride a bike so we helped her. All the children cheered her on. She took one of the children's bikes to the front yard and climbed on. I directed her by saying left and right and she did amazingly well. Later she took a class at Kansas State and I read her textbook for her over the phone. She and her husband eventually moved back to California and she hoped for eye surgery to restore some of her sight.

In 1969, we bought fifteen acres of pasture two miles up into the hills for our Pink Palace. It had an old, large wood and stone barn, and an old house. We traveled up to 'The Property', as we called it, every day to clean up the old rusted barbed wire fences and mounds of trash and brush from our newly purchased land. We had a great time as a family planning and deciding what we would build on our fifteen acres. The preschool children, Andrew and Tim, helped me paint the old house a red barn color. They wore their overalls and happily painted with their brushes anywhere they could reach; I was grateful for their help since I just wanted to get the bare boards covered. But when I left them for five minutes alone, they had turned their brushes on one another and thought that each other's hair and face needed some paint. When working with preschoolers you learn to take what you can get and clean up the mess.

We had Star bred and she gave birth to a black filly we named Starlight. We moved the three horses Frisky, Star, and Starlight, a goat named Mandy, and the chickens up to the property and enjoyed our future farm. Starlight was black with a star on her forehead like her mother Star.

Without our knowing, she became sick and we could not save her. She died of encephalitis. The kids loved her, and we were so disappointed to lose her. They had looked forward to having another horse to ride. We found the chickens roosting on the horse's backs when we went up in the evenings. There were many coyotes and that was the safest spot they could find.

We had a pond built in a ravine in front of the area where we planned to build our house. When it was finished and had enough rain to fill it, we brought small catfish from a fish hatchery to stock the pond. We located an architect in Manhattan, Ray Cruble, and started drawing our house plans. It was an exciting time to think about having our first house on fifteen acres with a barn for our horses. By summer we had our basement dug and started. I was now pregnant with Eric since we decided that one more child would be within our plans for a family, and I was growing larger by the week. We could build as many bedrooms as we needed for our expanding family. Tim would start kindergarten in September and Eric was due in July of 1970.

# Chapter 9: Follow Me

**IN ORDER TO SAVE ON LABOR COSTS,** we decided to do most of the finishing work on our new house ourselves. The older children helped with much of the work and even picked out their own special rock to put in our fireplace in the kitchen/family room. It was not yet ready for us to move in, but we were trying to hurry things along to finish before school started in a few days. I felt the first labor pains while I was out in the front yard of our new house on the evening of August 18th as we were all helping to stain the trim, with the long strips of wood laid out across sawhorses. I had begun to think that I might be permanently pregnant, and no woman could face that. Relief in the form of childbirth was on its way. I mentioned to Kenny that I should go home and rest awhile before going to the hospital, for I knew that the baby was near. Back at the Pink Palace, I packed my bag for the hospital and waited for Kenny to get home with the other children. About midnight, we thought that I might as well go to the hospital since the movers were coming and we would be moving out the next day. I was happy to avoid being in the middle of the moving mess. I didn't think that I could handle that, so the timing was just right. Eric Evans Long arrived on August 19, 1970. We had driven to Wichita the month before for a niece's wedding on July 18th, and I had thought the baby would come very soon then. Eric was a little later than expected, but a very handsome, healthy, dark-eyed baby boy. The younger boys, Andrew and Tim were in the car when Kenny picked me up from the hospital, and they checked out Eric's arm muscles on the way home. They were glad to have a baby brother.

Since our house wasn't finished I moved in with Dorothy and Bud for a week in Manhattan, and Kenny and the other children moved to his parents' house. Dorothy and

Bud had just moved to Manhattan from Arlington, Virginia where they had lived for nine years. Bud had been stationed at the Pentagon in Washington D.C. and now came to be on the faculty at Kansas State University as Professor of Military Science. We were very glad to have some of my family near for the first time. Dorothy and I spent many hours visiting on the telephone and making up for our long distance separation for so many years. It reminded me of my mother and her sisters, the Lucas sisters who loved to chat and visit with each other. Dorothy finished a degree from Kansas State that year which she had started before World War II.

We moved into our new walkout basement and house the next week when Eric was a week old. His first crib at Dorothy and Bud's had been a dresser drawer on the floor next to my bed. The boys enjoyed telling Eric when he got older that when he cried, I just shut the dresser drawer. It was very chaotic in our new house at The Farm as the children were starting their first day of school, and we couldn't find shoes for Andrew, who was starting first grade at Roosevelt Elementary School. There were still no doors or windows on our house, and we had to chase our goat, Mandy, out of our bedroom to reclaim it for human habitation. While the house was being built, Mandy had claimed that corner for her own. While the air conditioning/furnace worker had his plans all laid out to put it in the equipment and left for a lunch break, Mandy ate them. She had been the children's pet for quite a while, but I didn't know how much longer she would last. I cooked on a hot plate until the new stove was installed in the kitchen.

We had a bad storm with lightning that struck our new electric water pump in our well. We had drilled one hundred and thirty-five feet for water and had a good supply. We had a new house, but no water until a new pump could be ordered and arrived from Wichita. With lots of rain in September, we badly needed gravel on our winding, dirt, driveway through the pasture to our house. Our builder had admired our German grandfather clock in our home that we had bought in Stuttgart, Germany so Kenny made a deal for ten loads of gravel for our driveway for the grandfather clock. We were tired of wading through the mud to the house, carrying sacks and sacks of groceries, since we had to park so far away. We had run out of money and the clock was expedient and became our new drive.

We were really out in the country now in a valley between two hills with no close neighbors. We had very tall hills behind the house that the children climbed frequently. The one-and-a-half-mile narrow gravel road from our mailbox led only to our home on a dead end. The fields of grain came right up to the road with no ditches. We needed to keep the weeds mowed that grew up on the sides. Later we would have cars come up our drive that thought the road would go through the hills to Manhattan. We had a lovely red wood and old stone barn that we had considered remodeling into a house. It had a beautiful view of the valley from the hayloft, but we planned to raise more horses, cows and pigs. In a few years we planned to add a second story with plenty of bathrooms and bedrooms to our walkout basement. The old frame house on the front of our fifteen acres still stood, so we stored our extra furniture in it. It was in very sad shape inside, but served as a good storage place for our things. Among many other things we stored a portable dishwasher, and four years later when the second story of our home was finished, I found some dirty dishes of our last meal at the Pink Palace still in it. I was in the hospital with Eric when Kenny and the children had moved from the Pink Palace.

The builder had left a huge pile of trees stacked by our pond from clearing the land to build the basement. It took a while and many bonfires, but we finally got it burned over the next year. When our neighbors from miles away saw our frequent bonfires, they just said, "The Indians are burning again." In fact burning became a favorite and necessary outside past time for Kenny and the boys. We called them pyromaniacs. There were times when their fires got away from them, and we had some accidental burnings; those are some of our funniest stories to tell.

Now that the children were at the Farm, they seemed a little intimidated by so much space and hills to climb. But it didn't take them long to get on their horses and ride them up and down the hills. We leased three hundred more acres so that we could have more cattle and horses. The children had much freedom to play and built campsites and tree forts wherever they chose. Kenny's tools were always in use. The pond did not hold water yet, so we raised pigs to pack down the dirt in the bottom. We were told that pigs would pound the dirt to seal it. When it was time to sell the pigs or butcher them, we had a hard time getting them up the hill from the pond. I never realized what short legs they had and how hard it was for them to climb hills. We had to drag those pigs out of the pond, and it was not a pretty sight. Later the pond filled up in the rainy season and dried up in the dry season.

When Chip got his first car, an old Volkswagen bug, he parked it on the patio one Saturday night and forgot to put on the brakes. The next morning I noticed that it was gone and went out to look for it. I saw it resting at the bottom of the pond where it had rolled to a stop against a rock. When I shook him awake that morning he was very upset with this information. He jumped out of bed and went outside to see that lonely little VW at the bottom of the pond. There was no water in the pond yet, but that morning while we were in church, it started to rain and the pond started filling up. After getting home from church Kenny put a chain around the bumper and pulled the VW up the side of the pond and out with his tractor. I think Chip remembered his brakes after that.

Later when the pond held water we brought ducks and geese to decorate and keep it clean of the algae. We added more horses and cows to our farm and the younger children joined the older ones in 4-H and had their own projects. We had a large garden and everyone worked in it. Although we had no extra space inside the house, there were limitless possibilities for the children to entertain themselves outside. It reminded me of my own childhood on our farm.

The boys all owned B-B guns and shot everything they could find. They would never run out of things to shoot at. The guns were usually kept in the mud room and kept handy when someone needed one. Many of their town friends would come out to shoot with them. There are many stories to tell about these guns, but I never heard them all.

We had lots of family come for visits, family reunions, parties and pig roasts. Kenny had the boys dig a deep hole, they burned trees in it until there were enough coals and hot rocks in the bottom to roast our butchered pig that we had killed and cleaned. It roasted all night on the coals and hot rocks covered in sand. By evening the next day, we had nearly one hundred friends and students from Manhattan Christian College and our church come to our Pig Roasting Party. The meat was smoked and so tender and delicious that a slight gentle rain did not discourage anyone from coming. This was our first try at a Luau and we were so happy to have it a success. Kenny had stayed up all night to cook the pig. He did this many more times over the coming years for special occasions and we became well known for our pig roasts. More people came each year.

Phillip wrestled in junior high and broke his elbow in practice. The school nurse called me and I met him at the hospital. It was a difficult break and the orthopedic doctor put a pin into his elbow. He gave up wrestling and ran track. We prayed that he would have full function of his elbow again as it healed, knowing future problems could appear as he got older. His elbow did give him problems twenty years later and he had more surgery.

I had a new bright yellow VW Bug to drive and enjoyed the bright color sitting on the carport. Dorothy and I often talked on the phone, and one morning she called to see what I thought of all the rain we were having, since it had rained the entire week. She knew that our dirt road was very muddy in this weather and created many problems for getting out to the main road. I told her that I hadn't really noticed all the rain since I had been so busy. She replied, "Phyllis, you just put on your little yellow bug and go in the morning and don't even notice the weather." She was right. I really enjoyed driving that car. Eric as a preschooler would stand in the back with his head at my right shoulder and we would sing on the way to town. I sang "Jesus Is the Sweetest Name I Know" with gusto, and Eric tapped me on the shoulder and said, "Mother, my name is Eric." There were times when this car was our only transportation on Sunday for church. We all layered in and unfolded out when we arrived at church. I think it was an amusing sight to see. The children suffered through the fifteen-minute ride and didn't complain too much. Later we had many different vans and several station wagons to drive, especially when the teenagers were driving their own cars.

Kenny's father was diagnosed with leukemia in the early 1970s. He quit work and became thinner and thinner. It was a very difficult time for his whole family to see him suffering. He came out to our farm often to see his grandchildren play until he had to go into the hospital. He died in April of 1974 in Manhattan when Eric was four years old and was buried at Sunset Cemetery. Eric went with us to the funeral at the cemetery. Afterwards in the car on the way home, because there had been an old war cannon parked at the entrance of the cemetery, Eric asked me why it was there. I told him that I didn't know and he replied, "I think it is to shoot the dead people and keep them there when they try to get out." All my previous explanations of his granddad being in heaven seemed to have not been enough for him. A four-year-old evidently comes up with his own concrete conclusions. I was very glad that Kenny had those last few years near his father after we got out of the Army. They were very close, and we all loved him very much. He was quiet and had a great sense of humor. Kenny was able to help his mother with her finances and she soon moved into a retirement home.

In 1974, we asked Ray Cruble, our builder to add the second floor to our house. We planned five more bedrooms, a living room and two bathrooms. The children drew up their own plans and we gave these some consideration. They all wanted their own door from their bedroom to the outside balcony. We had liked the Swiss chalets built into the Swiss Alps that had stayed in when we vacationed in Switzerland. So we decided to have a long balcony across the front of the house with double sliding glass doors going out from the living room and sliding glass doors from the front three bedrooms. The older children were very excited since these were there rooms. We finished before summer and many friends came out from the church to help us paint the inside. Kenny had a car accident just a few days before we were to move upstairs and had broken a few ribs. He was in a lot of pain and unable to lift anything. Everyone enjoyed having new bedrooms and we had plenty of space for everyone. The two new bathrooms with three additional showers were quite an addition. With a new teenager joining the family each year, hot water in the showers was their first priority. We turned linen closet in the upstairs hallway into a telephone booth for the teenagers. The boys' old bedroom downstairs off the kitchen soon had a pool table and ping-pong table in it. We also used it to store saddles and horse tack and a freezer.

The horses loved to run in the hills, and the children enjoyed riding them cowboy style around our property. The children also built many campsites, some quite elaborate, and I was often invited to see their handiwork. When they tired of one site, they built another. Many tools must still be buried up in those hills. Most weekends there were extra children, their friends and neighbors that came out to camp. We usually had plenty of canned Vienna sausages, beans, bacon, eggs, marshmallows and hot dogs on hand.

By June, we were settled in, and I was the director of our Vacation Bible School at our church. We decided to try an outside Vacation Bible School Day Camp at the farm for two weeks. We rented a school bus to bring children from three churches in Manhattan and also from Yuma Street, where some of the children's friends lived. We put up tents in the yard and had classrooms in the barn. The children were all excited. One hundred children came to the camp. In the mornings at break, I looked out over the hills and they were covered with children, a beautiful sight. All were using and enjoying God's beautiful creation. The Bible story dramas they enacted in the woods were very authentic. Our theme for the week was:

God Is!
Jesus Lives!
We Are His!

We offered swimming in the pond, horseback riding, and hiking in the hills for recreation. By the end of the first week, we couldn't find the horses in the pasture, and we thought they were in hiding. It turned out Frisky decided to have her colt when we went to find her. She timed it very well and all the children got to see a brand new black filly, very wide-eyed, gangly, and unsteady on her feet. It must have been frightening for her to see so many children. We had rain on one occasion, and we were glad for our barn and the tents. A large black snake attempted to join a class of teenagers, dropping from the rafters into the hayloft of the barn and landing right in the middle of them. The teens did not mind the interruption. Something happening unexpectedly was part of our daily routine; adults and children all enjoyed it.

A week after camp, all the children and I drove to Virginia to see my twin brother Philip and his family. Kenny couldn't take all that time off from work, so Chip who was sixteen, helped with the driving. Philip and Irene had three children, and we hadn't seen them for a long time. Philip had just brought property about the same time we did and built their house and barn on some acreage in the country. He worked at a bank in the city, but was raising horses. We had a wonderful time and went into Washington, D.C. to show the children the tourist sites. Irene was working and so Philip and I took our ten children to the Lincoln and Washington Memorials and Smithsonian. It was a fun time.

Kenny flew in for a few days and we traveled home in our van. We let Grace stay with her aunt and uncle for a few weeks, and we brought Jeff, Philip's boy back to the farm with us. We ran into tornadoes along the way home and I was sure glad to have Kenny driving. Later Jeff rode back with Dorothy and Bud when they went to sell their house in Arlington and Grace rode home with them.

Kenny fed his catfish in the pond each morning before he went to work. They were really growing big with all that attention. He and the boys had built a dock out to the pond, and he kept a big barrel of Farmers CO-OP catfish food on the end of the dock. Each morning with his cup of coffee in his hand, he would scatter food out on the pond for them and they grew and grew. But when he tried to fish for them, they didn't want to bite. So our spoiled catfish grew larger and larger.

Kenny enjoyed burning off our pastures each fall. He and the children would go on horses and with the tractor on a Saturday or Sunday afternoon and light the fires while they all helped to control them. But the wind in Kansas is always hiding out somewhere and arrives at the most unexpected times. Just light a fire anytime and you'll see. Many of Kenny's fires got out of control and burned the ditches along our road and occasionally the neighbor's stubble field after the wheat had been cut. This was an exciting time for the children and they loved to go with him.

In the summers the boys found jobs with the farmers that were our neighbors and went to work in their fields. They carried machetes and cut weeds in the rows of corn and milo. Tim cut his leg once by accident and had a few stitches. They also spent a lot of time riding their horses and camping out with friends. August was the month for the Riley County Fair in Manhattan and a big event all the children eagerly waited for. They had gone to monthly 4-H meetings all year at the Club House nearby with all the other children in the area; they had fun and learned how to keep their record books. They chose their animals to raise in the spring for their projects that weren't already our pets, and showed them at the fair, which lasted a week. They kept their animals at the fair and sometimes slept in the stalls with their horses. They washed and groomed them every day and practiced putting them through their paces for showing. The children usually wore blue jeans and white shirts with a red kerchief, and cowboy hats and boots. All their friends had animals there too, so it was an exciting and happy time with lots of competition. Some animals were sold at the end of the fair for butchering or we butchered them ourselves. The joke at our dinner table was which one we were eating tonight. Even though they named their pigs and steers, everyone knew that they were destined for the table.

Many years later when we sold all our animals and left the farm, I went to the supermarket to buy meat. As I looked at the stacked meat cases with all the saran wrapped choices, I realized these were strange cows and pigs, and I didn't even know their names. It really seemed a little risky to buy these, but I soon got used to it. The coyotes often came to our pond and carried off our purple-ribbon winner ducks for their dinner. We lost many ducks and geese. The possums had a good nose for baby geese and our babies didn't last very long. The coyotes and possums didn't seem to discriminate, but usually took the best. The children showed horses, pigs, steers, calves, ducks and geese. They had wood and leather and metal projects, gardening and cooking and sewing. The last night of the fair was a fun rodeo, called a "showdeo," that they enjoyed the most. After the fair ended, they all caught up on their sleep and slept for a couple of days. Once a year was enough.

Not long after the fair I usually bought new school clothes for all the children. I made a trip to JCPenney in Manhattan and tried to do it all at one time until the children were old enough to drive and do their own shopping. Shoes, socks, underclothes, shirts and jeans, coats, caps and sweaters; we were large consumers. I sewed a lot for the girls. Girl cousins on the Long side often added clothes for Amber and Grace. After I'd enroll the children at Theodore Roosevelt Elementary School, I made another trip shopping trip with lists in hand for needed school supplies. We were definitely in the children's business.

While living at the Pink Palace, Kenny had found restaurant dispensers that held three to five gallon containers of milk that we bought for the children. They loved getting their own. One small room inside the front door served as the mud room and it always had plenty of gear in it. Kenny had made rows of pegs on a board that stretched the length of the room. It held jackets, coats, hats, bridles, saddle pads, curry combs, baseball gloves, kites, ropes, coveralls, and sweatshirts. The floor was cluttered with cowboy boots, shoes, rubber boots, running shoes, ice skates, camping equipment, folding army shovels, tents, hockey sticks and pucks, B-B guns, balls and bats, bows and arrows, skates, fishing poles, fish bait, mittens, work gloves, snow saucers and tools. And occasionally, small domestic and wild animals. There was a sink with a mirror for washing up and a medicine chest supplied with Band Aids and Neosporin. It was the most popular and busiest room in the house with so many children coming and going. There was excitement in assembling everything they needed for camping trips and relief in having a place to dump all their used and muddy supplies when they were finished.

Kenny decided to start his own business, Bittersweet Auto Farm, in 1974 and used the red house on the front of our property as his office. He liked to tell people that he was in the transportation business and enjoyed solving their transportation problems. I think he knew most everyone in town. Some families bought three or four cars from him. The children worked for him during his first summer, and they all learned to drive cars early. There were nests of wasps in back rooms of the old house, and Grace went berserk one day with swarms of wasps chasing her. When the cows or horses got out of the barnyard fences they wandered through his parked cars for sale.

Chip had joined the Manhattan High School Pops Choir that traveled and performed around Manhattan and different areas of the state. It was a lively and talented singing and dancing group. He also ran track in his senior year and won the half-mile at the Kansas State Track Tournament in Wichita. We gave him a blue VW Bug for a graduation present when he graduated in 1975. Chip spent that summer working with a mission on an Indian Reservation near Show Low, Arizona. After spending the summer there, Kenny, Tim and Eric flew out to see him and drive an old antique Hudson car that Chip had purchased back for Kenny. A few days before the left, I had a miscarriage and was in the hospital overnight. I was resting and told Kenny to go on the trip with the boys. When they got back, Chip planned to move out of the house and start classes at Kansas State University in Manhattan in August. When Kenny and I had decided to leave the military in 1966, we knew that we needed to settle close to a college for our six children to be able to afford their education. Now the time had arrived much sooner than we had imagined. This was a momentous occasion for the first child to leave home. Kenny said that for the first time all his children would not be "under his roof." It sounded to me like something from *Fiddler on the Roof.* He was very sentimental, but I had grown up in a family where children were anxious to leave home and be on their own. I thought luggage was the appropriate high school graduation gift. We made a happy combination. Chip's room was already claimed before he walked out the door.

The Roosevelt Elementary School was called the Roosevelt Rough Riders after Teddy. They always hosted an annual school carnival to raise funds for various projects. Eric, at preschool age loved attending these with older brothers and sisters. One event was smashing an old car that had been brought to the school grounds. Tickets were sold for ten cents apiece and he had so many chances to wield a hammer and smash away at an old car. He loved it. He got ten swings with a regular hammer, or five with a large ball peen hammer, or two with a sledge-hammer. He looked forward to this every year and put all his heart and muscle into this endeavor. It was a time when he got the experience of not having to worry about scratching the car. He could bang away all he wanted. What an experience for a little boy who loved to bang on things! Eric often spent time at work with his Dad, which he loved.

In June 1976, Kenny planned our special twentieth wedding anniversary celebration at the Historic Alma Hotel. This was a well-known hotel in the small town of Alma, Kansas right off Interstate 70. It catered to special occasions and special group dinners. The nine of us were definitely a special group. It was to be a surprise for me. We drove there with lots of mystery involved, and Kenny only said that it was a special place out of town. All the children had arrived secretly without my knowledge in two separate cars and when we were seated at a table, the seven children came to our table and shouted "Surprise!" It really was a surprise to me, something I had never suspected! We had always celebrated our anniversary with dinner out alone, so the children knew that this was quite a privilege. It was really a different twist for us. The children were so excited that they had surprised me and they were enjoying this famous fancy hotel dining room. Kenny told them that they could order anything off the menu that they wanted. These were not McDonald's prices! Eric, six years old, decided that he would try lobster and everyone ordered their favorites. It was a wonderful evening and we all had a great time as Kenny and I talked about the past twenty years. Everyone was proud to be a part of this family, and we gave thanks to God for his love and generosity to us over the past years. Kenny also had been very generous. It was one of those very special family times that all of us remember.

At Christmas in December of 1976, we told all the children that we were expecting another baby, our eighth. I convinced Kenny that we needed one more. He thought I was crazy, but said that is what we would do. What class! Chip went over and shook his Dad's hand and congratulated him. After the initial shock, the older children

got on the phone and told all their friends. In preparing for
the arrival of a new baby brother or sister, Eric was seven
years old and helped me paint a red chest of drawers that
we had used for the last three boys, lime green and yellow
for the nursery. I knew better than to go all the way with
pink, but I had hopes. We had made a small room under the
stairs for the new baby with a baby crib and chest near the
kitchen.

Phillip ran track in high school and also joined the
Manhattan High School Pops Choir his senior year. He was
president of his senior class, loved riding horses and playing
his guitar. He had a special talent for music and often
played and sang for church. Phillip soon graduated from
high school in May 1977, and planned to start college at
Kansas State University in Manhattan in August. He would
be living with Chip in our house on Hillcrest. Kenny had felt
that it was a good investment to buy a house in Manhattan
for the children to stay in while they were in college. Phillip
and Chip both needed a place to stay closer to college, so he
bought a house near the campus. Chip was manager and
they both lived there and found friends to live with them.

It was a beautiful spring morning in 1977, and all the
children were at school. Eric, the youngest was in first
grade. Chip, our oldest was twenty years old and attending
Kansas State University. Phillip would soon be graduating
from high school. Amber and Grace were in high school;
Andrew and Tim in junior high. I could see the lovely red
bud trees with their soft, delicate, pink colors across the
pond along the hillside. I had tried to transplant some of
these trees closer to the house in the front yard with no
success. But they were my favorite at this time of year. The
purple iris standing tall and elegant; white, pink and dark
red peonies getting ready for Memorial Day; and bright
orange and delicate poppies were all shouting gloriously of
a Creator. I had recently planted petunias, marigolds and

pansies in the round rock enclosed flower bed surrounding the large honey locust tree that shaded our front yard. After planting petunias down by the entrance of our drive, I found that the deer also enjoyed the taste of these. Sometimes there would be thirty to forty white tailed deer in a herd that munched and sauntered their way across our front field by the driveway. I could count on them to eat the petunias that I planted at the entrance. I had a lovely view of the grassy dam and wooden dock that stretched out to the pond. The natural stone and red painted barn with bluish hued tin roof peaked just across the barnyard. Depending on the time of year, the barnyard was full of wild marijuana plants or tall bright yellow sunflowers. Cedars, locust, walnut, oak, maple, cottonwoods, Osage orange and Dutch elm trees covered the hillside. It was an artist's feast of line and color and form that I drank in every morning. What a beautiful place God had given to us to enjoy!

I was very much aware of life in all its forms as I was seven months pregnant with our eighth child. I had risen early that morning as usual and had my devotions at our large kitchen table while the house was quiet and before the busy day began. After Kenny had gone to his office and the children left for school, I sat in the upstairs living room to read. I felt such gratitude to God for all His blessings as I picked up a copy of World Vision magazine to read of missions around the world. We had kept many missionary families in our home, and our church had a number who were good friends of ours. We often talked about where God wanted us. My world was so lovely and my blessings overflowed.

Reading of the poorest people in the world in the World Vision magazine, who had no access to any kind of health care, I felt moved with compassion to pray for them. As I was on my knees praying, a definite voice came from outside me that said, "Phyllis, you could be a nurse." I was alone in the house. I had not chosen nursing in college and had never had any desire to be one. It just didn't interest me. I thought that this was pretty crazy! Where could this have come from? The quiet, passionate, insistence of His "Follow me" was spoken to my wide-awake senses of God's love and majesty and beauty that morning, and I was aware of His presence and power. I had learned that the life of a Christian is a life of quiet listening to that voice. As I now considered what I had heard, as crazy as it sounded, I never questioned that it was the Lord speaking to me. Those words were the beacon light for the years ahead of me, getting me through some very difficult times and keeping me focused. God was in control and if that was what He wanted, I would check it out.

I quickly dressed and drove to the University in Manhattan to check out the possibilities for a nursing degree. Meeting with the department-head, I found that all my sciences were recent enough to be counted toward my pre-nursing requirements, and that I could begin a course in microbiology in the summer. I could finish it before the baby came. I saw no obstacles. It would take two years to finish all my nursing requirements for a Bachelor's of Science in Nursing. So I enrolled for the summer semester starting in June at Kansas State. On my way home, I stopped by Kenny's business to let him know what I had done. He said that he thought that was a fine idea and we could go to the mission field together when I was finished. He was happy and supportive and would lease out his business when that time came. We were confident of God's calling.

Kenny and I celebrated our twenty-first wedding anniversary on June 10th and instead of going out for dinner, he sent the children out to McDonald's and told them not to come home. He was always very creative. He fixed a wonderful gourmet seafood dinner of lobster and crab, and we had the whole house to ourselves, which rarely happened. He gave me a new Bible with my name inscribed on the cover and 21 years. The time had really flown by. Very pregnant with our eighth, we were still romantics.

I started a pre-nursing microbiology course at Kansas State in June of that year and finished August 5th. There were times during that last week when I thought the baby might arrive either in the lab or on the way up the stairs before I could finish the course. I'm sure that I was the most pregnant lady on campus. It was a very hot summer, and I was pretty miserable. While I attended the Riley County 4-H Fair and all the children exhibited their animals and projects, I usually found somewhere to sit and rest. As my neighbors walked by, they all looked upon me with compassion and asked me when I would have the baby. Kenny tried to raise my spirits one evening when he said that he was making me a special milkshake. I rested on the couch while he was busy in the kitchen working with the children making quite a production of it all. He had bought a huge bag of fresh, dark purple Bing cherries and had the children cutting and pitting them for my milkshake. They were delighted to help and ate all the cherries that they wanted. It was the best milkshake that I ever tasted, but most important, Kenny was very understanding about how miserable I was feeling. When my labor started at home, I called his office to let him know and he jokingly said, "Drive to the office and I'll take you on to the hospital." I was not in the mood for a joke and he quickly closed up shop and came and got me.

Our eighth child, Sarah Emily, was born August 6, 1977, at Saint Mary's Hospital in Manhattan. We all gave our choices of names, and Kenny made the final decision. I had thought of Octavia for the eighth but decided against it. Chip was twenty years old and had a job as a Riley County Ambulance Emergency Medical Technician. He was on duty in the ER the night I went into the hospital to deliver. As I checked in at the front desk, the receptionist paged him and said his mother was going to Labor & Delivery. His friends heard this and said "Your Mother!" His friends were astonished that his mother was in the delivery room. So he kept his father company in the waiting room and was the first to congratulate us on Sarah's arrival. With brown eyes and lots of brown hair, she was a healthy and beautiful little girl and a happy last addition to our family. What a blessing to have another little girl! Kenny put up a sign in the front of his office window to let everyone driving by know "It's a Girl." We were all very happy. We had eight children now, but still had room for guests.

We invited an American Field Service Exchange Student to stay with us that year, and she arrived the last week of August. She was from the Island of Barbados and named Inger Leacock with a nickname of Delly. She was a senior at Manhattan High School. We all enjoyed her different accent because she spoke English with a British flair. I had enrolled for another course and would be taking ethics at K State and Sarah was with me in her infant seat. I was still nursing her but also took a bottle to class in case she became hungry and a noisy distraction. I was forty-two years old and the oldest student in the class. I knew that in twenty years, Sarah would be in college classes and these college students in my class would be forty-two years old, so it helped me keep time in perspective.

In September we all drove to Colorado Springs to my sister Betty and Pats' to attend my niece, Melanie's wedding and Delly went with us. We wanted to show her a different part of America. Sarah was just a couple of months old and Kenny had bought a motor home for our vacations. The children all loved to travel in this and it was very comfortable for our family with a television, kitchen, table and benches, bathroom and beds. We usually drove overnight to Colorado Springs.

Kenny bought a couple of motorcycles and said that we would take some vacation trips on them together. I could not get up the courage to ride one by myself, but I rode behind him while he steered. With a new baby, vacations didn't seem a priority right now. He had brought home a chocolate-brown convertible car that we took out occasionally. Kenny always provided me with a wide assortment of cars to drive. The only one I refused to drive was a purple Cadillac. I drove many different cars and sometimes didn't know which one to look for when I came out to the parking lot with my groceries. When the boy bringing out my groceries asked me what kind of car I had, I couldn't always remember.

Our lives with eight children, the business, the farm, and an exchange student from Barbados, seemed to be racing along at an exceptional high speed while we trusted God's leading. Communication was the key and Kenny and I usually went out each week for dinner, just to be alone and visit. We had a lot to talk about!

# Chapter 10: Hospitality

A NEW YEAR WITH MUCH PROMISE was always exciting. I was making progress towards my nursing degree. I finished my second class at Kansas State University and started a statistics class in January of 1978. Kenny said he had found statistics difficult for his business degree 12 years before me. He challenged me to get a better grade than his; I accepted, but since it involved math, I worried a little. Later in the semester I wrote Amber in South Africa saying, "my class is stretching my little brain to its mathematical limits, and it is groaning under the load." I turned to our high school and junior high kids, Grace and Andrew for help in a refresher course in Algebra. I could actually feel the gears creaking as my brain coped with the unfamiliar math language. It was very humbling. Kenny celebrated all my successes with making dinner or taking me out. He knew that I could do it even when I had doubts. I took Sarah to many of my classes as long as she was quietly playing or eating her cheerios. Chip and Phillip watched her whenever they could. When I received my final grade of a B in May, Kenny was very proud of me and we really celebrated. I was convinced that the Lord could do anything.

Amber had applied for and been accepted as an American Field Service Exchange Student her senior year at Manhattan High School and left for Johannesburg, South Africa in January of 1978. She enjoyed playing tennis for the first time in the fall and was on the Manhattan High School tennis team. Before she left for South Africa, she worked for a short time for Kenny in his office, which he really appreciated. She had all her requirements for graduation finished and would be gone a year. It was an exciting time for her, making preparations and seeing all her friends. We saw her off at the Manhattan Airport and she called me from New York City, where the students from around the country gathered together for orientation. I realized seventeen was very young to be going so far, but it was too late to change plans. Cautious about applying for the program, she was now very excited about going. She stayed the year with a lovely Christian family, Ray and Dorrian Stafford with four daughters, and I wrote letters to her once a week. We all prayed for her every day. We sent pictures and kept her up to date with all the news of the family. Her boyfriend, Larry, spent a lot of time at our house while Amber was gone.

We had over six weeks of below freezing temperatures and the pond had been frozen solid with thick ice. While ice skating on the pond, the children noticed dead catfish in the ice below the surface. This hadn't ever happened before since having the fish in our pond. They told their Dad, and Kenny cut out a block of ice to see if we could defrost and eat the catfish. He used the chain saw and cut out a thirty-six-inch block of ice with a fish frozen inside the block. The children brought it up to the house on a sled and we defrosted it in the shower. The smell was so bad that we knew it had died before it was frozen. The catfish had first been caught in an air pocket in the ice, died from lack of oxygen, and then froze. We lost all our large catfish because the pond had been frozen for so long. When the pond defrosted, they were all floating on the top and we ended up with piles of dead catfish on the sides of the pond. That was the end of our catfish farming adventure.

Sarah was six months old and weighed nineteen pounds. She had a system of motivation by arching her back and neck and pushing with her legs, so she crawled across the living room floor very fast. Everyone enjoyed holding her and carrying her around. She had a playpen, but was rarely in it. With brown hair and eyes, she looked a lot like Amber at that age.

On February 17th, Chip and Phillip came out to the farm to cook Kenny's forty-fifth birthday dinner. It was very cold at eight degrees below zero. We celebrated with a wonderful dinner and all missed Amber in South Africa. She had sent Kenny a lovely card, and I'm sure that he was missing her very much. Chip began making plans for a backpacking trip to Europe and to meet Amber in December of that year in South Africa. On one occasion when the boys came out to visit, Kenny and Chip decided to put on the younger boys' boxing gloves and go a round. Kenny ended up with a broken thumb.

We had a great amount of snow that winter and there were fifteen-foot drifts on top of the hills. It made sledding great for the kids as they used their toboggan, sleds and large tractor tire inner tubes. They had removed some rocks and built a very fast sled slope from the top of the hill to the bottom of the ravine. Many of their friends from Manhattan came out to sled on their great sled slope. Eric ended up hung by his stocking cap in a tree on one of his fast trips down the steep hill. Ice hockey on the pond was at its best and we had to constantly shovel off the snow to keep it clear. The children kept the outside light above the dam turned on at night and played ice hockey until midnight. Many friends came out to join us and the games got very competitive. Andrew ended up with a cut above his eyebrow one night when it became especially violent.

In the spring, Andrew and Tim played soccer and ran Junior Olympic track events and I drove them to all their practices. They were both fast runners. While I waited in the car with Sarah for them, a friend challenged me to start running and participate in the Masters Running Events. I had not run since grade school but thought that I might give it a try. My first run of half a mile down to the walnut trees showed me that I needed a lot of practice to get in shape.

Over the summer I worked up to jogging three miles, and it wasn't as hard as I thought it would be.

Tim had started playing the trumpet in the honors band at school. He seemed to really enjoy it, so I bought him the sheet music to *Star Wars*. In March, Grace and Andrew and Delly went skiing in Colorado with a youth group, and Kenny and I took a trip to Wichita, Kansas with the three younger children, Tim, Eric and Sarah. We stopped by to see my twin brother Philip and his family in Independence, Kansas. They had moved back to Kansas from Virginia and eventually bought another farm, built a new house, and raised horses. We stayed at a very elegant downtown hotel in Wichita with trees and an indoor swimming pool right outside our tenth floor room. Adren and Sally, my brother and sister-in-law, joined us for dinner. This was a special treat and we enjoyed a good visit with them. Kenny bought a very nice light blue western suit at Sheplers Western Clothing for Easter on our way home. He really looked very handsome in it. It had been a few years since he had bought a new suit.

In the spring I got my first traffic ticket in my driving career on a Sunday evening coming home from church. The police car with its blinking blue lights pulled in behind me and parked alongside the highway and wrote up my ticket. Eric, seven years old and very embarrassed complained, "I wish that he would turn off that dumb blinking light." We also saw deer crossing the road in front of us as we drove to the house that night, their white tails shining in the dark as they jumped the road.

With spring coming, I felt like I needed to wallpaper or paint or something. In June I started repainting Sarah's room which Delly had just vacated. It had been a medium blue so it took six coats of yellow paint to finish. Sarah and Eric moved in and shared a room together.

On Mother's Day I was really surprised when the children came driving up the driveway in a brand new 1978 silver Subaru station wagon. Kenny had bought me this knowing that I would need it to drive to nursing school in Salina, Kansas when I finished my pre-nursing requirements at Kansas State. He had suggested that he buy a helicopter and fly me to school each day. I thought the Subaru was more practical. It was four-wheel drive, which is just what I needed for the mud and snow on our road. I was very happy and felt very special. The children were just as happy as I was and were delighted to be able to give it to me. They learned a lot from their father's generosity.

Chip turned twenty-one on the first of May, and we had a special family dinner for him. He received a nice check from the Miami Indian Tribe, which had been invested for him. All the children received checks on their eighteenth and twenty-first birthdays. The government settlements with our Miami Indian Tribe were invested and each child received theirs. Kenny cooked out on the gas grill and Grandmother, his mother, came out for dinner.

We always hunted in our woods for wild mushrooms in the spring called morels. There were more of them if we had a lot of rain. We often gathered large bags and brought them home to cook in butter in a skillet. They had a distinctive taste and were delicious. Andrew and Tim made a pizza for dinner one night and put these on top with sausage. It was very good.

Delly graduated from Manhattan High School and returned to Barbados in the summer. She had learned much about American family life and we learned a lot about her family. Her family owned a large sugar plantation in Barbados, and she had many brothers and sisters. She had gone to an all-girls school in Barbados but enjoyed our co-ed Manhattan High School. She didn't talk much when she first arrived and it was three months before I noticed that she had not said a word at the dinner table. When she finally asked, "Please pass the jam," we were shocked. So we worked on communication, of which there were many opportunities in our house. She stayed with another family in Manhattan the last month of her year. She enjoyed her year in America and did not want to return home, but she hoped to return someday. We were glad to have her with us and we learned a lot about her culture and the needs of exchange students adapting to a new culture. Explaining to her why we did things the way we did helped us to examine our own traditions and beliefs.

We took our motorhome and enjoyed camping and fishing on a trip to Madison during Memorial Day weekend. We visited the cemetery where my parents and sister were buried and the children all enjoyed fishing in the Verdigris River. We had taken fishing trips there many times before and slept in tents along the river. We cooked our fish as we caught them and they were fresh and delicious. It brought back many childhood memories with my family. We also restocked our own pond with bass in the summer after losing so many catfish in the winter.

Strawberry picking time came and we brought home many gallon-buckets of strawberries that we had all picked from Britt's Farm and Vegetable Market. I made five gallons of strawberry freezer jam that always tasted so fresh in the winter. We had two large freezers that kept our meat, garden vegetables and jams. We also made many jars of bread and butter pickles that everyone loved.

Phillip worked and assisted our preacher with summer camps at our Christian Camp near Abilene, Kansas and helped with the Campus Life organization at the high school. He got very good on his guitar and did lots of singing. He and Amber sang for church services and other groups. Grace spent the summer working with dad at his business and doing some office work that Amber had done before she left. Andrew and Tim kept up with the large area that we had to mow.

We invited some new couples that were attending our Home Bible Study to our house for a fish fry in the front yard. It was a good way to become acquainted with new families in town; many of them were with the military at Fort Riley. Most people loved coming to the country, and Kenny and I enjoyed giving hospitality. Kenny was a great cook and enjoyed cooking on our new gas grill. Fish was always a favorite with our family.

Kenny and I celebrated our twenty-second wedding anniversary on June 10th. He had recently gotten a crew cut as he had when we were first married in 1956. We went out for a wonderful seafood dinner, our favorite, and saw the movie *All Things Bright & Beautiful* in his chocolate-brown convertible. Twenty-two years had passed so quickly, but seemed like a long time. We had eight children and had covered a lot of territory. He made a new large redwood picnic table with benches for our patio. Andrew and Tim helped him with this project and we used it every day.

In July we drove to Independence, Kansas in our motorhome to visit my twin brother Philip and his family and spent the night with them. Their children Erin, Jeff, and Elaine were the same ages as our children Phillip, Amber, and Grace. They always enjoyed being together. They had built a beautiful brick home in the country sitting on a hill, and just finished a large pond behind the house. Philip had quarter horses that he raised and rode. I always remembered our riding Black Beauty together as kids and we often talked about it. He had developed his property with four homes along one side of the drive, which he had sold. We enjoyed visiting them when we could and had also stopped by to see them in March on our way to Wichita. We all had a great time and then drove on to Beaver Lake where we visited my older brother Richard and his family.

Richard had built a house on Beaver Lake in Arkansas and invited us to spend 4th of July with them. We spent the 4th of July on a houseboat on Beaver Lake and shot many fireworks that Phillip had brought along. He had been in the fireworks business the year before and had plenty for everyone to shoot. The children all had a wonderful time with their cousins, Rick, Melissa and Michelle Evans, fishing and swimming in the Lake. Michelle was just two years older than Sarah.

It was very relaxing for Kenny to get away from his work and enjoy all the children. They jumped from high cliffs into the water and the older boys thought their Dad pretty daring. We enjoyed Richard and Carols' hospitality and their beautiful new home and scenery. I think this was the trip where we lost Eric at the pinball machines in a Howard Johnson's near Kansas City. Everyone thought he was with someone else and we didn't miss him until we were on down the Interstate for a while. But we turned around immediately and came back and he was right where he had been left, still watching the pinball machines. There are always so many blessings and risks with so many children.

Amber wrote frequently of her South African family, school and experiences in Johannesburg. She also sent us a tape and it was so good to hear her voice. Although it was a dangerous time there, we trusted in the Lord and knew that she had a Christian family to stay with. We kept up on the political situation through the news. We had an AFS dinner in Manhattan in July and shared her news with the other families and members. She seemed to be adjusting well and enjoyed the challenges of adapting to a new culture. She had many opportunities for public speaking and took many slides and photos. This was good news for the other members. The success of the exchange program depended upon how well the students adjusted in another country.

Amber kept a political notebook where she noted the happenings in the country. She wrote mostly of what was going on at school, church and trips that she took. We were very grateful for the Staffords and the hospitality they showed her.

The children and I tried to work in as many trips to the beach that summer as possible for picnics and swimming at Tuttle Creek. We ate a lot of watermelon, corn on the cob, and ice cream in the summer. I could bring home a box of twenty-four ice cream bars at noon, and they would all be gone by supper. I also planned and worked on a playground for children at our new church. We had plenty of space but no outside play facilities for Sunday school classes or Vacation Bible School. We were given donations of playground equipment.

My interest in running grew, and I enjoyed the challenge of improving my time. I kept a log of my miles and ran 1,000 miles in my first Brooks running shoes that first year. I ran five miles each morning, starting at 6:00 a.m., to the highway and back from our house. Everyone else in the family was running, so I felt like joining the team too. I got faster over time. Kenny drove the motorhome to our track meets and Sarah watched from her playpen. I tried to get Kenny into running with me and he said that he would later. I knew he would be very fast and would have no trouble outdistancing me very quickly. With Grace, Andrew, Tim, Eric and I, there were five of us running at events. I remember one very difficult 10K run in Kansas City called Heartbreak Hill. We all ran in our different categories, and it was one of the most difficult events that I ever ran. Grace ran with me and encouraged me to keep going. They all won medals in their categories.

That summer, Kenny's Aunt Alice from Oregon and children came for a visit. Amber's room was empty, so we had quite a few visitors. Kenny had spent his summers as a child on their farm near Salem, Oregon and had many happy memories there. This was the first time I had met these relatives, but had heard a lot about them. Kenny was glad to show them our farm and his mother was very happy to have her sister come to Manhattan for a visit. Later in the fall, we heard news that Aunt Alice was diagnosed with colon cancer. We were so glad that she had come for a visit and we all prayed for her.

Eric and Kenny took a trip in the brown convertible to Kansas City to see the Kansas City Chiefs play a football game in the fall. I waved goodbye to them as they drove off down the driveway and thought about what fun they planned to have together. Kenny, who was so young at heart, and his youngest eight-year-old son. They took off their shirts and got some sun on the way to Kansas City and had a wonderful time together. Eric loved being with his dad and they talked about their trip and what fun they had for a long time. Eric especially remembered the hotdogs at halftime. It was a special time that Eric will never forget.

Kenny brought his tools and helped me put up bookshelves in my classroom at the church, and I brought many books from my library at home that I had collected to start a church library. Other church members also donated books. A library just seemed like a necessary part of Christian education that we needed to offer and everyone was free to use the books. The playground was finished and looked very cheerful and inviting for the children. It contained a swing set, slide, two large tractor tires filled with sand, two cast iron shaped mushrooms for climbing painted with polka dots, a cast iron racing car painted bright blue to sit in and steer, and other assorted tires. Sarah and all the other children at the church enjoyed the playground.

The year before, the land adjoining our fifteen acres was for sale and we had decided to buy those forty acres. The land cost more than we wanted to pay, but we felt like we should take advantage of the opportunity. There were ten acres of meadow and thirty more acres of woods and nice building sites. There was an underground spring on the land, and Kenny planned to build a barn and pond in the meadow. We also planned to build our smaller underground home on a hillside in the woods in the future. We just called it "the forty."

We found out that our building permit had been approved for a new house, and began working with our builder to pick out a suitable building site and began work on our house plans. We were in no hurry and planned to take all the time that we needed to plan our home. We wanted it to be smaller than our present one, but flexible for our children still at home, economical and energy efficient. Kenny also started building a storage building for his machinery and equipment beside the house. It matched the house and was the same color. The boys all worked with him on this and learned the process.

I had decided not to take any classes at Kansas State in the fall because I wanted to spend the time with Sarah. I only had one six-hour anatomy class with lab to finish before I started nursing classes at Marymount College in Salina, Kansas. I wrote Amber telling her, "I need an hour alone with the Lord before I'm fit for my day."

In September Kenny and I were invited to join the Kansas State football team on their trip to Phoenix, Arizona for a game. Kenny was an avid supporter of the Kansas State football team, although they weren't doing as well as his team had when he played, and he was good friends with the coach, having played football with him in college. The coach's wife, Shirley, was a good friend of mine from Columbus High School, and we played clarinet in the band together. She was one of my first friends there in Columbus, Georgia when I moved there with my sister. They were unable to find a house with sufficient acreage, and we kept their quarter horses for them in our pastures. They had five children and we enjoyed getting our families together for dinner and picnics. I didn't want to leave Sarah at home, so we flew with the team to Phoenix, Arizona and took Sarah with us. Chip came home to watch the other children, and Grace was old enough to do some cooking. We had a wonderful time in Phoenix, and Kenny enjoyed the camaraderie with the football staff and the team. He still had a good suntan from the summer and wore a new lemon yellow polo shirt and matching shorts, looking very debonair. We rented a car and drove to the Fort Huachuca Army Base to see our old home and friends who were living in Sierra Vista. Had it really been that long ago before we had any children? It had grown so much in the last twenty years since we had left. We remembered our wish to return and live there again sometime and really enjoyed all the memories that it brought back. It was a fun time and we took some good pictures of our vacation there. Chip had been born at Fort Huachuca and we had our eighth child Sarah with us. It was kind of a "deja vu" feeling. It had been over twenty years, eleven in the military and eleven as civilians.

In August I attended the Billy Graham School of Evangelism in Kansas City. The meetings were held at an all-black Baptist church in downtown Kansas City. Grace had made out menus and did all the cooking for the week. I submitted a manuscript to the *Guideposts* Writers Workshop, but had not been chosen for their school in New York City. That had been my first attempt at writing. I felt a need to learn to communicate my faith in a way that would be helpful to others. I took Sarah with me to Kansas City, who was a little over a year old, and we stayed at the Holiday Inn in downtown Kansas City. When we checked into our room, there was a huge floral arrangement to welcome us with a note from Kenny. He said that they loved and missed us. I was so surprised and knew that I was very fortunate indeed to have such a loving husband who supported and encouraged all my endeavors. I learned most how blessed I was. Sarah spent much time in her stroller and we had a great time.

Chip and Phillip both exchanged their cars with Kenny, and Chip got a gold Volvo that he had always wanted. Phillip got a blue VW with a sunroof. They drove these in the summer and then drove Chip's Volvo to New York City the first week of November on their trip to fly out for Europe on their backpacking trip.

Sarah and I camped out in the hills with Eric after his eighth birthday in August. We set up a tent in the pasture and cooked supper over our campfire. We loved to listen to the bullfrogs at night croaking in the nearby ponds. The whip-o-wills were also a part of the nighttime noises along with the usual coyotes yipping and howling sounding like a hundred. When we awoke in the morning, we were surrounded with a group of cows, contentedly munching grass very close to our tent. Sarah was wild eyed and loved it and wanted to join them. It's no wonder "cow" was one of her favorite words and the first word she learned after 'ma ma and da da'.

Phillip received a letter in October from Arthur Moore in New Zealand, inviting him to come to New Zealand and work on a Christian ranch. We had met Arthur Moore in Manhattan when he was speaking in churches the year before. Kenny and I talked about this and decided it would be a good opportunity for Phillip. But Phillip didn't make any definite plans until the next year.

Kenny mowed the grass at the church for the last time that winter with his tractor and bush-hog. It was a large area to mow, but looked very good when he was finished. It wouldn't need mowing again until the first time in the spring. Even though it took a lot of his time, I know he enjoyed doing this.

I got my running up to eight miles and ran my first five-mile race in 50 minutes in October. Kenny was with Sarah in the motorhome and Grace and Andrew cheered me on. I was amazed that I could run so far. Tim was running regularly and set a faster record than Grace or Andrew had set for the same two-mile course. So Grace and Andrew challenged him. We decided to have a Family Track Meet at Warner Park. Grace got a stopwatch from the high school and Chip and Phillip cheered and timed us. It was very close, but Andrew won by 12 seconds, Tim next and Grace last. Eric and I raced the one-mile and he beat me by 2 minutes. His confidence soared and he thought he was the fastest kid around after that.

Donating blood was a usual event for Kenny and me both each year. But I had a problem this year with no one believing that I weighed one hundred and ten pounds. That was the minimum weight. When I arrived to donate, three different people asked me and I insisted that I did. After giving the blood, I weighed myself and I weighed exactly one hundred and ten pounds. But the next day, I didn't. That was the last time that I was ever able to give blood. The next year, my travels to Haiti and India disqualified me.

Kenny and the boys had finally finished the storage building adjoining the house and were putting on the roof one weekend. Kenny sprayed white foam that hardened and insulated it so it would be warm in the winter and he could use it as a workshop. They were all very happy when it was finished and had a pizza party sitting up on the roof. They had ordered and picked up the pizza in town and were celebrating all their efforts. It looked very nice with a sliding garage door on the front and matched the house.

We all had a farewell dinner in Manhattan with Dorothy and Bud for Adrienne and her husband Jim who

were on their way to Germany for three years. They were
stationed with the Army in Hahn, Germany. Chip and
Phillip planned to visit them there in November on their
backpacking trip. It had been fifteen years ago that Kenny
and I had lived in Germany. We had many good memories
of our three years there.

On November ninth, Chip and Phillip left Manhattan
and drove the gold Volvo to New York City, stopping to
stay with friends along the way. They called us before they
boarded their flight to London. They had delayed starting
back to college that semester so they could earn money for
trip expenses; they also had some Indian money to help pay
their expenses. In saying goodbye, Kenny asked them to call
each week to let us know where they were. I thought that
this was unnecessary but he insisted. They had a great time
travelling through many countries, south as far as Naples,
Italy, and north as far as Copenhagen to see many new
countries and some countries where they had been when we
lived in Europe. They went skiing in Austria on the border
of Italy and Germany. They also spent some time with their
cousin Adrienne and her husband stationed with the Army
in Hahn, Germany. They stopped in Stuttgart where we had
lived for three years when they were little. Chip especially
remembered the Black Forest across from our house. They
called us each week and from London before Christmas.
They were on their way to Johannesburg, South Africa, after
stopping in Nairobi, Kenya, where they would spend
Christmas with Amber and her family. We were so glad to
get their call and know that they would soon all be together.
This was the first Christmas that any of the children were
not with us. Our family would seem very small. I wrote my
last letter to Amber, the fourth of December.

We hosted a Cross Country Banquet at the farm in
November the track team and their parents. We had
finished up the season well; the kids ran many races and

won many medals. It was a nice evening of eating and visiting and the children all enjoyed having their friends there. It was very cold out, but I was still running five miles a day. I heard from a speaker at church about the need for medical evangelism on the Island of Haiti in the Caribbean. I was very anxious to go. I was confident that the Lord was leading us.

We invited my twin brother Philip and Irene and their family for Thanksgiving dinner. It was a lovely day with much food. After dinner I challenged Philip to a foot race in the front yard. We had raced each other since we were born. With my recent running experiences I thought that maybe I could finally beat him. The children were all out to watch this historical event and the dogs ran with us. I won the race down the front yard to the rock wall, but he passed me coming back up to the house. That was the first time I had ever been ahead of him in our lives, if even for a short while. Grace took pictures and I have the two of them hanging on the wall in my kitchen to remember. Me in front in one and Philip out front in the other. I think it might be time for another challenge.

I pre-enrolled for my last six hours of credit at Kansas State in an anatomy class called The Human Body, which was scheduled to start the next semester at the end of January. I drove my new Subaru to Salina, Kansas, about sixty miles, and checked on my transcript for Marymount Nursing College. I had chosen this smaller nursing school over the one in Topeka because of its excellent faculty-to-student ratio and their strong religious values. I met with the Dean of Nursing to make sure that I would have all my requirements finished. I planned to start next summer for my first Basic Nursing Class.

# Chapter 11: Home for Christmas

KENNY AND I WOKE UP the morning of December 23, 1978, and talked about all the things needing to be done before Christmas. He usually sat by our rock fireplace in the kitchen/dining room with a roaring fire, drinking his coffee and smoking his pipe before he put on his cowboy boots. The native rock wall had an opening for a wood-box on the left side that the boys kept stacked full in winter, and a larger-than-average forty-inch fireplace opening with grate. It had a wide hearth extending the width of the room, where quite a few children could sit. Kenny liked to cook Sunday evening dinner here in a black cast iron stew pot that hung over the fire. The smell of his tobacco, Mixture 77, was very familiar. Sarah, just one-and-a-half years old, considered her Daddy's boots very interesting and sometimes put her wooden blocks in them and other toys, so he always turned them upside down to empty everything out before trying to put them on. She also tried to load up the dishwasher with her own things. I always smiled when he, without even realizing it, emptied his boots in the morning. Each child found a way of making themselves noticed in unique ways.

We talked as I started putting out breakfast for the children. In the morning before the children woke up was our best time to find out what we each had going. The two most important things on our agenda was we wanted to call Amber and do last minute Christmas shopping. It was another very cold Saturday morning, so the children were home and able to help with things. Kenny got dressed in his well-worn jeans and plaid shirt with his light green down vest and Stetson cowboy hat that he wore to work in the winter. I sewed a small patch on his jeans and it was still holding and not too noticeable. I made him a new cotton flannel shirt for his birthday last February, a soft gold and olive green plaid, but he didn't wear it this morning. I had taken a long time to finish it and considered it a work of art. He was very pleased.

We called Amber in Johannesburg to wish her a Merry Christmas, and Chip and Phillip also, since they had just arrived from London to visit their sister for Christmas after backpacking through Europe. It was a good connection and wonderful to hear all their voices. They sounded excited and happy, and we were happy to have them all together safely. But Johannesburg, South Africa was still 9,000 miles away from home. Kenny and I talked about this and were feeling both happy and sad not to have all our children together for Christmas for the first time. We began to wonder why we had let them get so far away, even if their plans sounded reasonable at the time and we encouraged them to go. We had agreed together to let them go, but now silently blamed each other for the lack of their presence. Right now we wanted them home. Kenny was very sentimental about this, and we didn't feel like being brave at this point.

I remembered times during WWII when all my family couldn't be together and Bing Crosby's song "I'll be Home for Christmas" was our wish. I'm sure that we were both thinking, "Kids can grow up and leave and have all the adventures they want, but they should be home for Christmas." I guess this was the beginning of my "empty nest syndrome" with five children still at home.

We talked together about our plans for the day like we usually did, as Kenny drank his coffee and got ready to go to his office at Bittersweet. I had finished a lot of baking, but still had much to do and needed to encourage the children to finish making their Christmas gifts. Sarah was still asleep and all the other kids were still in bed. They usually made their gifts for all of us. Sometimes they were still trying to finish their gifts on Christmas Eve. They had many projects lined up to finish on this day since they were off school. I had a trip to make to town to finish up some last minute shopping myself. Kenny asked me to drop by his office and pick him up and he would go to Manhattan with me so we could do it together. I was glad to hear this and really appreciated having him with me and depended upon his choices for gifts for his family.

We had already taken one night the previous week to go out for a relaxing dinner together and do our shopping for the children. This was a tradition that we had started many years ago. We had the children make a list, then went out in the evening for dinner taking the list to help guide our shopping for them. We felt free to deviate from the list, but learned that our choices weren't always theirs. This was no fast and easy job for either of us, but we tried to keep the commercial giving within reasonable limits. I often threatened to leave the country or suggested that we all go to an orphanage that we supported and care for the children there, while the regular house-parents went off for a few days. Anything to downplay all the gifts and demonstrate the Spirit of Christ as we celebrated His birth. I was so glad that all their gifts had been bought and were in hiding. Christmas can easily get overwhelming with a family of ten, even if three are in Africa. That fact only added a little more stress to our own feelings.

Kenny left for the office and the children began to work on their Christmas gifts after breakfast. I started with my baking and finished many loaves of Christmas bread for gifts to neighbors and friends. During the morning, Grace and Andrew received a call from Kenny to come down and help out at his office. They went, and the children returned by lunch and we all ate lunch together. Around 2:00 p.m., I left the older children and home and took Sarah with me to Manhattan. I stopped to pick up Kenny on the way. He came out to our car to talk to us and said that he was expecting a customer to come in and pick up a car before Christmas. He was sorry but he could not go with us to Manhattan. I was disappointed that he couldn't go with us and felt like he should take the afternoon off, but I understood his business. A customer wanted to have a car as a Christmas gift.

Kenny filled up my car with gas from his pump and told me to stop back by on my way home and we would go home together. He leaned through the car window and kissed Sarah and we kissed goodbye. I told him that I would see him later. I drove off towards town and he waved to us and walked back toward his office. Those were our last words, and that was the last time I saw him.

When I started this book, if I had known how painful this would be, I would never have started. Reliving the joys and sorrows of my life have been emotionally and psychologically draining. To go through this once was enough.

I drove home from Manhattan about thirty minutes later with Sarah in her car seat and came to Kenny's office. Before I had turned off the highway, I could see three or four police cars parked in his office driveway, so I decided to drive on home. I was worried and knew something was wrong, but I never guessed in those few seconds, the magnitude of our loss. I had no warning. When I returned home, Grace told me that a policeman had called.

I drove back to Kenny's office and parked. Before I could get out of my car, a policeman came to my window. He said that a man had been shot inside and that I couldn't get out. I said that I was Mrs. Long and this was my husband's business and I wanted to talk to him. The officers had just arrived and there had been no identification yet. He asked me what Kenny had been wearing. I told him down to the last detail, with the small patch on his jeans. He said that Kenny had been shot and they had called the ambulance. I insisted that I needed to go in and see him and tried to open my car door, but he prevented me from getting out of the car. He said that I did not want to see him like this. I was in shock! This wasn't real! I had just seen Kenny alive and well thirty minutes before. All I could think of doing was to go home and be with the children.

I drove the few miles home in a daze. Grace, Andrew, Tim, and Eric were all there and Sarah was sleeping. They had been working on their Christmas presents. When the policeman had called our house from Kenny's office and Grace had answered, she knew something was wrong. Grace and Andrew had worked with him all morning. I asked them if anything had gone wrong, but they knew nothing. I called all the children together to sit at the kitchen table. I think that I hugged the children and told them what had happened and they all began crying. We read the Bible together at the kitchen table. I instinctively knew that there was no place else to go. God had promised to be with us in all our suffering and this was more than we could bear.

I had made Christmas bread for our best friends in Manhattan, so I asked Grace to take them the bread and tell them what had happened. I called Dorothy and Bud in Manhattan and told them that I needed them right now. They did not know what had happened, but came out immediately about 4:00 p.m. Bud's mother, Mrs. Hyle, had come to spend Christmas with them, and Bud had just gotten in from hunting; he came in his hunting clothes. None of us understood what had happened. The children were all in shock and just sat around the house, but Andy went to the barn.

There was nothing that I could do. I felt paralyzed. I held Sarah and cried. She was not aware of what was going on. Bud gathered all the children together in the kitchen and told them what had happened to Kenny and what had

happened when my parents had died. That I was thirteen
years old and the same thing had happened to me. I lost my
mother, father and sister. He advised the children that they
should look at me and see how things had gone in my life.
In time, they would get through this. Eric went up to his
room to be by himself. I found Bud talking to him on his bed
when I went to check on him.

I called the Staffords in Johannesburg, South Africa
and told them that Kenny had gone home to be with Jesus.
With the time change, it was the middle of the night for
them. Ray Stafford woke Chip, Phillip and Amber and told
them what happened. Dorothy talked to Chip and just told
him that Kenny had been shot and had died. We had no
information other than that, so that is all they knew until
they arrived home the next day. We later learned that
Kenny had been robbed; the crime had been a robbery and
shooting.

By evening I knew that I had to do something, so I
cooked hamburgers for supper. I didn't know what else to
do. None of the children wanted to eat, nor did I, but I said
that we needed to. I wanted to just run out of the house in
the dark and run for miles by myself up in the hills but
couldn't leave the children. I think that it would have
helped us all if we could have done this, but it was very cold
and snowy on the roads.

The pastor from our church, a good friend of
Kenny's, came out with Kenny's sisters and their families,
his mother and brother to share their grief. Kenny's family
was all sobbing and no one could talk. They hugged the
children and we just sat and looked at each other. Friends
and neighbors came to see how they could help. There were
many phone calls and Dorothy took them. We talked about
making the business secure for the night and the police had
done that. Dorothy stayed with us until late and then went
home for the night. She called the rest of my family and

relatives. We had a large fire in the kitchen/family room fireplace going all day as it was December and still very cold.

Bud stayed with us and sat by the fire all night, and I went to bed after the children, about midnight. He thought that we might be in some kind of danger and didn't want to leave us alone. We still had very little information as to what had happened. I don't think anyone slept that night. I could not comprehend what had happened. We took our grief to bed with us and I put Sarah in bed with me and cried.

Sunday morning I fixed breakfast, and we talked about going to church. Kenny was an elder and I taught a Sunday school class. I didn't know what to do. No one wanted to do anything, but I talked to the children and said that I wanted to go to church. They could go with me if they wanted. I think they all came with me. Dorothy called and said that she would go to church with me. I went to church and taught my class and we came home. Many friends expressed their sorrow and grief. I don't remember much, but felt like it was better to do something than nothing.

We all wanted to hold and play with Sarah. That afternoon after dinner, Dorothy and I went to look at cemetery lots for the burial. It was still hard to believe the reality of it all, and I just went through the motions of living. But I knew that I had to do this. My sister Betty arrived in the afternoon. The funeral was on Tuesday, the day after Christmas. Many friends and neighbors started arriving with food. Someone has said that food is the currency of affection; we were millionaires.

We opened gifts on Christmas morning. Kenny and I had bought all the children's gifts before, and I told the children that their dad had picked out these gifts with me. My sister Betty was with us and stayed through the funeral. I appreciated her presence and she was a great help at

Christmas. It was just good to have her there. Dorothy and Bud helped in every way that they could, and I never knew all that they did. Chip, Phillip and Amber arrived home from Johannesburg. They had many questions to ask, and I was exhausted and glad to see them. I hugged Amber like she had been gone for a year. It was wonderful to have them home safely.

Because of the unexpectedness of this tragedy, I felt like the sky could start falling any minute. I felt that I was in the middle of a war and I didn't know who would go next. I had switched to the survival mode of existence. Chip was twenty-one years old and took care of many of the details for the funeral. My twin brother Philip came on Monday, and it was so good to have him there. My whole family loved Kenny very much and they were like a rock of support and encouragement. We had all been here before. We were not inexperienced in family tragedy. Kenny's family were all together in grief and shock volunteering their help. I felt unable to give words of comfort to anyone in my state of shock. I would first need to mourn.

There was not enough room at the church, and guests were standing in the back of the church and outside. I remembered that Kenny had just mowed the church grounds in October. Kenny was very well known and respected and loved within our church and all of Manhattan. He had attended high school and graduated from college here as a Kansas State Football player and spent eleven years as an officer and pilot in the military. His many friends loved and appreciated him and enjoyed having him as a businessman in the community. His military service and record in Vietnam was well known to many.

The church had respected his leadership abilities, and Kenny was active in the Stewardship of Finances and had served as an Elder. He had contributed generously and helped build this church. His business friends were half the community. Manhattan Christian College had benefited from his generosity and hospitality. The neighbors all respected and admired his friendship and leadership in the community. He made a large economic contribution through the rearing of our eight children. He would be missed by most of Manhattan.

The funeral service and burial was so hard for us all. All my brothers and sisters and their families were there. They had all loved and respected Kenny. His family and relatives were all there. He was a much loved and devoted son, brother, and uncle. Chip, Phillip, Grace, Amber and Andrew, Timothy, Eric and Sarah all sat with me. We were all numb with grief. It was horrible at the cemetery. No one wanted to leave. There were many Scripture readings of hope and comfort. Kenny was with the Lord, but how could we go on as a family?

After all the relatives and friends left, we went through the motions of living. I didn't stop talking to God. In fact, I argued with him constantly. What was He doing, allowing Kenny to be killed in this way? Leaving me alone with all these children! What was I supposed to do? Why did he have to be murdered? And it was so unexpected, after returning home from the dangers of Vietnam. I demanded answers. And He said, "Phyllis, look at my Son." And I was quieted.

Then I blamed Kenny for getting himself killed while he was going about his business at his office. Why did he leave me alone to raise these children when God had brought him back from Vietnam so we could be a family? This was a job that we both had chosen and he had just left me in the middle of it. Who did he think he was, leaving me alone when our job wasn't finished yet? I was irrational, angry and confused. I usually shut myself in the bathroom and cried and prayed and yelled. My anger and grief was overwhelming while I still cooked and cleaned house, washed clothes and took care of the children.

But God was definitely with me, sharing my suffering and loss. The children were a blessing and joy as they helped and loved one another. Sarah climbed into bed with me and handed me a Kleenex when she saw my tears, so I could wipe my tears when she slept with me at night. And the angels ministered to me. I kept Kenny's pajamas with his smell, neatly folded on top of my bureau for many months where I could see them. We kept on doing the things we always did as a family. I forced myself to go to the indoor track at KSU and run together with the children. Knowing how much I suffered the loss of my parents as a child, I'll never know how much the children suffered. Only they can know how it changed their lives.

The random robbery and violence was deemed a homicide. Kenny died on the afternoon of December 23, 1978, in his office, just thirty minutes after I had left him, of a massive brain injury with hemorrhage. The police came out to our farm to question me. They asked me if he had any enemies, and I could think of none. We could never come up with a motive other than robbery. There were speculations. None of the clues ever produced the man who pulled the trigger. The case remains unsolved.

Kenny was buried at Sunrise Cemetery in Manhattan, Kansas on December 26, 1978. We had twenty-two-and-a- half years together. The year had been a wonderful, but this tragic closure was beyond comprehension for all of us.

# Chapter 12: Just an Ordinary Day

JANUARY 1979 STARTED OUT with all the children at home. Chip moved back to the farm to help for a short while. I ran physically for solace and to exhaust my bleeding emotions. My mind and heart were numb as I moved through my loss of Kenny. The whole family suffered, each navigating their gaping hole in their own, age-appropriate way. Could we ever be whole again? We were a functioning family, but horribly scarred and wounded from our emotional battle with grief.

The only thing that I could think to do as the sole parent in command was to return to routine. There would never be "normal" again. The everyday demands of running a household and caring for children provided structure and sanity for a life that had suddenly gone out of control and become incomprehensible. I functioned separate from my will, engaging the habits of putting one foot in front of the other, doing what was necessary from day to day, cooking, cleaning, washing and feeding. I was physically fit and could run for many miles without thinking, which helped keep me going. The world looked cruel, cold, empty and hostile to me. My life-mate, soul mate, protector, lover, and joy had been ripped from my heart.

January passed and Andrew's fifteenth birthday on the third and my forty-fourth birthday came uninvited. I found myself in a fog of daydreams and thought that I would soon see Kenny somewhere. When the reality of the truth hit me, I shut myself in the bathroom and talked to God and Kenny and cried. Or I went outside into the hills and cried out to God. Living each day was painful. I could understand why people retreat from reality. It is not pretty. But I believed that God was my Reality and I knew that there was no retreating from Him. He was there with me, and I talked to Him moment by moment every day. I knew that suffering was a part of the Christian life as well as all life, but I'd had enough.

I resented the unexpectedness of Kenny's passing the most. There was no warning, no premonition, nothing to prepare for. With Vietnam I was prepared. It could have been any day. I lived through that knowing and coped with the children for a year alone, so Vietnam itself was the preparation for this. A Mohawk pilot flying dangerous low-level reconnaissance missions at night over the Ho Chi Min Trail in the horrors of war and a world away, was very different from sitting in your office on a Saturday afternoon two days before Christmas, just a few miles from your family and home. He had lived through very difficult odds and then been shot by a random robber. There are no safe places in this world.

In January a Christian bookstore in Manhattan called to let me know that a set of books that Kenny had ordered me for a Christmas present had arrived. Did I want to come and pick them up? My throat began to close and tears came and I said, "Yes, I would." Kenny had picked out a set of Bible Commentaries that he knew I wanted for Christmas. I drove to town and picked them up, picturing the smile on his face and a secret light in his eyes knowing what my reaction would be. I cried all the way to town, vision blurred and tears streaming down onto the steering wheel. It was a set of the entire New Testament of *The Daily Study Bible Series* by William Barclay, a Scottish Minister in Glasgow, Scotland. They became a daily part of my morning devotions inscribed with "Love Kenny, 1978" in the front cover, and over the next twenty years they helped me "to know Jesus Christ more clearly, to love him more dearly, and to follow him more nearly." He wisely knew that I would need these.

Friends in the church had a party for me after services on a Sunday night on my birthday. I was not ready for this. A good friend, Laura Grenier, an artist, painted a large oil portrait of Kenny for me from our family portrait and other pictures. She had known him well and we often visited in their home. It was a lovely painting, but there was not much joy in my life and I could not appreciate it until much later. Sarah was a great comfort to me in just being the sweet baby that she was. Only eighteen months old, she could not comprehend my sadness. We were all getting a lot of comfort from her, but she would face this grief many times later as she grew up and learned what she had lost. Since she was little, Kenny often held her on his lap at the table as he ate in the evenings. She learned to enjoy salad with blue cheese dressing at an early age this way. But when she stood on the couch looking out the window for her daddy to come home in the evening at dinnertime, it cut to my already bleeding heart. If the heart is the center of our emotions and love, then mine had been cut in half and was hemorrhaging. I felt mortally wounded.

The boys continued with the chores and took care of the farm and animals. They had all worked closely with their dad on everything. They knew what he wanted done. I talked of Kenny often to them as if he was just in another place. I would say to them, "What would your dad want you to do?" Everyone tried hard to help each other and do their best. We survived and continued to run races. I had taken the semester off of school to take care of all the legal paperwork involving Kenny's business and properties and many details that I knew nothing about. I did not like this, but I learned. Fortunately, Bud stepped in immediately and helped me with financial decisions. He was vice president of the First National Bank in Manhattan. Dorothy and the rest of my family called frequently to check on me. The children were busy at school and coping in their own way, as I had done as a child after the death of my parents and sister. I knew that it wasn't easy for them. Life continued.

I picked out the color, type of stone, and words to be engraved on the headstone for the cemetery, and had all our names put on it. A brass military-plaque was put at the foot of the grave with Kenny's name, rank and date of service. We planted peonies from the farm on each side of the headstone on Memorial Day and gathered around, holding hands and prayed. It was very difficult for us all. We all shed many tears and I'm sure that it was still an open wound; Kenny was always in our thoughts.

I especially remember one incident during the winter when I went into the room off the kitchen to the freezer to select some meat to fix for dinner. As I held up the top of the freezer, staring at the contents, this decision just seemed too much for me as I began to think about Kenny being gone as the children grew up. I was overcome with the responsibility of our eight children. now, and grandchildren in the future. The future looked so very bleak and I felt so very weak. I prayed, "Lord, how can I be a grandparent all by myself, without Kenny?" He answered, "Just one day at a time, Phyllis."

My mother's sister, Aunt Marie, had written me, "God is greater than all our troubles." It didn't register in my numbness at the time. He is and I knew this. My family, Kenny's family, friends, and neighbors called to offer encouragement. God had showed me His plan for my work in medical missions, but now He was requiring I walk by faith. Day by day, step by step, Jesus took my hand and brought me back to life again. I would never be the person I was before; that person had died. But I would be more and more what Christ wanted me to be.

Grace graduated from Manhattan High School in May. She ran track and was hoping for a scholarship. She also applied for an AFS Student Exchange Scholarship. She found out that she was accepted to go to Tasmania in June for the summer. Tasmania is an Island south of Australia with the Indian Ocean on one side and the Tasmanian Sea on the other. I'm sure that I had seen it on the map before, but had never noticed. Amber enrolled at Kansas State for her freshman year when she returned from South Africa. She spoke to many civic and church groups in Manhattan about her AFS experience in Johannesburg, South Africa. She took over four hundred slides and pictures of her travels during her year there. South Africa was often in the national political news and many people were interested in what she had seen and experienced. Chip and Phillip both returned to college at Kansas State for another year. They looked into the Air Force ROTC Program and planned to fly when they graduated.

In addition to flowers for the funeral, I asked that as a memorial for Kenny, money be donated for an orphanage that we supported in Port-au-Prince, Haiti, where there were over one hundred children in desperate need. Over one thousand dollars was given for this memorial. Missionaries who had lived there visited our home and showed us slides and pictures of the orphanage and the children. A couple of American Christian missionaries were there now supervising the building and managing the orphanage, and they needed a medical clinic for the children. I decided to go to the orphanage in Port-au-Prince to see that the memorial money would be used for that.

After talking over my plans to go to Haiti with the four older children and the four youngest children, Andrew, just turned fifteen years, Tim, fourteen years, Eric eight years and Sarah one-and-a-half years, I decided to go to Port-au-Prince in June for six weeks with the four younger children. Sarah didn't have much to say about it except "bye, bye." I sent in the papers for our passports. Grace wanted to go with us, but decided to go to Hobart,

Tasmania with AFS in June for the summer. She turned eighteen years old in June and we would be many miles apart from the Caribbean to south of Australia. Our family was on the move again.

In order to simplify my life and prepare for mission work abroad, we arranged a garage sale at the farm in the spring. We sold much of our old furniture and things that we collected in Europe and stored at the Red House. I think we sold a horse and some farm machinery at this time also. I purchased our tickets and made arrangements for a place to stay in Port-au-Prince. The children received their updated vaccinations, and I consulted our pediatrician about preventive practices to keep them all healthy during the summer in Port-au-Prince. I think he thought I was a little crazy, but prescribed a low-dose antibiotic pill. We planned to be in Haiti most of the summer. We all prepared for our departure the first of June as soon as school was out.

Chip went to College Air Force ROTC summer camp in Wichita, Kansas and Phillip and Amber stayed to take care of the animals and the farm for us. I really looked forward to getting away from Manhattan with the children and seeing what was needed on the mission field. I knew that I would get back to our plans, and Kenny would be with me in Spirit for mission work abroad. My last classes at Kansas State could wait. The younger children talked about our flight and plans to spend the summer in Port-au-Prince. They were excited about the trip. I corresponded with missionaries from Haiti about all the necessary items to bring. Another family went from Manhattan. This was our first trip to a Third World country, the poorest in the Western Hemisphere. I foolishly thought that we were prepared.

Our time to leave in June 1979 came faster than I expected. We were ready to go and took a van to Manhattan Airport. In the hurry to get everyone into the van Eric had the tip of his thumb smashed in the sliding door of the van. He developed a blood blister and we drained the blood and put a Band-Aid on it. We got to Manhattan Airport for our flight to Miami and from there caught a flight to Port-au-Prince, Haiti. I hoped that I still might remember a little French. That was the official language there, with Creole spoken by most people. I don't remember how many pieces of luggage we took for the five of us, but I think it was a lot. We took extra used clothing to give children at the orphanage and plenty of diapers for Sarah. She was the first child I was able to raise with disposable diapers. The Lullaby Diaper Service was sold many years before, but I still had dozens of cloth diapers that I took to the orphanage.

Sarah was a toddler and hard to keep quiet and occupied on the plane. Toys, crayons and color books only last so long. During the flight she crawled around under our seats until the flight attendant came by. Sarah requested, "Coke, please." The three boys were great travelers and helped a lot. All of our travel with the four oldest children in Europe made this trip seem very short. I gave Andrew, Tim and Eric thirty dollars each in one dollar bills to use on the trip and in Port-au Prince. Their pockets were padded and their enthusiasm for spending it was hard to contain. Missionaries told us that American dollars were used in Haiti and it was hard to get money changed there, but small denominations of bills would be best.

In 1979, I read general facts on Haiti given to us by missionaries. The majority of the population spoke Creole although French was the judicial language. In 1804 it became the world's first black republic. It was the western third of the Island of Hispaniola in the Caribbean and approximately 27,750 square miles. It had six million people of West African descent. The capital of Haiti, Port-au-Prince, had been founded by the French in 1749. The largest of

Haiti's offshore islands was Ile de la Gonave. Haiti had what is known as a daytime climate, varying more during the course of a day than it does from month to month or season to season. We arrived before the hottest months of July and August, and missed the two rainy seasons of April to May, and September to October.

Haiti was the most densely populated country in the Western Hemisphere and extremely mountainous. The root of their problems lay in their poverty, overpopulation and the peasants' struggle to survive. Their need for charcoal as fuel had started the disastrous deforestation of their mountains, which continued for many years. I learned that the U.S. Marines had invaded in 1915, modernizing the sewage system, building hospitals, clinics and roads, but had pulled out in 1934, leaving behind an impoverished infrastructure. This ensured the shipping route between the newly opened Panama Canal and the U.S.A. Their use of forced prison labor for the building of roads caused an uprising. In 1937 the 20,000 Haitians living in the Dominican Republic were killed by the police on orders of the President, making it the worst massacre in their history. The Haitians took pride in their African heritage and reclaimed their religion, Voodoo, as a source of cultural identity.

The flight from Miami was fine, and before we could deplane, a mist came out of the air vents on the plane and scattered over all of us. That was a surprise, but then our first view of Port-au-Prince was a balcony of Haitians where hundreds gathered to wait for their friends and family. We quickly learned what it meant to be in the minority and we had never felt so white. There was not one white face in that sea of faces.

A hot wind blasted our faces as our feet hit the tarmac, and there was a pervasive odor of garbage in the air. We found out later why. But customs in Port-au-Prince was a nightmare. Every piece of our luggage was opened and searched and left for us to pick up the pieces. It took a long time for us to get through customs. Teenage soldiers the age of Andrew and Tim carried machine guns and rifles and looked angrily at us. The boys stared at them warily. We were swamped by the crush of people and taxi drivers and beggars. Tim said that he was scared to death when he looked out at the crowd and saw no white people and so many guns. He sure hoped that his mom knew what she was doing. Nothing could have prepared us for the deplorable living conditions of the people. Pictures and videos cannot describe conditions as they really are and leave out much. The filth, noises, smells, heat, and anger of the people spoke volumes.

A Haitian from the hotel, the Magic Bud Inn, met us and loaded our luggage into a van. Our van got a flat tire on the way to the hotel. When we did arrive at the hotel, they welcomed us and the children saw the swimming pool. They noticed a giant fish at one end of the pool with the water coming out of its mouth. We had two rooms side by side on the second floor. Andrew and Tim unpacked and settled themselves in one room with twin beds, and Sarah, Eric and I took the other with two double beds.

An enterprising Canadian lawyer named Bud operated and owned the hotel. During the 1970s, Haiti was put on the map as a holiday destination for the quickie divorce. Haitian law allowed foreigners to obtain a divorce within twenty-four hours. The decree arrived by mail to your home in two or three weeks, or in only two days if the client was willing to remain in Haiti. So Bud provided his clients a nice hotel to wait in with time to spend some more money. It was a mixed clientele at the Magic Bud Inn. There were missionary families and couples looking for a quick divorce. We were long-term guests and treated very well.

I had brought a stroller for Sarah so that we didn't have to carry her, but when I saw the condition of the open sewers and human filth on the streets, I knew that I could never let her feet touch the streets. Microbiology and seeing reality through a microscope had given me a heightened and frightened awareness of the tiny things that you cannot see. I knew that I had to take more control of her environment. When she wasn't in her stroller, Andrew and Tim took turns carrying her on their shoulders. The hotel seemed clean and hospitable. We had all our meals there and went out to attend church, visit people in the church in their homes and do shopping and sightseeing.

A young Haitian man from the church with a van took us on trips around the city to see historical places, like the Presidential Palace. It was very beautiful and heavily guarded in the center of the city. The President of Haiti in 1979 was Jean Claude Duvalier, "Baby Doc." His father, Francois Duvalier, called "Papa Doc," had a reign of terror as President for Life for fourteen years from 1957 to 1971. Papa Doc came as a modest country doctor but was one of the most infamous and notorious dictators in Haitian history. He had changed the constitution so that his son could follow him in office. There was a Secret Police of one million, known as "The Tonton Macoutes," who started as hooded thugs and emerged in denim jackets and jeans, red kerchiefs and sunglasses, enforcing the Duvalier reign and spreading terror among the people. No one knew when they were being watched. Thousands of Haitians either died or fled the country during this brutal reign. 'Baby Doc' followed in his father's footsteps later in 1971 in much the same way. The Tonton Macoutes had become the "Volontaires de la Sécurité Nationale," a private militia without salary who would use force and coercion with impunity in order to exhort cash and crops from a cowed population. In exchange for this privilege, they afforded Duvalier the utmost loyalty and protection. There would be no coup from the army or any group as long as he had the

Tonton Macoutes by his side. When we arrived in June of 1979, the people still called them by this name and showed much fear of them.

During Jean Claude Duvalier's reign, repression eased to a certain extent because he wanted foreign aid and investment and wanted to be seen as a liberalizer to the international community. But it was still the age-old struggle between the black middle-class majority and the mulatto capitalist minority. Those dissidents calling for democracy were silenced.

I taught the Bible to women's groups and Andrew and Tim helped in the construction of building a cinder block and cement church. After the first week was finished the boys asked when we were going home. They had already enjoyed spending most of their money on wooden carvings made from mahogany. I told them not for six weeks and they learned their way around town on the 'tap-taps', brightly colored pick-up trucks lined with wooden benches in the back used as taxis. These were also called "camions or camionnettes." The Haitians carried their chickens and pigs with them in these taxis. By the time we left Haiti, some of the wooden statues they purchased were eaten with termites and they left them.

Andrew and Tim, familiar with working with their dad, were amazed at the methods of construction. The Haitians had made different sizes of screen strainers to sift out the rocks and pebbles from the dirt that they scooped off the streets in making the cement for the church. They kept sifting until the dirt was ready to mix with the cement. Their building supports looked very flimsy. Andrew fell from a ladder, down the concrete stairs at the church construction site while helping with the electrical wiring. Hitting a corner of a step as he fell, he cut clear through his bottom lip and we took him to a doctor to get a tetanus shot. We saw another side of Haitian life as we waited at the doctor's office for a couple of hours in the shade by a luxury hotel; it had a swim-up bar that the children enjoyed watching. This was the top end of life in Haiti, and we had been helping with the lowest end where the poorest lived. Eric thought watching other people have fun was almost as good as doing it ourselves. When the doctor came and Andrew saw the six-inch needle his eyes got much bigger, but we had to keep out infection from the millions of bacteria.

We visited the Baptist Mission built on top of a beautiful mountain. It included a craft shop, restaurant and church. It was a long drive up the mountain with beautiful and elaborate French homes surrounded by walls along the way. We saw Haitian workmen sitting on piles of rocks with a hammer, breaking them into smaller pieces for gravel near the expensive homes. The men earned fifty cents a day for their work. The Mission compound was very cool and clean with the large green broad leaf banana trees and lush jungle where the Baptists had been working for many years. The kids played with monkeys and parrots, and we saw many varieties of birds and every color of bougainvillea flowers in a lovely garden. Missionary guest houses were for rent for respite from the heat and noise of Port-au-Prince. After we had been there for six weeks I understood what a blessing these were. A short visit here could restore balance and perspective to the psyche after working a few months among wall-to-wall people in Port-au-Prince. We also enjoyed meeting and visiting with other missionaries staying at our hotel.

We discovered a Kentucky Fried Chicken restaurant and had familiar food every Sunday after church. The children particularly loved this, and I let Sarah walk in the restaurant. We ate a lot of goat meat at our hotel. The Sunday morning service at the Haitian Mission Church included one thousand people pressed close together on wooden benches. All Haitians dressed in their best clothes, sang and prayed with enthusiasm and were all very friendly and happy to have us. Poverty didn't dampen their joy for the Lord.

The boys found a good ice cream place just across the street from the hotel where they went after dinner in the evenings. The hotel had many cats that played in the flowers, palm and banana trees. The children enjoyed playing with them. Eric said that after eating goat day after day, he had just gotten so he liked the goat meat and at dinner one evening, we had spaghetti and the meat tasted a little different. We suddenly looked around and all the cats were gone. We had a very creepy feeling that we knew what kind of meat we had just eaten. We lost our appetite for meat for a few days. I had taken a gallon jar of peanut butter that we used for sandwiches for lunch. We loved the fresh pineapple, mango and papaya, maracujas and the small sweet "figue" bananas. Lemonade and limeade were favorites too.

The boys enjoyed swimming in the hotel swimming pool every day. The water coming out of the fish's mouth didn't look clean. It looked rather green at times. Sarah wore a green dress that matched the water and was toddling along beside the pool one day and suddenly just disappeared. Andrew was in the pool swimming underwater and coming up out of the water as she had lost her balance and went down under the water and he caught her. We never let her get close to the pool again.

I brought powdered milk for the children that they didn't like, but Sarah drank it. We bought gallon jugs of safe drinking water each day. They drank a lot of soft drinks, especially coke. We would just have to make up for the milk when we got home.

We knew that our pigs and cows at our barn at the farm in Kansas had cleaner and better living conditions than most of the Haitians. We were astounded at the poverty.

There were concrete walls around the hotel and most businesses and nice homes. Broken glass was embedded in the concrete on the top, with barbed wire or iron posts. Our trips to the Iron Market, the large downtown market, for the largest selection and best prices, and to the main post office was always an adventure. Eric was fascinated looking at all the displays of watches and knives. I let the older boys ride the "tap taps" alone to mail letters or buy things. After many trips to the market in our first two weeks, Andrew and Tim served as tour guides for other missionaries who arrived at the hotel and needed someone to show them the way. Eric, almost nine years, went to the Post Office with Tim to mail letters, and Tim came back saying that a woman had approached Eric to ask him if he wanted to make love. It was pretty unbelievable! On another day Tim came back and said that a man had pulled a switchblade knife and held it to the throat of a woman that he had gone with when she started haggling over the price of baskets or wood carvings. There were other occasions when knives were used to scare Andrew and Tim and they got the message. So that ended their trips to the Iron Market without me.

When I asked small children in Creole how old they were on the streets many would simply stare. Time has no relevance and means very little there, so age is a concept that many didn't even know. And many did not know their age. We soon adjusted to the Haitian concept of time by saying that it could be anytime. Haitian time could be now, tomorrow, or never. Time took on a new meaning for us and we learned just to wait and see.

We brought soccer balls for the Christian schools and kept a couple at the hotel for the boys to play with. Andrew and Tim played on a soccer team in Manhattan, Kansas for two years. Phillip, their older brother, had been their coach. There was a big open soccer field near our hotel that the boys walked to, with rocks and broken glass scattered all around where they often played with the local Haitian boys. Sometimes they were welcomed and sometimes not. Tim went to the soccer field by himself sometimes and after being kicked and knocked down a few times, he decided it was time to go.

The boys also discovered that all the baseballs for the National Baseball League in America were made here in Port-au-Prince. There was a factory that employed Haitians to hand sew the leather baseball covers. Andrew, Tim, and Eric enjoyed collecting them and brought back several Haitian baseballs of their own. These were their favorite souvenirs.

The boys spent so much time playing in the swimming pool at the hotel that Eric, Tim, and Andrew got an infection under their fingernails. We soaked their fingers in hydrogen peroxide three times a day and they stayed out of the pool for a while. But all Eric's fingernails came off except the thumbnails. Fortunately this was not painful for him and he went back to swimming again. The boys spent time comparing how many fingernails they were losing.

After my course in microbiology I saw germs and disease everywhere. When Sarah sat on the wooden benches with us in church and chewed on the backs of the seats, I rescued her and tried not to have a panic attack and just prayed that the Lord would protect her from the worst. She also wanted to kiss all the little babies at church. Almost two years old, and I couldn't take my eyes off her for a minute. I knew that she could not kiss babies and stay well, so I guarded her closely. Most of my time was spent feeding, watching, and entertaining the children.

I brought spray cans of Lysol disinfectant for the public bathrooms, but there were no public bathrooms. But I kept our bathrooms very clean at the hotel. We took the antibiotic pills that our pediatrician Dr. Crane prescribed for us each day to prevent any parasitic infections. Eric had a terrible time with his first one that he took before we left the farm. He sat at the kitchen table a long time before he could swallow it and all the coating came off the pill and it tasted horrible. But he finally got it down. The children took two large antibiotic pills each day that they called horse pills, with a large glass of lemonade and continued to complain about the size of the pills. They still had occasional stomach cramps and diarrhea but were otherwise in good health.

The Haitian sun goes down quickly like a curtain at the same time every day. The poverty is hidden in the dark as it can be hidden in colder climates under a blanket of snow. At night it looks very beautiful with the coconut palm trees, bright fuchsia bougainvillea flowers and abundant flat, lush, green leaves of the banana trees. The conditions of poverty were in sharp contrast to the extravagance and richness of color and green plants everywhere.

There were black and intricately designed wrought iron gates in front of the hotel through which the children learned new skills and carried on their bargaining with the Haitian peddlers. The street children taught them many Creole words. Tim liked to do his trading with a one-handed kid each day. This young boy told Andrew that his parents had chopped off his hand when he was little so that he could be a beggar all his life. Tim had purchased a supply of souvenirs with his thirty one-dollar bills earlier that he kept trading. This was a daily pastime and education in Haitian culture for them. They swapped their supply of bright colored cotton running shirts from all their track meets, and clothes for souvenirs when they had run out of money. They had a six-week course in negotiating skills that would last them for a lifetime. Other missionaries and guests came to stay at our hotel and couldn't believe how many Haitian boys had been to Manhattan, Kansas and were wearing running t-shirts from there. It was one of the jokes the boys enjoyed.

We drove in a van to Jacmal, a beach town along the southern coast of Haiti, with our Haitian friend Leon. It is known for its thriving-artistic community and the most spectacular carnival in the country. Roads in Haiti are notoriously appalling and I was very glad to have a Haitian driver. The frequent and large potholes were amazing and there were no highway rules. The children had a great time getting out in the country and it was the first time that they had seen black sand on the beaches.

On our way back to Port-au-Prince after a long day at the beach, we stopped along the winding road and bought a stock of one hundred or more bananas from a lady in a roadside stand selling the small and sweet dark yellow bananas. We devoured them all on the way home. Eric was so hungry that he started taking some bananas off the stock before we paid for them. Leon warned the boys that the punishment for thieves was to have your hand chopped off. We bought the whole stock. The children had never tasted such good bananas and it was something clean for Sarah to eat that I didn't have to worry about. We left the van door open throwing our banana peels along the countryside for the goats to eat, and sang all the way back to our hotel the Beatles song "The Yellow Submarine." We were beginning to feel at home here.

We took the ferry to Ebo Island and spent the day at Ebo Beach where the boys snorkeled. They rented their equipment from a French lady in a hut on the beach. Both in puberty and counting the emerging hairs under their arms, they said that she had the bushiest armpits and longest hair on her legs that they had ever seen. I really learned more from the children's view than I realized. Haitians warned them to be on the watch for barracudas in the waters, but they only found sea dollars and starfish. During that summer they swam more than they ever had in their lives on our farm and got very dark tans.

Our next plan was to take a ferry to the Island of La Gonave. We made plans with other missionaries to meet at 6:00 a.m. one morning to catch the ferry. For some reason our plans were cancelled and we never went. The ferry went without us, and later that day we learned that it had sunk because of overloading and all the passengers drowned. It was a horrible thing to happen. It made us very much aware of the potential dangers here and the need to have many people praying for our safety and health. All the boys could think about were the barracudas and how grateful we were that many people were praying for us and we did not take the ferry.

I called Grace on her eighteenth birthday, June 23rd, in Tasmania, to wish her Happy Birthday. Although we were in the Caribbean it was a pretty good connection, but it sure reminded me how far away she was. She was living with a nice young couple in Hobart and said that she was having a great time. I was so glad for this opportunity for her and knew that she needed this adventure by herself. We would see each other again in September when she returned. She turned down a track scholarship to Cloud Community Junior College and was ready to start college at Kansas State when she got back to Manhattan in the fall.

I heard Andrew and Tim yelling for me to come into their room. A very large black tarantula was on their wall. They said that they had seen it in the hotel before on the walls and another one on the stairs, but they were afraid of it. I don't know how long it had been in their room, but they threw shoes at it and finally killed it, nailing it to the wall. They left its black and hairy very large body stuck to the wall for the duration of our stay. I was very thankful that they found it before they had turned off their lights for the night. Haitians warned them that some were poisonous and they were on the watch for them.

We sent the money from Kenny's memorial fund to the Cookson Hills Christian Schools who had missionaries and an orphanage in Port-au-Prince. Their greatest need was to build a medical clinic with the money that was given for Kenny. We visited the orphanage several times and gave out the clothes and toys that we had collected and brought with us for the children. It was a very primitive and bare place, but the children were being fed and cared for. The orphanage was made of cinder block and painted white. This was a home for the street children who had no place to go. The numbers of small children on the streets could fill up many places like this. The Haitian Director wanted us to visit one of the worst slum areas of Port-au-Prince, Cite Soleil and La Saline. I noticed that he wore a holster with a pistol for protection on our visit. Shocking our sight and senses, we saw places that words just can't describe. These were such horrible living conditions for the people here. I don't know how they continue to survive. It was absolute misery for them with no hope of moving to a better place.

The boys created very ingenious things to do at the hotel. The hotel roof was flat with a good view of the surrounding area and clotheslines hanging for the clothes to dry. When the boys were bored they frequently went up to look around. Giant almond trees with broad sweeping branches near the hotel towered over the top of the roof. They reached up and picked the green almonds and threw them at each other and off the roof. The crowded streets with people, carts, donkeys and women riding selling baskets stacked high on their heads, were below. Unknown to me, they threw the green almonds aimed at the donkeys going by. I'm sure that their good eye, after many years of practice with their BB guns, often hit their target. When the donkey felt the hit on the rear with the green almonds, the woman riding carrying all her baskets on her head was taken unawares. The donkey started up quickly trotting to get away and the woman yelled for it to stop.

Another American missionary boy, about Eric's age at eight years old, staying at the hotel wanted to come up on the roof and see what fun they were having. The boys decided that they had found this place and didn't trust him to keep their secret, so they didn't let him come up on the roof. Finally they consented to let him join their game of running around on top. As he ran past a clothesline he forgot to duck and the rope line hit him across the neck. He fell to the floor of the roof and Tim and Eric thought he was dead. But when he started choking and gagging, they knew that he was fine. He never wanted to come back up again, so the boys held the top of the hotel roof as their own fort with the women who came back and forth to hang the clothes. When we ran out of clean clothes I knew that I could send the boys to get them for me.

Hurricane David threatened the area with high winds while we were there. The radio announced that it was coming to Port-au-Prince and we took precautions. Everyone at the hotel gathered in a central area away from any glass windows, making sure we were wearing rubber sole shoes in case electrical wires were blown down. We waited out the strong winds and rain with prayer. We were spared any damage and grateful that this poor country didn't have the damage from a hurricane to deal with added to their horrible poverty. We had never been in a hurricane before, but we were in a tornado in Kansas and knew the fear and apprehension we felt waiting for the strong winds and rain to come.

We left all our friends in Port-au-Prince, excited about getting home again and flew back the last part of July, from Port-au-Prince to Miami to Wichita, Kansas where Chip came to pick us up in a van. Our flight from Miami arrived in Wichita very late in the evening, and we drove home getting back to the farm about 2:00 a.m. The whole drive home, the boys talked and talked of their experiences in Port-au-Prince. Chip had finished his ROTC Summer Camp Training and had many stories of his own to tell of his summer. He caught us up on all the news from Phillip and Amber at the farm.

The highways and streets looked wonderful and smooth with no potholes and everything looked very clean. We were amazed at not seeing piles of rubbish everywhere. We had accepted the reality of Haiti and almost forgot what Kansas looked like. Everyone was glad to be home and fell into their own beds. Home never looked so good. After receiving our warm welcome from Phillip and Amber, I went right for the bathtub and knew how fortunate we were to have clean hot water for bathing and clean drinking water from our faucets. I soaked in a tub of hot water for a long time and knew how rich we were. The rich of this world must include all Americans. The children all had many stories to tell of our summer in Port-au-Prince for many years.

Grace arrived home from Tasmania having enjoyed her time there. She told us many stories of her three-months stay. She was ready to start her first college classes at Kansas State in September. All four of the oldest children were at Kansas State where Kenny and I had both graduated in 1956.

School started for everyone but Sarah and me. I taught many Bible studies in the church at our home and in the community, so Sarah just went along to play with other children who came. Eric had done this for five years, and really missed it when he had to start kindergarten. Many families had small children in our rural neighborhood and mothers and neighbors got together for morning coffees and for the children to play together. It was a good time to swap recipes, find out who was pregnant, what people were planting, exchange flower bulbs, and locate available dogs, cats, livestock or machinery.

In September I attended a National Missionary Convention of the Christian Churches in El Paso, Texas. I met many missionaries from around the world. A missionary from Kotagiri, India, Heather Lacson, talked to me about their need for a school nurse for their Christian School in South India. She asked me to come for a visit to India. Although I had yet to do my nurse's training, I told her that I would go home and pray about it. She wanted to come and visit me at the farm in Manhattan before they went back to India. We made plans for her and her family to come in November. Heather and Jerry Lacson had two young boys, six and eight years old.

Phillip corresponded with Arthur Moore at the Christian Ranch near Christ's Church, New Zealand. Kenny and I had talked about this opportunity for him to work there and thought that it would be a good experience for him. The Moore family expected him to arrive in September to stay for a semester of work on their Sheep Ranch and Christian Camp. One of the young couples from our church was already working in New Zealand. In September, we saw Phillip off at Manhattan Airport in his blue jeans and t-shirt, rubber thong sandals, and carrying his guitar in his new guitar case that we had given him for his trip. He carried everything in a duffel bag and was traveling light. Knowing that Phillip did not write many letters, I did not expect to hear much from him. And he hadn't left any serious girlfriends behind.

Amber called from school and asked to bring home a friend from her English class at Kansas State, Elizabeth Sadler. I said fine, we wanted them to come for dinner. Amber told me that it was Elizabeth's twenty-first birthday, October 11th. I wanted to have a celebration so I called Chip at his apartment to ask him to bring ice cream when he came for dinner. I made a cake. Amber and Elizabeth arrived and Chip came later for dinner. We had a good dinner with cake and ice cream and sang "Happy Birthday" to Elizabeth. During our visit we learned that Elizabeth was from St. Louis, Missouri and a sophomore studying architecture at Kansas State. Her parents were teachers and she had one younger brother and sister. We all thought that she was a very lovely girl and were happy to get to know her. Elizabeth and Amber became very good friends and they roomed in an apartment together in Manhattan. Then Chip and Elizabeth became better friends and started dating. Chip still worked as an Emergency Medical Technician for the Riley County Ambulance Service and was in the Air Force ROTC at Kansas State. He would graduate in 1981.

The Missions Committee of our church talked about sponsoring a Vietnamese boat refugee family through Church World Service, a Christian organization relocating families from Vietnam to other parts of the world. Church World Service paid the transportation and we found jobs and housing for the refugees and they worked to reimburse them for part of their transportation. Many churches and families did this in 1979 across our country. Saigon had fallen to the Communists in 1975 and the Communists gained control of the entire country.

More than one million Vietnamese refugees fled by boats to neighboring countries. They often languished in boats waiting acceptance by a country. Refugee camps were quickly set up to care for them until they relocated to other countries. Some boats were towed back out into international waters as refugee camps were full or countries denied them access. The newspapers were full of stories about boats being hijacked by pirates in international waters and many were killed. Many Vietnamese boat people were sent to Australia and England for resettlement, and nearly a half-million Vietnamese immigrated to the United States.

The Missions Committee prayed about this and decided that we wanted to help care for a family with children, and I made the necessary contacts. Church World Service called me at the farm one morning when I was just finishing up breakfast dishes, to ask if we would take a Vietnamese family with four small children and I agreed. It was just an ordinary day on our farm in Kansas when I said, "Yes we would;" our "yes" saved the lives of six people and provided a future with many possibilities for four small children. Our lives were greatly blessed and enriched by these dear friends. And I knew that God would provide. We took care of the necessary paperwork and I signed to be their sponsor.

They arrived at the Manhattan Airport the middle of October and stayed at our farm until we found them an apartment and jobs in Manhattan. The family was presently staying at a refugee camp in Malaysia. They had fled Saigon by boat at night paying $2,000 for each person, leaving Saigon with nothing but their clothes. Their boat trip was a horror story lacking sufficient food and water. Countries denied their boat permission to land anywhere and it was towed back out to international waters many times. Desperate, they landed in Malaysia in the middle of the night and burned their boat. Because of the long journey and no water they had thought their oldest daughter would not survive. Many members of the church donated their time, money, clothes and food for the Tran family, and we began waiting for them. October was starting to be very cold. We knew of their need for warmth since they had always lived in Saigon before their escape and were in the Tropics on the Island of Malaysia for six months.

Since we did not know their physical condition, I decided that my large master bedroom suite with private bath was large enough for them all. It had extra electric-baseboard-heating they could control and have as warm as they needed. It also had a large walk-in closet, where we put the donated clothing and toys, with its own outside entrance. A queen size sleeping bed with sleeping bags on the floor would be sufficient. I thought the family needed to be together in such a strange place at first. They did not speak English, and we started teaching them English words. The children, two boys and two girls, were ages two, four, six, and eight years.

We were forewarned that the family had spent six months in the Malaysian refugee camp and were coming from crowded and terrible living conditions. They needed treatment for tuberculosis. The youngest was a boy Sarah's age and the oldest, a girl, was Eric's age. We were excited about having this opportunity to help a family with children, living in similar conditions like we had just seen that summer in Haiti. We collected clothing of all the children's sizes and adult clothing for the parents.

Kenny had shown us slides of Saigon when he returned in 1966, and we knew that it had been a large and beautiful city. He had many good memories of the kindness of the Vietnamese people. He sent the children silk pajamas, jackets, and straw hats from Saigon and beautiful pictures and vases. Soon we had a Vietnamese family of six living with us. He would have loved this. We met with other members of the church and prayed for their safe arrival and for God's help to welcome and meet the needs of the Tran family. We were all excited about their arrival.

On a cold, rainy day in October, Bud and Laura Grenier and I met the six members of the Tran family at Manhattan Airport: Tony and Son, the parents of two girls Mai, eight years, Linh six years, and two boys, Kahn four years, and Minh two years. We all hugged and greeted them. They looked so tiny, fragile and lost, and we brought them to our farm using the Grenier's van. We knew that they did not speak English, but Tony had some broken

English that he had learned while working with Americans in Saigon. We welcomed them warmly to Manhattan and our home, and we were grateful for this opportunity to care for them. Knowing the terrible hardships they had endured just to get here, we thanked God for their safe journey.

Tony and Son were very thin, each weighing not more than eighty pounds. The children looked very frail and fragile and clung to their parents, wide-eyed and solemn. We prayed that God would give us the wisdom and compassion to care for these special people of His that He had sent to us. We showed them to their rooms upstairs, and then I fixed rice and vegetables with chicken for dinner. Tony insisted that he serve me and would not sit at the table until I had. He always did this at every meal during their entire stay. He often fixed wonderful dinners of Chinese and Vietnamese food. Their two small meals each day at the refugee camp had barely sustained them. With three substantial meals a day, we overfed them and they were unable to eat all the food we gave them.

Tony's broken English helped us to communicate and all the children did very well at getting along together. Minh, their youngest little boy, and Sarah played famously together as two-year-olds will, with no language problem until Sarah decided not to share her toys. Then they really spoke the same language even better. It was much fun to watch them playing together, sharing and affectionate. Two-year-olds have no knowledge of social skills, but just think that everything is theirs. Tony and Son watched them with smiles, happy to see their children provided for. The rest of our children were in school during the day while the Tran family adjusted to their new home. The children were all very sweet, quiet and obedient to their parents. We knew they survived a tremendously dangerous ordeal of escape when Tony told us their story. While they stayed with us the two girls, Mai and Linh, did a lovely Vietnamese dance that we thought was really beautiful. We felt fortunate in having them with us. They showed us photos of their lovely home in Saigon that they were forced to leave. Son left an elderly mother that she was very concerned about.

Apple picking season was over, but hundreds of apples were still on the ground in our neighbor's orchard that the children picked up every day. They took the Tran family down to the orchard with bushel baskets and filled many of them for their family. Tony told us that apples sold for one dollar each in Saigon, and he was amazed at so many going to waste on the ground. Before they left our house and moved into Manhattan, they had picked up many bushels more. When they moved they put the apples in the kitchen of their apartment. They took pictures of their family sitting in the kitchen surrounded by bushels of apples and sent the pictures to their family in Saigon. All their letters were censored, but Tony said that they would see their wealth when they saw the apples.

Members of the church looked for jobs and an apartment for the Tran family while they stayed with us. Everyone prayed for them and was generous with providing for their needs. Tony and Son insisted on finding work to do for me in the house and were so gracious and grateful for their new home. In three weeks they had been to the health clinic to start their tuberculosis medication, received immunizations, learned more English, and won their place forever in our hearts. They had gained some weight and looked healthier.

Members of the church found jobs for Tony and Son, an apartment on Bluemont Street in Manhattan for the family, a bicycle for transportation, and helped the children get enrolled in Bluemont Elementary School just two blocks away. The Trans had arrived in 1979, and exactly three years later in November of 1982, the Vietnam Memorial in Washington, D.C. was dedicated. It was a wall of polished black granite bearing the names of 57,939 Americans who died or were missing in action in the Vietnam War, including many of Kenny's friends.

The Lacson family called to say that they were coming for a visit. Jerry and Heather with their two boys, Neal and John, were missionaries to Kotagiri, South India, whom I had invited to stay with us on their way back to India. I made my decision to return with Heather and her family to Kotagiri with Andrew, fifteen years, and Sarah, two years, for a short visit of three weeks. I thought this might be where the Lord wanted me to work in the future, as there was a need for a nurse and teacher. Andrew made arrangements with his teachers at the high school about missing his classes. I knew that he would be a tremendous help with Sarah and the Lacson boys and our luggage.

Heather arrived at the farm before the Tran family left, and Amber had a friend from South Africa arrive during this time, so we were an international guesthouse for a while. Heather and the boys stayed for a week and Tony, Son, Mai, Linh, Kahn and Minh moved into their Bluemont apartment in Manhattan before we left for India.

I decided to get Sarah a smallpox vaccination, even though the World Health Organization announced that it was no longer necessary for travel there. All of our other necessary immunizations had been updated with our trip to Haiti in the summer.

On November 19th, 1979, we flew from Manhattan, Kansas to New York and then on Pan American Airlines to London, England and then to Delhi, India. It was a total of forty hours flying. Our flight from New York to London had been delayed in New York before we left. I remember while in the waiting room Sarah enjoyed just walking around. She was two years old now. She walked up to another little Indian boy looking two years old and gave him some of her

bread and had hugged and kissed him before I could reach
her. She must have thought that he was Minh Tran.

## Kotagiri, South India

In November of 1979, more than one hundred
Americans were taken hostage in the American Embassy in
Iran, just a couple of days before we flew to India. President
Nixon demanded their release. They were still held hostage
as we flew to India, and Pan American Airlines was
forbidden to fly over Iranian airspace. We detoured around
Iran on our London flight to Delhi. During our flight, while
trying to sleep in the middle section of seats, I smelled
something burning and asked the flight attendant what they
were cooking. I told her that it smelled like something
burning in the oven. She insisted that nothing was cooking. I
told Andrew, then went up to the flight attendant station
and told her that I was sure something was burning. She
asked me to show her where I was sitting and I returned to
my seat with her. Then she asked me to come and tell the
captain flying the plane. After I did and returned to my seat,
we were immediately notified that we were making an
emergency landing and our cabin lights flickered off during
landing. The whole electrical system had burned out and
our emergency landing was in Bahrain, Saudi Arabia. We
were there for about eight hours having repairs done before
going on with our flight to Delhi, India.

Our flight was very long. Heather and I visited about
the mission work in Kotagiri, and I tried to keep Sarah
entertained. Andrew always read a book. Going through
customs, we were searched carefully. Heather brought
medicines and electrical supplies for the mission in Kotagiri.
Andrew made friends with a customs official when the man
found Andrew's hand-held spring forearm exerciser and
used it. He really liked it, and Andrew gave it to him,
having another in his bag. The customs official allowed us

through with no more questions, delighted and smiling with his new toy.

After arriving in the capital city of New Delhi as it said on our flight ticket, we stayed at a missionary guest house for two nights before we took a train for forty hours to Madras. So this was India! The poverty was overwhelming, but I had yet to see that which equaled Port-au-Prince, Haiti. Bicycles and people and cows and carts jammed the traffic on all the streets. It was very hot our first night in Delhi, and I could hear the eerie horns as they played into the night with the ceiling fans whirring above our heads while I fell asleep with my arm around Sarah. The next day Andrew went out into the street with a camera and took several pictures of children playing. He was taking a photography class at school and hoped to get some good pictures. A customs official seeing his camera, warned him not to take any pictures of bridges or roads. He also rode a bicycle belonging to a boy who he was friends with at the missionary guest house. They rode to a Hindu temple and other places in our part of the city.

Heather purchased our train tickets and we boarded our train the next morning for our forty-hour journey to Madras in the south. Jerry, her husband, planned to meet us with their van and boys, and drive us on an eight-hour ride up into the Nilgiris Hills in South India. I had not seen much of Delhi, but was ready to make our train trip to Madras.

India has eighteen official languages besides English, which is still the official language of the judiciary, fifty years after the British left. Hindi is the most important Indian language and spoken in the north, with Tamil being spoken in the South. Urdu is spoken by a large Muslim population, and Bengali by the people of West Bengal. Heather spoke Tamil.

Heather, Sarah, and I had a sleeping compartment on the train, but there was no bed in it for Andrew at night, so he shared our compartment by day and slept in the next compartment. The train stopped often and we had a wonderful panoramic view of the landscape from the north of India to the south. India has been often said not to be just a country, but a continent. I can certainly verify that. We passed every kind of landscape imaginable in our forty hours on the train. I have never seen such amazing diversity anywhere else that I have traveled since. There are few countries where I saw the enormous variety that India has to offer. We saw the crowded squalid areas of Delhi around the train station, and the vast areas in the country reaching from north to south as we traveled by train. Had we not already spent a summer in the worst poverty in the world, the poverty here would have seemed much worse.

I used disposable diapers for Sarah, but there were no trash cans anywhere, so Heather just threw them out the window of the train. It was a real challenge to entertain Sarah in our small compartment. I brought her books and a few small toys. Andrew spent his time checking out the train and brought his own books to read. While looking from the window of the train, I watched the village workers going to their rice fields each morning at sunrise. I watched the children playing, the women washing clothes in the rivers and streams or cooking on the outside fires. We saw the passing bicycles, carts, donkeys, oxen and horses and watched the slow progress of the day as the train went south, and then saw the workers return to their houses in the evening. After forty hours I felt that I had seen the heart of India. At every stop, beggars came to our window to ask for money or food. Heather bought food in the city of Delhi for us and bought more at stops along the way and we ate in our compartment. Sarah enjoyed standing at the window and watching the children play when we stopped.

We finally arrived in the very large city of Madras. We stayed a few days with missionaries there and attended their church with them. We saw how the Indians were building and smearing cow dung on the outside of their houses by hand. Sarah and I shared our bed with a trail of ants going across one end. I just decided not to bother them and stuck to our end.

Andrew made friends and hung out with a boy his age at the mission. They lit and threw firecrackers from a balcony and scared some cows in the street. The American Embassy had a bomb threat and we were told to stay away. We went to the beach on the Bay of Bengal and it was very beautiful. But the many shark bones lying in the sand reminded us that it was one of the most dangerous beaches in the world for swimming. We shopped at a large underground shopping mall and bought gifts for the other children. Heather asked me if we wanted to go see the Taj Mahal, but I said no. Many years later I realized that we should not have passed up this unique opportunity. At this time I didn't realize the significance. Not thinking about the cultural benefit to Andrew, I was single-mindedly focused on missions. I knew that our time was limited, and I wanted to spend it at the mission.

Jerry Lacson and Neal and John met us with their van. The drive to the small village of Kotagiri was fun and we stopped for a picnic. Heather bought food in Madras for our trip. The countryside was very green and lush and beautiful with lovely tea plantations. Thousands of tea plants terraced down the hillsides and there fields of broccoli and cauliflower plants. This was a very lush and beautiful place to live. We arrived at their Christian School late in the afternoon and stayed in the Lacson's home. It was a short distance to the village of Kotagiri. Heather and Jerry explained the work of their mission and how long they had been there. They needed a school nurse for over one hundred children in their school.

A walk into the small village of Kotagiri to look at the hospital was very interesting. Heather introduced me to a doctor that took me on a tour and said that they would like to hire me for nursing if I moved there. They always needed nurses. There were very few nurses at the hospital, and relatives provided most of the patient care. Family members cooked all patient food and provided for their needs. After seeing the hospital we shopped for food. I loved the fresh custard apples and coconut cookies. Heather had a cook who cooked hot and spicy Indian dishes, which she served with steaming piles of rice. Everyone ate with their hands.

We took a trip to a larger town, Coimbatore, to check out the schools that were available for missionary children. We visited a private school run by the British. If I was to live and work in Kotagiri, the school was too far away from Kotagiri for the boys to commute daily, and they would have to live at the school and just come home on weekends. I didn't think that would be feasible since I had no plans to put them in a boarding school where we would be separated. The roads were very dangerous and commuting was out of the question.

We enjoyed our time with the Lacsons and they made us feel very welcome. Their school and work area was very beautiful, but I was not planning on giving my child rearing responsibilities to a boarding school. I knew that I wanted to return to the U.S. and finish my Nursing degree and then ask the Lord to provide the direction for my work in missions. We drove down the mountain by the light of the moon and left Kotagiri on our way to Bangalore for a flight on Air-India to Karachi, Pakistan. It was very beautiful and I thought about Kenny and our life together, wishing that he was by my side to enjoy this with me. I missed him very much. I knew that I needed to pray for

God's guidance, but I did not feel that I would return to work there.

On our drive to Bangalore we came upon a horrible accident of a German tour bus with a flatbed steel truck that had just happened in front of us. Jerry and Andrew got out to see if they could help, and I stayed in the van with Sarah. Andrew said it was a horrible nightmare scene with thirty dead bodies lying around and twenty more people dying and cut to pieces by the overloaded truck carrying steel bars. Many people were cut in half when the steel sheared the bus in half; limbs were scattered everywhere. It was an unbelievable terrible sight in this country with no medical help. Other people had stopped to assist and later Jerry drove us on to the airport. Andrew said that he had nightmares about the scene for a long time.

Our return flight stopped in Karachi, Pakistan, and we were not sure when our flight to London left. We waited a long time with all the passengers' luggage piled up in the middle of the bare waiting room floor. Andrew sat on our luggage and read while Sarah and I explored the airport. Our flights all went well to London and New York with no more burning electrical systems and we arrived in Manhattan safely with the American hostages still held in Iran. Family had been worried about us.

Back at the farm again for Christmas we had the Tran family join us and celebrated with all but Phillip, who was still in New Zealand. After returning from India, I decided to continue my nursing classes and finish my Bachelor's Degree in Nursing before I definitely moved to a Mission Field to work. I also made the definitive decision that wherever I worked the children would be with me and not at a boarding school. God was leading me each step of the way as He said that He would. The needs were great for anyone who could go to India. And wherever I went as a trained nurse, I wanted to bring the kind of help that the

Lord had asked me to do. I needed to get as much training as possible to be the most effective.

# Chapter 13: God is Good

MY YOUNGER BROTHER CHARLES died on January 17, 1980. He was discharged from the State Hospital to a halfway house in Wichita, Kansas to live with a group of men. Against all medical and family advice, he moved out of the halfway house and found an apartment of his own. He was found dead in his apartment shortly after his move, and my brothers in Wichita were notified. They saw him often, but Charlie was not able to handle schizophrenia alone and refused living under supervision. We were all worried about him and talked often about what we could do for him, not knowing what to do. We were so sorry that we were unable to help him as all families of schizophrenics feel. The doctors had tried different kinds of medication and treatment in the hospital without success. We had graveside services in Madison, Kansas, and Charlie was buried near our parents and sister in the Madison Blakely Cemetery. Recent medical literature is looking at schizophrenia as a chronic infectious disease and progress may be made soon for families who feel so helpless in watching their loved ones suffer.

Phillip returned from his semester in New Zealand and started back to Kansas State. While there he grew a moustache, worked hard, traveled the North and South Islands and had many new songs to play on his guitar. He was busy in New Zealand, sheep ranching with the Moore family and working with the pastor of a local church. He had many stories to tell us. He found a serious girlfriend soon upon his return home and began dating Pamela Lowe from Manhattan, a freshman at Kansas State. They had dated while they were in Manhattan High school together.

In January Amber went on a Semesters Abroad Program through Trinity College in Deerfield, Illinois to

Seville, Spain for six months. She received sixteen credits of Spanish for her Bachelor's Degree with a minor in Spanish from Kansas State. She had many good experiences, perfected her Spanish language, and invited her sister Grace to join her at the end of the semester for a trip through France and Germany. Grace left for Spain as soon as her classes at Kansas State were finished in the spring. They traveled through Spain, France and Germany and visited their cousin, Adrienne, and her husband, Jim, in Germany, and returned in time for summer school at Kansas State. While Amber was in Spain, Chip and Elizabeth were engaged and called to tell her their good news. She was very excited and happy for them, having introduced them last year. We all looked forward to their wedding.

We all worked together to put a redwood three-tiered split-rail fence around the pond and on both sides of the driveway up to the house at the farm. It was a hard job, but with all the children helping we got it done. It looked very nice, but a few cows and horses still managed to get out occasionally. We were plagued with high jumping cows.

Andrew and Tim took care of the outside work at the farm and built barbed wire fences. We had a good friend, Jim Forwood, and his family who came to our house for Bible studies, and Jim was working on a PhD at Kansas State in Pasture Management and Agriculture. Jim and the boys fished together, and he helped the boys put up fences and burn off the pastures that we did every year. All of our kids had enjoyed helping Kenny burn off the pastures for many years. This year Andrew, Tim, and Jim started their burn with a butane tank strapped to Jim's back, lighting fires along one fence line on top of the hill of our forty acres. Andrew and Tim had water tanks on their backs to control the fire, but an unexpected wind came up and fanned the flames and the fire got out of control. It spread rapidly beyond their control and we called the fire department. It spread to neighboring pastures and we thought that it might even go all the way to Manhattan.

Five fire trucks responded from Manhattan, Riley County, Ogden and Junction City to contain the raging fire. We were a little embarrassed. Small fires had gotten away from us before, but this one was definitely the biggest. As the fire was being extinguished, there was a common agreement from all the fire departments that since they were already there, it would be a good time to burn everyone's pasture and they would keep it under control. So they lit the fire again, and we had a Saturday afternoon of firemen camaraderie burning pastures for all the neighbors. Some of the pastures had not been burned off in many years and with good pasture management, should have. Jim must have convinced them that this was a good idea. Everyone went home happy.

In the summer, Amber and I both enrolled in a course in Cultural Anthropology at Kansas State. I thought I might need this learning for my mission work in Port-au-Prince and elsewhere around the world. We took Sarah, now three years old, with us. Sarah had Microbiology in utero, Ethics as an infant of two weeks, Statistics at six months and now I thought she could handle this class. She could sit still for an hour, and all the other children had jobs and were working. Sarah did well and we enjoyed the class. Amber had friends from Johannesburg, South Africa come to visit the farm after summer school, Brian and Debbie Wood. They were youth group leaders in her church in Johannesburg. I enjoyed getting to know them while they stayed with us. They all took my Subaru station wagon on a trip to California and the Grand Canyon, along with a young Spanish boy, Juan, who Amber was teaching English. Brian and Debbie toured many other states and enjoyed their time in America.

I often thought of tearing down the Red House that was filled with junk, and it was beginning to look like it needed another coat of paint. Tim was a hyperactive child and it was a challenge to always find something for him to do. I told him that the wood was his for selling if he wanted to take the summer and tear down the Red House. So he started, working very hard at it. He was lifting weights, so had enough muscle to get the job done. He was fifteen years old and really wanted some hard work so I told him just to take the summer and do it when he wanted. He finished the job quicker than I expected and sold the lumber for a lot of money. I eventually filled in the hole and planted grass. With the Red House removed we had a very nice view of the fields from our house. Tim bought a used silver Camaro with his money, but it didn't last too long. We bought another car for him to drive to school after Andrew went to New Zealand.

We had other children's friends visit from Spain, South Africa and Tasmania stay with us that year. I went upstairs to the children's bedrooms one morning after everyone had left for school and found a strange person with very long curly hair in Grace's bed. Not knowing who it was, I asked and it was a young man who had arrived at the Manhattan Bus Station at midnight from Tasmania, a friend of Grace's. She picked him up from the bus station and gave him her bedroom while she slept on the couch downstairs. She forgot to tell me before she left for school.

In September I started my anatomy classes in Human Body at Kansas State. I really enjoyed these classes and thought learning the different body systems was awesome. God's miracle in Creation was even more astounding to me as I understood how the Creator made it especially wonderful to see the complex systems of life in the human body. I could understand the Church in a new way since the Bible calls it the Body of Christ. Amazing insight! The course was six hours of lecture and lab with time on a cadaver team. Not everyone was chosen for the cadaver team, and I felt fortunate to have this experience. At first I was hesitant and queasy about cutting my scalpel deep into the flesh of a dead body. Then in reading the Bible scriptures I came upon a reference that said, "All flesh is like grass, and all its beauty is like the flower of the field. The grass withers, the flower fades when the breath of the Lord blows upon it." Then it didn't seem so difficult.

The cadaver was on a table in a small room off our laboratory classroom. Six students silently surrounded, dissected and studied the body with me every week. Sarah went to my laboratory class with me when I didn't have a babysitter. I sat her at my desk and gave her a coloring book and crayons or the box of human bones on my desk that we used to identify different bones. She was happy. But when I went into the cadaver room to start dissecting, or to identify the position of the cranial nerves, she got lonesome and peeked her head around the corner asking to come in. I did not think seeing a dead body and all our enthusiasm for dissecting would be a good influence on a three-year-old, and didn't let her come in, but diverted her interest to other things. She just wanted to be where all the excitement was.

Sometimes Grace did not have a class and kept Sarah when I had my lectures. Grace carried her in a child's seat on the back of her bike to Dillon's Supermarket where she worked, to buy Sarah a soda and small, multicolored chicklets, which she loved. Sarah loved to do this and remembers those times with her sister. Sarah also attended a preschool afternoon group on campus twice a week with her peer group, since she had always been with teenagers. I thought she might be surprised to find out that she wasn't a teen. She wore her own tiny red Jansport backpack that her sister Grace had bought for her. She looked funny walking around campus with her backpack. She walked around campus with Chip, Phillip, or Amber who were attending K State and they took her to their own favorite places.

<u>1981</u>

Chip and Elizabeth and Phillip and Pam were all going to a formal Military Ball at Kansas State one Saturday night. I asked them to drop by the farm on their way so that I could get pictures of them all together. The boys were wearing their Air Force dress uniforms and looked very handsome. Kenny and I went to this ball and had a wonderful time dancing while he was in ROTC at Kansas State. They arrived and we went upstairs into the living room to take pictures in front of our large natural stone fireplace. Elizabeth and Pam looked very beautiful with the boys so handsome and tall. As I focused the camera, I could see that everyone was the same height. Elizabeth and Pam wore high heeled shoes, so all four of them looked six feet tall. I was aware the girls were tall, but it was a unique picture with all of them the same height.

In the spring we decided to build a barn for the horses near the developed, fresh water spring that the county had helped build for us on the forty acres. It provided shelter for our horses and storage room for the winter bales of hay. Phillip drew up the designs and ordered lumber for us to start. Andrew, Tim and Eric worked alongside Phillip in this project. Pam often came out with Phillip and worked with us. Sarah and I also rode over through the woods on the trailer behind the tractor when Phillip and Pam came out to work. We had a good time and made a campfire to cook hot dogs and make our family favorite, S'mores; roasted marshmallows between a square of Hershey's chocolate bar and two graham crackers, very sticky and sweet but delicious. We were all very proud of our efforts when the boys finally put the tin roof on. With the fresh spring as a water source and the barn shelter, the children used this area for their campsites.

Chip graduated from Kansas State in June with a Bachelor's Degree in Biology and received his commission as an officer in the Air Force. Chip and Elizabeth Sadler from St. Louis had been engaged for a year and planned their wedding for June 13th in St. Louis, Missouri. The whole family went there for the weekend staying in a lovely downtown hotel near the church. Chip had made all the arrangements. Phillip, Andrew, Tim and Eric were all in the wedding and wore tuxedos. Elizabeth was a beautiful bride. Amber and Grace were bridesmaids, and Sarah was the flower girl. It was a very beautiful wedding, and some of our military friends that we had known in Germany, the Rademachers, were able to attend. After a two-week camping honeymoon to Victoria Island, British Columbia, they returned to Manhattan for a visit. Chip started his Air Force flight training in the fall, so they moved to Wichita Falls, Texas to await flight training at Sheppard Air Force Base.

I took a course in U.S. History in the summer at Kansas State. Phillip and Pamela Lowe were engaged and planning their wedding for August 2nd in Manhattan. They both had two more years until graduation and until Phillip, in the Air Force ROTC Program at Kansas State, would receive his officer's commission in the Air Force. Pam was majoring in Geology.

It was a lovely and very large wedding at the First Methodist Church in Manhattan. Phillip and Pam had both grown up in Manhattan and had lots of friends and family here. Pam had two brothers and two sisters in the wedding. Chip was best man; Andrew and Tim and Eric were groomsmen in the wedding and Amber and Grace bridesmaids. Sarah was the flower girl. Phillip and Pam went off to Colorado for their honeymoon. They returned to Manhattan in time for college and lived in a nice mobile home that Phillip had purchased near our Vietnamese friends, the Tran family. Tony and Son bought a mobile home and lived there with their four children, Mai, Linh,

Kahn, and Minh. Tony often cooked delicious Chinese food for Phillip and Pam. They loved his wontons and egg rolls.

After the wedding, Eric, Sarah, and I and Mrs. Long, Kenny's seventy-one year-old-mother, took a three-week trip to England, Scotland, and Wales. Mrs. Long always dreamed of returning to the place of her father's birth, Edinburgh, Scotland.

We flew from Manhattan to Kansas City to London, England. We found a nice bed & breakfast in a good location with a sign on the front gate that read, "Free Kittens." I could hardly believe it. Sarah had been asking for a pet kitten for a long time. She wanted to stay there and play with the kittens, which were more interesting for a four-year-old than London. It could not have been more perfect for her. She enjoyed them while we were there and we left them behind after the trip. While we stayed at the bed & breakfast we took the red double-decker buses everywhere. Eric and Sarah always ran up the stairs and loved the top view.

Sarah had her fourth birthday with a picnic at the London Zoo and Eric had his eleventh birthday in Cardiff, Wales with dinner in the Cellar Restaurant at Cardiff Castle. We traveled to Wales by train and saw the gently rolling hills and the beautiful green countryside. It was in the Cardiff Historical Museum where I saw posters and historical documents with the very common name of my father's family Evans. I knew that his grandfather had come from Wales to America in 1844. Sarah enjoyed the refreshments on the train, especially the tomato sandwiches and Kit-Kat chocolate bars. Eric and Sarah both enjoyed riding the trains on our trips since they never rode them in the States.

Kenny's mother's father, Thomas Smith, had been born in Edinburgh, Scotland, and immigrated to America as a teenager. She was excited about going back to her father's birthplace. We were at Victoria Station in London to catch the train to Edinburgh, and I sent Eric to a nearby Kentucky Fried Chicken restaurant to get food for our trip. He just barely made it back in time and we raced for the train. I jumped on with Sarah and helped pull Mrs. Long on board while Eric pushed from behind and jumped on himself. It was a close call! Mrs. Long caught her white cardigan sweater in the door as it closed but we were able to retrieve it, and we all leisurely enjoyed our fried chicken picnic on our ride to Edinburgh.

We loved riding the train and seeing the spectacular fields of lavender heather covering the miles and miles of hills. We chose a very beautiful time of the year to visit Scotland. It was rugged and breathtaking country, very spectacular. I felt very much at home in this country. I remembered that this was the country of Oswald Chambers, the author of my daily devotional book, *My Utmost for His Highest*. A friend in one of my Bible study groups gave this to me, and I read it each morning with my Bible.

We stayed a few days in Edinburgh and walked to the Municipal Courthouse building from our bed & breakfast. We inquired about the ship's passenger lists, but Mrs. Long didn't have sufficient information to find her father's name listed and the date of departure on a ship to America. The building was very large and filled with large volumes on shelves stacked high to the ceiling. There were many people on tall ladders retrieving volumes for waiting customers. She was a little disappointed, but just so happy to be there in the city and country of her father's birth. He had died when she was six years old, the youngest of four children. She loved meeting and visiting with the people and walking the streets where her father was born and grew up as a boy. He immigrated to America as a young man, and his brother immigrated to Australia. She enjoyed shopping and seeing the Edinburgh Castle, an ancient historical place. We took lots of pictures. We have a picture of Sarah sitting astride the back of a lion statue in front of the castle. She looked so tiny. Mrs. Long seemed very content that she had made the journey, and I was very happy that we she came us. She learned much about her heritage and said that it was the most wonderful trip of her life.

We traveled as far north as Inverness, Scotland, and stayed a few days there. We took boat trips on the Ness River and watched them lower the boats through the Locks. Eric had heard a lot about the Lochness Monster and wanted to travel down the River Ness, but we saw no monster. August was a lovely time in Inverness, and we met many friendly and helpful people. The bed & breakfast where we stayed was right on the river and had delicious food. We all enjoyed the large breakfasts with sausage, bacon, eggs, toast with jam and orange marmalade, beans and fried tomatoes, tea and coffee. The family running the B&B invited us to a church service with them and we went. They offered us great hospitality and were so friendly.

Awakening early one morning, I dressed and went for a long walk alone over the bridge on the Ness River at sunrise. Eric, Sarah and their grandmother were still asleep. There were very few people on the streets. The first sun rays of the morning cast a golden glow on the river and the bridge as I stood looking down at the water. They made the bridge look as if it was made of gold. It was a beautiful moment. I felt at one with creation and the Creator. It was a quiet and peaceful time where God confirmed my coming on this trip, and I felt at peace with my plans to pursue my Nursing degree. I knew that I was following His plan for my life.

I sent out many letters of inquiry to Nursing Midwifery schools in England during the previous year. I thought about attending Nursing Midwifery School as soon as I got my Bachelors of Science in Nursing. The Hospital for Mothers & Babies in Greenwich, London had replied that there might be an opening for me to study and were interested in my attending there. I wrote back that I planned to visit London in August and was given an appointment to see the hospital.

Other friends from Manhattan who had lived and worked in London invited us to their home for dinner. We took the London Tube and enjoyed seeing my friend's beautiful home and had a wonderful visit. Mrs. Long, Eric, and Sarah stayed with them while I rode the train to Greenwich and had my appointment at the Hospital for Mothers & Babies. I visited with the Nursing Administrator and they assured me that I could find a place in 1983 to study Midwifery when I graduated with my Bachelor's in nursing. I felt that our trip to England had been very rewarding and successful in many ways. We flew back to Kansas City, tired but happy with many fun and wonderful memories of our time in England, Scotland, and Wales. The summer had been filled with weddings and trips.

In the fall of 1981, after returning from England, I started my first Basic Nursing lecture class at Marymount College of Kansas in Salina, Kansas. It was an hour drive from the farm, and I usually took Sarah with me. We left very early in the morning for my 8:00 a.m. class. She remembers me carrying her to the car pretending she was asleep so I would let her lie down. I brought an overflowing cup of hot tea to drink on the way and breakfast for Sarah along, and our drive went quickly. A couple of times Sarah stayed with a babysitter in one of the girl's dorms, but most of the time she went to class with me. On one occasion the old paint on the radiators in the classroom was cracked and peeling, and Sarah helped remove most of the paint during one of the nursing lectures, leaving the yellow dried flakes of paint on the floor. She also had a bag of toys and colored plastic army soldiers, her brother's stuff to play with. She tried to carry my purple and blue eight-pound Basic Nursing textbook each day but didn't get very far. Amber had decided to take the class, too, as she had planned a pre-medical degree and rode with us.

Andrew was running cross-country track and played football on the Manhattan High School football team. He was a wide receiver and especially fast runner. We enjoyed going to his football games and watching him run cross-country meets. He won many medals. Running was his best sport. Tim had wrestled and ran cross-country, and later played on the Manhattan High School football team also, and we enjoyed going to his games. He played for two years and made many touchdowns.

Max and Carol Hartman, a young couple from Hutchinson, Kansas, moved into a mobile home that was moved to the pig farm on our road and were now our closest neighbors. Max was in the School of Veterinary Medicine at Kansas State University and Carol worked at a local bank. Max managed the pig farm and they were breeding and raising many pigs. Carol came up to meet us and brought a plate of cookies. We got acquainted and invited them to our News Year's Eve party and often to our house for pizza. Carol rode her horse to our house and gave Sarah horseback rides, which Sarah loved. Eric rode his bike, and Sarah often rode her big wheel down to their house for visits, and Carol fixed special Jell-O Popsicles for them. Sarah loved to see all their newborn pigs.

One day after Sarah was two years old, she asked to go see some new baby pigs that were just born. We drove to the pig farm and stood by the pen and Carol reached down and picked one up for Sarah to hold. It was one week old. Carol and I visited for a while and then Carol said it was time to give the baby pig to her so she could put it back with its mother in the pigpen. Sarah hugged the baby pig tightly to her chest and looked up at Carol with her big brown eyes and said, "But I'm the mother." She really wanted a baby animal to raise. Later Max and Carol gave her a newborn pig that was a runt for her very own to raise. She called it Miss Piggy. Sarah kept it in a box of straw on the patio and fed it with a baby bottle until it got too big. Then kept it in a pen under the dock near the pond. She was very good at feeding it and didn't get too upset when it grew much larger and had to be butchered for meat. Her affection dwindled the larger and dirtier it got. She even ended up taking packages of pork chops to her Sunday school class at church. She had taken the live baby pig for show and tell months earlier, so we thought it appropriate for her to share the bounty.

Sometime that year we finally sold all our cows and just had four horses left on the farm. We had a long checkered past history with horses, the good, the bad, and the ugly. We had many of our own and kept those of friends for quite a few years. My brother Richard gave us one called Sweet Pea that we bred, which gave us a colt. My twin brother Philip gave us a very large palomino quarter horse called Blaze. Kenny bought both Amber and Grace a horse of their own when they were fifteen years old. Every child grew up learning how to ride and fall off horses at an early age. Eight children and over twenty horses later, we had no broken bones. We had many angels riding up and down those hills with the children. I loved to see all the horses brown, black, white, dappled grey, palomino and sandy colored, charging down the hills in the morning, snorting and neighing with their powerful muscles rippling, mane and tails flying, and eyes wild with excitement as they came to the barn for some hay and feed. It was a beautiful sight, and I thought that alone earned their feed. But when they declined to be caught and saddled for the children to ride, I had second thoughts.

The children had all shown horses at the Riley County Fair starting with Frisky and Star, the original POAs that Kenny had bought for Chip and Phillip, when he returned from Vietnam. They all had interesting names. Friskey, Star, Starlight, Sweet Pea, Little Speck, Blaze, Balam, Diamond, Li'l Bailey, Husky Boy, Devil, Money, Thunder, Santana, Jeanny, and Old Blue that Kenny rode. We could fill a book with horse stories. Phillip bought a set of books on how to train horses and may have had the most success and scars. They pulled buggies, rode through fire, chased cows, swam in the ponds, ate our newly planted grass in the front yard, ate the dog food in the dog dish bowl on the patio, carried us through snow, tried to come into the kitchen, bit children, refused to show up for the fair, threw a kid into the barbed wire fence, ate the apples in the neighbors orchards, got lost, went to the neighbor's barn and ate their feed, tore down fences, tried to behead their riders through woods, fought with each other, ran away after dumping their rider, fought the loading trailer, threw themselves over backwards, refused the saddle, and provided many hours of riding fun and entertainment for the children.

I started my psychiatric nurses training at the Veterans Administration Hospital in Topeka in the locked ward for long-term psychiatric patients in September of 1981. You might think that after eight children and my past history that I would be a patient instead of on the staff. It was very interesting and there was never a dull day. The patients' behavior was not predictable and every day was full of surprises. Since I had raised eight two-year-olds, I felt prepared. I enjoyed the variety, but it was quite a challenge requiring a special alertness. The patients were very clever and often smarter than me.

Nearing Christmas, I was asked to plan a Christmas party for the patients with refreshments, songs, gifts, and activities. We had the Christmas party on my last day of clinical and we sang many Christmas carols. It was a very moving experience as all the patients were very touched with the singing and joined in with the staff. I noticed many patients with tears in their eyes, probably remembering their childhood and happier days when they were young and with their families. For that short time we were one, patients and staff as we sang of the baby born in Bethlehem. I experienced a great compassion for these seriously ill patients who had so little future to look forward to, and I knew that God loved them as He loved me.

On December 16th, 1981, I finished my semester of Psychiatric Nursing in Topeka at the Veterans Administration Hospital and took my final exam. I was exhilarated, having survived the semester of commuting and Psychiatric Nursing and feeling that I had done well on the final exam. I was really happy and ready to hit the road before the weather became worse, since it was already snowing. I stopped to buy a ham for dinner and a few toys for the Christmas stockings. The weather wasn't too bad that morning when I left about 7:00 a.m. on the drive to Topeka.

I was cautious and driving very slowly on I-70 just outside of Topeka as the snow got heavier. The ice built up and my windshield would no longer defrost. I knew that this was bad. I tried to ease gradually to the side of the highway in the blizzard to stop because my windshields were covered with ice. I must have barely touched my brake, causing me to swerve around into the path of an oncoming blue semi-truck that hit me broadside on the driver's door. Because the highway was glazed with ice, my silver Subaru spun around in midair and landed in the median on its four wheels between the two highways. Seeing the semi come towards me out of the corner of my eye an instant before impact, I knew that I would never survive this and just closed my eyes and said, "Here I come, Lord" and hung on to the steering wheel.

With my shoulder harness seat belt on, it was very quiet when I landed. I opened my eyes to find that I was still alive, but the door smashed in on my left hip and the windshield was shattered. I was so surprised to be alive! I quickly unfastened my seatbelt, and unable to open my door, crawled out the passenger side. The silver Subaru that Kenny and the children had bought for me in 1978 for Mother's Day was totaled.

I was in a daze and in shock and walked around the car when the truck driver stopped and ran back to my car and found me. Other vehicles had stopped because of the weather, and I was put on an Army bus to keep warm until the highway patrol arrived. They called an ambulance, and I was taken to the emergency room of the Wamego Hospital near Manhattan. I asked the highway patrol to call Grace at home, who was taking care of Sarah, and to meet me at the hospital before I left in the ambulance.

Grace and Sarah raced to the hospital to pick me up and brought some clothes. Seeing me in the hospital bed, Sarah was very frightened and thought I was dying. I assured her that I wasn't and would be around for a long time to see her graduate from high school. But I knew that I had a very close call. My clothes were cut off me to look for injuries and they found glass in my clothing. The car was filled with broken glass. Phillip and Pam also came to the hospital to give me moral support. The x-rays showed no broken bones, but I had severe whiplash of the neck and wore a cervical collar. They wanted to keep me overnight for observation, but I insisted on going home. I went home with a much bruised body and a throbbing, aching head and neck, literally feeling like I had been hit by a truck. This casual remark had a new and vivid personal meaning for me.

After arriving home, I stayed down on the couch for a few days and suffered. I was so grateful that my Psychiatric Nursing Clinical was finished. Chip and Elizabeth arrived from Wichita Falls, Texas for Christmas on December 23rd. Everyone was home. It was a wonderful Christmas together, and I was so glad to be alive. God is good! When I was feeling better I went to Junction City, Kansas to buy another Subaru, bright blue and new four-wheel drive where Kenny had bought my first one. Phillip took me and helped me make the decision. When I drove again, I drove with fear and trepidation for a while and broke out in a cold sweat when a semi passed. I knew that I had barely survived this year.

## 1982

Cautiously, I started driving again to Salina each day for my nursing classes. Even with my new blue Subaru, I wasn't sure how long I wanted to continue to do this. A flat tire on the highway early one morning with the temperature at eight degrees below zero convinced me that this would be my last semester to drive. We would have to move to Salina if I was to finish my last year for my nursing degree.

Andrew applied for an AFS Exchange Program in January and left for Auckland, New Zealand. He spent his senior year there and graduated. He helped build a boat with his host family and played on a rugby team. He looked forward to travelling and seeing other parts of the world. He had spent a summer in Haiti with me, and had gone to India with Sarah and me. His best friend, Artie, had plans to join him in New Zealand for a vacation and they took a trip together. Since we had sold all our cows, Tim and Eric just had the four horses to feed and care for.

Phillip had plans to fly in the Air Force after graduation from Air Force ROTC at Kansas State, so he decided to put an ultra-light airplane together and get some experience flying. He ordered a kit with all the parts from the manufacturer and asked Jon Howe, a neighbor, if he could use his apple barn in the winter to put it together. Jon owned the Pink Palace where we lived for six years, and had apple orchards and used the barn for storage. Phillip had a great time and worked on it by himself, nights and weekends when he wasn't in school. It took him awhile, but he finished it and took it for a test flight over the forty acres. We watched him fly and he was so excited. He took off in the pasture and stored it in the barn when it was finished. He was delighted with his success and had many good times flying his ultra-light around Manhattan. Later, interviewing with Delta Airlines after seven years in the Air Force flying T-33s and C-135s, he mentioned his ultra-light flying experience in his resume and got the job as a Delta Airline pilot.

Amber and Pat Theobald made plans for their wedding to be at the farm in August. Pat was a basketball coach at the Christian college and they had been dating since she came back from Spain. I finished my semester of OB/GYN with clinical experience at Memorial Hospital in Manhattan. I got Sarah out of bed early in the morning to take her to be with Amber while I worked. My time in the nursery was interesting. It was a totally different viewpoint of babies. Amber bought a mobile home and lived in Manhattan with a kitten named Nina that Sarah loved to play with. Sarah says they ate sausage and crackers and cheese for snacks in bed. She loved going there.

Amber had some Spanish skirts she had brought from Spain and showed Sarah her Spanish dances. Sarah thought the dances were very beautiful. Sarah also attended a Montessori School for a semester.

Dr. Crane, our pediatrician for many years for all the children, asked me when I planned to go back to Haiti. I had no plans yet, but soon began to make plans and he said that he wanted to go with me. I knew the orphanage could use a pediatrician for the time period that he could go and was pleased that he had offered to go. So we started making plans for a mission trip there to work at the orphanage in June. Two other medical students wanted to go with us, so we had a team of four that would leave in June for three weeks. We collected donations of medicine and clothing to take to the orphanage. A medical clinic had been built so we would have a place to work.

We made plans to move to Salina after Amber and Pat Theobald's wedding in August. Because of my serious accident commuting to Topeka during last winter, I knew that it was not a good idea to continue commuting. Tim and Eric did not want to change schools. But my last year of nursing classes required early morning and late night clinical experience at the hospitals that would be hard to attend from this distance. There was no other way than to move to Salina.

Max and Carol Hartman came to the house often and were wonderful neighbors. We played practical jokes on each other and Carol's birthday was coming up. I wanted her to be surprised, so the boys took a sign that said, "Today Is My Birthday" to Manhattan on their way to school early and stuck it underneath her drive-up window at the bank where she worked. The drive-up window opened first thing in the morning and drive-up customers wished her "Happy Birthday," and even brought her gifts. She was really amazed that everyone knew until finally a customer told her about the sign. She came home that night after work with the sign stuck to the bumper of her car.

We had tall wild marijuana plants growing in our barnyard and over the years could never get rid of them. One rainy day the boys came up with an idea of transplanting some large stalks to our neighbor's front yard after dark. Tim and Eric cut down the tall plants and stuck them in the Hartman's front yard after the rain late one night. They had a great time doing this and could hardly wait for the Hartmans to wake up and see their new plants that had grown in their front yard. Max and Carol were very surprised. They returned our pranks with toilet paper wrapped along our split-rail fences on the driveway and water balloons over our front doors to the house.

Classes finished in May, and Sarah, Eric and I went to Port-au-Prince for three weeks. We lived on the top floor of the orphanage that had apartments for missionaries. Carre-Four was a different part of the city than we had lived in before and much poorer. We took many more supplies for the orphanage, clothing for the children, medicines for the clinic and powdered milk and toys. Dr. Pete Crane arrived and worked at the orphanage giving physical exams along with the medical students. The children were well taken care of and received all their immunizations.

The last week of our stay we were invited to live in the home of Haitian Missionaries, Etienne and Betty Prophete and their family. They had Christian schools and found sponsors for children in need of special care. They had small children Eric and Sarah's age and they played together. Sarah remembers playing in the backyard together and hiding in the mango trees and under the bed in the house. We went to their church, and the children remember the services as lasting for hours and hours, which they did. The Prophete family had a lovely home, were very kind and generous, and we enjoyed being with a Haitian family. Etienne drove us to one of the highest points of Port-au-Prince to look down on the city at night, which was very beautiful. We loved the beans and rice, fried plantain, mango, papaya and breadfruit. We stayed healthy and returned to the farm after our three-week stay.

Ray and Dorrian Stafford, Amber's host family from Johannesburg, South Africa, visited us at the Farm in the summer. We were happy to return their hospitality that they had offered Amber in 1978. Amber, Grace and the Staffords went on a long trip to California together in my blue Subaru, seeing the western part of the United States. They always stopped for afternoon tea, as was the custom of the Staffords in South Africa. This was the Stafford's first trip to the states and they enjoyed all their travels.

I received a letter confirming that I was accepted for midwifery training at the Hospital for Mothers and Babies in Greenwich, London, starting September of 1984. I filed it away for future reference and never found it again. After my graduation in May from Marymount College in Salina and the children finished their year of school in the summer, we moved to London, England.

We celebrated Sarah's fifth birthday on August 6th, the day before the wedding. She received a pink and white Strawberry Shortcake bicycle. She was delighted. Amber and Pat's wedding was August 7, 1983, in the front yard at the farm. Amber planned everything. Near the pond, tents and tables were set up for the refreshments. We roasted a pig for the reception, and Tony Tran, our Vietnamese friend, helped with the carving and serving. Chip with Amber on his arm, walked down the aisle of a hundred chairs placed in our front yard. She was a lovely bride. Grace was maid of honor, and Judy, a high school friend, and a friend of Amber's from South Africa, Renee, was one of her bridesmaids. Sarah Emily was flower girl again carrying a pretty white parasol. It turned out to be an unusually beautiful August day with a slight mist in the morning to cool everyone. Many of Pat's relatives from Nebraska were able to come. Most of my brothers and sisters and families were there. All of our family was present but Andrew who was in New Zealand. He called Amber and talked to her before the wedding.

Max and Carol Hartman offered to help us move to
Salina so we started moving the week after the wedding. It
was a huge job. I found a house to rent on an earlier trip, not
far from Marymount College where I would be attending
my last year. We used the Hartman's large trailer to move
our furniture. The boys wanted to take the pool table, which
was very heavy. Tim, Eric, Sarah and I moved. I had not
lived in the city since New Jersey in 1964 and the children
never had, so it was an adjustment. Tim was a junior in high
school; Eric in seventh grade; and Sarah started
kindergarten. I knew that it would be a difficult adjustment,
but it was more difficult than I imagined.

Tim enrolled at Salina High School and started
football practice. Now he played against his football friends
at Manhattan High School. Instead of starting junior high in
Manhattan, Eric started in Salina. Seventh grade had been a
difficult year for the other boys in Manhattan. We lived one
block from Sarah's kindergarten and she walked to school
with girls in the neighborhood. She felt very independent
and grown up. She rode her pink strawberry shortcake
bicycle on the sidewalks in front of our house and parked it
in the garage, too close to my Subaru on one occasion and
broke one of the tail lights. We all had to get used to living
and working in less space than a huge farmhouse and sixty-
five-acre farm.

Granddad Long, Kenny's father, had a sister Aunt
Reva, and her daughter's family with three boys lived in
Salina; we had just met a few times. Eric had one cousin in
his class and another cousin one year older. He enjoyed
having these cousins to be with and go to their house. The
oldest cousin, a year older than Tim, played on the football
team. These cousins were often at our house playing pool
and acquainting Tim and Eric with Salina. We found a
Christian church nearby and joined. I enrolled in my classes
at the university and knew that it would be a difficult year. I

had a 7:00 a.m. shift to work at St. John's Hospital one semester. Tim got Sarah ready for kindergarten after we had an early breakfast together.

Tim enjoyed the football season very much. Eric enjoyed his cousins most of all, but he never liked the school and had a difficult time. I went to the school many times for consultation with teachers. After football season Tim got a job at a restaurant. We had found a car that he fixed up in the garage and drove. We were living so close to the high school that he could walk.

We all drove to Wichita Falls, Texas to spend Thanksgiving with Chip and Elizabeth. Chip was graduating from flight school and soon got his orders for his first assignment. They were hoping for an Air Base in England.

Andrew came home in January from New Zealand, and Grace went to Costa Rica to study the geography of Latin America. She had taken Spanish in high school and at Kansas State. She lived in Heradia, a suburb of the capital San Jose, and studied at the University of San Jose. She lived with a Costa Rican family and she was gone for a semester with plans for a degree in Geography from Kansas State. Andrew visited us in Salina and planned to get a job and work a semester before he went to college. While visiting the farm, where Phillip and Pam were managing and living, he broke his foot on a snowmobile ride. I took him to the hospital in Salina and he had a cast put on. He bought a VW bus and decided to drive it to Texas to warmer temperatures and find construction work. He dropped by to tell us goodbye as he started off in January with a cast on his foot, driving his VW bus. He came back in the summer before we moved to England.

Sarah made many friends in the neighborhood and really enjoyed kindergarten. She was doing very well. Her first parent conference showed me some of her personality growing up with five older brothers. The teacher remarked that, "Sarah won't take nothing of nobody." The kindergarten children were exchanging friendship pins, which were safety pins with colored beads on them. She gave and received many of these. She rode her bike a lot and played with little girls who lived close by. When the older children visited from Manhattan, she enjoyed dressing up in old clothes and acting for them. Amber and Pat lived in Manhattan, and Amber sewed a quilted blue print cowgirl skirt and vest for Christmas that she loved. She had a gray baby kitten that she dressed up in doll clothes and treated like a baby. She always had someone to play with and was having a wonderful time. She had long, light brown-blond hair, and I curled it each night.

Phillip and Pam, Amber and Grace all planned to graduate in the spring from Kansas State while I graduated from Marymount College with my Bachelor's in Nursing Degree. Phillip was graduating with a Bachelor's Degree in Social Sciences and a commission as an officer in the Air Force and would go on to flight school. Amber was graduating with a Pre-Medical Degree with plans for medical school and a minor in Spanish. Grace was getting a Bachelor's Degree in Geography and Pam a Bachelor's Degree in Geology. After graduation, I needed to sit for my Kansas State Boards in Nursing for my Registered Nursing license before moving to England. I had lost my letter of acceptance from the Midwifery School during our move to Salina, so I had not replied yet and it didn't occur to me again in all the plans for the children and graduation and the move to England.

We all decided that Salina was a nice place to visit and a nice place to leave. All of us missed the farm and were so anxious to get out of town. It was just not where we would choose to be. We enjoyed getting to know Aunt Reva and her daughter, Mary Sue and her boys William, Ray and

Tom. When the kids were out of school and I graduated, Tim, Eric, Sarah and I took a road trip to California in my Subaru. Tim and I drove and we visited Huntington Beach near my sister Elaine in Lynwood, California. I had not seen Elaine for a long time and we were glad to get together. We enjoyed our trip together and then moved from Salina back to the farm. I prepared to take my Kansas State Board of Nursing Exams in July.

We had four graduates from Kansas State University in the family in 1983, and I graduated from Marymount College. Amber had the highest GPA and was a member of the honorary Phi Beta Kappa. We attended graduations for Phillip, Amber, Grace, and Pam in Manhattan, but I was on our trip and didn't attend my graduation.

# Interlude: Family Photographs and Memorabilia

Adren and Amber Evans Family

Riverside Park
at
Wichita, Kansas

Family Group (1941)

Junior, Dorothy, Norma,
Mom, Pop, Dale, Dick
Phillip, Charles, Phyllis
Dwight, Sharm, Betty

Madison Farm Home

## Cattlemen Banqueters To Hear Manhattan Man

Dr. Howard Hill Has Been Chosen For Annual Affair on Friday, October 29.

## METHODISTS TO DEDICATE NEW ORGAN SUNDAY

The new Hammond organ and Maas memorial amplified chimes will be dedicated at a special service next Sunday afternoon at 2:30 at a part of the homecoming celebration of the Madison Methodist church.

## HONORS FOR MISS MARKS

Miss Mahlon Marks, daughter of Mr. and Mrs. Guy Marks, was one of four graduates of the class of 1947 of the Independence junior college who was the recipient of honors.

## DR. J. A. BUKWALTER TO SPEAK IN EMPORIA

Dr. J. A. Buckwalter, associate secretary of the American Temperance Society, will speak at the First Christian church in Emporia Friday evening at 8 o'clock.

## B TEAM WINS MONDAY

The Madison B team defeated the Burlington B team in a football game at Roothook Field Monday night by a score of 13 to 6.

# Three of Family Killed in Highway Accident Sunday

Mr. and Mrs. Adam C. Evans and Daughter Are Victims—Three Others Injured.

## Bulldogs Winning Streak Intact; Defeat LeRoy

First Quarter and Fourth Quarter Touchdowns Spell Defeat For LeRoy Gridders.

## Community Happenings of Interest

## Election Day Interest Centers On Repeal Issue

Interest in State, District and County Races Are at Low Ebb. Voting to Be Heavy.

## CANDIDATES VISIT MADISON

## RETURN FROM LONG TRIP

## LINE THORNTON SALE FRIDAY

## NELLERS BRANCHING OUT

## WORLD COMMUNITY DAY

## W. S. C. S. RUMMAGE SALE

## HALLOWEEN NOTICE

## CHICKEN DINNER

## EMPORIA ATTORNEY SPEAKS

## ALF VANKHAUSER SELLS FARM

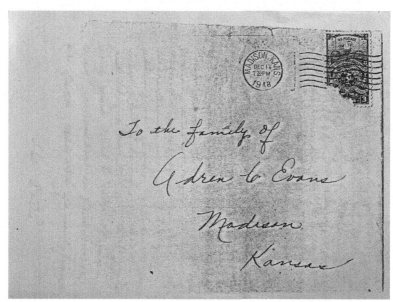

# Season's Greetings

Dear Evans:

Today while doing Grover's Christmas cards; in going down the list I came upon the name of Adren Evans and I thot of writing you this little note

Without a doubt, so soon after your great loss, none of you will feel much Christmas spirit this year; but you must know that although they can not be with you in body, they are in spirit because of the wonderful heritage they have left you.

You won't believe it now but you are so lucky. So many youngsters you will see about you, never have a chance — regardless of lack of, or the over abundance of worldly goods. That doesn't matter; but believe me – it wasn't an accident that, as you say – people have been so good to you! That is a part of that priceless Heritage left you by a thoughtful, good, loving parents that by living a good life they make for you such a wonderful example for each of you to live by. Not only were they wonderful parents, neighbors and friends but really good people who enjoyed living a good life that I'm sure was as model a Christian life as He Above would ask of any of us. Not only did they live a wonderful pattern to live by but to each of you, good books plus a head containing brains. I know each of you will use yours advantageously & wisely.

It's too bad the gang must be split up but time passes swiftly and each family is split up anyhow after a fashion, in time. It's nice tho to have a general gathering place so all can get together at times.

You know I always envied your Mom. Each new youn'n I wished was mine. I envied her boundless energy that made it possible to go so many places and get so much food cooked, canned, raised & etc. Her constant cheerfulness I marveled at her each new baby (a term) was welcomed and enjoyed in a already (bulging) home. How she seemed to get out of her money, more than any of the rest of us. Your Dad always said when asked "How?" "Oh she's the manager but I've always guessed that he was pretty good at it too. I always secretly as well as openly laughed with him when he told some of the tricks some of you "pulled"

So long now and if discouragement comes, don't forget, there is one who help us to beat anything if only we ask—if we remember to ask—regardless where you may be—at school, shopping, driving down a road, in our secret chambers—washing dishes or whatever we are doing—just get the habit of asking—it works! And if ever you need a bit of help of any kind— just let me know— any or all of you. and good luck to each of you and remember, in fair weather or foul—this old familyfriend

The Sites

**MISS PHYLLIS EVANS,** whose engagement is announced by her brother-in-law and sister, Maj. and Mrs. A. R. Hyle of Ft. Leavenworth, will become the bride of Mr. Kenneth L. Long of Manhattan, Kas. Miss Evans is a member of Alpha Xi Delta sorority at Kansas State College, and Mr. Long is a member of Sigma Alpha Epsilon fraternity. They both will receive their degrees from Kansas State next spring, and an early June wedding is planned.

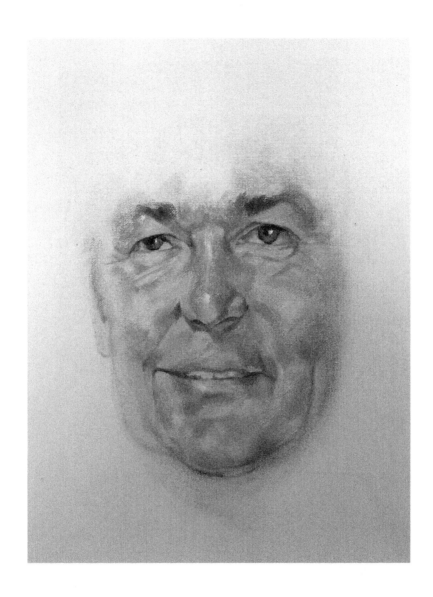

# Long's Country Inn

### a country Bed & Breakfast Inn near Manhattan, Kansas

Kidodobo Mission station is strategically located in the mountainous area of eastern Zaire (formerly the Belgian Congo). Only fifteen miles from Bukavu, the capital of the Kivu Province, supplies and medicines can be brought in that are essential for the orphanage. There is an agreeable climate of 60-70 degrees F. the year around. Fresh fruits and vegetables are available.

This area is peopled with the prolific Bashi tribe who live in huts made of grass and shaped like huge bee hives. They have very little food or clothing.

Zaire, Africa

Home Address:
Phyllis E. Long
893 West Side Road
Manhattan, KS 66502
Tel. 913-776-3212

Forwarding Address:
African Christian Mission
African Christian Mission
7900 Sandia
El Paso, TX 79924

Mission Address:
African Christian Mission
Box 956
Nairobi, Kenya

Field Address:
Phyllis T. Long
African Christian Mission
P.O. Box 175458
Nairobi, Kenya

*Phyllis & Sarah Long
To
Zaire, Africa
1989-1991*

*"For we are ambassadors for Christ, God making his appeal through us."*

2 Cor. 5:20

Back row, L to R: Amber, Eric, Drew, Chip
Front Row, L to R: Grace, Tim, Phyllis, Phil, Sarah

# Chapter 14: An Ounce of Prevention-A Pound of Cure

**THE SECOND WEEK OF AUGUST,** Eric, Sarah, and I packed up all that we needed for a year in London. I invited Tim to come to England with us to finish his senior year, but he was going to turn eighteen years old in one month and preferred to stay at the farm and graduate from Manhattan High School. He wanted to live there with Andrew and play his senior year of football and be independent. I didn't want to make him come with us, but I thought it might be a difficult year for him whether he went with us or stayed in Manhattan. Andrew returned from working a construction job in Texas and planned to manage the farm for me and find more renters. It was a boy's dormitory of students wanting a place to live with horses or dogs. Andrew's best friend, Artie Shaw, who had visited and traveled with him in New Zealand, moved into the farm and they both were freshman at Kansas State in the fall. They shared a room together. The farm provided a place for Andrew and Tim to live, since I had no plans to sell it yet, so this worked out for the present. I left my blue Subaru station wagon for them to sell for me at a later date. Andrew was in charge of the maintenance and finances for the house. Carol Hartman, our good friend and neighbor, had agreed to do some housework and keep the house in good condition while we were in England. The boys were glad about that.

I finished my Kansas State Board of Nursing Exams while visiting with my brother Richard and sister-in-law Carol in Topeka, but I didn't hear the results until September when I would be in Midwifery School in Greenwich, London. Chip and Elizabeth received orders for an Air Force base near Ipswich, England north of London. They were joining us in England in October, and we were excited about having some family there to visit and enjoy. After graduation and receiving his commission in the Air Force, Phillip and Pam were off to flight school, and Amber and Pat were moved to Pittsburg, Kansas. After returning from Costa Rica and graduation, Grace moved to a Chicago suburb to find work. She wanted to go on for a master's degree in Geology, but I thought it was better for her to find a job and help pay her way. I agreed to start building a swimming pool in the front yard at the farm and it was under construction. Andrew and Tim were planning to help with this.

We took some very heavy large suitcases on our flight to London. On landing, Sarah became sick and vomited into one of the sick sacks provided. Arriving at Heathrow, it took two taxis to hold the three of us with our luggage. One of the taxi drivers asked what was in one piece because it was so heavy; "A dead body?" he asked. We arrived in Greenwich / Blackheath and stayed at a B&B close to the Cutty Sark. We planned to stay here while looking for a flat to rent. Eric and Sarah were very good about adjusting to all our new circumstances in a new culture. But when they had poached eggs every morning and no cold cereal, I had mutiny on my hands. After a week or so they never wanted to see another poached egg looking at them at the breakfast table. I was much more tolerant since I didn't have to cook anything but just show up for breakfast. After a while I began to know how they felt. I went to the Hospital for Mothers & Babies to find out when my courses started. They apologized but had given my place to someone else since they had not received a letter of reply from me with my acceptance. I lost their letter in my move to Salina and forgot to do this. Instead of September, I needed to wait until January. They assured me that I could start then. I was disappointed but they directed me to the Nurses Course at the London School of Hygiene & Tropical Medicine. I called about getting into their next course, and they said yes, it would start in September. I asked if I could pay my tuition in dollars or if I needed pounds. The director said that I could pay in 'chickens or cows or anything that I wanted'. I decided that I liked this kind of school. After I read more of what was offered at this school, I knew this was what I needed if I worked in the tropics, especially Haiti. I was happy that I had the time for this. Now all we needed was to find a flat. I opened a bank account at the Barclays of London Bank in the Greenwich area using a letter of introduction from my bank in Kansas.

Eric thought that the Observatory in Greenwich was pretty neat because he was able to stand in two hemispheres at the same time. He said it made very clear why time zones worked. We also went on board the Cutty Sark and looked around and walked across the Thames River. London through the eyes of a seven and thirteen year old records many interesting things. Our first trip had been two years ago, and the children remembered our trips to Scotland and Wales and to the London Zoo.

We looked around Greenwich for a flat but decided to locate out of London. Other Americans were staying at our B&B in Blackheath and gave us the name of a realtor in the small village of Sevenoaks outside of London, who had helped them find a house to rent. The Americans, Bill and Paula Thetford, had two boys about Eric's age and Sarah and Eric enjoyed playing cards with them. They were from Maryland and were relocating their family. Bill had a business office in London with an American firm. We took the train out to Sevenoaks and a realtor made an appointment with the owner to show us a house that was available for rent in the nearby village of Otford. The owner picked us up at the train station in a red convertible and we all got in and rode a very fast on small winding roads to Otford. Eric thought this was a great way to see our new house. The roads seemed very narrow and crowded to me. There were good schools for both Eric and Sarah in the village. I was about a forty-five minute train ride from Otford to Victoria Station in London where I would get the red double-decker bus to Gower Street and walk to Keppel Street to the London School of Hygiene & Tropical Medicine. It was part of the University of London. I also planned to work at the Hospital for Tropical Diseases on St. Pancras very close by. We all decided this was a very nice house and made the arrangements to rent. We rode back to the realtor's office with the young man and happily settled on the house in Otford. We now had a home but waited a few days before we moved in.

Ray and Dorrian Stafford, our friends in Johannesburg, South Africa gave us the telephone number of their two daughters working in London and asked us to call them. When I called to let them know that we arrived, they invited us to their flat to stay a night and go out for dinner. It was Eric's thirteenth birthday and we decided to go to a Chinese restaurant together and celebrate. We enjoyed meeting Gill, who was a nurse, and Leigh, who was a teacher. They offered to help us move into our new house. We went back to our B&B and soon moved into our new house in Otford. We rented our lovely three-bedroom brick home with attached garage from the young doctor in the red convertible, Mike, who lived in London. It belonged to his parents who had left the country and he was taking care of it for them. The house was on a very lovely quiet wooded street with a circular drive lined with rose bushes, and had a nice large brick patio in the back with a picnic table and large backyard. They left a working, self-propelled mower for Eric to keep the grass mowed. It was just right for us and completely furnished. Gill and Leigh Stafford helped us bring our many pieces of heavy luggage out on the train to our cottage at 28 Greenhill Road in the small village of

Otford. We had a good visit with them and invited them back. We were very happy to get unpacked and settled. We already had friends and a new house. God is good!

I enrolled Eric in the local boy's prep school at St. Michael's for his eighth grade year, and Sarah in a private elementary school called the Greenhill Road School. After paying for their tuition we took the train into London to buy their school uniforms at Marks & Spencer. This was a well-known London department store that sold all the school uniforms for the private schools in the area. The sales people knew exactly what they were doing and were very efficient, appearing to have done this same fitting for thousands of school children for many years. They had everything that we needed. Eric was outfitted with the St. Michael's uniform. His was gray corduroy shorts, matching knee socks with dark gray leather shoes, a long-sleeved light gray shirt, a striped maroon and dark-gray tie, and gray wool blazer. Sarah wore the Greenhill Road School uniform of a brown wool jumper, white shirt and brown leather shoes, tan leotards, and brown wool blazer. I thought they looked very nice, but they both complained about uniforms. I knew that it would take them time to adjust to their different clothes and this new school system. I'm sure that Eric thought it was pretty ridiculous. The uniforms were a good beginning. Books were supplied, so after we bought the clothes they were ready for school.

Upon arriving in Otford one of the first things we did was join the village library find out what was going on in the village. After working in the Kansas State library for three years I always felt very comfortable in libraries. It turned out to be the best thing that we could have done. We got much information on the activities, churches, trains and schools, and I saw a notice about a baby-sitting club for moms to join. I took the number down and noticed that the address was a neighbor on our street. I called her and she invited us to come for a visit. I knew that Sarah got out of school before my classes were finished, and I needed someone to watch her until I got home. The neighbor said that I could join and we took turns caring for each other's children. It helped us to become acquainted with other neighbors on our street and I kept their children.

We visited the Village Anglican Church for two Sundays, and I discovered why the Pilgrims left. I would have been on the first boat. We next went to the Village Methodist Church and enjoyed the singing and preaching. This became our regular place of worship, and Sarah loved her Sunday school class and teacher. We were the only Americans in the village and they gave us a warm welcome. I participated in a Bible study with many friends from the Anglican Church later and learned that they were very committed to studying the Word of God.

We took the train to the near-by village of Swanley to shop for a bicycle for Eric to ride to school each morning. St. Michael's was an Anglican boy's boarding school, but Eric was one of the few day students. Eric picked a black bicycle that he liked and was right for him and we brought it home on the train with us. He was glad to have wheels and rode it to the village and around our neighborhood and learned the way to school.

The first day of school came and I fixed an early breakfast to get them started. Eric came out of the shower saying that he felt dizzy and not well and didn't want to go to school. I felt him and he didn't have a temperature. I knew that he didn't want to wear his uniform with tie and was dreading the first day and I understood his reluctance. But this was something he would have to deal with and might as well face it head-on, so I told him that he was going to school if I had to call an ambulance. I guess he heard the determination in my voice and decided not to fight it. He didn't know how to tie his tie and I didn't either.

Your guilt over the inadequacy of being a mother has no bounds! After dressing in his uniform and eating breakfast we prayed together, and he got on his new black bicycle in full uniform with his tie looped loosely around his neck. When he got home that afternoon he said he found another student and asked him to tie it before school started. He came home the first day excited about the sports offered and met his coach and many friendly boys. The boys were from many countries, and Eric was the only American. Most of the boys were boarders whose parents had left them in St. Michael's to pursue activities in many different countries around the world.

I walked with Sarah to her school and she felt very dressed up and loved her new school clothes. Little girls can feel so happy in a new dress and shoes. I think that she felt very comfortable looking like everyone else. We met her teacher and found that most of the children there had been reading since they were four years old. Sarah had a good kindergarten in Kansas but needed to catch up. I knew that she was a quick learner and was not concerned about this. She was very excited about going and came home the first day with news of a nice teacher and many new friends. I attended a parent's meeting one evening at a local pub and wore a favorite red cotton sweater, ready to take on my responsibility of a new parent in the village. I found out that red was too bright and flashy for my conservative English neighbors. Education seemed to be the most important and serious business for parents. Everyone thought that Eric and Sarah were my only children.

The first week after the children started to school, I had an attack of severe weakness and fatigue and aching joints. One morning I was barely able to raise my head out of bed. I knew that I was worn out from our move, but I had never felt this way before. England has a National Health Service, and I knew that they also took private patients. I decided to visit the local village physician and he determined that I might have a bout of malaria after finding that I worked two summers in Port-au-Prince, Haiti. He commented on my good suntan and suggested Chloroquine. I quickly regained my strength and attributed my fatigue to the hectic and physically challenging summer that I had just gone through. It was only now that I gave myself permission to notice the effects on my body. After both of the children were settled in their schools my classes started at the London School of Hygiene & Tropical Medicine. If I was going to have any problems with malaria this was the best place in the world to be.

Eric rode off to school on his bike each morning, and I walked Sarah to school. Then I caught the train across the street from her school and rode to London in time for my first class. I think the whole male population from Otford commuted. I caught the bus across the street from Victoria Station and rode it past St. Paul's Cathedral; I got off at Gower Street and walked to Keppel Street where the University of London was located. From day one, I liked my classes and enjoyed my professors. The program was very practically oriented toward medical work on the field--basic health, sanitation, and medicine needed to survive. The teaching doctors and professors had worked in many parts of the world with experience in all tropical diseases. The other students were international health workers, nurses and missionaries who were doing the same thing that I planned to do. I was the only American in the class and often suffered the negative effects of American Foreign Policy. I browsed the huge Dalton and Walden Book Shops in London, which was such a treat and purchased three books for my courses: *Medicine in the Tropics* by Woodruff; *Tropical Medicine for Nurses* by Adams & Maegraith; and *Medical Laboratory Manual for Tropical Countries* by

Cheesebrough. They looked very interesting and I was eager to learn all that I could.

My daily trips to London gave me an opportunity to explore much of the city that I never could have as a short time visitor. I felt very fortunate to have this opportunity to study tropical medicine at the oldest and most famous school in the world. The Ross Institute was also located in the School of Hygiene & Tropical Medicine and provided useful and inexpensive publications on every subject concerning health in the Third World. I knew I could take all the resources that I could carry with me for my work to the mission field. This was a new adventure in my life.

Part of my coursework was sessions in Parasitology and Practical Medical Laboratory Techniques. We fine-tuned our microscopic techniques to identify malaria, other parasites, and many diseases. I was intrigued with this aspect into a deeper understanding of microbiology and looked forward to each week of my laboratory sessions. The professors were top-notch. They encouraged questions. I was learning about diseases that I had only read about and wondered about all my life that were not included in my nursing textbooks.

I knew the Lord led me to this course in Tropical Medicine, and the philosophy of disease prevention was parallel to my own. Basic health and sanitation are most cost effective and economical in the Third World where I planned to work. There will always be millions more needing healthcare than the available resources to provide it. The medical approach is curative and not preventive and so much more expensive, available to only those who can pay. I was excited about common sense health and disease prevention that was the basis of my Tropical Medicine Course. I knew that it was something that I could sink my teeth into, and I wanted to learn all I could to be the most effective with limited resources on the mission field wherever I worked. The sheer numbers of people in the developing world without healthcare is what had brought me to nursing. And it was most useful to not only my work, but for the health of myself and my family. I often mentioned a Ben Franklin quote, "An ounce of prevention is worth a pound of cure," to my children and really believed it. Now I was learning how to practice this in medicine and disease prevention. I looked forward to my classes each day and devoured my textbooks since this was all so new to me.

My courses required that I complete my clinical work on the wards at the Hospital for Tropical Diseases or in the outpatient clinic at Hospital at St. Pancras. It was a short walk from the University of London. I chose the outpatient clinic so I could schedule my hours during the day when the children were in school. People from all over the world came here to be diagnosed with every tropical disease known. I worked with one of my professors and did histories and exams before he saw the patients. I learned to ask the most important questions of all such as "Where have you come from?" "Where have you traveled in the last year?" and "How long were you there?" We learned the worldwide geographical distribution of leprosy, filariasis, leishmaniases, schistosomiasis, trypanosomiases, cholera, smallpox, dengue fever, yaws, typhus, and the five different strains of malaria. But dysentery, fungal infections, hookworm infections, and nutritional diseases were the most common everywhere in the Developing World.

I learned how to take an accurate medical history for tropical diseases and had the opportunity to help diagnose leprosy in a woman patient. I was intrigued with the simple ways of diagnosis preliminary to microscopic laboratory examination of the nasal mucous membranes. When noticing pale patches of skin on people in a village, especially children, have them run around the village to develop a sweat and if the pale patches don't sweat, prick them with a pin for pain and nerve sensation. If there is no pain and no sweat then it most likely is leprosy. Leprosy, or Hansen's infection, is the slowest growing bacteria of all the tropical diseases and attacks the nerves. Leprosy is not spread easily and it is not readily acquired, especially by adults.

Malaria transmitted by the bite of the anopheles mosquito, has evaded all attempts of science to develop immunizations. The disease still kills millions each year in the Third World. It comes in five different varieties around the world identified by microscopic examination of the blood taken by a finger prick. In 1984 we learned how to do thick and thin films for malaria identification. A preliminary definition of the species can be seen with the examination of stained thick blood films, and the species confirmed by examination of thin blood films. Plasmodium Falciparum, Plasmodium Vivax, Plasmodium Ovale and Plasmodium Malariae, all take on different shapes under the microscope. But they can all manifest symptoms of fever, chills or rigors, headache, muscle pains, cough, abdominal pain, and vomiting. Common signs are sweating, shaking, anemia, jaundice, tender liver, splenomegaly, herpes labialis, abdominal rigidity, stupor, coma and anuria.

The common measures of prevention still include wire mesh across windows, air-conditioning, mosquito netting around beds, insecticide aerosol spray, insect repellent, long sleeved shirts and long trousers and staying indoors at night. New drugs have been developed for prophylaxis and prevention. I have used all of these modes of prevention and some drugs in the last twenty-two years of work and living in the tropics and have avoided getting malaria in Haiti, Africa, the former Soviet Union on the Black Sea and South America. While taking the antimalarial drugs of Paludrine and Chloroquine, my youngest daughter Sarah had a light case of malaria while we lived in Zaire in

1990, which I treated with Chloroquine. A *Wall Street Journal* in July, 2001 announced a donation by Bill Gates, the computer soft-ware billionaire, of forty million dollars to the London School of Hygiene & Tropical Medicine to be used for research and development of an immunization for malaria. Having been there, I think this money will be put to good use. That would be a tremendous for the sake of millions who die each year.

There is a general lack of knowledge about the immunity that people can develop. There is some immunity and acquired resistance to infection for those people who have always lived in endemic areas. An attack of malaria promotes some degree of resistance to further infection with the same strain of the infecting parasite and repeated frequent infections enhance the degree of resistance. But the 'immunity' so acquired is not absolute. Re-infection is not entirely prevented, but the clinical attack from subsequent infection is usually considerably modified. Therefore survivors in highly endemic areas are able to resist the serious infection so long as the 'immunity' persists. So the species of the malaria and the state of "immunity" determines the clinical picture of the disease in the patient.

I subscribed to the *London Times* so I could keep up with the British news and what was going on in America. It was delivered every morning, and I enjoyed reading it on the train as I traveled from Otford to London, but most of my neighbors took the *London Guardian*. Arriving early for a cup of tea in the cafeteria before my classes started, I had a chance to skim other London newspapers. I had many interesting and stimulating conversations with other doctors and nurses around the world on the politics of healthcare in the developing world. I decided to study nursing so I would not have to deal with politics; I found that healthcare was the most volatile political subject that I could engage in.

Later, I also learned how dangerous it was for me personally.

With the children in school I decided to look for a used Austin-mini car for us to drive from a dealer in Swanley where we had purchased Eric's bicycle. I rode the train to Swanley by myself and shopped. I found what I wanted at a price I thought that I could pay. I had driven Volkswagens, but had never seen such a small car as this. The Mini was the most common and inexpensive car that I saw on the motorway. It was two-tone in color with metallic green on the bottom and burnt orange top, reminding me of a pumpkin.

After I signed the contract, wrote my check, and had my car, I realized the only way to get it home was to drive it home! I was scared to death of the motorways and the traffic around London; I didn't even know if I could find my way back to Otford. Never having driven on the left side of the road, I was equally frightened of the very busy M-16 motorway. I asked for directions and with much fear climbed behind the wheel on the wrong side of my car and drove slowly on the wrong side of the road feeling very uncomfortable and vulnerable. It was just a short distance on the motorway to Otford, but I felt that I was risking an accident every time a car passed me or I came to a round-about at an intersection. I often went two or three times around in order to decide when to get off. Staying focused to remain on the left side of the motorway was demanding. I was drenched with sweat by the time I made it to Otford and so glad the children were not with me. I parked in the front drive of our house and went in and collapsed on the living room couch. I had time to recover before the children arrived home and drove the car to pick Sarah up from school. Eric and Sarah were delighted and loved to ride in it.

Although we had just had a month of riding trains and buses and walking around the village, we were all ready for wheels again. After I finally got used to the driving and did not feel that I was an accident waiting to happen, it was fun to drive. When I called my auto insurance in the States that we had used for many years after being in the military, I was amazed at how simple I could have my car insured over the telephone and drive it that day, with my policy in the mail. That gave me a lot more confidence knowing that I was insured. The British drivers followed very close on my tail and the roads were one narrow lane with a line down the center and shrubs enclosing the sides of the road.

Andrew wrote from Manhattan that his best friend, who was sharing a room at the farm with him, was killed in an auto accident while he was driving with his father back to Manhattan from Virginia over a weekend. He was devastated. It was hard for us to believe. Artie was just eighteen years old and had traveled to New Zealand to stay and travel with Andrew just the year before. We were all very sad for his family. I regretted not being there to help out at this time. Andrew forwarded to me my Kansas Registered Nursing License and my passing score for the Kansas State Board Nursing Exams. I was very excited to have passed and have my license in my hand. I submitted a copy to the General Nursing Council of England and Wales to practice nursing in England, Scotland & Wales.

Chip received his orders for England and he and Elizabeth arrived in October. We met them in London at Victoria Station on their arrival and brought them to Otford. They were so happy to be in England and excited about getting settled close to their airbase near Ipswich. They just stayed a few days with us. Elizabeth and I went to a theatre production of "Fiddler on the Roof." It was playing at a theatre across from Victoria Station where I had purchased tickets on my way to the School of Tropical Medicine, with the original leading actor who played Tovia. Chip stayed with Eric and Sarah at our house. We enjoyed taking the train to London and got back very late.

I let Chip drive my newly purchased Mini to the airbase to use in locating housing until they could find a car. They would be back when they had found a place to live. They came back in a couple of weeks and had ordered a brand new light-blue Mini of their own to drive. They rented a three-hundred-year-old thatched-roof house in the country near the small village of Parham and moved in. It was called Mill Cottage. Chip was a close drive to work. We looked forward to driving there to visit them when the children were out of school, and we were able to get together many times during the year.

Eric was having a great time with soccer games, cricket games, track meets and rugby matches. He was so good at rugby that he later played on a Kansas State University team in Manhattan, Kansas. He didn't arrive home in the evening until around 7:00 pm. They had afternoon tea at St. Michaels's with a couple of hours off and then sports. He talked about some good friends that he made and looked forward to going to school.

Sarah had made friends with another girl in her first-grade class on our street named Caroline, and they played at each other's homes. I was glad that she had found a good friend. We enjoyed the church service each week at the Village Methodist Church and got acquainted with our neighbors. They were very friendly. We still took the train into London to shop and eat at Pizza Hut near Piccadilly Circus. We missed our pizza night at home each week, and I hadn't found all the right ingredients yet. We also found a Pizza Hut in the village of Bromley just a short train ride from Otford. I kept my driving to the villages around Otford. On one of our tube rides in London, Sarah left a small package and everyone thought it was a bomb. There was a bomb explosion later at one of the tube stations that year.

Sevenoaks was an interesting village nearby, and we enjoyed visiting the outside markets there. I drove either there or to Swanley for food shopping at a large supermarket, but I ordered my meat from the butcher in Otford. There was also a Green Grocer truck that came on our street that sold fresh fruit and vegetables twice each week. The man would open up the back of his truck and it was stocked with produce displayed in pretty open bins. Our milk was also delivered in small glass bottles on our back door step. With just the three of us we could handle that, but I remembered the five-gallon containers that we used to buy for the children at the Pink Palace. We could also call the butcher and have our meat delivered to our back door. Otford was a very small village with churches, a library, a shoe repair shop, butcher shop, bakery and tea shop where you could buy sandwiches. We stopped often at the bakery, and Sarah and Eric loved the fresh jelly donuts the best. It had a duck pond in the center of the main street at the roundabout. When we went to Sevenoaks we often bought fish and chips which we all loved. Sarah particularly liked the After-Eight chocolate-covered thin dinner-mints for a treat.

Our neighbors were very kind and friendly. When I was able to locate all the ingredients, we introduced the Martins to our homemade pizza which they enjoyed. Our back yard was large, but Eric had no problem keeping it mowed. With all the rain it grew fast. He kept the rose bushes trimmed and then had to cut up the branches to fit in the trash can. He enjoyed working outside and there wasn't very much to do compared with our farm in Kansas. The neighbors also worked in their backyards and we enjoyed visiting and getting to know them over the fences on each side. Malcolm Quail raised bees and often gave us honey.

Sarah really loved this. We had not encountered the stinging nettle plants before and that was a real shocker when I tried to walk around barefooted. Sarah also had unpleasant encounters with the stinging nettles. The large magpies were our most frequent and numerous visitors. They sounded so silly but looked very pretty with their bright red heads. Their large bodies were about the size of our black crows in Kansas and their noise about the same.

Since Eric usually left for school first on his bike, I drove Sarah to her school and then parked my Mini at the train station and took the train into London each day. When I arrived home I picked up Sarah from the neighbor's house, and we met Eric at home. I usually cooked a late dinner and we ate about 8:00 p.m. Eric enjoyed riding his bike to school but the roads were winding and so narrow and the large Lorries came dangerously close. There were no ditches and he had to stop at the side of the road and try to get off as far as he could. It would get dark at 4 pm in the winter and there were no streetlights, only the tiny light on his bike. Riding home at 8 p.m. seemed like midnight to him. He recounted many interesting adventures during the year with so many turns in the road on his bike rides.

With study time in the afternoons, Eric didn't have homework at night since he finished it at school. We had a library in the house of a variety of books and Eric was an avid reader. He had a wonderful selection and read many books that would never have been available in an American home. He picked up an interest in history and later at Arizona State University when he needed to declare his major, history is what he liked most. We had a piano in the upstairs hallway and Sarah enjoyed trying to play. We also had a radio in the upstairs hallway that gave us Radio Moscow each morning with its different slant on the world news. We listened to the news when the Korean jetliner was shot down and the Americans were portrayed as the scum of the earth.

Sarah had a tape recorder and started a collection of the tapes and books called the Storyteller. She got a new tape and picture book each week with stories that I ordered from the Newsagent in the Village. She loved these and listened to them many times each day. I had them practically memorized. A couple of her favorites were *Stone Soup* and *The Frog of Toad Hall* were some of her favorites. She looked forward to going each Friday to pick up her new tape and book. I think it helped her with her reading and understanding the different words used and British accent. Sarah had a loft bedroom but often came downstairs and slept in a twin bed in Eric's room. She said that the toilet upstairs did not always flush right. I had a nice large bedroom with French doors out to a brick patio. With no television again, we played a lot of card games like Uno and listened to the radio in the evenings and read. We had also brought Scrabble and some board games from home. There was no movie theatre in the village so we occasionally went to a movie in Sevenoaks. It had a small theatre that allowed smoking. The smoking was kind of unnerving and seemed so dangerous.

I remember one night in particular when we went for Chinese food and a movie. The Tran family from Saigon who had stayed with us in Manhattan had cooked our family great Chinese food and whetted our appetites. The Chinese restaurant was very nice and we enjoyed the food. Eric and Sarah laughed and laughed in the movie and we all had a great time. I enjoyed watching them laugh more than the movie. There was a group of mentally handicapped children behind us who didn't seem to understand much. Their teacher seemed relieved that Sarah and Eric were laughing so much and making enough noise to cover the noise her students made.

Chip and Elizabeth drove down from Parham in their new blue Mini for Thanksgiving, and we invited our American friends the Thetfords, whom we had met at the B&B in Greenwich. We became good friends with the Thetfords during this year and visited with them often. Going through the same cultural adjustment, we had a lot in common. We enjoyed England, but often laughed at the lack of creativity in their way of doing things. The Thetford's boys and Eric always enjoyed playing together. Bill and Paula wanted to do what was best for their kids as I did. We cooked a turkey and made pumpkin pies and celebrated our forefather's good judgement. We felt a lot closer to the Pilgrims and their decision to leave England and seek religious freedom. Chip got off the American holidays, but since Thanksgiving wasn't an English holiday, Eric and Sarah were in school. It was a fun time together, and Chip brought their new Golden Retriever puppy, Rex. Eric and Sarah had a great time playing with him. It was so good to be with family, but we missed those at home.

My classes and courses went very quickly, and I enjoyed the camaraderie of my colleagues. We were a motley group ready to take on the challenges of the Third World. We had a woman officer from the famed Scotland Yard Bureau to visit us in one of our classes at night to give us training in self-defense. We learned how to repel dangerous attacks of all human and animal sorts. I remember one specifically that I couldn't imagine needing to put into practice and prayed desperately that I would never need to. If confronted with and surrounded by men wielding sharp knives in the jungle, we were to get into a crouching position with our backs to a tree and protect our vital organs with our arms and hope that they gave up or yell for help. This was the most extreme of all the instructions, but it was all very good common sense and helpful. We took turns coming up behind each other and putting a stranglehold on each other's neck and escaping. Since we were all women it wasn't all that realistic, but we got the idea. I came home on the tube from London after dark alone and mentally just dared anyone to bother me. I learned new skills that I planned to put to work. Fortunately I never had to use my expertise and was very grateful. I felt that prayers were just as important, and I would continue to trust in the Lord and remember all the good advice that I had been given.

I signed up to run the London Marathon in the spring, so I continued to run many miles each week. I found a couple of neighbors on Greenhill Road who ran and we ran around the Otford roads and fields together. Richard and Pamela were a very friendly couple and encouraged me. I had a blue running suit and could be seen running from Otford to Seavenoaks and other villages trying to get sixteen miles of practice in. I was forty-eight years old and knew that I needed to do it now or never. I was in the best running condition that I had ever been in my life and I was excited to face the challenge of the marathon. I knew many of the London streets very well by now, since I was commuting each day to school, and I looked forward to running them with other runners from all over the world.

Christmas break came and London looked so beautiful with all the decorations. I purchased a very large, bright purple and pink, fuzzy stuffed elephant on my way to classes. I saw it in the window of the Woolworth's across from Victoria Station. I bought it for Sarah and got it in a large plastic bag. Taking it to school with me it filled the seat next to me when I sat in the lecture hall and listened to the morning's lecture on Anaemias & Mal-absorption in the Tropics. Some of my friends just looked at it and laughed; it appeared so jolly and incongruous in the lecture hall. The purple and pink elephant looked very bright and cheery with its small beady glass eyes staring straight ahead at the lecturer for the day. I don't think elephants ever have any problems with anaemias or mal-absorption, but it wouldn't hurt for him to listen. I carried it home that night on the train and hid it under my bed. I felt so happy to find this unusual Christmas present for Sarah. She also got a pretty new china tea set for Christmas and more Storyteller tapes.

We enjoyed all the Christmas carols and festivities at the church. The pastor asked Eric if he would read the Christmas Story from the book of Luke at the Christmas Service, but we told them that we would be out of town with our children near Ipswich. I thought it was very complimentary for him to ask Eric, and I knew that Eric would have done a good job. These very dear people in the church had become very close to us. They accepted us wholeheartedly and greeted us each Sunday morning with affection. We learned that the Otford Methodist Church never missed a Sunday Service all through World War II even with German Bombers flying over, but they did at times get under the pews when the air raid warning sirens sounded. What faith and commitment to God! I had not brought any Christmas decorations, but we bought a few things and decorated the house. I mailed Christmas presents to all the children in the States and some Christmas cards to my family. Chip and Elizabeth invited us to spend the holidays with them and we were very excited to drive there and see their new house. After Eric and Sarah finished their classes we drove to Parham and our Mini gave us no problems in the two-hour drive with no ice or snow on the roads, as we were accustomed to in Kansas.

We had a wonderful Christmas with Chip and Elizabeth. Eric and Sarah helped prepare a live goose for the Christmas dinner. We met many of their friends at the airbase and their neighbors. We saw their village and the airbase where Chip flew and attended their church. It was a different part of England, rural with lovely fields and green paddocks. We also drove to Norwich with them on the North Sea and visited the fishing villages and had fish and chips. Their house was just like those depicted in children's storybooks with a thatched roof and a loft where we slept.

They had a coal fire in their fireplace each morning that Chip started first thing upon rising. Elizabeth had a very nice kitchen with low ceilings and very modern considering the age of their house. The rooms were small but cozy. It was a very fun and relaxing time for us all. The visit was a nice change from commuting to London by rail and bus every day and studying Tropical Medicine and identifying parasites under the microscope. We were so grateful to have them there and they were enjoying the Air Force. God abundantly blessed us all. I sure missed all the other children and we called to wish them Merry Christmas.

Eric and Sarah returned to their schools and I studied for my final exam in Tropical Medicine. It went well in both Lecture and Laboratory and I passed and received my certificates. I felt that I had learned a great deal in a field that was totally foreign to me, and I was eager to put this knowledge to work. I celebrated with two young girls from the course with dinner at an Italian restaurant in London. Midwifery took second place now and I was in no hurry to start. I wanted to adapt to the hospital scene here and even take a job until I chose to start a course. I had inquired at other hospitals closer to Otford about their midwifery programs and found that I had a large selection to choose from. It was just a decision to make around when I wanted to start. There were other courses at the London School of Hygiene & Tropical Medicine that I wanted to attend now that I had gotten my feet wet and knew the school. A doctor's course in Tropical Medicine was offered that I could audit and learn more about courses of treatment. A course in "Refugee Camp Health Care" was offered, so I signed up to start immediately. But I didn't get in. The instructor from the World Health Organization told me that Americans were the reason refugee camps were necessary, and they didn't understand why an American would want to be in this course. I knew I could not have kept quiet while we were blamed for all the refugee camps in the world, so it is a good thing that I didn't get in. I felt that was discrimination and would have to choose something else.

I chose Pediatric Priorities at the Institute of Child Health in the University of London. It was at the Tropical Child Health Unit on Guilford Street, very close to the Tropical Medicine School. Since forty percent of a population in a developing country may be children, I knew that this was a large part of a nursing job. I attended and learned that most deaths in the developing world are children under the age of five years old. In some rural areas, one-half of all children born die during the first five years of life. The facts were shocking! Preventive health care for children was the most important.

"Nutritional diseases and infectious diseases were the two main problems. And doctors and nurses with relevant pediatric training can organize a service which will prevent more than one-half of the deaths in infancy and early childhood without awaiting any great changes in environment. The large numbers of young children and the small funds available for child health services is a most daunting challenge. A challenge to design and evolve services making the best use of the small budget available is worthy of the most intelligent."

This course stressed the logical rational that the best way to improve a nation's health in the long term is through the care of young children and women of child-bearing age. In this way you can earn the cooperation and respect of the local people. Success in reducing child mortality will depend upon nurses willing to disseminate skills and knowledge and to teach local health workers and the village worker. The practical training that I received in this course was invaluable for nursing in developing countries.

I wanted to attend a course called "Organising Primary Health Care in Developing Countries," but it would have to wait for a later date. In the summer of 1989 before we left for Zaire, Africa I was able to return to London and finish this course. While trying to decide between midwifery school and a job in a London hospital, I received a letter from Etienne Prophete asking me to work in Port-au-Prince, Haiti with their mission. After much prayer I made the decision to leave London and work in Port-au-Prince, Haiti when the children finished school. I knew that I could keep preparing forever, but now was the time to get started.

I enjoyed having more time at home and became involved in a women's home Bible study with women from the Anglican Church in different villages. We met for tea in different homes and studied the Bible. I made many new friends as we studied together in our homes and I shared my plans for work in Haiti. They were all very encouraging and supportive. I had missed this camaraderie with local women raising their families while I was studying Tropical Medicine.

Eric played many rugby matches and was very excited and good at this new sport. He always watched his older brothers play football and loved it, but rugby was a different matter. Sarah and I attended many of his rugby matches at St. Michael's School. It was fun to watch him run the ball frequently and score even if we didn't know the rules. We just knew that he was always in the action, whether running or on the ground. We got so excited. But the English don't show such excitement on the sidelines and the most exciting encouragement they gave was "well done." Sarah and I looked like maniacs as we cheered. Chip and Elizabeth came for one of his games and cheered with us. One game with a team from Seavenoaks ended in a very high score, and I think Eric got tired of scoring. But the cricket games were not very exciting and Sarah, and I declined to go after the first one. They lasted so long and with so little action. They even stopped for afternoon tea. But the boys all looked very nice dressed in their white shirts and trousers standing on the green with their wickets. We just could not maintain our interest. We invited Eric's coach for dinner at our house and he was a very nice young man who took a lot of interest in Eric. He appreciated Eric's enthusiasm and good sportsmanship.

Some of our neighbors on Greenhill Road who attended our church invited us for dinner. They had two children and were very nice and friendly. Others invited us for tea and we felt well accepted in the village. I started a Bible study on Tuesday evenings in our home and the pastor from the Village Methodist Church came and other friends. We talked about and prayed for the need for evangelism in England. He said that about one percent of the population attended church services in 1984.

Our landlord, Mike dropped by to see how we were getting along. He said that his mother would be pleased with the house. We loved the house and he was grateful for us as renters. We felt at home in the house as soon as we moved in. It was furnished with everything that we needed and we enjoyed the neighborhood.

On January 28th, 1984, Chip and Elizabeth arrived from Parham, knocking at our door as a surprise for my forty-ninth birthday. We were so surprised and happy to see them! They spent the weekend with us and we had many good times together. Chip was doing well in his flight school learning to fly the A-10 aircraft called the Warthog, an ugly twin engine aircraft that carried rotor cannons and cluster bombs at low-level flying during the war. They were enjoying their new home and making many good friends. We walked a short distance to an old mill on the road to the next village called "The Oat House" that had been converted to a restaurant. They took us out for dinner, and I had a wonderful birthday celebration. It was a beautiful evening and we enjoyed them being with us that weekend.

After receiving my certificate in Tropical Medicine I felt that I could relax a while and just enjoy staying home. It was good not to have such a hectic schedule. I was running more and ran six miles in fifty-six minutes, which was probably my best. I found out that I was not selected in the computer elimination for the London Marathon and this was a disappointment. Americans were only given so many slots and the ones travelling from America got priority. But a Paris Marathon was coming up that I could run at night under the lights in Paris. I was thinking about this. Eric, Sarah and I drove to the coast earlier and took the very speedy Hovercraft to France on a weekend and stayed outside Paris at a small hotel in the countryside. I would have to think about this too. If I couldn't run in the London Marathon, Paris would be better. The two-hour drive to the coast, ferry ride and drive on into Paris to find a hotel to stay might be exhausting. Could I then run a marathon and find a place for the kids to stay? And what kind of shape would I be in when I finished. I knew the answer to that one — absolutely dead! There were obvious obstacles in making my decision to run. Later a ten-mile run in Tunbridge Wells came up and I decided to run it. Paris seemed to have too many obstacles just to get there, and I couldn't leave the children without supervision. Running was fun and I enjoyed it but I had greater priorities right now. I continued running with my neighbors Richard and Pamela Pitcairn-Knowles. They were such nice people and I was glad that I had gotten to know them.

I read one of my favorite Psalms in the Bible and decided that it would influence the direction for my life. It was Psalm 62:5—

> "For God alone my soul waits in silence,
>     He only is my rock and my salvation.
> On God rests my deliverance and my honor;
>     My mighty rock, my refuge is God."

Sarah started swimming lessons at an indoor pool in Swanley, and I took turns with other mothers driving the children from the school to the pool each week. We had received invitations from other friends in the village and invited them for dinner in our home. I started pruning the rose bushes in front of the house along the drive. As I was pruning the rose bushes, I realized God seems to prune our lives to give opportunity for the fresh new green shoots to bring glorious and lovely new roses in the coming spring. Flowers were blooming everywhere reminding me of God's beauty and grace.

I called Kenny's mother and talked with her in Manhattan. She enjoyed visits from Andrew and Tim, and she was moving into a new apartment in her building. Phillip and Pam sent us a tape with all their news. Phillip sang and played some country western songs that he wrote on his guitar. We sure loved their tape and Eric and Sarah loved to listen to his songs. England didn't have any country music and we had missed it on the radio. We were always glad to hear a touch of home.

By this time I said no to midwifery and I was looking forward to working in Haiti. Tropical Medicine was my specialty as a nurse and I was sure to need it there as a community health nurse. Decisions are hard to make, but I was happy with this one and knew God's guidance in order to make it.

We met a family at church who were from the Netherlands and who had two small children. Mickolein and Yip and Otelien and Daan. We enjoyed visiting with them at church and they lived near Greenhill Road. In March Chip and Elizabeth came for a visit and we invited Yip and Mickolein and family for dinner. Chip and Elizabeth got to attend one of Eric's rugby matches with us.

Knowing that God was leading us to Haiti, I was not ignorant of the risks, hardships and difficulties. I just felt better prepared now with all my courses on working in the Developing World. Our two mission trips earlier showed me the hardships and now I hoped to be able to make a difference through nursing and teaching. I just needed to take things as they came and trust in the Lord to provide.

In England "Mothering Sunday" was in April and Eric and Sarah gave me a beautiful chocolate egg and a box of chocolates. They were so pleased with themselves. Chip and Elizabeth called to wish me a "Happy Mother's Day," and I call the children in the States. It was a lovely Sunday.

Chip called and said that they were coming on the following weekend. We always looked forward to their coming and had such fun together. We had dinner with Bill and Paula Thetford and Bill's mother who was visiting. I called my sister Dorothy on her birthday and we had a good visit. She hoped to come for a visit in August. Amber called to say that they were to Houston, Texas and Pat starting Chiropractic School there. This was a big decision for them. They were very excited.

A journal entry in April: "So we are going to Haiti with courage and a real desire to help, but most of all, depending upon the Holy Spirit and resting completely upon God's strength for our resources, adaptation, culture adjustment, language and service. We have been trusting in and depending upon God here, but it has only been a small lesson compared to the type of dependence that will be required in Haiti. It will take all our courage and trust in God to make it work for us."

Our passports needed to be renewed, and we took the train to London and went to the American Embassy in Grosvenor Square. It did not take long and it was necessary before we went to Haiti. I began thinking about what it takes to adapt to a new culture.

From my journal entry: "I can see that it is hard to live in a new culture and use wisdom for what you accept and what you reject. It would be so easy to stand apart and condemn that which is different from what you know without trying to understand and weigh its value. Or to accept everything new in order to please others, even that which is not right for you. The middle way of respecting others behavior and ideas without condemning: weighing and deciding the value of new ideas and customs and how they can enrich your lives and your understanding of people and God is the most difficult but the means by which God can bring us to maturity. We can maintain our own cultural identity and still enjoy the wisdom and benefits of a different culture, maintaining our own choices and integrity."

Easter came and we had a lovely church service. The message was wonderful. My journal entry: "Thank you Lord for Easter and the message of the resurrection. That is all we've got – and that is more than enough to save people from sin and eternal death. Every day must be Easter in our hearts as we experience the power of the Living and Resurrected Christ."

We met a young couple who lived in a cottage in the country and were working on finishing their house. Tony and Ann Shelly were a very nice couple who had lived and worked in the tropics of South America. Eric and Sarah enjoyed going to their house in the country to play. Ann and I had Bible studies together each week. Later we fixed a birthday dinner for her and celebrated. She brought flowers by the house the next morning. The Matthews family, who lived across Greenhill Road were in our church and we enjoyed visits with them. They often came to our Tuesday night Bible studies at our house. Behind their house was a tall hill that Sarah and I enjoyed hiking. I had missed being out in the open and it was so nice to be out in the country again.

Eric's friend Coki Manella at St. Michaels who was from Spain, came to spend a few days with us. Eric was looking forward to his visit for a long time. The boys had a great time together and talked about all the things they liked to do. Eric made many good friends, but I think that Coki was his best. Coki gave me a beautiful Spanish fan to use.

The children were off from school for a few days and we decided to take the train to the Isle of Wight in May. It was a good trip and the water was a little chilly. We stayed at a nice B&B and just played on the beach. Elizabeth's parents came to England for a visit. On one of their trips up from the coast, they stopped by our house for a visit. We enjoyed their stay and they liked our village of Otford.

In June, we started clearing our house and moved out on June 30th to a B&B in Sevenoaks until Sarah and Eric finished school the first week in July. Eric did an excellent job on getting the rose bushes trimmed and the yard cut and trimmed. Sarah came home the afternoon before her last day of school very excited. She said that her teacher, Mrs. Williams, said they did not have to wear their uniforms on the last day, but could wear anything that they wanted. She chose to wear jeans and the next morning she arrived at school and saw that everyone else wore their regular school uniforms. At first she was very upset, but she got to clean the floors of the school since she had jeans on. She thought it was a great job and came home happy from her first grade year.

We drove to Chip and Elizabeth's to keep their house and Rex their dog while they went on a trip. While we were there we met their neighbors and found a nice big picnic table to buy for their backyard. Eric and I tied it upside down on the roof of the Mini and drove very carefully down the road to get it to Mill Cottage. Chip and Elizabeth were so surprised when they arrived home and used it all the time and even brought it back to the States with them. We drove to the coast and the children loved taking care of Rex and throwing sticks in the water for him to retrieve. After we celebrated Sarah's seventh birthday on August 6th together, we left for the States. I left my Mini with Chip to sell for me. Chip drove us to Heathrow, and we said a tearful good-by as we knew it might be a long time before we saw them again. We appreciated our family time in England so much. We were on our way to see the rest of the family at the farm before we went on to Port-au-Prince. Later Eric summed up his time in Otford. "I am sure that the year there in England and all the historical sites and figures piqued my interest in history. It made my major a fairly easy choice later when I decided to just choose something." It had been a very fast but good year for us all, with many new friends and new opportunities. We had another adventure on the horizon.

# Chapter 15: Kindred Spirits

**OUR TRIP FROM LONDON TO KANSAS** went well and we were happy to get back to the farm for a couple of weeks before we left for Haiti. Eric and Sarah enjoyed seeing everyone and swimming in our new pool. It was a very large, vinyl-lined pool about forty-four feet long and twenty-four feet wide, with a nice diving board at the deep end and cool decking around the sides. The pool was at the end of the right side of our front yard. It looked very nice, and Andrew and Tim helped in the construction and were enjoying it while we were in England. We relaxed and enjoyed our two weeks, then packed up what we needed for our move to Haiti.

While in Otford we had met a couple from the Netherlands in our church and became good friends. They had worked abroad in many countries with non-governmental organizations. They were also making a move, and Mickolein and the children wanted to come for a visit and help out at the farm while we were in Haiti. I thought that to have her taking care of the place and Jip join them later was a great idea. Mickolein, Otelien, and Daan arrived, and we met them at Kansas City Airport. They brought their large wolfhound dog with them and the children's bicycles. We got them settled in and showed them around the farm. Andrew and Tim were planning on moving into Manhattan.

We flew to Miami and on to Port-au-Prince where Etienne and Betty Prophete met us. This was our third trip here, and I thought, again, that I was prepared for meeting the desperate situation of the poor. But it was always such a shock, worse than I had remembered. Professionally prepared now, I knew that there were things that could be done. I felt there was hope for improvement in the health of the children. While we stayed at the Prophete's house, we tried to find a house to rent. Etienne took us around to many places and the schools where the children were enrolled. But we realized that renting a house was not wise and settled on an apartment at a guesthouse with garden and pool within walking distance to the mission and clinic. There was also a nice restaurant and lounge and television room. We came with the bare necessities, so Eric and Sarah enjoyed the pool and television. With the children enrolled in the Haitian-American School, I started my work with the Haitian Christian Mission. The children were picked up each morning at our guesthouse by a van that picked up the children of Americans working at the American Embassy. The van brought the children back in the late afternoons. So I went off to the health clinic at our Mission Church when the children left for school.

Each morning the roosters crowing all over the city woke me up very early around 5:00 a.m. Our small apartment had a trail of ants in the kitchen that I never managed to get rid of. I brought a few of my pots and pans with me from the farm, just enough to cook essentials. We ate beans and rice and a lot of fruit and vegetables.

First I met with the Director of the Health Department in Port-au-Prince and presented my RN License in order to work with the Haitian doctor now working at the clinic. I started an immunization program for the five hundred school children in the Haitian Christian Mission. There were so many starving and malnourished children that I was very concerned when I gave immunizations. I prayed that none died from these and we didn't lose any. The children at the orphanage where I worked before in Port-au-Prince, were in better physical condition that many of these children.

We also offered a feeding program where seventy to eighty of the sickest children came into the clinic to eat a bowl of gruel mixed from powdered milk, mashed grain and oil. These children were so lethargic and starving that a few couldn't even hold up their heads. Many of the mothers came to feed them. It was very pathetic to see the large sad eyes of the children as they sat at the tables eating bowls of gruel with their hands. We knew this was the only meal the children received each day. It was definitely a rescue operation for many of these children died. But we were so glad that we could give them that much. We also added peanuts for more protein. In time some became more alert and active and could join the others at school. The work required much faith and a tremendous amount of energy to keep a positive attitude to only see the little amount of improvement each day, knowing that it was saving the lives of these children. There were just so many in need.

One of the government doctors who worked up in the mountains asked me to work with her on one occasion. We rode out a long distance from Port-au-Prince in a truck, and I was advised to take some food with me. I took a peanut butter sandwich and coke for a break during our day of immunizations. We found our location that looked very deserted in the mountains, with no houses or Haitians around. We set up our table under a shade tree and got out our vaccines, given to us by the Health Department that we kept in coolers. I was in charge of the table to keep the needles and supplies going along with the immunizations. We had two health workers to assist in the immunizations. I thought very few people would come since I saw no one to begin with. But we arrived early and a few Haitians came trickling in from the mountains. They formed lines and soon we were vaccinating hundreds. It was not going to be as easy as I thought. We worked for a few hours and stopped for a break. Mothers with babies stood all around us. As I got out my peanut butter sandwich and coke, they moved closer with the babies and children staring at my food. I realized that I could never eat this food and broke it into as many pieces as possible for the babies and children. I took one sip of coke and passed the bottle around. Feeling very depressed at how little I had to give, we went back to work for the afternoon. The table was piled high with used needles and I tried to bring some order to our work place. That was a very bad decision. In handling the used and dirty needles, I pricked my finger and gave up trying to create any order. We finished the day and drove back to Port-au-Prince having immunized over five hundred Haitians. I never guessed that many people were living there in the hills.

As I rode along with the doctor, I told her that I had pricked my finger with a used needle and asked her what I could do. She said that there was nothing to do about it now. I did have bad dreams about the risks that I took and prayed that God would protect me from any disease. This was the end of 1984, and AIDS came on the scene the next year. Haiti was in the news when the international press mistakenly accused Haiti of being the crucible of the disease. Just working here was a huge risk in itself, so I got used to the dangerous situations that I found myself in. I concentrated on keeping Eric and Sarah well.

Amber and Pat were living in Houston, Texas where Pat was in chiropractic school. They were expecting their first baby in December, so we planned to go to Houston and spend Christmas with them. This was our first grandchild, and we were excited about going. I thought that after four months of this physically and emotionally draining work, I needed a vacation.

I started taking a language course in Creole at the Haitian-American Institute in Port-au-Prince after I finished work at the clinic. This made for a very long day, and I didn't get home until after dark a couple of nights each week. The children swam in the pool after school, and I usually fixed dinner after I got home. It stayed around 96 degrees Fahrenheit all the time we were there. School was going all right for them and they usually did their homework as soon as they arrived home in the afternoons.

Etienne and Betty Prophete, directors of the Haitian Christian Mission, invited us to their house often and encouraged us in our work. Their two young boys were close to Sarah's age. They also had two older children, Yves and Madaline who were college age. We had stayed at their house for a few days while we were here in 1981. I talked with them about all the problems for the Haitians to survive. They told me that the poor people living around the church had to buy water for fourteen cents a bucket, and it was from contaminated wells. This was just awful, and I couldn't see how their health could ever improve with contaminated water. I asked Etienne if it was possible to dig new wells for water. He said that the World Bank allotted money for that. I remembered that my neighbor on Greenhill Road in Otford, England was an engineer for the World Bank and had told me to write him if there was any way that he could help. I did write him a letter asking for assistance in drilling new wells, but never heard directly from him whether he received my letter.

Haiti's population was six million, and there was a 53 percent literacy rate. Only 40 percent of the school children actually attended classes. There were 1.5 million Haitians residing abroad in places like Miami, New York City, Boston, and Montreal. They sent more than $300 million a year back to help their families who remained in the country, which went directly to the people. Without this family aid many Haitians would starve.

We all became very sick with diarrhea and vomiting. I was most concerned for Sarah because she lost weight since we had been in England. But we made it through and recovered. We were taking Chloroquine anti-malaria pills for Falciparum malaria, the type that was here and the most dangerous. I was very careful with my handbag, but my passport, billfold and driver's license were stolen without even knowing it when I was at the market.

Right before Thanksgiving, Sarah came down with chicken pox. It was so very hot and she was really miserable and missed school. I found baking soda to put in her bath and she just sat in it. One nice cool morning when Sarah was home sick and sleeping in, I reflected on our time in Port-au-Prince. I realized how God was with us in all the things that happened since we arrived. Not all was pleasant, but He protected and kept us in His care. We were very grateful. Chicken pox was very familiar and seemed like such a blessing when the diseases and problems that the Haitian children had were so devastating. Sarah got lots of rest and missed a week of school.

The Prophetes invited us to their home for Thanksgiving dinner and made us feel very much at home. We had an abundance of food in a country that was so poor. While we were at their house, Etienne reminded me that an army Major lived next door and to talk quietly and say nothing about the government. It was still a terribly repressive regime under "Baby Doc" and everyone lived in fear. The Secret Police took people away in the middle of the night and they were heard from again. They just disappeared. Before we arrived I cautioned the children if they ever hear what sounded like popcorn popping on the street that it was probably gunfire and to get down immediately. We were very fortunate never to hear the sound of gunfire on the street while we were there.

We took time on the weekends to visit some of the areas around Port-au-Prince. On Sarah's first day out after chicken pox, we all went and enjoyed the Yellow Bird Boat Trip. It was a beautiful, warm, sunny day with smooth water and a cool breeze. We cruised around the beautiful

purple coral on our own private boat. Eric and Sarah got out
in the warm water and found nine starfish. Eric said this
was the best time and had discovered what he liked to do
best in Haiti. We also visited the Haitian Art Museum.
What vivid and bright colors! We saw a different view of
Haitian life here.

News from the farm came that Mickolein and
children were leaving. They were going to join Jip in Africa.
She wanted to stay longer but with winter coming she
needed to make a decision. I think she didn't know what
harsh winters we have in Kansas, and I am sure this was
best for their family. If Jip couldn't join her and help out
with the work there, it was too much for her. So Grace was
coming to the farm to stay until we got home. I wanted to
rent out the farmhouse so that we could come back to Haiti
after Christmas, but there are no renters and it looked like
that was not possible. Our stay here was short and we
planned to leave on December the 18th. The children would
have time to finish all their exams. Amber was due to have
the baby on December 8th, so we would miss the birth.

While sitting by the pool on a Saturday afternoon I
received a telephone call. There was no telephone in our
apartment, but the owner brought out a mobile telephone
for me. Chip and Elizabeth were on the phone calling from
England with wonderful news! They were having a baby in
May! Another grandchild! Our family was continuing to
grow. We were very happy for them. I hoped that they
would be able to visit the farm the next year. We also had
news from Andrew in Spain where he had been studying
for a semester at the University of Seville and was travelling
in Portugal.

I enjoyed my Creole classes and started learning
quite a few phrases. It seemed like it was a combination of
French and Spanish and English. The French I knew, but I
had never studied Spanish. When I went to my class it was

very common for me to be the only white person on the streets where there were hundreds of Haitians milling about. I became used to being a very small minority in this country, but I always felt too glaringly white. Late one night as I was walking home from class, a Haitian lady with a basket of fruit on her head was singing a song. It sounded familiar, and I knew the English words. She passed by me, and I started singing in English and she just smiled at me. It was an old spiritual called, "Nobody Knows the Trouble I've Seen, Nobody Knows but Jesus." It was late, and I was very tired and she really picked up my spirits. Her life was so difficult, and she could sing too. The Lord was her strength living in this very poor country. And that is why I had come; I came because He was my strength also. We had a lot in common. We were kindred spirits.

No matter how late at night it was, the streets were still packed with people. I asked Etienne when they all went to sleep. His answer was one I'll not forget. He said that most poor houses just don't have enough space for so many people or beds and they take turns sleeping. Those who didn't have houses slept in the streets. And the streets always seemed to be full. It was impossible to estimate the number of beggars on the downtown streets and around the Iron Market. Certain areas of Port-au-Prince also had garbage stacked as high as a two-story building. The stench and rat population that these produced were beyond my comprehension.

The mornings in December turned refreshingly cool at 70 degrees, but the temps warmed up during the day. That felt good after hot temperatures in the 90s. An excerpt from my journal: "What these people here need more than anything else is not drugs and medicine, but adequate food and a means to grow food or buy it for their families."

Reflecting on my work here now that there was just a short time left, I wished that I could have done more to help. Whatever I did never seemed like enough. No matter how many you feed, there are hundreds more who need food. It was an endless job to try and find food for so many people. Not only that, but the food was not a permanent solution. They needed the land and resources for growing their own. I did not see how conditions were going to improve with the present repressive government. Any assistance with agriculture and farm projects would give the most help for preventing further starvation.

On December 4th, we received a call from Amber saying that I had a new granddaughter. They were both well and happy. I felt very blessed with our first grandchild. I was sorry that I couldn't be there, but the Lord had done a wonderful job without me. We were very excited to be on our way to Texas and see our new granddaughter, Alexandra Kelly Theobald.

We met quite a few people coming and going from the guesthouse in Haiti. I had tea with a woman who was an American lawyer from New York City, visiting and working with the United Nations. She said that she was to determine whether aid was needed for the country since she hadn't seen people starving on the streets. She wanted to know what I was doing here and what I thought. I guess that she only visited the wealthiest parts of the city, and I told her about the people in the villages and in our clinics. She had only been here for two days, but I couldn't imagine how she could ask the question and have missed the poverty. But missionaries see the bottom end of the life scale where they work, and they learn that the obvious is not always obvious to others.   Another American family moved into the guesthouse with children the ages of Eric and Sarah. One of them worked at the American Consulate. We became friends and helped each other when our water went off. Life in Haiti is adjust, adapt, or die. Before we left they gave us a going away party in their apartment.

While writing in my journal one morning, Sarah walked by and asked "if I was writing about life." Now as I read my journal for this book, I have found that is exactly what I was doing and can now put it all down. She was a very wise little seven-year-old girl.

Eric took his last French and Algebra exams and did well. He went out to a party with high school friends and told them all goodbye. Eric was looking forward to leaving and being back in Manhattan. His school picture taken here at the beginning of school did not look the happiest. He didn't complain, but I knew endurance was more on his face than enjoyment of his life here.

Just a few days before we were to depart Haiti, the Director of the Health Department and a nurse that I met there when I first arrived who inspected our Mission Clinic, came to my door about midnight. We were all asleep and they knocked on the door waking me up. I got up to open it and asked them what they wanted. They wanted to come in and ask me questions. I recognized them, but I would not let them in since the children were asleep. They stood at the door, and asked me if I liked the Haitian people. And why had I come? They seemed angry at me, and I couldn't think of what I had done. I didn't know what their purpose was in interrogating me at midnight, but I didn't get much sleep that night after they left. Eric, awakened from a sound sleep and curious, went into the bathroom by the front door, stood on the toilet and looked down on them through the screened window while we were having our conversation. He wanted to know what was going on. I really didn't know myself and decided to contact Etienne Prophete the next day and find out.

The next day we went to Etienne Prophete and let him know about our midnight visit from the Health Department. He said that the government feared any foreigners and that they were trying to intimidate me and it might get worse. He said that the children and I should leave immediately. So we finished our packing quickly and Etienne took us to the airport. We left sooner than we planned and knew for sure that it wasn't safe for us to come back. I was glad when we checked our boxes and bags through and were not detained by the police. I tried not to be too fearful in front of the children, but I wanted to get out of Haiti as fast as possible. I did not feel safe even in the departure lounge while we waited for our flight, but kept looking over my shoulder for the police to come. I was so relieved and happy when our plane took off, and we were on our way to Miami. I had no way of knowing that Haiti's revolution was coming soon and all foreigners made them very nervous. I never found out if they considered me a friend or foe, but I knew that I didn't want the children involved. They may have received a copy of my letter with my signature from the World Bank at the Health Department, stating the problems of contaminated wells by our church and asking for new wells to be drilled. If so, then they considered me a trouble-maker and wanted to get rid of me. I was glad to go.

On our descent into the Miami area and landing at Miami Airport I could see the orderly rows of houses and thought how nice it was to have straight streets and nice roads. We arrived in Miami, and I literally felt like kissing the ground when we disembarked from the plane. The customs official's smiling, "Welcome to Miami" had a wonderful significance to me. We caught our flight to Houston and began adjusting to life back in a free country again. Freedom always got higher on my priority scale on each return.

Amber and Pat met us at the Houston Airport, and I immediately grabbed my first eight-day-old grandchild out of my daughter's arms without thinking. Since our standards of cleanliness had suffered these past months, I had planned to go to the restroom and wash my hands and clean up a little before I took the newborn Alexandra for inspection. But my emotions of gratitude and thanksgiving took over my professional caution, and I held her in my arms while thinking, "So this is a grandchild and what it is like to be a grandmother." I had not had a lot of time in Haiti to prepare for my grandparent role, so I just took it as it came. Sarah was an aunt at seven years and loved holding Alexandra. Eric thought it was great to be a teenage uncle.

Back at Amber and Pat's new apartment, we relished in such luxuries as nice paved streets, sidewalks, carpet on the floors, drinking water from the tap, wonderful bathrooms with a bathtub and nice toilet paper, a refrigerator, cleanliness everywhere, space and an abundance of food. We missed a few things in the last months we were in Haiti. It was a wonderful time of enjoying the new baby and preparation for Christmas. Grace drove from Kansas to spend Christmas with us and take us back to the farm after New Year's. Eric and Sarah forgot all about carpet on the floors and loved to sit on the floor and play. We all had a wonderful Christmas and New Year's together in Houston. Andrew and Tim drove to Mississippi to spend Christmas with Phillip and Pam stationed there with the Air Force. Eric, Sarah and I were very grateful to be back together with our family again.

# Chapter 16: Of Pigs, Pizza, and Hope

WE ARRIVED BACK IN MANHATTAN, KANSAS, the first week of January 1985, and the landscape was such a vivid contrast to our tropical vegetation in Port-au-Prince. Sarah said all the trees had died on our drive to the farm. She missed autumn in Kansas for the last two years and had forgotten that the leaves returned in the spring. The temperature was ten degrees below zero with snow on the ground. I knew there was a period of adjustment for us ahead as I remembered this cold Kansas winter weather. There was sufficient wood cut and stacked on our patio for our wood stove in the kitchen/family room, and we kept it filled and blazing all the time. We often gathered around our wood stove and enjoyed the heat. We were all so grateful to be safely back at the farm that there were no complaints about the work. But fortunately there were only a couple of horses to care for.

The first week back the children and I were invited to a 4-H meeting with refreshments in a neighbor's home. We went to see everyone again and could not believe the abundance of food on the table. We had forgotten the bounty of America and abundance of everyone during our time in working with the poor in Port-au-Prince, and I found tears in my eyes. It was such a drastic change. The starving children at our clinic in Haiti were still on my mind. Kansas seemed a world away from the hungry streets of Port-au-Prince. I thought how wonderful it was to live in peace and prosperity without worrying about the Secret Police, midnight interrogations, or a repressive government. Freedom became very precious to me, and I was reminded not to take it for granted. I knew that we were in real danger in Haiti.

The children went back to Manhattan Public School, and Eric started thinking about football. He missed two seasons and wanted to play on the Manhattan High School team next fall as a sophomore. Eric picked out a used blue Chevy pick-up truck that we bought for him to drive to school after he got his driver's license. He was happy to have his own wheels. Sarah quickly made a good friend in second grade that is still her best girlfriend.

We sponsored a newborn baby girl, Barbara, who was found on a trash heap and taken to an orphanage in Port-au-Prince while we were there. Her picture was on the refrigerator and we provided for her care through a child-sponsorship program through the Haitian Christian Mission. We knew that if even one child could be rescued, our time there was well spent. Eric and Sarah helped pick out gifts for holidays and birthdays that we sent Barbara. Over the next many years she sent us pictures and wrote us many letters.

After returning from Port-au-Prince I knew that I still wanted to be involved with the Haitian Christian Mission to help with projects, even though I couldn't live there. There were 1.7 million indigenous Creole pigs that had been destroyed in Haiti a few years previous because of the swine flu epidemic with no compensation for the peasants. A whole breed of livestock was eradicated and they needed more breeding stock to restart their pig breeding programs in the country. Before I left Port-au-Prince, Etienne Prophete asked me if I could help with that. I talked to some of my neighbors who raised pigs and the one pig farm closest to our farm. Every day that I drove by the Pig Farm I thought how wonderful it would be to get some of these to our mission at Fonds Parisien, Haiti.

After discussing my plans with the owners they were very positive about donating pigs for the project and discussing the merits of a breed that would have the best chance of surviving in the Haitian climate. Fond Parisien was the location of a farm outside of Port-au-Prince where the pig shelters for the Haitian Christian Mission were built and waiting. I started making arrangements for the pigs to be selected, vaccinated and shipped to Port-au-Prince. I located the Suarez Shipping Services in Miami, Florida who took care of the necessary papers and details of having them trucked to Miami for shipping and then sent by boat to Port-au-Prince, Haiti. The Kansas State University School of Veterinary Medicine donated the vaccine and people to help with the project. In May, forty-five young fifty-pound gilts, a Yorkshire-Chester white cross breed, and five Duroc Jersey or Hampshire boars, were sent from the Gary Alee Farm In Manhattan, Kansas to the Eglise Chretienne Des Rachetes DHaiti in Port-au-Prince. They were selected by our neighbors for their hardiness to survive the trip and establish themselves for a breeding project in Haiti.

When all the pigs were tagged and vaccinated at the Pig Farm, they were picked up by the trucking firm and taken to the loading docks in Miami, Florida. Andrew was interested in the project and helped to load them. They were put in disposable double deck containers on the ship. They weighed 1,200 pounds and were insured for $7,000 by Lloyds of London against loss. Our church, the Zeandale Community Church, paid for all the shipping costs, which totaled $2,291. All the farmers in our church were enthusiastic about this project. The pigs made it to Miami and all survived the boat trip to Port-au-Prince.

The pigs stayed in quarantine for six weeks at the shipping docks in Port-au-Prince, and Etienne Prophete hired guards to protect them from being stolen. They were a very expensive commodity in a poor country that had none or very few. After quarantine they were taken out to the newly built concrete pens and shelters at Fonds Parisien, the Haitian Christian Mission farm, where they were cared for. Everyone involved in the project was very happy to have the pigs arrive safely and waited for the first pigs to be bred. Many prayers were offered on behalf of the continuing safety of the pigs knowing that this would provide an income for families and their starving children.

Sarah decided to be baptized at our Easter Sunrise Service at the Zeandale Community Church when she was eight years old. Dr. Harry Baird was our friend and pastor. She was in my Sunday school class and asked many questions about the Bible. I was very happy for her. She helped out at the farm with all the work. When we opened the pool in April she enjoyed catching the frogs and toads in the pool skimmers and getting them out. They usually left the pond and hopped across the driveway to the swimming pool and Sarah took them back to the pond. We often sat out on the screened in porch at night after dinner and listened to the locusts, screech owls and whip-o-wills and watch the moon reflecting on the shining pond. We were enjoying the summer night sounds as I had when I was her age. We loved watching the summer thunderstorms on the screened in porch or on the upstairs deck where we could see the rain coming in sheets across the valley. The Tran Family was happy to have us back in Manhattan. Eric and Sarah loved the Chinese food that Tony Tran often brought out to us, especially the wontons.

In the summer first thing in the morning when she got out of bed, Sarah put on her swimming suit and cowboy boots and went to the barn to feed her animals, then took off her boots and went swimming. She wore that every day most of the summer. When girlfriends came to camp out they always had bonfires and cooked hot dogs and roasted marshmallows. If they stayed in the house they often played hide-and-seek and Sarah hid in the laundry chute. That was her favorite place. Dorothy's grandchildren, John and McCord Cox, came out most every weekend to spend the night or camp with her. Adrienne my niece was working on her doctorate in education at Kansas State University. Sarah loved having them to play with and hike in the hills. They thought it was great to get out in the country too and play around the pond. They liked catching frogs and all kinds of insects. It took them a long time to agree on what things to take on the camp outs. A neighbor, Lori Michaels, was Sarah's good friend and Sarah would often walk to Lori's house through the woods on our forty acres with her dogs Jesse and Babe. Lori and Sarah were in 4-H Club together and played together after school. Sarah loved the farm and especially the barn where she kept and fed her animals and played. She also liked hiking to the apple orchard nearby for unlimited apples to eat.

Jesse was Sarah's constant companion outside and I never worried when Jesse was with her. Jesse was a very large, coal black, with a broad-chest, Labrador/St. Bernard/German Shepherd mix puppy of six weeks when we got her. Her sister that was a golden yellow, Tasmania, was Grace's dog; that dog had cancer and had to be put to sleep. Jesse was Andrew's dog until he left home. She was definitely a hunter and brought every kind of dead animal that crossed our property up to our front yard to show us her trophy. Even a deer. Neighbors, friends, strangers, Kansas Power and Light meter readers, everyone would ask us if it were safe to get out of their car if she was napping peacefully in the front yard not paying any attention to them. She loved the sunshine and always took her naps in the front yard near the drive.

All of us knew of Jesse's feats of bravery. I discovered and had her kill a snake behind our freezer on the screened in porch and carry it out. She cautiously and quietly nosed behind the freezer where I saw it, bit and snapped the snake in her mouth. She slowly backed out of the screened door while I held it open with the snake hanging limply from both sides of her mouth. The whole process took about one minute. I was amazed at her professional and rapid snake-killing ability. She was not afraid of anything and Sarah knew that she was safe with her. We saw mountain lions on our forty acres and Jesse ran them out. Later Jesse lived in California with Andrew in her retirement, and swam after deer in the American River in Sacramento. She amazed many people trying to catch them at the ripe old age of twelve years old. She had an undaunted spirit when it came to hunting. She was loved by us all.

My sister Dorothy and I drove to visit some of Mom's sisters in Chetopa, Kansas. On our way home, I started discussing the possibility of opening up the farm as a Bed and Breakfast for guests. We stayed in many of these throughout England and Scotland on our trips there. I knew that we had extra bedrooms and a lovely place in the country with a pool that guests could enjoy. Eric, Sarah, and I did not fill up a six or eight bedroom farmhouse. Eric had his bedroom downstairs and there were three empty bedrooms upstairs with two baths.

I prepared a brochure and asked an artist do a charcoal sketch of our home, barn, pond, pool and the hills around our house. It turned out lovely, and I organized brochures printed with this sketch on the front and "Long's Country Inn" as our name. A short description inside the brochure described our farm and location. We were listed in the Country Inns & Homes Guidebook for the U.S. in 1986, 1987, and 1988. Eric made a beautiful red wood sign for our Country Inn as his project for the 4-H fair, and helped with all the mowing and maintenance of the farm. His sign looked professional with white lettering hanging at the entrance of the drive and he kept everything mowed and looking very neat. Maintenance and cleaning of the pool itself was a big job. I refurbished the three upstairs bedrooms that we planned to use for guests. We distributed our brochures around the Manhattan area and soon had calls for reservations.

In May of 1985 Morgan Elizabeth Long, our second beautiful granddaughter, was born to Chip and Elizabeth and arrived in Ipswich, England. Chip invited me to come and I flew with Sarah to London at the end of May to meet Morgan. Jean Sadler, Elizabeth's mother, arrived and stayed with them the first week and Chip drove Jean to Heathrow Airport and picked up Sarah and I for our visit. It was fun to be back in England and meet our second granddaughter. Morgan slept most of the time, but we enjoyed holding her. Sarah missed a few days of school in order to make the trip. She was in a group of girls that sang and did a dance for their talent night at her school. The moms made all the girls matching hot pink and white stripped circular skirts for their dance. Sarah loved being in this group, but missed her last dance so she could go to England with me.

Yves Prophete, Etienne and Betty Prophete's son from Port-au-Prince, arrived in the summer and stayed with us at the farm. He planned to attend Manhattan Christian College and live with us. He worked with Eric and helped in the maintenance and we helped him with his English. We met him in Port-au-Prince and he was much older than Eric was, but they became friends. Yves bought a car and eventually moved into a dorm room at Manhattan Christian College where he graduated. This was his first car and he was really excited. Chip and Elizabeth were able to come for a visit from England that summer when Morgan was just a few months old. Everyone came back to the farm for a few days and we had a family reunion with lots of pictures. There were two grandchildren, Alex and Morgan, and one on the way with Phillip and Pam. Chip planted a small birch tree by the pond for Morgan. It was good to all be together again since 1981 at Phillip and Pam's wedding.

We entertained guests at our B&B and spent the summer and fall with many family members visiting.

Eric had a good football season his sophomore year and we enjoyed going to his games. His father and brothers had all played at Manhattan High School. The engine of his blue Chevrolet truck went out, so he received a new engine for Christmas. Sarah asked for a horse for Christmas, and I bought her a new colt, a brown and white paint from Clarence and Ruth Dobson, our neighbors. They delivered it with a red and white checked ribbon tied around his neck. When Sarah got home from school and saw him, she was really excited about getting her first horse. She made plans for feeding, caring, and training him to ride. She named her new six-month old colt Money, and he was very frisky.

Amber and Pat and their daughter, Alex, came to spend Christmas of 1985 with us. Many of the children were home and it was a wonderful Christmas together. Tim and Andrew, and Grace and Amber and Pat and family were with us for the holidays. Phillip Jacob, our first grandson, was born in November of 1985 to Phillip and Pam, but I hadn't seen him yet, so Phillip and Pam invited me to their home near Oscoda, Michigan for New Years. Amber and Pat were able to stay with Eric and Sarah while I traveled. I flew into Saginaw, and Pam and Jacob picked me up at the airport in their four-wheel drive. We drove their jeep through very deep snow to Oscoda. They lived in the woods and the snow covering all the trees was just beautiful. This was my first trip to Michigan at probably the coldest time of the year.

Phillip spent New Year's Eve on Wurtsmith Air Force Base on alert status near Oscoda, but we picked him up on New Year's Day. Phillip and Pam loved their home and Jacob was a healthy and handsome little boy, so alert and eating all the time. The snow was piled high in

Michigan, and Phillip had a wood stove to heat their house and kept logs cut and stacked outside. Pam spent much of her time feeding the baby, the fire and large watchdog Prince, while Phillip stayed on base on alert status, frequently flying KC-135 Tankers with the 920th Air Refueling Squadron with the Strategic Air Command. Later in June while flying during the Pacific Tanker Force exercise, he coordinated air traffic control for emergency recovery and landing for a crippled Phantom jet that had developed a massive fuel leak. He also managed the fuel systems for both aircraft, which was critical to keep the Phantom from flaming out. He was decorated with the Air Medal for his part in helping the NC Phantom jet fighter stay in the air until it could safely land in Hawaii.

In 1986 Andrew bought a mobile home to live in Manhattan with a friend and dated Shawnae Cox from Manhattan. They were both attending Kansas State University. Tim decided to leave Kansas State after finishing one year and moved to Seattle, Washington to work with Domino's Pizza, later managing a store in Oregon. Shawnae frequently came out to the farm with Andrew and then later started coming out to study the Bible and asking many questions. She soon made the decision to accept Christ and was baptized at our church. We were very happy for her. Yves Prophete also studied the Bible with us at the kitchen table.

I taught a class at our church and decided to work with teenagers as a youth group leader. We took special orders from members of our congregation and made pizzas in the kitchen in the basement of the church on Friday nights after school. There were two large ovens for baking. I bought the fresh pizza ingredients; mushrooms, green pepper, onion, black olives, sausage, hamburger, pepperoni and mozzarella cheese, and mixed the dough for the crusts. The teenagers met at the church after school to make the pizzas. We had lots of two liter bottles of coke and 7Up to drink, and their music blared while they grated cheese and sliced onions, green pepper, olives, pepperoni and sausage. I gave them lessons on the procedure, slapping out the dough to fit the large round pizza pans; putting on the tomato sauce, Italian seasonings, hamburger, sausage, pepperoni, onions, mushrooms, green peppers, olives; and grating the cheese to put on the top. When finished the pizzas were a work of art.

With six to eight teenagers working in the kitchen and two ovens going, we put out a lot of pizzas. Some of the members of the congregation picked up their pizza and the boys delivered pizzas to other members. Then the teenagers all made pizzas for themselves and cooked and ate all they wanted with plenty of coke to finish their night. They enjoyed their pizza party with much horsing around. Sarah joined us for these Friday nights with a friend of hers and they had a great time. We were very excited when we made eighty dollars our first night. With the sale of our pizzas over the next two or three months, the Zeandale Youth Group made enough money to finance their trip to an amusement park, Silver Dollar City in Texas. The teenagers all worked hard and earned their vacation. A young couple from the church took them and served as their sponsors.

Sarah invited a friend out and they went to the barn to play. Jesse went with them and found a badger in the barnyard right before the girls came upon it. Jesse lunged and started fighting with it. We thought it was a stray cat at first with its fluffy tail and made her leave it alone. Then when Sarah and her friend got close to it they found it was a very fierce badger that tried to attack them. Jesse jumped in and fought it and the girls came screaming back to the house that they had found a badger. I had never seen one before but Jesse had. That is the only one I ever saw at the farm. But it never should have come on Jesse's turf.

I was contacted in January of 1986 about our church donating grain to an organization, Brother to Brother International. This organization was shipping loads of grain to Port-au-Prince, Haiti. When the revolution came in February the grain was needed even more. The revolution destroyed much of the economy of this country and the poor were in even worse condition than when we lived there, which I could hardly believe. There were many starving people. We talked about this project in youth group and the teenagers were enthusiastic about wanting to help.

The farmers in the church donated wheat and the teenagers from the youth group met together to fill the 384 one-hundred-pound bags to be shipped by Food for the Poor for relief purposes to Port-au-Prince. We met together as a group in September at a farm to clean and fill the bags of wheat, and the wheat was stored until arrangements were made for a truck to pick them up. A shipping truck arrived in Manhattan, Kansas on October 3, 1986, from Miami and picked up the bagged wheat weighing 40,000 pounds. It was shipped through the Mercandian Exporter Vessel from Miami, Florida to Port-au-Prince, Haiti. Food For The Poor Inc. of Pompano Beach, Florida took care of all the shipping charges and the wheat was valued at $3000. As the motivation for their work, Food For The Poor Inc. quotes Matthew 25:40 in the Bible where Christ says, "As often as you did it for one of my least brothers you did it for me." The people of Haiti were still very much in our prayers.

My fifty-first birthday came and Andrew brought me a beautiful bouquet of fifty-one red roses from all the children for my birthday party. Eric and Sarah woke early and fixed me a pot a tea in bed and they all fixed a wonderful dinner. Kenny trained them all well and I was grateful. Along with my birthday was the sudden shocking news on television of the Challenger Space Shuttle plummeting in an explosion and flames to the ground. Many civilians, the first to go, as well as the astronauts died on the space shuttle that day when our American pioneers risked their lives for others. I will never forget that day as our country mourned for all their families. The Nation was horrified, stunned, and humbled at the loss of life. We were not yet in control of the universe, but still hindered by human error. We were all in shock. But yet that is one of the reasons that America remains the strongest free country in the world. Our freedom is priceless. It will always cost the lives of many.

Phillip stored his ultra-light airplane in the pole barn on our forty acres and we received calls for people to look at it. Now in the Air Force and flying, he eventually sold it. I started a basic computer class at Kansas State and learned along with other freshman students. When I went into the computer lab to practice for my final exam, I went over and over the practice exam on the computer three or four times. To my amazement the actual Lotus 123 Final Exam came up on the computer! I was embarrassed and didn't know how to get rid of it. I complained to the students sitting on either side of me who responded immediately and almost broke my hand hitting the "print" mode on my computer. Needless to say, I now had the reputation as the finest hacker in the class. I guess the instructor thought if anyone was dumb enough to do the practice exam three for four times, they deserved having it.

When the Haitian government was overthrown in a revolution in Port-au-Prince in February, Etienne Prophete called to say that the orphanage and medical clinic had been destroyed. The country was in chaos. The Haitian director who ran the orphanage turned out to be a Ton Ton

Macoute and the people all tried to kill him. It was such a tragedy that the children at the orphanage all had to leave. But there was good news, too. There were twenty-six newborn pigs and more newborns expected every day at the farm in Fonds Parisien from the shipment that we sent last October.

Sarah got her first bucket calf in April of 1986, a sweet-looking, soft, black and white, one-week-old registered Holstein from the dairy farm of a family in the church. She got calf settled in the barn with straw, water, food and hay and did a great job. She now had her own calf. Sarah at eight years had taken on a big job and named her calf Lucy. She planned to show Lucy at the 4-H Riley County Fair in August. She loved her baby calf and took very good care of her, mixing the milk supplement in a bucket and pulling it in a wagon to the barn and feeding her. She put her hand into the warm milk in the bucket and then into the calf's mouth and let her suck her hand. She kept doing this until the new calf got the idea and put her head into the bucket and drank the milk. This was the exciting part of her day each morning and evening. She played with her calf whenever she wasn't in school. Jesse was her best friend and followed her and her calf everywhere they went. Sarah had grown up with this dog, and often taken her naps in the front yard lying on a blanket with her head on Jesse.

There was a tree by my bedroom window and a red cardinal saw its reflection and kept trying to fly into it. The woods came up behind the house within just a few feet of my window. There were no drapes at the windows, and I often woke up in the morning hearing the thump as the bird hit the window, but it never gave up. One morning, I looked out a bedroom window and noticed a large tawny-colored cat sitting in the grass by the end of the house near the woods. I had never seen such a large feral cat and thought it was beautiful. By the time I realized there was something strange about its bobbed tail, the bobcat turned and took off into the woods. We always had coyotes come up close to the house and when the dogs played with them, they seemed more brazen. We heard them every night howling and yipping back and forth together. The howls and yips of their young always sounded like there were more than there actually were.

Grace started a job managing with Domino's Pizza and was transferred to Seattle, Washington where she managed a store and then was an area supervisor in Oregon. She met and married Dan Brentano from Kansas City at our church in Zeandale the next year. The whole family, except Chip and Elizabeth who were still in England, were able to be there. Sarah picked out a new lavender lace dress from Sears for the wedding that she loved to wear and helped at the wedding. Amber was the matron of honor. Grace looked lovely in her dress and was a very beautiful bride and they went back to live in Oregon. Phillip walked her down the aisle.

My brother Richard and his wife Carol, with their daughter Michelle, moved to Rossville, Kansas near Manhattan, and we drove to visit them frequently since it was just an hour from our house. Sarah and Michelle were the youngest of all our parents' twenty-five grandchildren, and enjoyed getting together. They bought a pretty farmhouse with five acres in the country and were busy planting fruit trees and blueberry bushes and a garden.

Eric became very active in the Campus Life organization at the high school and ran for class president for the next year. He enjoyed the politics of running and was elected President. He hosted parties at the farm, and he also played on the Manhattan High School football team. It was a busy year for him.

I ran a 10K race in fifty-seven minutes in March, the best time that I had in a long time. I began running more and started thinking of a return trip to Haiti without the children now that the revolution was over. Etienne Prophete called to say that they needed me in Fonds Parisien in Haiti at the medical clinic. They would give me anything I needed to come back and work with the Haitian Christian Mission. But I knew that I could not take Eric and Sarah back there to live. It was still too dangerous.

In the spring I decided to replace our old 1948 tractor with a new one. I visited the Ford tractor dealership and bought a brand new 1986 blue and white Ford tractor. It was fun to pick out. They delivered it to the farm and I was soon in business after I got the mower hooked up. I enjoyed mowing the front field and the forty acres. It went fast, and I was especially glad to have the roll bar. We had so many potholes on the forty acres and I often got in trouble. Eric loved using it to mow and grade the gravel road.

Pam and Jacob came for a short visit with us at the farm and we really enjoyed having them. Jacob was our first grandson and had brown eyes and blond hair. I started making plans for a trip to Haiti to do some projects at Fonds Parisien and Pam said that they could come and stay with Eric and Sarah while I was in Haiti. I talked to many churches in the Manhattan area about a sewing project with the many villages in the country around Fonds Parisien. Churches donated money and supplies for the project. Chip called to invite us to Morgan's first birthday party at the London Zoo on May 24th. He asked if Sarah and I could come.

School came to a close and we hosted a class of twenty children at the farm from Ogden. They enjoyed all the farm animals and the picnic, especially the mothers. These children were culturally deprived in many ways and learned a lot through petting the animals. Their smiles and enjoyment made the day. Etienne Prophete called to say that it was safe in Port-au-Prince. Chip called to say that they would meet us in one week at the London Zoo for the birthday party and then take us to Mill Cottage. Sarah and I planned to fly into Heathrow and catch the Tube to the London Zoo.

Sarah and I flew to London just a few days before her school was finished in May and took the Tube to the London Zoo, arriving just in time for the Morgan's first birthday party. This was our third trip to London and we knew our way around very well. Sarah had spent her fourth birthday with her Grandmother and Eric and I at the London Zoo in 1981. We met Chip and Elizabeth and Morgan at the zoo and their many friends who had come for the birthday party. Morgan had grown to a walking toddler, and it was a fun time for us all. We visited and enjoyed our time with them at Mill Cottage that week and it was good to see them after a year. We only stayed a week and would have loved to stay longer, but I had a ticket for Port-au-Prince the next week.

## Fond Parisien, Haiti

Pam and Jacob came to spend time with Eric and Sarah while I was in Port-au-Prince. Amber and Alex and Kelsey surprised us and came to the farm. Eric and Sarah had lots of company. Amber drove me to the airport in Kansas City with all my boxes of supplies. After we left the farm, Chip called from England to say that he was watching television and saw riots and shooting in Port-au-Prince and wanted to tell me to cancel my trip, but I was already on my way and would not find out that he called until I got back. Grace's husband wanted to go with me and met me at the Miami Airport. We arrived in Port-au-Prince amidst much violence and chaos. I couldn't believe that this was the way it was when Etienne had called before telling me it was safe! Etienne picked us up at the airport and there were mobs of people burning tires, throwing rocks at our car and destroying buildings. Etienne said that he had wanted to call and tell me not to come but it had been too late. I could only remember how we fled this country just a year ago, and here I was again in a very dangerous situation, but fortunately without the children.

After we arrived safely at his house, Etienne advised us to stay there for two days and not go out of the house for any reason or let people know that we were there. It was a chaotic and frightening time for everyone. During this time Etienne showed us videos of the revolution that had taken place in February when the President, Baby Doc Duvalier, had to flee the country and many people were killed. It was horrible watching these videos where people were chopped up with machetes. The Haitians on the streets were taking out their revenge on the Ton Ton Macoutes who were the Secret Police, and had held the Haitian people in terror for thirty years killing thousands. It was not a pretty sight, and I got physically sick watching the videos as the Haitians laughed. Their need for revenge in this Third World country was understandable, but not something I could stomach. It was quite an introduction to my fourth trip to Port-au-Prince, and I thought that I had already seen the worst before this. Each time I came it seemed to be getting worse.

After spending two days in hiding, we travelled by car over roads that couldn't even begin to qualify for the name, and arrived at Fonds Parisien in the country near the lake. Etienne asked me if I was sure that I wanted to stay there for the two weeks that I planned. I knew that not much would get done if I tried to go back and forth to Port-au-Prince each day, so we made ourselves comfortable in the rooms that were available in the church. I brought boxes of sewing supplies and materials to start a sewing project for the five different villages surrounding the mission.

The women must have had prior notice of my coming and were lined up in long lines outside the mission very early in the morning. I was close to getting killed with their enthusiasm for the supplies and was guarded by mission workers just in time before I got trampled. We handed out small sewing scissors, sewing thread, colorful red, green, purple, pink, yellow, orange and blue embroidery thread, sewing needles and cotton materials in many colors that were cut into small cotton baby shirts for the women to hand sew and decorate. I showed some women how to use the scissors.

The women from five villages walked long distances to get there and be a part of this sewing project. They were grateful and happy to receive these supplies, hoping that I would pay them for their work. I planned to sell them in the States and pay each woman a dollar for her work. Each morning more women came and I handed out more supplies. When I went walking in a nearby village, and all the women were sitting out on the front steps of their houses sewing, smiling, singing, and waving to me. It was a beautiful sight!

They were doing their best. I guess I thought hope was the most important thing to give them and they were responding with much gratitude. Later they used their scissors to cut each other's hair. They were all setting up barbershops in their front yards! There were many things that you could do with your first pair of scissors.

Each night I collapsed on my cot exhausted and fought off the mosquitoes. It was terribly hot with mosquitoes and flies and rats everywhere. I slept in a room with open rafters and watched the rats running above my head every night, so didn't sleep much. I slept with my hand on my flashlight and when I heard a sound, I took my flashlight and shined it in the rafters to scare them away. I think that I would have died of a heart attack if one had fallen on me in the night. We swam in the lake and then were later told that they had lost many children to the crocodiles there. Some days I worked with a doctor in the medical clinic. We had very few supplies but a room had been set up to see patients who came in from the villages. I saw one woman with terrible burns and scars all over her body. She told me that her husband threw her into the fire to chase out the evil spirits because a witch doctor told her husband that she was crazy. There was much voodoo and many witch doctors in the country.

We saw the Pig Project and took pictures of the nicely built concrete pens and the hundreds of pigs that had been bred from those sent from our neighbor's farm in Kansas just last year. It was a beautiful sight! They gave one pig to each family to raise. The family raised this pig until it was ready to sell and then took it to Port-au-Prince and sold it for the beans, rice, and clothes and school supplies that their children needed. The pig was their bank account and they took especially good care of them. They lost extremely few pigs and many families had received one. Etienne was thoroughly pleased with the Pig Project. It gave them hope for the future where there was no hope before the pigs arrived. I had never known how one pig could mean so much.

After two weeks we rode back in a truck to Port-au-Prince to spend the weekend before we left for home. The village women were able to sew many shirts that I took back to the States to sell for them. The city looked calmer and so much better than two weeks previous. It looked much better than the countryside. I remember swimming in a hotel pool thinking this water was just wonderful. And eating a normal meal of beans and rice and bread and fruit for the first time in two weeks. We stayed at the Prophete home with Etienne and Betty again and rested up for our trip home. We appreciated their generous hospitality.

A neighbor arrived to visit with us saying that there was much excitement in the neighborhood where a sorcerer was found. I asked what the sorcerer was doing and the young man told me that the sorcerer was stealing children and putting them in a sack and taking them to a shop to cut up and sell. I heard enough and didn't want to know any more of that story, but the neighbors caught the sorcerer and tied a rope around his neck and dragged him through the neighborhood that day. The young man told me that after they killed him, they ate him. I told him that I was living in the country the past two weeks, and I didn't believe that. He said they did much worse things out in the country. I saw many shrines along the road where animals were sacrificed, usually a chicken. I knew instinctively that this was more than I could cope with and just wanted to get out of the country. We left Port-au-Prince in a couple of days, and I heard enough of the horror that the people suffered to last me a lifetime. I brought back pictures. While a picture is worth a thousand words, pictures are not able to tell the real story. And thousands of words could never describe the impact of poverty on the lives of the people in this country.

## Back at the Farm

Arriving back at the farm was like coming into another world again, and I was glad to see that Eric and Sarah were fine. They had a good time with Pam and Amber and the grandchildren, swimming every day in the pool. I spent the next few months marketing the clothing that the Haitian women at Fonds Parisien sewed and sent them each a dollar for each shirt they made. I brought back other Haitian crafts to sell in the gift shop at our B&B and sent the money to the mission. Many friends helped me sell the Haitian crafts and sewing for the mission. But marketing the handmade baby shirts that the women sewed was harder than I thought. I could not find a shop that would take them on consignment, except one gift shop at St. Mary's Hospital in Manhattan that was run by a friend. I tried to find a larger national market that I could continue to sell to. Many friends and members of churches in Manhattan wanted to help and bought Haitian crafts. I did not plan to return to Haiti, and I realized that the quality control for the sewing project was a problem. Some embroidery and sewing was very nicely done and others not very well. So I just bought all the shirts the women made and tried to sell them later. Some of these ended up at an orphanage in Africa.

Sarah had a wonderful time at the Riley County 4-H Fair and showed her calf, Lucy. Lucy won a blue ribbon and Sarah was very proud of her. She also showed her white ducks and they won blue ribbons too. She was excited and happy to do so well on her first animals to show. Eric helped her transport all her animals and showed a beautiful wooden sign for our Country Inn for his wood project. Sarah was not having any luck with training her horse. Money was a beautiful paint gelding but had developed some bad habits and would not let Sarah ride him. Sarah and I just did not have the expertise to train him. We later hired a professional horse trainer who thought he could help us, but we had to sell Money. She then bought another paint and named him Ace. He was a nice riding horse for her and she and Jesse rode all over the farm and forty acres. We bought some white crested ducks with a fringe on top for the pond and for Sarah's 4-H Project and for her to show at the next Riley County Fair. All but one were white and they had crowns on their heads that made them look like they were wearing a hat. She got a BB gun for her birthday and thought that she was Annie

Oakley. She told me that I didn't need to buy any more meat, but most of her shooting involved shooting the pigeons that roosted in the hayloft of the barn to keep them from ruining the hay.

Sarah and I flew to Houston to be with Amber when she gave birth at home with a midwife to another beautiful granddaughter, Kelsey Leigh in September. There were now four grandchildren. What a sweet baby; Sarah had a wonderful time. We stayed just a week to help Amber and flew back to Manhattan. There were three more grandchildren expected next year with Grace expecting in March, Pam in April and Elizabeth in May. Our family was growing by leaps and bounds.

When Eric closed the pool in the fall and there was no grass for him to mow, there was a lot less work to do at the farm. Cutting and carrying in the wood for the wood stove was his main job. When the pond froze over Eric and Sarah loved skating and sledding. They invited the kids from 4-H to come for parties.

In 1987 Andrew decided that he didn't want to finish college right now and moved to Sacramento to work in the pizza business and start a store of his own. He sold his mobile home and drove an old gray pick-up truck, which he nicknamed the "Gray Goose," to Sacramento loaded with all his belongings. I wasn't sure that it would make the trip, but he arrived safely and got a job and found a place to stay. He worked hard and became manager and then made plans to start his own store.

The news from Haiti was very discouraging. The TonTon Macoutes was reinstated and massacred innocent voters in a polling station, and General Namphy of the Army took over. He was the general in charge before the revolution. He was overthrown the next year. There was an estimate that $700 million of cocaine passed through Haiti every month.

I decided to brush up on my French with a couple of courses at Kansas State University. With all the children in school, I enjoyed taking a class that spring semester, and I still ran some 10K races. I liked to run early in the morning when it was nice and crisp with a beautiful moon still out. Sarah sometimes ran to the walnut trees on our road with me. I wrote in my journal "the sweet fresh days of spring are nice to relax in before the heat of summer presses down. The sun comes up at 7:45 a.m. on another lovely day April 26, 1987." I began keeping a journal a few years before.

A brochure came in the mail with an opportunity to attend a Professional Nursing Seminar. I could receive thirty-five hours of continuing education credit for renewal of my Kansas Registered Nursing License while evaluating the healthcare in cities of the Soviet Union. Nurses were going from across the United States to visit hospitals, maternity homes and children's facilities in Leningrad, Moscow, Kransnodar and Sochi in Russia, and the Medical University of Leningrad. They brought information and research to exchange with medical professionals there. It was in the fall for three weeks and I really wanted to go.

Amber said that she could come and stay with Sarah and Eric, and I signed up for the seminar. Although the Cold War was still in progress, Soviet-American relations had begun to thaw and this was one of the educational exchange programs the government was allowing. I asked my sister Dorothy if she wanted to go with me as my guest and she did. We made our plans to go together for three weeks in August/September of 1987.

Since Eric was graduating from Manhattan High school next May, he took his ACT test for college entrance. He also started taking a freshman speech course at Kansas State University in the summer. Sarah always went into his room to look at the Sports Illustrated Calendar Girls hanging on his wall and bounce on his waterbed. She was always interested in his girlfriends. She got lice from her classmates at school in the third grade and Eric would never let her forget it.

Andrew and Shawnae decided to get married in June and asked to have the wedding outside at the farm. Andrew came back from Sacramento, and Shawnae graduated from Kansas State University with her Bachelor's Degree in Elementary Education. They planned to move to Sacramento, California. We were very happy for them. We planned a family reunion for all my brothers and sisters and all the children planned to be there since Chip and Elizabeth had returned from England.

Eric, Sarah and I came home one day and found a very small dog on our deck. We saw it on the road a day earlier and it appeared to be lost. It was definitely not a farm dog, and Sarah took it in and fed it and made a bed for it on the front deck outside the door to her room. It looked very young and well cared for and was grateful for all her attention. She started calling all her girlfriends at school to find a home for it since we already had two dogs. I took it to school the next day to show her class and a friend of hers took it home. Sarah was happy that one of her best girlfriends adopted and kept it and called it Rocky. Sarah enjoyed playing with Rocky when she spent the night with her friend. Rocky had found a home for many years.

Sarah loved corn dogs, watermelon, and corn on the cob and popsicles all summer. I think that she ate her weight in watermelon that summer. She often invited girlfriends out for slumber parties or camp outs. They went to the neighbor's pond early one morning to skinny dip and quickly ran away naked through the woods carrying their clothes before they were discovered. Anything for a little excitement. They always took Jesse and Babe with them for company when the coyotes started to howl. They felt safe with the dogs beside them.

A friend helped me to work out another sewing project to send to Haiti for the village women to sew. Margaret was a quilter and after we designed some baby quilts, I bought $550 worth of cotton quilting print material. We cut the fabric into squares and sent them in boxes to the Haitian Christian Mission in Port-au-Prince, Haiti. They were taken out to the villages for the women to sew and then shipped back to me when they were finished.

We had Campus Life meetings at our house since Eric was active in the group and usually attended all the meetings. We replaced the pool liner and opened the pool usually in April. Many of the kids' friends came out to swim. Eric, Sarah and I flew to Kirkland, Washington at Spring Break to be with Grace, and Jason was born on March 14, 1987. Jason was a handsome blue-eyed blond baby and grew to be very active.

Tim was also living in Washington and working in their pizza store. Andrew met us there with plans of opening his own pizza store with a friend. They were ready to start their own business in Sacramento. Then Dirk was born to Phillip and Pam at Williams Air Force Base in Phoenix on April 28th. A month later Kenny was born at Davis-Monthan Air Base in Tucson to Chip and Elizabeth on May 29th. Spring of 1987 added three more grandsons to our family. There were seven grandchildren by the beginning of summer.

May was an extremely busy month at the farm with guests at our B&B, three Head Start picnics, and other school picnics. Eric, Sarah and I worked hard getting the mowing, flower beds, pool and house all finished. And we got everything ready for Andrew and Shawnae's wedding in June. They didn't know it, but they had picked my sister Betty and Pat's wedding anniversary as their date. Betty and Pat were married in June of 1948, the year that my sister Norma Jean and my parents had died in October.

Many of my brothers and sisters and their families came and it was a beautiful wedding in the front yard by the pool. Phillip and Amber sang and played their guitars. Morgan and Alex were flower girls, and Jacob carried the ring. Sarah graduated from flower girl to keeping the guest book. Shawnae fixed a green arbor on a white trellis by the woods at the side of the house with an altar where they had communion. Shawnae was a beautiful bride. We roasted a pig as our family tradition at the reception for all our friends and relatives. All our grandchildren were there, and five of them were still in diapers. The trash barrels just filled up with disposable diapers.

Everyone enjoyed the swimming pool, and Andrew was thrown in, clothes and all the night before the wedding. I looked out at the pool one day and saw many small, blond haired, bobbing heads of my grandchildren, floating in the pretty blue water in colorful inner tubes near their parents. It was a beautiful sight! Jason was just three months old and discovered color and talked to a bright red scarf that my sister Dorothy wore around her neck. Dirk was just two months old and looked so sweet in a gray suit that Pam sewed for him to match his brother Jacob's suit. Kenny was exactly one month old and the youngest of all the grandchildren. Alex and Morgan, the oldest grandchildren wore pretty white brimmed straw hats with pick ribbons and lovely pink and white-flowered dresses that Shawnae had sewn. Kelsey just watched everything. Our B&B and farm was stretched to the limit with family and friends. It was a wonderful time visiting together.

# Chapter 17: Born in the USA

IN MID-AUGUST, DOROTHY AND I drove to Kansas City where we left her white Cadillac at the hotel and then flew to J.F.K. Airport in New York meeting the other nurses going to Russia with our group. Amber had come from Texas with Alex and Kelsey to be with Eric and Sarah. We talked to some Russian experts at KSU in Manhattan about the country before we left, and learned a little of the language for traveling purposes. We were eager for this adventure. I took some Haitian beads that were made out of seeds and dyed many beautiful bright colors. I planned to use these as gifts for the Russian women. Our flight was very long with a change of planes in Shannon, Ireland, where we spent one day touring the city and then boarded Aeroflot, the Russian airline for Moscow. I think there was some apprehension for us all since the Cold War had been going on so long and few tourists were allowed to travel. Chip and Phillip jokingly told me not to let anyone know that I had two sons who were Captains in the U.S. Air Force.

Flying on Aeroflot and looking down over the city, Moscow seemed to be carved out of a huge dark green forest, with many trees in the city. After landing at the airport we boarded a bus to take us to customs and heard American songs from the forties in English being played on the loudspeakers on our bus. We were quite surprised and pleased with our welcome. I think it helped us relax a little for the unknown that was ahead of us. Familiar music can make you feel at home in strange surroundings. There were armed guards with dogs everywhere, and it was a tense time as we were exhausted from the long flight. Customs was extremely thorough and slow, but I managed to get my two Bibles through in my checked luggage. We were cautioned to bring only one Bible in our luggage along with other strict rules to adhere to during our visit. I brought my own Bible and an extra one in Russian that I received from the American Bible Society to leave at a church that I planned to visit.

When we arrived at the Cosmos Hotel in the morning and were assigned to our rooms, they were not ready for us. I don't think the hotel expected us so early with the large amount of time difference or just didn't keep track of which rooms were ready for guests. When we opened the door to our room and went in we could see that it was not cleaned or prepared for us to check in. Clothes scattered on the floor: dirty glasses and towels in the bathroom and unmade beds in need of clean sheets greeted us. We asked for help and a maid came to our room to start cleaning and began changing the sheets. She was an older woman and dressed very poorly with worn shoes resembling house slippers. She worked hard and finished our room quickly. After our room was ready I reached into my suitcase and gave her a brightly colored bead necklace from Haiti, and thanked her in Russian. She took it and clasped it to herself with such appreciation and joy. Then she grabbed me and gave me a very strong hug and kiss on both cheeks, thanking me profusely. I was surprised and a little embarrassed with such extravagant thanks for a small gift but so glad that I brought the Haitian beads with me.

That initial encounter told me a lot about what was not available in the Soviet Union. We later saw many long lines of people on the streets for food, potatoes, fruit, cabbage and shoes. This was 1987, and the Soviet Union had been such a mystery to Americans for many decades that there was very little information reaching us about the conditions of the Russian people on the streets. Because this was a Professional Nursing Seminar, and we were expected to write our evaluation of the healthcare system of the

SovietUnion at the conclusion of this trip, I kept a journal of my observations. From my studies at the London School of Tropical Medicine, my nursing work in Haiti, and my travels in India, I learned that there were many basic indicators of a country's health. The medical facilities were obvious, but I also evaluated the way their system met the basic needs of the average person. The availability of food, water, clothing, sanitation and the attitude of the people were all significant indicators.

Our nursing professors from the School of Nursing at the University of Kansas gave lectures and seminars each day early in the morning before breakfast and then our touring schedules began. Our first visit to a medical facility was to Maternity Home in Moscow. The Chief Doctor Irena Revantovskya, who was the administrator, was very cordial and answered our questions as we were shown through the building. Our translator Alex assigned to us through Intourist, the government tourism organization, spoke good English and went everywhere with us. We were all shocked with the conditions of the buildings and the lack of beds, blankets, and medical equipment. As Alex translated for us, we could tell that he became a little embarrassed at the medical questions we asked concerning pregnancy, labor, and delivery.

Moscow was at that time a city of eleven million people with thirty-three boroughs having maternity homes. Each borough was divided into neighborhood welfare centers where expectant mothers received pre-birth consultations. Obstetrical nurses also visited some mothers in their homes. Mothers received classes at their closest neighborhood centers to help them take care of themselves and their babies. Mothers came to the nearest maternity home where they lived to deliver and stayed for five days for a normal birth, with midwives doing normal deliveries. Fathers were not allowed to be present at delivery or to see their wives until the mother and baby returned home. They just dropped them off and picked them up five days later. At that time they had a six-percent rate of cesarean sections. Most mothers breastfed, but there were "Milk Kitchens" where formula was prepared.

After discharge the mother and baby had follow-up care by the doctor who saw her at the neighborhood clinic. There was a high rate of abortions causing complications for further pregnancies, including excessive bleeding and longer labors. Their average number of abortions for one woman was eight and the highest was twenty-two. They used hormones, contraceptives and intrauterine devices to prevent pregnancies but these were not always available. No tubal ligations were allowed by choice. We watched a C-section and abortion in the operating room. The rooms were all very bare, dark and gloomy. Sterile technique was not always used and the sanitation was lacking. There were no visible disposable medical or health care items. Our entire group of twelve American nurses was silently and deeply grateful for not having to work or experience a delivery in those conditions. Some of the older nurses agreed that the conditions resembled our own American hospitals in the 1940s.

Our hotel was across the street from the Soviet Achievement Park with Space and Medical Exhibits and we toured with a guide in the afternoon. There were beautiful stone fountains and some impressive buildings. The people of Moscow seemed to be very proud of their parks. Everywhere we traveled in Moscow, there were many beautiful gray and white birch trees along the streets and in the parks. My love for trees was heightened to a greater appreciation, and I took in this beauty. August was a very lovely time of the year with the birch leaves turning all colors of yellow, orange and red, looking like a painter's palette of gorgeous colors.

We had good food with lots of fish served with a sauce made of mushrooms in sour cream. It was very good, and the soup was especially delicious. We always had good tea but milk was not available. When I asked for a bit for my tea, I was told that "We keep it for our children." I felt very guilty wanting to use milk in my tea. We were even served chocolate cake and Pepsi Cola at one meal. One breakfast was hot dogs and cheese and we decided that they were trying very hard to please us.

The Moscow Ballet gave a lovely performance at our hotel and it was breathtaking. The next night we attended a performance of the Moscow Circus that was unbelievable. There were many high wire and dangerous acts without nets. A trip to the largest GUM department store showed us what was available to buy on the market even if we didn't recognize what it could be used for. Designed as the first shopping mall in the world, GUM was a huge shopping center with many floors and was all under one roof; it was open with wrought-iron bridges.

The Kremlin was a huge complex that contained the tomb of Lenin across from St. Basil's Cathedral. Across the cobbled square St. Basil's was a beautiful collection of many tall towers with golden round onion domes reflecting the sunlight at the end of Razina Street. We went into the first floor of the KGB building. It was very dark, massive and impressive reminding me of a bank, and I felt that this was the center of Soviet Power from what we read. We were watched very closely and could go no farther than the first floor, but all of us felt a little shaky and wanted to get out. The ride on the Moscow Metro was quite an experience as we went down very deep under the city. The swift trains transported this city of eleven million people around, running every fifty seconds. It was really a surprise to see beautiful marble floors and mosaics on the ceilings and gorgeous chandeliers. I wasn't prepared for the beauty of it after the dreary and colorless buildings and streets. We went to the Lenin Museum and I was really getting tired of his face. I enjoyed the magnificent performance of the Ukraine Dancers the most. They were just fabulous with beautiful brightly colored costumes, beautiful singing and many clashing swords and men dancing in tall boots. I hated for it to end and hoped to see them again sometime. They were my favorite. We saw so much in Moscow that it seemed like we were there for two weeks instead of just a few days.

Our seminars continued each day with different subjects. We discussed the different aspects of the Soviet health care system as we traveled to other cities. Our next visit to Krasnodar was a two-hour bumpy and noisy flight on Aeroflot. It was a welcome weather change, very nice and warm in a southern atmosphere. It was on the Kuban River and the Sea of Asur with a population of under a million people. The Kuban Cossacks lived here, Russians who wanted to be free. It had a tropical and subtropical climate with many rice fields. We saw large numbers of women working in the fields of the collective farms, which were the peasants' individual farms put together. A man was cutting with a great hand-saw and I recognized huge fields of sunflowers, our Kansas flower. The Volga River was used for irrigation and the rice crop was harvested in September. There were also people scavenging for corn left from the harvest in the cornfields. This was considered the granary of Russia.

We rode through the woods and park in Krasnodar and ended up at a very nice restaurant where we ate dinner and danced. Lots of western music was played and we danced all evening. The food was good and the music loud and I think that everyone had a good time. A middle-aged Russian man came over to our table early in the evening to see if any of us wanted to dance with him. I did first, then

Dorothy and another friend. Then numerous men asked us to dance and everyone was dancing in different groups of two, four and six. I danced and spoke to a young man in French. The Russians were very informal in their dancing and loved to dance every dance. They seemed to want to make sure that we were having a good time. Dorothy said that she really enjoyed the dinner and dance. We all left exhausted but happy that the Russians wanted to be friendly.

The next morning we walked from our hotel on the Great October Socialist Revolution Square to the Russian Orthodox Church. It had beautiful gold towers and was made of red brick. We walked in with the many people going in, mostly older women. I gave the Russian Bible that I brought to a middle-aged woman in a red suit who started talking to us in Russian. She tried to talk to us and kissed me and was very happy. Krasnodar being in Cossack country was a more relaxed city on the left bank or the Kuban River. We had a very sumptuous lunch at the hotel. So much food! Men played the Russian balalaika, a musical instrument. Many of the famous Russian painters were from here.

After a few days we flew for about forty minutes to Sochi on the Black Sea for our next visit. Sochi was in the Western Caucasus Mountain range and became a city in the twelfth century. We were traveling and seeing great distances in Russia. Aeroflot was very noisy and our seats could only be in reclined position, but the safety belts worked. After landing, the pilot strides down the aisle and off the plane first. We enjoyed the warm balmy weather, ninety miles of beach on the Black Sea, and the tropical fruits. Subtropical plants were brought from all over the world about eighty years ago and planted here and were not native to Sochi. It is the world's largest tea growing area. All the Russians come here for the emphasis on natural cures with the healthy climate, sanitarias, and natural springs, seawater, special diets and exercise.

We visited Bath House #4 and Youth Sanataria, and we were able to ask many questions. There were 340 children in the Youth Santeria. It had bright green painted walls, yellow curtains, and red patterned rugs on the wood floors. There were paintings on the walls; large potted tropical plants and flowers; fish tanks with fish; a bird atrium; and many large windows gave the rooms a light, airy, cheerful look. They said all their treatments were scientifically based using special diets, mudpacks and the sulfur in the Black Sea. September was the best time of year to come and one and one-half million people came each year. The small country of Georgia was only forty kilometers away where Stalin was born. Eight years later in 1995 when I was asked to go to Georgia to work after it was an independent country, I didn't remember this.

I enjoyed the lush subtropical scenery with palm and banana trees, and gorgeously colored flowers everywhere. Much later in 1995 while living in the adjacent country of Georgia, the Georgians told me that Sochi had been a part of Georgia and Stalin gave it to the Russians. The dinner that night in the Cossack Restaurant was just beautiful and the people quite friendly. We could see the Black Sea from our Intourist Hotel balcony and ventured into it once experiencing the cold waters. The beautiful forests and hills and mountains around Sochi were very refreshing and lovely to look at. I can understand why the Russians have their Dachas here and flock here each year. Krushev had a Dasha here. I heard enough Russian music to always remember it and have it ingrained in my soul. As we took off from Sochi to fly to Leningrad, I couldn't tell where the Black Sea ended and the clouds began. A fishing boat chugging along almost appeared to be drifting on the clouds. It was a two hour and fifty minute flight from this southernmost point in Russia to Leningrad in the north, our last visit in the Soviet Union.

We landed in Leningrad and stayed at the lovely Pribaltiyskaya Hotel where we had a room on the tenth floor. The hotel was very elegant and beautiful with a view of the Baltic Sea from our window. Across the street was a Brozosky Shop, the only place where tourists were allowed to purchase gifts. We stopped at these shops in all the cities during our visits. There were large selections of their best crafts. Our nursing lecture was with a Russian doctor, Dr. Leonit Brokarius, Scientific Secretary, Institute of the Academy of Medical Sciences of the USSR. There were twenty to twenty-five medical schools in Leningrad. They had special midwife schools here for nurses that were started three hundred years ago.

One of our nursing lectures was on the treatment of HIV/AIDS, and we had questions for the doctor about the situation here. He said, "We live now in our country in such an interesting period. The medical care of the public health is one of the main problems of the state. To have a better life for each person is our main task. There are common human laws that cannot be avoided. We knew about HIV/AIDS several years ago. Three days ago, the decision of our Supreme Soviet Union published a report on the profusion of AIDS in this country. There will be no blood transfusions without testing."

When our meeting concluded with the doctor, he wanted to know if we brought any new Robert Ludlum books with us. He read two that were translated into Russian and wanted more. I'm not sure if anyone brought one.

We took a hydrofoil to the Summer Palace in Peterhof. The weather was just right and it was a beautiful trip on the Neva River. The magnificent number of beautiful fountains, one hundred and forty, many overlaid with gold leaf, was more than our imagination could conceive. We saw the fortress on the island where Peter and Paul had been imprisoned. We thought this palace was magnificent and then saw the Hermitage the next day. Words cannot do justice to the chandeliers, marble, woodcarvings, gold, brass, silver statues, furniture, tapestries and paintings. Rembrandt's paintings of "The Prodigal Son," "Madonna and Child," "The Last Supper," and "The Crucifixion," and so many more from the Gospel stories were exquisite. All were painted with dark colors and exquisitely beautiful. We only had a day here and could have spent a week or more. The French Impressionists paintings had beautiful bright and light colors.

There were many stairs to climb in the Hermitage; many beautiful well-polished inlaid wood floors of intricate designs, gorgeous glass chandeliers, and hundreds of beautiful statutes. There was so much gold leaf on the ceilings, walls, doors, chandeliers, statues, stairways and doors, that it was unbelievable. I had not seen so much gold anywhere in the world, even in the Palace of Versailles in Paris. The senior citizens, mostly women, sat at the entrances to the doors and exhibits in the Hermitage watching over their national treasures in their shapeless black dresses. I thought about the many poor houses and people I saw and the terrible shortages, and wondered about all this gold in one place. We saw the Bolshoi Theatre, which looked very elaborate, elegantly decorated with heavy dark fabrics, drapes, and dark, carved wooden seats.

We stood on the beach of the Baltic Sea and looked across to Finland just one hundred miles away. The medical doctor told us that many of the rich Russian women go to Finland to have their babies. I asked our guide and translator if the Russians kept pets in their homes. I didn't see any walking on the streets. He said that the dogs did not want to come out. I thought that was a strange answer and decided that they didn't have any because of the food shortage.

While visiting in our hotel after dinner one evening I asked the tour guide why customs restricted us to just one Bible in our luggage. He replied, "We don't need your Bibles here." He looked very upset, then went out to smoke a cigarette. I followed him out to talk, and he explained that he personally had no objection to the Bible, but he was to give the official position or lose his job. I apologized for upsetting him, but was just curious. Eight years later I was teaching the Bible in Russia.

I bought many gifts for all my children and their families. I especially liked the balalaikas and bought two. On the flight back, I boarded the plane with them hanging across my shoulders. We all did our share in bolstering the economy of the USSR, and Dorothy and I enjoyed purchasing many of their beautiful crafts. The beautiful, delicately hand painted flowers on the black enameled trays and crafts were bright and vivid colors. I brought back many for the children.

Our weeks in Russia were something that we never forgot. We had a crash course on Russian history, language and geography and traveled vast distances. It was a very long flight back. Dorothy and I arrived in Kansas City from our trip late at night to find that her white Cadillac that we left in the parking lot of the hotel had the rear window knocked out in a storm while we were gone. We drove to Manhattan with the September wind whistling through the car and very cold. It seemed like a long trip home and we arrived back in Manhattan after midnight. The children were all awake at the farm to welcome us with their stereo blasting Bruce Springsteen's song "Born in the U.S.A." and a party ready. They were right. We were very grateful to be home safely and deeply grateful to be born in America.

# Chapter 18: Time to Move On

I RETURNED HOME thinking about the USSR military that we had feared this whole year. I thought of the last thirty years of the Cold War, especially when we were living in Germany and in the military when it was the Cuban Missile Crisis, and the many books that I had read. So many things were not working in their best hotels in the country. Doors, televisions, and lamps weren't working, and the carpets in their nicest hotels were poor and shabby and would not lay flat. I noticed that there were no square corners and shoddy craftsmanship in many places. There were tall weeds in front of the hotel and only one entry door that worked. There was lack of food, shoes, and common items in the cities. Medical facilities were so archaic. The maternity home I visited looked like something from long ago. There was one shared public cup for a drink dispenser that gave you a bit of the local drink, kvass, for a kopeck. I saw rows and rows of very poor houses and huge, lonely, nondescript colorless graying apartment buildings on our way from the airport to Moscow on our arrival.

Back at home I had seen an advertisement in the *Economist Magazine* for a job with the World Food Program in Rome and sent in my application and resume. I found that there were two hundred other applicants and realized there was little to no chance of my getting the job. I looked into the faces of the hungriest people in the world and worked with them, but that didn't qualify me for political problems and distribution. I knew that it was a job involving many reports and paperwork, which was not my forte. I really didn't want to work with the politics of feeding hungry people. I wanted to work with real needy people. I knew of the need for medical missionaries in Senegal and Zaire, Africa. And I was just praying that God would give the guidance that I needed. I was beginning to feel restless, and my feelings of going back to the Third World were growing stronger as I took care of my children and the farm and B&B. I mentioned to Sarah about the possibility of working and moving to Africa and her reply was, "I do not want to go to Africa. It will be a dirty and stinking place." Children can be very honest and brutal when they speak the truth.

Amber, Pat and their family were visiting our old neighbors at the farm who had moved near Springfield, Missouri, so we drove there to see them and visit other friends. We had a good visit with the Hartmans, Washburns, and Theobalds.

Eric started college courses in the summer of 1987 at Kansas State and continued throughout his senior year of high school until he graduated. He also played on a Kansas State University club rugby team his senior year and really enjoyed traveling to games out of Manhattan every weekend. Since he played rugby at St. Michaels in Otford while we were living in England, he knew the rules and had some experience. Sarah and I went to watch him play rugby as we did in England and wore our red "Rugger Hugger" t-shirts to cheer him on. I think that Eric enjoyed rugby better than football, but Sarah and I still didn't know the rules of the game.

Sarah was born into this family with many teenagers and grew up listening to all kinds of loud music. The girls all played in the band. She loved listening to every sort of music on her radio and played the flute in the school band in fourth grade. Grace gave her the flute that she played in school and Sarah enjoyed being in the band. I went to her concerts at the end of the school year.

I learned in January of 1988 that the African Christian Mission of Zaire was looking for a Registered Nurse for their orphanage in Zaire, Africa. Since I decided not to go back to Haiti with the children, this was an opportunity that I prayed about. Eric planned to graduate in May 1988 and move to Phoenix, Arizona for college, so Sarah and I were the only ones at the farm and B&B. There was much to pray about for God's leading and guidance. About this time I wrote in my journal from my favorite place at the farm that "a rocking chair by a nice warm fire, a cup of tea, and my Bible, is not very risky living." This ongoing Bible reading and dialogue with the Lord in my journal was the first priority of my day.

On February 8th, I received the first Haitian-sewn baby quilts made in Fond Parisien by the women in the villages whom I taught on my last trip to Haiti. I sent boxes of cotton quilt pieces for them to sew together and they did a great job. The colorful print patterns of the cotton and their interesting designs looked very well done. They were put on display at the gift shop at the St. Mary's Hospital in Manhattan. Knowing the villages and the circumstances in Haiti, this was a miracle of gigantic proportions. I bought many of these for my new grandchildren who seemed to be coming quite rapidly in our family, and sold many to members in the churches. I also displayed them at our B&B gift shop at the farm giving additional income to the women in the villages of Haiti.

This was also a time of waiting upon the Lord. My application was sent in for the job in Rome with the World Food Program, but I also sent an enquiry about the missionary nursing job in Zaire. I was doing well in my French class and knew that I needed French in either role. But only the Lord knew where He wanted us.

I helped Eric buy a used red Chevrolet car for $1,500 to drive to Arizona for college after he graduated in the summer. He took care of all the arrangements and was learning a lot. A friend on his rugby team had an uncle in

Phoenix in construction and he was making plans to get a summer job there.

I decided that I needed to do spring cleaning in the closets and took out boxes to sort through. I came upon all Kenny's letters that he'd written to me during our courtship and separations. There was an especially large box from Vietnam when he wrote me every day. I took the box to the trash barrels and read them again one by one and burned them all, committing my memories to the Lord of all the wonderful times that we had together. I cried a lot and decided that this was a time to burn some bridges behind me. It was hard, and I experienced a healing time. I had been greatly blessed with a loving and caring husband. He was always with me in my heart and in the faces of our children. I knew that part of my life would always be recorded in my memories, and I didn't need to hold on to it on paper. These personal letters were only for our eyes. All the good things in life have a tendency to just want to hang on and not let go. Jesus has asked us to lay up our treasure in heaven and not here.

Sarah found her new calf born to Lucy in the barn at the end of March. She was watching Lucy very closely for two weeks and knew the exact time that it came. She stayed up very late watching them and took good care of Lucy. She was so excited and called everyone she knew with her good news. We decided to start milking Lucy and took turns, but we were very slow and gave up before very long.

We were having many guests and the B&B was going very well. Each year the number of guests increased. Most of the guests were very nice but we did have some strange ones. One woman called from the bus station in Manhattan and asked me to pick her up. After she checked in, paying for a week in advance from a briefcase full of fifty-dollar bills, I told her that we only served breakfast and no other meals. She said that her car was being repaired in Manhattan and it would soon be ready. I visited with her that evening and decided that there was something strange about her behavior. Her head was shaved and she seemed to be healthy. After doing some checking, I found that she was sleeping in a car and had escaped from a Topeka, Kansas mental hospital and her brother was looking for her. When I suggested that she stay in Manhattan and returned her money, she did not want to leave and became very upset with me. We took her to a motel in Manhattan for the night and her brother was notified and came to pick her up. On another occasion three men from Boston booked two rooms and stayed a few nights and kept changing rooms all night. They asked about reservations for returning with more of their friends next year, and I said that I would be in Zaire. But we had many wonderful and interesting guests over the past few years. A news reporter with her family stayed with us and we were recommended by a very satisfied guest in the *Los Angeles Times* Newspaper.

I was getting closer on a decision about working abroad. While I was considering Zaire, I wrote in my journal, "To go to Zaire for three years means to go back to 18th century living conditions and to be without modern medical care for Sarah when she gets sick. That is a tough decision. And from eleven years to fourteen years is a pretty life changing time to absent from the 20th century." And a week later I wrote "Thank you for Sarah's spirit of adventure in thinking about Rome or Africa." I received a letter from the World Food Program that I was being considered for the job and would hear nothing else unless I was selected.

Amber and Pat welcomed their third child and first boy, Lance Patrick, born in San Marcos, Texas in April.

I got to meet this handsome grandson when I drove there to pick up Alex and Kelsey via Stillwater, Oklahoma and visited Adrienne, and her family. I brought Alex and Kelsey back to the farm for a couple of weeks to visit. Pat graduated from Chiropractic College and later worked at a new job in El Paso, Texas where they moved. Sarah and I enjoyed having the girls at the farm and we were having a wonderful time. I finished my two-hour French final exam, including a thirty-minute composition and twenty-minute oral exam. I was happy to be finished, and we all celebrated at McDonald's with Sarah. Sarah really enjoyed having "two little sisters." Amber and Pat came to get the girls and we saw Lance Patrick again.

In May, Phillip and Pam welcomed their third baby, a handsome boy, Simon Andrew, born at Williams Air Force Base Phoenix, Arizona. There were now six grandsons and three granddaughters. Phillip was an instructor pilot in the Air Force T-38 aircraft. Chip and Elizabeth were living in Tucson, and Chip was flying the A-IO aircraft called the Warthog.

I encouraged Tim to get back in college and he signed up for diving school in Seattle, Washington and found a girl that he wanted to marry, Colleen Keehner. He had ten months of diving school at the Institute for Diving in Seattle and then planned to get a boat for a fishing business.

Eric graduated from Manhattan High School and planned to leave for Arizona as soon as he could. Sarah and I knew this is what he wanted and thought about how much work he did. I knew the farm was just a launching pad for all these children who found so many different places to go and things to do. As it was intended. And Sarah and I planned to launch soon, too.

After much prayer I made the decision to work in Bukavu, Zaire and a mission family came for a visit at the farm to meet me and give me more information on the work and job in Zaire, which had been the Congo. We enjoyed their visit and later worked with them at Kidodobo Mission Station up in the mountains of Eastern Zaire near the border of Rwanda. They told us that they really wanted us to join them at the mission station and looked forward to our working with them. It was good to meet a couple who had been there for a long time. They worked there for forty years and needed some relief from their responsibilities at the orphanage so they could be away on evangelistic outreach in the jungle areas. We got along well and enjoyed our visit together. Now that we knew where we were going, what job I planned to do, and met the people I would work with, all that was left was our preparation.

Eric, Sarah, and I drove to Phoenix, Arizona in July in Eric's red Chevrolet, pulling a trailer with all his things. He also took some furniture Phillip and Pam left in Manhattan. It was an adventurous trip and it was exciting for Eric to be going off to college and living in Arizona. We were glad for him and happy to see the grandchildren. We had a get together in Tucson at Chip's with Phillip and Amber's families on the fourth of July. What sweet grandchildren! Eric had a good start since he finished one semester at Kansas State University in Manhattan. He always wanted to go back to Arizona since his dad had taken him when he was eight years old. Now with two older brothers there in the Air Force, Chip in Tucson and Phillip in Phoenix, he was ready. He planned to stay with Phillip until he found a job and an apartment. Phillip and Pam looked forward to Eric being with them and their three little boys, Jacob, Dirk and Simon.

Sarah showed her registered Holstein cow, Lucy, and her calf, Daisy, at the Riley Country 4-H Fair in August after we returned from Arizona. She took Grand Champion on her calf Daisy, and Reserve Champion on Lucy. Sarah had cleaned them both until they were spotless. They were a very pretty pair and when the calf nursed while they were being shown, they looked so beautiful and healthy. A perfect picture. While trying to help Sarah with Lucy, I sprayed her hooves with hair spray trying to make them look shiny. I forgot that cows kick to the side and Lucy kicked me in the mouth. I didn't lose any teeth, but had a bruised and fat lip for a while. That was a bad summer for me because her horse Ace had already bitten me on the arm and it was bruised. We didn't get him trained in time for the fair. I was glad to survive that summer with nothing worse. She took a purple ribbon on her ducks, blue on her banana bread, and red on her gathered cotton skirt.

After Eric left the farm, Sarah and I had much work to do. I should have known that I would run out of boys one of these days. It was definitely time to sell the farm.

Later in August we went to Illinois to an African Christian Missionary Retreat and met more missionaries that were working with this mission. I was approved by the Mission Board and took the MMPI Psychological Testing Exam and my credentials were sent to the African leaders. Sarah and I planned be on our way to Zaire, Africa in June 1989, pending the approval of the African leaders. I looked up Zaire on the map and read up on more history of the country and mission. I decided to sell the farm and move on to a job in Zaire for two or three years. Life was changing drastically, and Sarah and I were becoming eager to start a new challenge.

Bujumbura, Burundi, the capitol of a tiny country near Zaire, was our flight destination. Then we would be met by missionaries and drive through Rwanda, another small country, to get to Bukavu, Zaire on the eastern border. Nairobi, Kenya would be our mailing address and Missionary Aviation Fellowship flew our mail into Bukavu each week. These places were now in our everyday vocabulary as we made our plans. If there was war in Burundi when we left for Zaire, then we could fly into

Kigali, Rwanda and be met by missionaries. And if both countries were at war with each other, then we had to find another route. I sensed that life was not going to be too predictable.

Tim finished his diving school and now had his boat and crew for a fishing business in the Seattle area. Chip resigned from the Air Force and planned to fly in the Air National Guard and take a job with the airlines. He had an offer with American Airlines and started his new job. The year went so fast with many changes in our family.

Three of the boys, Chip, Phillip and Andrew, met for a family reunion in San Diego at Mission Beach in September. Sarah and I flew out to join them for a few days. There were five grandchildren that I got to babysit at Sea World while Sarah and their parents saw the dolphin show. They all took naps on blankets on the grass and I counted my blessings. What sweet grandchildren! We knew that our time as a family together was getting more difficult to manage.

Tim and Colleen drove from Seattle for Christmas, and Grace and family, expecting another baby in January, joined us. We attended church together on Christmas Eve. We were very glad to meet Colleen from Duvall, Washington. Jason was a toddler who loved to climb the stairs and managed to fall down and have a few stitches. Such a sweet grandchild! I cooked a large turkey and we all had a great Christmas dinner together. Grandmother Long joined us too. Tim and Colleen announced their wedding in May.

Grace and family had moved to Kansas City the previous year and another handsome grandson, Eric Daniel, arrived in January. He was the tenth grandchild in our family. I predicted that in ten years, there would be twenty grandchildren in this family.

Sarah and I kept Jason for two weeks and really enjoyed having him. Grace came to get Jason and their family left for Tallahassee, Florida where they planned a pizza business.

Eric found a job and called to say he loved Arizona and was having a great time. Sarah and I started our yellow fever vaccinations. All the material that I read on Zaire sounded much like Haiti. Sarah was getting straight A's in school, and I realized that our departure time in June was coming quickly. I received a letter from the nurse at Kidodobo and the job there sounded more than challenging. It was minus three degrees here in Kansas and I knew that I would like the tropics again.

Chip and Elizabeth came to visit with their children, Morgan and Kenny. We had a great time. What sweet grandchildren! I sent in my registration for a short course in London at the London School of Hygiene and Tropical Medicine, "Reorganizing Health Care in the Developing World." I wanted to take this in 1984 before I left for Haiti, but couldn't. I had friends in Otford who invited me to stay with them. I planned to go to London at the end of May before Tim and Colleen's wedding. I would finish just in time to fly from London to Seattle for the wedding.

Sarah and I had our picture taken together and put on a brochure that we sent out for support for our time in Zaire. With a map of Zaire and a short description of the mission, we hoped to find others who were interested in the work. Kidodobo Mission station was strategically located in the mountainous area of eastern Zaire (formerly the Belgian Congo). Only fifteen miles from Bukavu, the capital of the Kivu Province, supplies and medicines could be brought that were essential for the orphanage. There was an agreeable climate of 60 to 70 degrees F. year round. Fresh fruits and vegetables were available. The people were known as the Bashi tribe who lived in huts made of grass and shaped like huge beehives. They had very little food or clothing.

Sarah and I finished our yellow fever vaccinations at Fort Riley and also had our cholera shot. We talked about the things that we were going to take to Africa. I ordered homeschooling books for Sarah's seventh grade year. We talked often of Africa.

No one was ever convicted of Kenny's shooting and the police called to say that they were reopening his case. The television station in Topeka called to say that they planned to do a television special on the case to see if they could find more information. Phillip arrived and went to the Manhattan police department to go over the files. We enjoyed his and Dirk's visit, and I really appreciated Phillip being with me. I hoped that there would be a positive outcome, but nothing was found before I left for Africa.

Potential buyers came out to see the farm while we were still having B&B guests. If it did not sell, I planned to rent it out to the Campus Life Organization Director to use. I shipped our household goods in footlockers to Zaire along with two new mountain bikes that I bought for Sarah and myself. These were sent on ship by container and we would take two large suitcases each on the plane. Chip had left active duty in the Air Force and flew with the Wisconsin National Guard. Since Chip was flying with American Airlines, he had tickets for us on Sabena Airlines to Brussels, Belgium, and then we would buy tickets on Kenyan Air to Bujumbura, Burundi.

A call came from Etienne Prophete in Port-au-Prince asking me when I would be coming back to work in Haiti. I told him that I planned to work in Zaire, Africa and wasn't coming back. He said, "Phyllis you don't belong in Africa." But I knew that there were so many places in the world where the needs were great and others could go to Port-au-Prince.

Eric decided to work the summer with Tim on his fishing boat in Seattle and earn more money for college in the fall. They had many good times together. The children all made plans for returning to the farm in June when Sarah and I left for Zaire. We planned our last family reunion here, and I let them all take the furniture and things, except for a few antiques that I planned to store. It was time to travel light and keep only that which I needed for a smaller house for just Sarah and me on our return. I sold all the animals and rented the pasture to a neighbor. Sarah sold Lucy and her calf and her horse Ace. She gave her dog, Babe, to friends in the church. Andrew planned to take Jesse back to Sacramento with him when he came in June. She advertised Ace, her horse, in the paper and someone came out to buy him. They paid her $500 cash and she stuck it in the back pocket of her jeans. Later that night I asked her where she had put her money and she pulled it out of her pocket. She was playing in the hayloft of the barn all day with some friends and carried it around with her. I thought that an eleven-year-old had very little concept or how much money that was. We planned for her twelfth birthday in Zaire.

Our last B&B guests arrived in May. I enjoyed running Longs Country Inn and met many interesting and nice people. It was good for us all and helped in the maintenance of the farm. We operated it for four years, and I learned a lot, but it was time to move on.

## Otford, Kent, England

This was my first trip to London without any children. I had been dragging children all over the world for thirty years and it seemed rather strange. Otford and Greenhill Road looked so much the same as when we lived here in 1983-1984. Greenhill Road seemed steeper with more trees than I remembered. I stayed with our neighbors

Martin and Margaret Matthews who were very kind and generous Christians and delightful people. They made me feel warmly welcomed and like it hadn't been long since we were together. They had a unique ministry with young people and worked very hard. I went to Otford Methodist Church with them, and many of our friends welcomed me. I visited many other friends on Greenhill Road and it was really good to see everyone.

My one-week course in London was just what I needed to update me on conditions that I would meet in Zaire in healthcare. I met many doctors and nurses working in the same situations in many other countries. I also met District Health Officers from Tanzania who gave me a good idea of what I would meet with in Zaire.

My train and bus connections from Otford to London went well and it was good to be back. I remembered London and my way around quite well. I enjoyed the city again. I knew that I was becoming better prepared for the job that I needed to do in Zaire; new ideas, better methods, and a plan of action helped give me confidence. After I finished up the course, I did some shopping for a dress for the wedding and bought my antimalarials that I wanted to have for us in Zaire.

On my return from London, Amber and Pam brought Sarah to meet me at the airport in Kansas City and we flew to Seattle. All of Tim's brothers were able to attend Tim and Colleen's wedding. After the wedding on a beautiful lake near Duval, we stayed a few days and went out fishing on the boat with Tim. We learned much about sea cucumbers, "cukes," as he called them. We didn't know that such interesting creatures lived in the water. Sarah enjoyed our time there and getting to know Colleen. The girls and grandchildren were at the farm taking care of things while we were gone.

When everyone arrived at the farm in June, we did a lot of cooking out, swimming and visiting. One evening sitting on the screened in porch, we divided up all our household possessions in about thirty minutes that Kenny and I had collected over the past thirty-three years. There was an enormous amount of junk to clear, but everyone pitched in and cleared it all out. It was very liberating. Everyone took whatever they wanted. Dividing up the household things was amusing and interesting for everyone. I felt like I was really traveling light from here on. Andrew found a truck and loaded up his and other siblings' furniture that he took to their homes later. He finished up hauling off the last loads after we left.

We took lots of pictures at the farm with us all in the front yard to bring to Zaire with us. All the flowers were blooming at the farm and it looked the prettiest that I had ever seen it. All eight children with five spouses and ten grandchildren were there. When we were all together we made quite a crowd. It was so much fun to have all the children together and grandchildren playing and swimming together. There were ten blond towheads, three very small, under one year, and the rest running and enjoying the farm. It was a sentimental but happy and historic time for us all. We all had many wonderful memories there as a family and would carry them with us throughout our lives. It was our last family reunion together at the farm as a family. Kenny had built a wonderful place to raise our family, and I knew he would have been happy for us. We all too the farm with us in our hearts and the children knew what a blessing it had been for our family.

# Chapter 19: Risky Living in Afrika!

**CHIP, ELIZABETH, MORGAN AND KENNY** all took us to the Chicago O'Hare Airport to see us off for Africa. Kenny, only two years old, started crying when I held him to kiss me goodbye. He was afraid that he was going with us. We flew out on the 23rd of June for Brussels, Belgium on Sabena Airlines.

Having the whole day in Brussels, we decided to take a bus and see the suburb of Ghent instead of trying to get some sleep. Many missionaries going to Africa get a room at a hotel and sleep that day, and we should have. We left that night around 11 p.m. for a nine-hour flight to Nairobi, Kenya on Air Kenya. I didn't get much sleep. While we waited there for our flight to Kigali, Rwanda, I noticed that Kenya looked much like the scrub country of West Texas to me.

Our flight to Kigali went well and we deplaned for an hour there and took on a new crew for our flight to Bujumbura, Burundi. I had not slept much at all since we had left on the 23rd. Sarah and I arrived safely and on schedule on the 26th of June at the airport in Bujumbura, Burundi in Africa. The three-day trip was quite exhausting, but we encountered no problems. Customs was slow, and they opened and checked our luggage. I had brought medical supplies, Ampicillin, and syringes that caused some excitement and interest, but no problems. We were met by a young man from the African Christian Mission in Bukavu, Zaire who greeted us warmly and helped us load all our luggage in his Volkswagen van. There were very few white people on the plane, we were not hard for him to find.

It was a long, six-hour drive to Bukavu, but a beautiful trip through very green and tropical countryside; all the children walking along the roads waved to us. Sarah and I waved out the windows and were excited about being in Africa. We passed through the border guards at Burundi, Rwanda and Zaire on our way. It was a test of endurance just to get to our destination. The countryside did not look as poor as Haiti and much cleaner. The people we passed along the roads were dressed well.

The beautiful, bright bougainvillea flowers were everywhere on the streets in Bukavu, and the fragrant smelling frangipani blossoms, reminding us of Port-au-Prince. The flowering hibiscus bushes and bright red flowering poinsettia trees greeted us in abundance. We had loved all the fresh tropical fruit in Haiti, especially the mangos, papayas, fresh pineapple, and breadfruit.

Arriving at the guesthouse in the city of Bukavu, we received a very warm welcome from many members of the mission who lived there. Although it was the middle of the day, we went to bed to get rested from our long trip. Sarah and I settled into two bedrooms with our luggage. We lived at the guesthouse for eight weeks while we attended language school and studied Swahili, the local language.

We soon took a trip to Kidodobo, the orphanage, and mission station where we planned to work. It was a long way on a winding and very dangerous road up into the mountains. That was my first impression. Much later I drove that dangerous road like the one at the farm thinking that it was quite safe. I met the American nurse from Michigan who soon went back to the States on furlough. She was doing a great job, and I could see that this was quite a challenge involving much health education and training for the Africans. Sarah saw all the farm animals, but no goats or rabbits and decided that when we moved there she wanted to have a goat and rabbit project. We felt very welcomed and very much needed. We looked forward to our work there. The sanitation and hygiene was a real problem at the orphanage with so many children.

Learning Swahili was my first job. We started in school immediately with our Swahili notebooks and tackled the combinations of 'kw' and 'mw' words that sounded so unfamiliar on our lips. I felt like I needed to do lip and mouth exercises to warm-up before I started class each morning. We had a good teacher named Bisemwa. Sarah met some younger girls and started making plans for them to join her for a slumber party since her room had four bunk beds.

The locks on the doors of the houses are in direct proportion to the level of fear and security in a country. The doors on the guesthouse in Bukavu were made of steel and had the biggest steel locks that I had ever seen. They looked like they would need to be blown open for anyone to get in after we locked up at night. A Zamu, an African man armed with a machete, was stationed right outside this door and stayed up all night. He slept in a small hut guarding the guesthouse. I also noticed many armed soldiers on the streets.

After a few days at our language school we went back to Kidodobo and stayed in their guest camper trailer near the Crowl's house. We thought for sure we heard lions and tigers outside during the night, but it was only their horse and some dogs. We were happy that only domestic animals got that close to the houses.

The 4th of July came and we went to a picnic with all families of the mission on Lake Kivu, instead of school. I thought the roads in Haiti were horrible, but these roads made those look almost civilized. It was a beautiful lake, and Sarah swam with other teenagers. After the first week, Sarah was adjusting well to Africa; she took life as it came.

It seemed so unbelievable that here we were in the heart of Africa that I read and heard so much about all my life and it was really not that different from other places. People were much the same everywhere with the same basic needs. The missionaries were all very kind and helpful and we made friends with the Africans very easily. After a month of language school, we took a week off for a camp meeting of many missionaries from different countries and missions in the area.

In language school, I discovered that I was trying to think of the French equivalent to the Swahili word first, since it was the most recent foreign language that I learned, and then the English. This slowed me down some in learning Swahili until I realized what I was doing. I also spoke French in doing business and read the French newspapers.

The Christian Missionary Fellowship flew our mail in from Nairobi every Thursday and took any mail we had back with them. Our first letter that we received took three weeks to get there. All the children wrote, and we had ten letters the following Thursday. Mail was coming faster.

On August 6th, we had a special birthday cake, made by one of the missionaries, and dinner for Sarah's twelfth birthday. I was so glad to have her with me and we were having a good time. She learned Swahili very fast, getting very good with the language. She acquired two kittens, when we were at Kidodobo, and kept them in her room and backpack when she took them out for walks. Sarah also took them to language school and played and fed them on the patio outside the classroom when she got bored. They were her constant companions and she named them Ebony and Rascal. She took very good care of them and even made a growth chart for the littlest one, Ebony. She sewed hats and dresses for them and dressed them up like babies; she was very creative in making their costumes.

I finished my dental work in Manhattan before I left for Africa, and my teeth checked out very well, but the unexpected happened and I developed a very bad toothache. I was told not to go to the local dentists, so instead went to a dentist in Kigali, Rwanda with others who were taking missionaries to the airport flying back to the States. All trips anywhere needed to be coordinated for many purposes in Africa. So I had to wait to see the dentist. It was a six-hour drive through winding and beautiful hills in a rainforest and we saw many monkeys along the road.

The African hotel in Kigali where we stayed was quite an experience with no water. The next day we stayed at the Baptist Missionary guesthouse, and I went to the dentist. But it was too late to save the tooth and it had to be pulled. I needed to come back in six weeks for a bridge to be made and sent from Nairobi, Kenya. By this time I was glad to be relieved of the tooth and the pain.

Compared to no telephones or roads or dentists in Zaire, Kigali looked like a modern city. There were many things here that did not exist in Zaire. We were surprised by a herd of goats that came right down the middle of the main street of town at 6 a.m. on our first morning there, to remind us that this was Africa. We had our Rwandan visas renewed while we were there since we planned to come back again. We ate most of our meals at the Tam Tam Restaurant while we were there.

We came back to language school and Swahili and it went well. When Sarah and I were walking on the way to school one morning, a young boy on a bicycle ran into me and broke my glasses. I had tried to move to the other side of the dirt road, but he followed me and hit me head-on. I had a few cuts on my legs, but the broken glasses were worse. These were my new ones that I bought before leaving Manhattan. I had an extra pair, fortunately. The whole city was without either electricity or water for a week. This is Afrika {Swahili spelling).

Our first phone call to the states for Eric's nineteenth birthday on August 19th, was quite a production. We took a taxi to the Zaire border, walked across the bridge over the river, through the border guards and showed our passports, and into the country of Rwanda and found a hotel with a telephone that we could use. We changed our money to Rwandan francs and made the telephone call collect. With the time difference, it was five in the morning in Phoenix and we got to talk to Eric, Phillip, Pam and Jacob. We could hear them so clearly, and it was wonderful to hear their voices and know that we could call. Phillip said that he had a pilot from Zaire in one of his flight classes that he was teaching at Williams Air Force Base and the Air Force flew planes into Kinshasa, the capital of Zaire. They hoped to come sometime. We sent Swahili words in our letters each time that we wrote everyone. We wanted them to know what we were learning.

Our first visit to the Soko alone, the large outdoor market in Bukavu, was a challenge to our language skills and we bought some bright colored purple and green material for skirts and two straw hats. We were very proud to have a very limited vocabulary and negotiate those purchases. Sarah loved shopping and enjoyed all the strange items. The bright colors caught her eye and she thought it was wonderful. She bought some pink plastic sandals that she loved wearing to splash in the mud puddles after a big rainstorm. I borrowed a sewing machine and made our bright purple and green splashed material into matching skirts. I had sent my sewing machine in the container on the ship and it had not yet arrived. None of our household things that we sent in March had arrived.

Sarah and I came up with our first hard decision to make. The Zamus were our house guards, very poor and skinny with ragged and shabby clothing. It was cold at night and they had no warm clothing. Our kitchen leftovers from dinner were being left in the refrigerator and then thrown out. Sarah had given some food to one Zamu and all the other missionaries said no. We talked about it and decided that we could not let the food go to waste. We left it in the refrigerator for a few days and if it wasn't eaten we gave it to the Zamus. We knew that we were only here for a short time in comparison to others and no one would probably feed them when we left. But it was what we needed to do.

We went to dinner at a friend's house and a bat was flying around in the house while we ate. Sarah noticed it first and our friend didn't blink an eye and just said that she sleeps under mosquito netting, no other explanation. It amazed us what people became accustomed to here in Afrika. I think that the stress of living and working here was very wearing on relationships and people could easily become depressed.

We went across the border to Cyangugu, Rwanda again to call Tim on his birthday on September 17th and our connection was again very clear. I talked to Colleen, too, and she was pregnant. They were both so happy and expecting in May. Amber was due in January, so there were two new babies arriving in 1990. Sarah talked to them and told her version of Afrika. With occasional telephone connections, we did not feel that Afrika was so far away if we didn't look at the map.

We attended church services in Bukavu in French and Swahili. It was an exciting Sunday when I could understand the church services in both French and Swahili. What an achievement! It was the encouragement that I needed. I was really heady with my language skills when I came home and realized that this language wasn't all that difficult. A little knowledge goes a long way when you first learn a language. Sarah helped the younger children in a Sunday school class and was having fun with the children. She loved helping the two- and three-year-olds, the same ages as her nieces and nephews. She was experienced and really loved them.

We finished our language studies and went to Kidodobo to start the next phase of our African culture orientation. We left Sarah's two kittens at Kidodobo with their mother for the week that we lived in the village. It was our "bonding experience" with an African family to help us understand the needs of the village families that we worked with.

We moved to the village of Kahanda with Kabanja and his family. It was quite different from the hills of north central Kansas, to Eastern Zaire of Central Afrika. We stayed in the foothills of the Mountains of the Moon. Sarah and I were invited to be guests in the small village of Kahanda, elevation over 7000 feet, near the mission station of Kidodobo. The hills and mountains were so lush and green and spectacular in this beautiful African rainforest. Our host was Kabanja and his family of three children Musa, Imani and Zowadi, with his wife expecting another next month. We arrived there by Land Rover and by foot with two cots, mosquito netting, sleeping bags and boiled water. And enough clothing for a week. Kabanja and his wife made us feel welcome and fed us very well. We were very grateful for the mosquito netting as malaria is endemic in Zaire.

Bugali is the main dish in Zaire. It is made of flour from the root of the cassava plant, which has been pounded with kutwangio, and then sifted and formed into dough. Then each person breaks off a chunk and dips it into a sauce. We also ate sweet potatoes, beans, rice and avocado with bananas from the grove in which we lived. Kabanja took us around to meet all his parents and grandparents nearby. This family is Christian with some means of support since Kabanja is employed as a cook by the mission. The family does not normally eat so well, but we helped ease the financial burden of feeding two extra people.

* * *

The kitchen is a hut where a wood fire burns under a metal frame that holds the cooking pot. The mama and the children and relatives sit around the warm fire to chat and sing songs while they cook the meal; the wood smoke surrounds us. It is a happy time when there is food. Some hungry children wander in hoping for some food too. They even have a wash house with rabbits on the other side. Little girls of five and six carry young babies on their backs wrapped in kikwembe, while the mothers work in the fields. The young boys and young men do nothing since it is the custom for them only to study. On visiting with a young man in the village who studies English at the University in Bukavu about an hour away, I found that his old mother works in the fields while he does nothing on his school holiday. It is the custom. The young girls and women work very hard. Life is not easy in the village, but if women make it through their childbearing years, they live longer than men it seems. Although the average lifespan for a woman in Zaire was in the early fifties. Many older widows live in the village, but maybe only look older.

* * *

We arrived in Kahanda after two months of study in Swahili, but after getting here we found that the whole village speaks Mashi, another tribal language. Fortunately our host understood and spoke Swahili. This was not surprising, as there were over 250 dialects in Zaire. Being there just part of our preparation for our work in Zaire. After I completed a six-weeks nursing "stage" in the hospital at Nyankunde in northern Zaire near the Ugandan border, I would work as Director of the Orphanage at Kidodobo where there were as many as seventy children.

One child was brought in recently weighing one kilogram whose mother put her in a cooking pot. The mother killed three previous children before the neighbors decided that she was crazy and brought the infant to the orphanage to be raised. This is not too uncommon. Most children at the orphanage have lost their mothers in childbirth. And fathers of families cannot provide for them. The mother feeds the family with her hard work and when she is gone, the family often goes hungry.

Kabanja's house was made of mud with a white wash over the walls. A dirt floor, which had hardened to a mosaic pattern, was swept out and very practical for the muddy environment with so much rain. They kept it looking very clean. After a heavy rainstorm the muddy paths to the choo were pretty deep. I cautioned Sarah not to track the mud into the house and then realized how stupid that was. After thirty years of trying to keep Kansas mud out of the house, it just didn't work that way here. She immediately caught me on this slip of culture, and I saw how ridiculous it sounded. We both enjoyed a good laugh at ourselves. As life is hard here, laughter is essential.

Sarah was the main attraction here, and many children followed her everywhere she went. When we went for a walk to all the surrounding villages and to the Chief's house, they invited us in for tea and stared at us like we were from another planet! It was humorous being the first white people to visit the village. About fifty children with ragged clothing followed us everywhere we went. Two or more boys came up to be with Sarah, but she brushed them off. She didn't have a problem expressing her real feelings. We gathered a mob wherever we went and everyone wanted to greet us. We knew only two words of greeting in Mashi.

The Mashi Tribe greeted each other with "Have you eaten today?" That would definitely tell you how people are doing. Might as well cut to the specifics of life here in Afrika and not mess around with formalities. It also seemed to imply social accountability to each other or why ask. We were doing well communicating in our freshly learned Swahili, and people didn't seem to mind that our Mashi was non-existent and were very friendly. Hearing the "cockle doodle do" of the roosters our first morning in the village reminded me of Port-au-Prince since that was my alarm clock there. Sitting in the main room of the house, the chickens walked in and out. It took all my sense of control not to shoo them away and just to watch them. I just sat and watched their meanderings. Everything co-exists in Afrika. The first day I wore a clean skirt, the second day it was slightly dirty with red mud, the third day it was much wrinkled and very dirty with red mud. But it is amazing what you can get used to.

Mama Zowadi brought us a pan of hot water to wash with every morning and night. That was very considerate of Kabanja and we really needed it. Sarah learned early how to go with the flow of the village. It was wash day in Kahanda and she made two trips to the river for water on the first day with two other girls. I helped Mama wash the clothes. They were just rags and such a pathetic wardrobe, but were washed a long time with lots of soap and put out on the bushes to dry. Sarah went with the children to help cut some leaves for the cooking pot. They asked her to have an English class for them. After dinner in the evenings, we sat around the table and showed our family pictures that we brought with us. They all asked many questions about America.

We learned that the only boy in this family was the parent's insurance policy for old age. They pampered and doted on him and worked the little girls starting as soon as they could walk. Their hopes for a good life in their old age are pinned on Musa, their only son. He will take care of them as Kabanja looks after his parents and grandparents in the village now. Kabanja and his wife Zowadi are about twenty-three years old.

Kabanja went off to his work from his mud house with a mud floor wearing clean jeans and a clean yellow windbreaker. That was surely such optimism and a triumph over their limited circumstances, with mucky, red mud everywhere. They taught me about victory over circumstances. We ate a delicious meal of beans with sweet potatoes cooked in them, rice and linga-linga, which was greens with ground up peanuts cooked in it.

We found the nights were pitch black in the village with only the moon and stars. They only had lanterns in the evenings in their houses. A man who we were later told was crazy, was right outside our window screaming and shouting and woke us up very early one morning while it was still dark. The mentally ill people in the village here are left alone and wander around alone to be laughed at and tolerated by the people. And they are usually fed out of compassion.

The view in Kahanda was spectacular and similar to the movie we saw on the plane flight here, *Gorillas in the Mist,* since it borders on the tiny country of Rwanda where the movie was made. The mist covered the mountains and foothills each morning and an approaching thunderstorm was spectacular to watch. Since we were there in the rainy season, we got to watch that every day. We loved the rainstorms in Kansas, so we really enjoyed that. With eighty-four inches or seven feet of rain falling yearly, it beat down hard when it came. The day before, the rain turned to hail as we watched it cover the ground and the tops of the beehive-shaped thatched huts. The hail came down hard and fast piled up to look like snow. Everyone was so excited. We were not prepared to see hail and it took us by surprise. It looked so funny and incongruous to us in the jungle. The children loved it and dashed out to eat the ice, running and laughing as I remembered I used to do in the rain at our farm as a child. I definitely knew how they enjoyed this. The hills with mounds of hail covering them created an unusual and lovely picture with the banana groves close by. The wood smoke from their kitchen fires curled up through the thatched roofs covered with hail. It made a lovely picture.

Early on the second morning as I went to the outside "choo" toilet, I discovered chicken feathers all over the bamboo covered hole in the ground. I thought that a chicken had met its untimely death down the hole after a terrible struggle. I went to tell Mama Zowadi and found her cutting up the chicken in a pan. So only the head had made its way into the "choo" and we had the kukoo, chicken, for dinner that night.

On the third day of our stay in the village we walked about two miles to the big Soko market. We felt very conspicuous in a multitude of Africans. All the farmers and villagers brought their produce and crafts to sell each Wednesday and Saturday. It looked like an outdoor Walmart with everything laid out on tables or on the ground. Food was plentiful if you had the money to buy or goods to exchange for it. Sarah was tired from our walk but really perked up at the possibility of shopping. She decided to buy all the family gifts with our 2,500 Zaires. I thought that was a great idea and let her do the choosing. She bought a bag of candy for the children, a round tray for Mama Zowadi, two notebooks for Efranse, Kabanja's sister, three Bic pens for Kabanja and a small can of oil for herself to keep her Swiss Army pocket knife that Phillip gave her clean and working. On our walk home it started thundering, and Sarah ate maracujas and candy while we hurried to beat the rain.

The candy was a good choice and a big hit with everyone. That evening, after the three children, Musa, Imani and Zowadi finished their baths, I put antibiotic ointment on the sores on their legs and feet and Band-Aids. They were enjoying their candy very much. Sarah brought a bottle of red fingernail polish and offered to polish their fingernails. They all wanted this, Musa the little boy included, and their toenails also. One child had an extra digit on their hand and she polished all their nails and the nails of some older girls who arrived too. Sarah usually knew just what the children liked.

All the fruits and vegetables were vibrant colors and very large. Sometimes they didn't look real. I will never forget the bright colors of the beans. All I had known was the brown and white beans that we had cooked on our farm. I was amazed and could hardly believe that beans actually grew in so many different bright colors. They looked like an assortment from a Dr. Seuss book that were colored from fantasy. We sorted beans of every color you can imagine out on broad green banana leaves on the ground. Pink and black striped, black and white striped, orange and brown striped, yellow, green, gray, brown, white, pink, blue, and purple beans looked like they had been painted for a picture. They were so pretty that I thought it was a shame to cook them. But they tasted so delicious cooked with sweet potatoes.

I was nervous the first time I was asked to pray in Swahili one night before our meal. I did the best I could with Sarah often prompting me. She picked up much Swahili from the children playing on the street in Bukavu and had more words in her vocabulary than I had in mine. The prayer was a start, and I became more comfortable each day in speaking this new language.

We had much time during the day to think about what we could do to help. One day I got out my sewing needles and thread and offered to mend some of the children's clothes. Mama Zowadi brought me a few and I started mending. A crowd of women and children gathered to watch me sew. One mother took off her baby's shirt and gave it to me to mend. I sewed all afternoon until I realized that they did not have any needles or thread like the village women in Haiti where I did the Sewing Project. I passed out a few needles and some women began sewing. They were curious and willing to learn, but I could tell that they did not know how or see this as necessary. Ragged clothes were just accepted and worn.

I dropped my toothbrush in the dirt the first night in the village and stopped using it. After unsuccessfully trying to boil and disinfect one in Haiti on an earlier occasion, and have the plastic and bristles twist into a corkscrew, I decided that I would have to go without one. After a couple of days, Sarah shared hers with me and it felt so good to brush my teeth. Sarah cleaned and oiled her pocketknife every day and always kept it with her and we cut everything with it.

A group of boys set up a drum-beating contest just outside our room in front of the house. I thought this was their contribution to our entertainment and a way to get Sarah's attention. One day there was a long line of older boys who lined up in front of our house waiting to get in. Kabanja was home and I asked him what they wanted. He smiled and replied that they were asking for Sarah for a wife and offered cows and goats and anything they had. A twelve-year-old girl that was as tall as the adults here was fair game for the African custom of wife bartering. I didn't tell this to Sarah until after we left the village. An older boy attending the university in Bukavu was very insistent and especially annoying to her, and wanted her to teach him English. He knew it very well and she just ignored him. As her kindergarten teacher told me "she won't take nothing from nobody."

Our last day in the village Sarah woke up with a fever and vomiting and had vomited the night before. She was eating so many different things outside with the children and not always washing her hands, so this did not surprise me. I decided to take her to the clinic at Kidodobo and we walked. Since it was foggy and drizzling rain and I didn't know the way, Efranse, the sister of Kabanja led us. I could never have found the way by myself. The fog and rain obscured the path through the jungle, and I supported Sarah since she was feeling so bad and dizzy. We walked very slowly and rested often. The crazy man followed us yelling the entire way to Kidodobo and it was very unnerving and I felt so sorry for Sarah. It probably look us an hour to walk and it was a nightmare. When we arrived at the clinic we did a test for malaria and worms and found that she had Ascaris, a parasite infection. I started her on medication, and she was glad to rest on the couch in the home of the nurse that day and just play with her kittens. We went back out to the village with Kabanja in the late afternoon for our last night there.

Many people came that night and ate with us. They knew that it was our last night in the village. Sarah took her medication again that evening and felt better. We got up early the next morning, and after bread and tea and bananas with the family, we told everyone good-bye. We packed most of our things and left for Bukavu. Sarah left many of her things with the children there. We stopped at Kidodobo just long enough to pick up her two kittens, Ebony and Rascal, and arrived in Bukavu, happy to have our week finished and able to enjoy a hot bath. Now we knew how the people lived in the villages.

We were grateful for the opportunity for bonding with Kabanja's family and their hospitality. People in the village with hardly anything enjoyed life and practiced neighborliness at a very basic level. To have enough food to eat and clothes to wear and warm shelter was the luckiest of all. And there were very few assurances that these would be provided.

As soon as we came back to Bukavu, we left for Kigali, Rwanda to have my dental bridge made for my tooth that was pulled last month. The dentist made the imprints and sent them to Nairobi for a gold bridge. I would have African gold in my mouth from this missionary trip. I hoped that is all of the country that I carried out of here in my body. The streets and restaurants of Kigali with all kinds of modern shops were a welcome sight. The six-hour drive was long, but we were getting used to it and it was a beautiful drive through the rainforest again. The last week in the village of Kahanda and this week in a modern city was a vast distance to bridge, culturally. We went to the American Club at the Embassy and watched a movie and ate pizza. It seemed like we were jumping back and forth to such startling contrast of lifestyles. It was no problem for Sarah; she loved the pizza and movie and swimming pool. The few days there were restful, and we drove back to Rwanda. I took my language exam when I got back. Sarah brought her schoolbooks but didn't start her formal study yet.

In just a few hours, a Missionary Aviation Fellowship Pilot came to pick us up early in the morning to take us to the Bukavu Airport and our flight to Nyankunde Zaire. Another young nurse from a Baptist Mission in Bukavu flew with us. We were delayed taking off at the airport waiting for a father and his four-year-old child to arrive. The child had been very sick and vomiting blood for three days. Two hours later we took off with a Swedish pilot, Sarah and I and the other nurse sitting in the middle seats. Sarah was holding her two scared kittens on her lap in a straw hat, with the father and sick child sitting in the back seats. The sick child slept most of the way. Sarah had gotten special permission to bring the kittens to Nyankunde with her.

We soared through the African skies at 7,500 feet going 250 miles per hour in a small plane. It was pretty noisy and we didn't do much talking. We made one stop to let the sick child and his father off and pick up an elderly doctor and his wife. We saw herds of buffalo, lakes and rivers with many hippos, and hillsides crawling with baboons. There were many thin lines of dirty brown rivers snaking through the dense jungle. The jungle looked like a massive broccoli patch of different shades of greens at this height.  One area had orange and brown trees mixed together. We flew over Lake Victoria in Tanzania and hugged the shoreline on one side. I almost lost it all a few times as we hit wind currents and bounced along. I saw no life jackets on the plane. We had a smooth landing and take-off at Romguba at a Heli-mission airstrip. Sarah was really enjoying the flight and feeding her kittens bits of roast beef that she had along for them. She received some Starburst candy in the mail from her sister Amber that came just in time before we left. She brought it with her and shared it with everyone in the plane on the trip. I was glad to have something for my queasy stomach.

It was very hot in the afternoon when we arrived at the grass airstrip in Nyankunde. We took a bus to the guesthouse where we planned to stay. They weren't expecting us so soon, so Sarah and I shared a house with a Japanese lady, Katsuko, for a couple of nights until our room was ready at the guesthouse. The two kittens survived the trip well and shared our bedroom with us. The long fringed bedspread scraping the bare floor provided hours of entertainment for these two playful kittens. Katsuko had three large cats that she let into her house. Sarah's kitten Rascal played the villain for a while until they got wise to him. Gordon Hunt, a Canadian doctor from Bukavu, greeted us at the guesthouse where we ate our meals.

It was very beautiful up here in the mountains close to the Ugandan border. The water pressure in the tub was absolutely fantastic! Sarah and I could hardly believe it. We saw the video *Chariots of Fire* on our first night at the guesthouse. We were all asked for blood donations of "O" type for a missionary who was undergoing surgery in the hospital. One of the nurses donated blood and the electricity went off during surgery. The back-up generator went on, and surgery was completed. The patient had a ruptured spleen from a motorcycle accident. Risky living here in Afrika! Our plane had no radio while flying to Nyankunde and flying over such vast areas of jungles and mountains without one seemed rather risky to me. But we stayed close to the coastline of Lake Victoria should we have any problems and needed to be found. I think the MAF pilots were ready to land anywhere.

Sarah brought all her schoolbooks and started her classwork early every day while I worked until one in the afternoon. She couldn't put it off any longer. When all the other kids who lived here got out of school and she went swimming. She met many kids at the pool and played soccer with them. It was a very nice pool, beautifully kept grounds and there were nice houses dotting the hillsides. Missionaries who lived here had very nice facilities. Swimming, mountain climbing, hospital, nearby city, and Lake Victoria were all available. Sarah's bicycle was coming up on the next plane and she looked forward to riding it.

My six-week orientation to African nursing started out in Intensive Care, OR and Women's Surgical the first week. The Intensive Care Unit was clean by African standards, but there were not many medical supplies. I assisted with the motorcycle victim with the ruptured spleen and also a broken jaw that was wired together in the

Operating Room. The African surgeon was very kind, cheerful and patient in dealing with his surgical patients. In the Women's Surgical Ward, families did much of the caregiving and all the food preparation for their relatives.

My next job was Community Health, which I enjoyed the most. We walked out into the villages, carrying coolers of vaccines and supplies for a prenatal and well-child clinic. After arriving we had someone in the village beat on a drum and then held our clinic in a schoolhouse. Women slowly started coming in groups of three or four with their children until there were about seventy-five. We read the Bible and a scripture teaching to open the clinic, followed by Health Teaching, and answering questions while we took care of the patients. I started out doing history taking, blood pressures and record keeping, counting and tabulating the children of the villages reached by the clinic.

There were 526 children in 23 locations receiving follow-up care, Daraprim (Pyrimethamine) for malaria, and immunizations. I really enjoyed this exchange with the mothers and their children and was able to use my Swahili. Teaching mothers how to care for the health of their children and prevent diseases was my greatest interest in nursing. I knew that I could make the greatest and most significant impact in improving the health of the people in rural areas. The outcome is multiplied greatly in giving the mothers the education and tools that they need to care for their families. They are the hardest workers and needed the most help.

I met a young girl in the Peace Corps who started a health center in another area. Janet really seemed to know what she was doing and had been here for a year and spoke good Swahili. I hoped to speak as well after a year. She lived alone in a small house on the edge of town and rode a motorcycle out to the villages. There were many Peace

Corps workers in Zaire living in very difficult situations. Later, I rode with her on her motorcycle to see one of the villages where she worked. It was a long ride where there were no roads. I saw cases of leprosy in one village. I had met Peace Corp workers in Bukavu who were studying Swahili before going to difficult places to work, and I really admired them. Janet was the daughter of missionaries who had lived in Africa.

The BBC from England came while we were in Nyankunde to make a video of Helen Roseveare, who started the nursing school at the Nyankunde Hospital many years ago while she worked as a missionary here. She pioneered this work and now the Nyankunde Hospital trains African nurses from many countries. I read her book at the guesthouse and was glad to meet her at dinner one night. She talked of her early years working there and was very interesting. The hospital had grown into large facilities and ministered to hundreds of Africans.

Our first week there, African boys came to the front door of the guesthouse with a cloth sack with a baby baboon for sale. Sarah wanted to buy it to add to her pet collection. It sure was cute, and I knew that she would really love it, but my good common sense said no. She had enough to take care of right now with her two kittens. Since she loved all animals at the farm I knew she really wanted this baby baboon. But I had to think of our purpose here and not get bogged down in too many pets for her to take care of. Later we heard how difficult and mean the baboon becomes as it grows older.

Sarah and I worked a long day of math, and I helped her with her long division. She caught on quickly and was feeling competent with it by the end of the day. There were many children to play with here and things to do. She especially liked a canteen nearby where they bought cokes, milk, juice, and snacks. She enjoyed her growing kittens,

Rascal and Ebony, and played with them and took them out for walks. The kittens policed our bedroom every day and kept the large cockroaches chased away or ate them. We played cards in the evenings with Karrie, the other young nurse who came with us from Bukavu.

In October, Amber and Grace sent out our first newsletter to all our friends and family who supported us in Zaire. I wrote the newsletters and sent them to Amber. Amber was our forwarding agent and took care of our finances. She kept the master list and mailings, and Grace was good with the geographical drawings. We kept people informed of our mission and how things were going.

During my Community Health visits we walked to the village of Kalingi with a local African health worker and a student. It was a two-kilometer walk along a road that soon turned into a narrow path through the jungle. We met in a church with a dirt floor and saw forty-six children with their mothers. Heavy rains came while we were there and beat hard on the tin roof of the church. When we were finished, we walked back by the same muddy path, trying to jump over the mud puddles and walked through tall grass. Fortunately I was able to stay on my feet while I slid in the mud, but still had mud up to my knees before I got back. It was a good experience seeing how the Africans organize their clinics. It was utter chaos, though, and the work really needed three people.

No mail came for three weeks, but then we finally got a number of letters from the children and friends. We learned with the mail that it was either feast or famine. Pictures and news of the grandchildren were especially devoured and appreciated. We also enjoyed the warmth of the jungle a little bit more when we learned that Manhattan, Kansas recorded the nation's low of minus twenty-three degrees with a wind-chill factor of minus sixty degrees. Living in the jungle of Zaire close to the equator, we had come to the opposite end of the world temperature wise. Sarah and I just looked at each other and knew that we were very happy here. We would have had to chop through six inches of ice on our pond at the farm for the animals to have water.

On weekends we went off for hikes and picnics in the surrounding jungle with groups that lived in Nyankunde. We enjoyed the hiking. After stopping to rest by a river, there was the choice of crossing the river on a rope-and-vine bridge or returning to the guesthouse. Sarah and I were all for the bridge, and it was an exciting event of our time there. We started out on the bridge made of ropes and vines, and crossed a very wide dark brown river, with foaming turbulent waters when we looked down through the vines and ropes. The noise was so loud that we couldn't hear each other talk and just kept going, with no chance of changing our minds once we got started. Our hands and feet had to go together. We made it across and even back again on our return hike.

Sarah and I both developed headaches, diarrhea, and stomach cramps and were very sick. I could hardly get out of bed and decided that we both needed to go to the lab for a malaria test and a stool culture. We ate some things on our hiking trip that I felt was highly suspect. I had terrible pressure in my lower back and stomach and knew that I either had malaria or amoebiasis. Sarah got well but I continued to feel weak with a lot of pain that Tylenol didn't touch. The electricity went off and we couldn't get our lab results back, so I thought about starting my treatment for malaria with or without positive blood tests. But I waited and lab tests confirmed that I had amoebiasis. I started taking medication and felt much better, although pretty weak for a few days.

The next week, Maternity Clinic and Leprosy Clinic went quickly. I particularly liked my days in the lab and pathology department, learning about the large numbers of AIDS cases in Zaire, although there were no tests given for confirmation. Africa always had its "wasting disease" as we learned in Tropical Medicine. There were still many cases of leprosy here in Zaire and it was treated with Dapsone. I was able to spend a day at the pharmacy and ordered medicines for the orphanage at Kidodobo. Sarah went with me one day and fixed up her own First Aid Kit.

Sarah's schoolwork was going well and she spent each morning with her books. She met many new friends and really enjoyed our time here. But we were both looking forward to moving on to Kidodobo and the orphanage and starting our work there.

We often sat around the dining room table drinking coffee and tea in the evenings in Nyankunde, and just visited with the many guests who came and went at the guesthouse. I learned about a kerosene refrigerator in storage here with the household goods of a missionary family who went back to the States. I was pretty excited about this news and got permission to take it back to our house at Kidodobo when we left for Bukavu. A refrigerator in the house would make a huge difference storing food and preparing meals. I inquired about transportation, and Missionary Aviation Fellowship was able to take it on one of their planes for us. It was good to see how all the mission groups supported and helped each other in the many different locations in Zaire. I had never used a kerosene refrigerator, but checked on their price in Bukavu and knew they were about $1000 new. I remembered the one Mom had on the porch at our farm in Madison and was sure that I could learn how to use it. I was reminded that God was able to do anything for anyone, anytime or anywhere. We were grateful for the kerosene refrigerator and for all those who made it possible for us to find it, clean it up, get it running and shipped to Bukavu.

We knew no one before we arrived here, but the world becomes smaller and smaller as you move around in it. In the first week after we arrived Sarah and I were walking on a path up to the guesthouse, and I heard someone call my name from behind us. A young girl recognized me from Manhattan, Kansas who was a member of our church there. Her husband was a pilot with Missionary Aviation Fellowship and they lived in Nyankunde with their two children. I was amazed to hear someone calling my name in this new place in Zaire and I remembered her family. She and her sister visited our farm and were in the same high school and youth group with our children. We talked and visited and she invited us to their house for dinner. We had a nice dinner with their family and talked about their work with MAF and her family in the States.

We left Nyankunde and took another MAF flight back to Bukavu. It went fast and again I was amazed at the enormous distance across the jungle. We were glad to get back. Our refrigerator made it back in good condition and waited to be taken to our house at Kidodobo. We waited for a trip to Kigali for the dentist to put in my gold bridge since it arrived from Nairobi, but we didn't have the necessary papers yet for the border.

Our household goods arrived from the States that we shipped so long ago. We enjoyed sorting and unpacking everything and Sarah appreciated getting her rubber rain boots. We decided to call some of the children for Thanksgiving from the hotel in Cyangugu, Rwanda just across the border where we called before. It was so good to talk to them and catch up on their news. They were all getting together in Phoenix for Thanksgiving and making us a video of all the grandchildren. That would be great to see sometime.

We moved all our things to Kidodobo and lived in a camper-trailer until Diane, the nurse left for the States. We were sure glad to be there after talking about it for a year and all my time spent in training here in Zaire.

We received a Christmas box from Grace, Tim and Colleen and some pictures from Chip. It was great to have mail again. I painted the trim inside the house and put in two folding directors chairs that was in our household goods. My portable sewing machine arrived, so I was able to sew an hour during the day when the gas generator was running to create electricity. I bought some bright African prints at the Soko and made couch and chair covers for the living room. A carpenter made a large comfortable rocking chair for our house, and I added a foam-covered pad. I miraculously found black and white gingham material and made curtains and covered the rocking chair pad that finished off our house decorating. It looked very cozy and comfortable.

I started making 6:30 a.m. rounds at Toddle Inn, the orphanage, with Diane and learning about the procedures. The children ranged from birth to seven years old and lived in houses according to their age group. There was a male African nurse, Ntabala, who ran the clinic and helped me with the children. There were young girls called "Bintis" (Swahili for young girl) who cared for the children and slept in the houses with them on mattresses on the floors.

Our kerosene refrigerator arrived from Bukavu, kerosene and wick added, and was running beautifully. I was so amazed and happy to have acquired it at Nyankunde. It was a cheerful blue and white that added a modern note to our very primitive kitchen. Diane enjoyed having it for a short time before she left and appreciated our help in cleaning up the house. She sometimes had six preemies in bassinets with hot water bottles in the spare bedroom to care for with helpers. She was so swamped with work and the children that it left her no time for anything else. We were glad to be there and helped her before she left on furlough. I was very grateful for all her instructions in preparing me for the work at the orphanage.

The driveway that led to the mission was lined with beautiful large Eucalyptus trees on either side, their silvery leaves and aromatic smell very inviting. We rode our bikes on the dirt roads after they arrived, and Howard Crowl put them together for us. Sarah and Amy, the adopted African daughter of June and Howard, enjoyed riding the bikes together. They were bright hot pink and white and we picked them out in Manhattan and sent them ahead with our household goods in April. Sarah and Amy were about the same age and went to Bukavu to attend classes at the Christian School.

We made our last trip to Kigali to the dentist with John and Sylvia Ross, and my dental bridge was put in, which was very painful. The dentist did not have an easy time. He used a rubber mallet to pound it in since my teeth had shifted. We went to the American Club to have pizza and saw a movie, which Sarah really enjoyed. We shopped and I brought some Christmas presents for the children, some Batiks of African animals, rural scenes and people in the villages. They were brightly painted on a stiff cloth that I thought was interesting and later I hung some in our house. I found some blue paint in a shop in Kigali and mixed it with white to get a nice soft country blue color for the kitchen cupboards after we moved into our house.

On Christmas Eve we slept in our house for the first time. Diane moved her things out and we moved into the house after spending three weeks in the camper trailer. She prepared me well for the many medical problems that I encountered at the orphanage. I learned the schedule for the children at Toddle Inn, and what was needed. I knew that it was challenging and required all of my attention along with checking Sarah's schoolwork. But I knew that I needed to clean and organize our house first to provide our privacy and refuge from the limitless demands of the orphanage.

We enjoyed running water into the house as long as the fifty-gallon drum outside was kept filled from the nearby spring. A roaring fire in the evening directly under the drum even heated up the spring water for a warm shower. We had a toilet and shower in the bathroom that we appreciated greatly. You really needed to work at staying clean in this environment. Our water filter in the kitchen filtered our water after it had been boiled and cooled in a pressure cooker each morning. Drinking the water was the fastest way to get very sick.

We enjoyed a nice Christmas Eve with Howard and June Crowl and their family with food and games and a gift exchange. We were still amazed that we were so far away in Zaire, but now settled in our home. We missed all the children and grandchildren. We opened our gifts on Christmas morning that arrived earlier from the children. All the children were very generous and we were loaded with treats and nice gifts.

After doing the rounds at the orphanage and checking all the children and wishing them Merry Christmas, I fixed a broccoli casserole to take to a potluck dinner in Bukavu with all the missionaries. All the children and workers at the orphanage received gifts and special treats. Since this was the rainy season, the rain came down in buckets very hard and we canceled our trip to Bukavu because of the muddy roads. We did not want to spend Christmas Day stuck in the mud. But we enjoyed our Christmas Day at Kidodobo and enjoyed all the nice cards and gifts that we received from friends and family. We also received a Christmas tape from Chip, Elizabeth, Morgan and Kenny, and Andrew and Shawnae, which added much to our joy. It was so good to hear their voices, and we were able to listen to it often with our battery-operated tape player. I gave Sarah an African drum that she beat on all day.

We gave all the children a banana at ten on Christmas morning and gave the Bintis candy. The rain kept coming and we ate dinner together with the Crowls. Although I hoped to call the children, it had to wait until later. Not much in Africa was dependable except the rain, and the roads were probably the most risky.

Our house was white washed with black painted trim with a red tin corrugated roof. There were windows on the front of the house facing the orphanage and windows on the back looking out on our flowers and grassy backyard with a clotheslines and a fence where the jungle and banana grove started. The bright shining stars in the pitch-black night were just spectacular. I had never felt so close to them or seen so many at once. They seemed so bright like I could reach out and touch them. We were up in the mountains, ten degrees from the equator here in Zaire. I was amazed that wherever I lived or traveled in America, Europe, Haiti, India, England, Russia, or Afrika, that it was the same familiar moon and stars in the universe. I felt at home.

We both slept on waterbeds in our bedrooms, but since it was cold at night, we had to sleep on a sleeping bag on the bed to stay warm. There was no way to heat the water. Eric had a waterbed at the farm, but Sarah had never had one before and really liked her waterbed. She spent a good amount of time organizing and fixing up her bedroom with plenty of space for her things. Her large window looked out to our backyard. She slept in her bed the first night and felt very much at home. A baby that was kept in a crib in her room had head lice, so I moved her out to the orphanage and treated her. That was Sarah's room now and all the babies were kept in the orphanage. I decided that Sarah needed her own private space. Our transition here was gradual with all our moves and adjustments since we had arrived in June.

Sarah liked to fix omelets for breakfast and people in the villages brought us fresh eggs. We were told to put the eggs in a large bowl of water, and if they floated they were rotten and we should not buy them. But the villagers brought us fresh eggs every day. We also bought flat round, huge mushrooms, twelve inches across and all kinds of vegetables as they brought them to our back door. Each day we got a little more settled and moved in. We kept our bikes outside in front of our house, but soon found everyone was riding them and they wouldn't last long, so we moved them into the front entryway of our house.

I decided that I needed to treat all the bad cases of scabies in the orphanage, then start a prevention program to keep it under control. With the children living in such close quarters and lack of sufficient water and sanitation, we never got rid of it, but we could keep it under control. Many of the children had swollen and infected hands and were put on antibiotics. But it was cheaper to use the powdered Chloramine solution mixed in water to dip their hands in three times a week and prevent the infections. With so many children, this took a determined and consistent effort. The babies' heads were often infected with scabies when they arrived, and their heads were shaved regularly. I also used a mixture that I made of Vaseline and sulfur in large jars and kept the jars in the houses for the Binitis to use for treatment.

There were three large houses of children at the orphanage: Kubwa meaning big, for the older children, Kati-Kati for the toddlers, and the house for the infants. There was a separate cookhouse where all the food was prepared, and the chickens wandered in and out among the vegetables spread out on the palm leaves on the ground. Kwashiorkor and bwaki was very common with all the children when they arrived. Their stomach muscles had become so weak during starvation that they continued to have pot-bellies even while they were getting sufficient and adequate amounts of protein food.

With our house cleaned and freshly painted we felt very much at home. Sarah turned her attention to starting her rabbit project. She tried riding the resident horse Duchess, but decided that she was too wild for her. The children at the orphanage were all afraid of Duchess. I purchased the wire screening for the rabbit cages, and Sarah asked one of the African workers named Jaa to find the lumber and start on building them. She wanted enough built for thirty to forty rabbits for her project and was soon ready to purchase her first pair of rabbits at the Soko.

Lighting the kerosene lantern each night about six o'clock was a routine we quickly established since we had no electricity. Sometimes it was easy and other times it took a while. Keeping the water boiled in our pressure cooker and filtered was another daily task that was important and very essential. We didn't want to run out of drinking water. I bought a case of the small, glass-bottled cokes when I went to Bukavu shopping and they lasted a long time. Water and lights took a high priority in our health and lifestyle. We were definitely down to the basics here. We cooked with palm oil, bright orange color peanuts, locally grown and in abundance, and Sarah enjoyed sucking pieces of sugar cane like the rest of the children.

An African girl who needed work came in from her village to hand wash our clothes and scrub the floors of our house. I don't think that she had seen a large mirror before because she always enjoyed passing it and smiling. Keeping the concrete floors clean was a big job and needed to be done often to keep out mud and disease. Staying healthy and preventing any sickness was my number one priority for Sarah and I so we could help the children and do the work. But we still occasionally got diarrhea and stomach cramps.

When one of the boys in Kati Kati, Byamungu, became very sick and did not respond to my treatment, we sent him to a doctor in Bukavu and a missionary came to take him. Many children developed ear infections and they went unnoticed by the Bintis until drainage was coming out of the ear. So I provided the girls with ear drops to use and told them to watch the youngest children closely who couldn't talk and use the ear drops frequently. I used liquid Chloroquine for the smallest children and gave one cc per kilogram. A little girl, Nzigera, refused to eat and we helped her until she started eating her meals each day. Heavy worm infections made the children nauseated and they often refused to eat. I used Vermox medicine as the drug of choice for mixed worm infections. This was given regularly since all the children had worms. The older children over six years old took one tablet twice a day for three days, and the younger ones a liquid of 5 cc twice a day for three days. The older children could go home for weekends, but if they were on medication they had to stay at Kidodobo so we could supervise them.

We felt weekend visits with their extended families were important for them to keep in contact because they were returned to their villages when they were seven years old. They received all their immunizations, healthy food and health care in order to help them survive the first dangerous years. Half of the under-five population living in villages died before they reached five years of age.

Sarah started going into Bukavu three days each week for school. I bought a white Toyota truck with a stock rack in the back that was for sale by a missionary leaving to go back to the States. We needed 4-wheel drive since the road to Bukavu was often muddy and dangerous in the rainy season. We needed our own transportation and space to haul all the supplies for the orphanage when we shopped at the market in Bukavu. The truck turned out to be very good transportation for us. During one of Sarah's school days, her mama rabbit had her first batch of baby rabbits. Sarah was delighted!

We hosted a Bible study and prayer meeting in our home on Wednesday evenings for the African workers at our mission. We sang songs and prayed together and studied the Bible and then popped popcorn before they went home. Popcorn was a real treat for the Africans. It was a fun time for us all and we got to know them better. They liked to look at our family pictures displayed on our kabati (cupboard). It was a good time for us to ask them about their families and concerns and we learned much about their work during the social time that we spent together. Sarah and I felt very close to them and they helped us in many ways.

Sarah had a small black mole growing on her left lower lid before we left the States in June. The eye surgeon told us to keep a watch on it and if it increased drastically, we should have it removed. It grew considerably in the last six months and would soon be in her line of vision, so I made the decision to take her to Nairobi, Kenya for outpatient surgery and have it removed. We caught a Missionary Aviation Fellowship plane from the Bukavu Airport after we got the required papers called the "sortir de retour" that allowed us to go and return. Sarah was so involved with her rabbit project that she didn't want to go, but I talked her into going. We flew again with MAF from Bukavu to Nairobi.

We stayed in a missionary guesthouse with electricity and water and had delicious meals while we were in Nairobi. Sarah's eye surgery was completed as an outpatient at the Nairobi Hospital and I brought her back to the guesthouse from the hospital. She had gas for the surgery and was still dizzy for a while and laughed a lot. We were able to make a telephone call to Amber and Grace and were told that Grandmother Long had died in Manhattan. We were very sad. I remembered how happy she was when we had the Long Family Reunion at the farm in Manhattan before we had left. That was the last time we saw her. She was so kind and loving to all the children and we would miss her. Jordan Theobald was born in January in El Paso, Texas and we rejoiced with his parents Amber and Pat. We appreciated another grandchild in the family making eleven with another one coming in May.

Our week in Nairobi went quickly and we accomplished a lot. Surgery for Sarah, a doctor's check-up for me, shopping at the Central Market downtown, a visit to the Game Park, and telephone calls to all the children kept us going. We learned that Eric hurt his lateral collateral ligament in his knee playing touch football and wore a cast on his leg for six weeks. We flew back to Bukavu with MAF and saw spectacular scenery over Kenya and Tanzania. We flew into Tanzania and landed on the runway on the edge of Lake Victoria at the last minute. That was exciting! We picked up passengers and flew on to Bukavu. Coming back to Kidodobo was sad in that two small children had died from typhoid fever while we were gone.

We celebrated my fifty-fifth birthday on January 28th, and Sarah fixed a nice steak dinner with vegetables and rice. She also made Jell-O and whipped cream cake. Sarah bought me a beautiful pink quartz necklace and bracelet in Nairobi while we were shopping. She was so thoughtful, and I was very grateful to have one child here in Afrika to celebrate with. Howard and June turned on the gas generator for electricity and we watched a movie at their house. With the movie in the VCR, popcorn, and some Africans looking through the windows, we almost forgot where we were. It was a very nice birthday.

Our house was comfortable, everything was working and we were able to keep it clean. The orphanage was going well and the children were getting the help that they needed. I felt that we settled into the routine and were doing the best with what we had. Sarah got homesick for her brothers and sisters and wanted more children her age to play with. She made friends with Vumi, a girl from the nearby village. She made a slingshot and liked to climb trees and shoot it.

We received an invitation to attend the opening of another orphanage in Bukavu and decided to attend. After we arrived, we realized what an important occasion this was when the wives of the Presidents of Zaire, Rwanda and Burundi were introduced. There were also the well-dressed mamas of the rich, widely in attendance. There were many dancers, singers and other dignitaries and the famous Leopard Dancers of Zaire, all dressed in large leopard skins and doing a wild high jumping dance and chants. We were so glad that we came. The power and influence of the three presidents' wives created much preparation and show, but their short visit only showed disinterest as they smiled their way through the crowds. I thought, "How can the fat and healthy ever appreciate and really care about the hungry and orphaned in this world. They have probably not missed a meal in a long time." Or maybe they started out hungry and decided never to be that way again. You never know.

We took a tour through the orphanage and it was beautifully built with eleven houses and well-kept grounds. The many soldiers with machine guns under their arms were a little disquieting. But I guess this was all necessary to protect the rich and powerful. The soldiers, looking very lean, became very aggressive over the food and beer. I was glad we left before they became rowdy. The road back home was still unbelievable. Twenty miles an hour was just too fast most of the time, and to go twenty-five makes you feel like you are racing. But we arrived home and made a nice warm fire and a cup of tea. I considered that I was happy to drink tea with the poor rather than champagne with the rich.

Howard and June Crowl took off in their four-wheel-drive red and white Land Rover for a six-week trip to reach tribes in the jungle. It was only Sarah and me at the mission with the Africans to keep everything going. We radioed to Bukavu each morning how things were going at Kidodobo. Two new babies arrived at the orphanage in one week. I drove a lady to the hospital over such bad roads that ten miles an hour was too fast. I was lucky to get her there and back.

From my journal, "Sarah is acting like a wild African, building forts and cutting down trees, and she killed her first adult rabbit for the cooking pot at the orphanage. She was very proud and kept the rabbit skin to dry and use. She is reaping the profits of her rabbit project for the orphanage and has many more rabbits happily fed and mating in their cages." Her 4-H leaders would have been very impressed with her record keeping.

A father from one of the villages appeared at our kitchen door with twin girls who were four years old but weighed only sixteen pounds. Their skin was stretched tightly over their skulls and bones, with large stomachs and the saddest eyes that we had ever seen. They were named Namuto and Nymakuro. They were lethargic, never smiled and broke our hearts. We kept them in our house during the day and fed them often, small meals of high protein foods, peanuts, eggs, milk, meat, cheese and bread and vegetables for many months. We had to teach them to eat like humans since they had just eaten their food off the floor. Sarah wanted to be in charge of them while they were at our house. We first needed to give them baths in our shower and find clean clothes for them. We treated them for lice and scabies and gave them all their immunizations. Within a few months they were smiling, playing games with Sarah, coloring and singing songs. In six months they had gained weight and looked like the other children at the orphanage and could spend all their days there. Sarah and I learned so much in seeing how starving children responded to a well-balanced diet and sufficient food with tender loving care in such a short time.

A new orphanage building with larger space to accommodate up to one hundred children was planned for a long time and it was almost finished. Arrangements were made to have electricity brought to the building. With happy enthusiasm we started painting the trim and doors on the new brick orphanage located near the present buildings. I found paint in Kigali and Nairobi on my trips there to paint the wooden cribs in the nursery for the youngest babies. Everyone was so excited about having larger rooms with fewer children and more light that could be kept cleaner.

All the children wrote often and gave us news of the grandchildren and all their plans. While Sarah and I spent the year on the continent of Afrika travelling through Zaire, Rwanda, Burundi, Tanzania and Kenya, all the other children were crisscrossing America on American Airline passes. Compliments of Chip, they visited one another in Seattle, Sacramento, Florida, Texas, Phoenix and Chicago at Thanksgiving, Christmas or enroute to jobs. It was a busy year of travelling for the whole family and there couldn't have been many times when one of us wasn't in the air. As Chip said, "Anyone that would give free passes to a member of the Long family would be crazy." Chip was flying with American Airlines and weekends with the Wisconsin Air National Guard, and Phillip an instructor pilot in the T-38 at Williams Air Force Base. He greet his student pilot from Zaire with "Jambo" every morning.

Amber with a new baby and Grace expecting a baby, were both busy with preschoolers. Andrew ran his Red Runner Pizza business and worked to finish a Business Degree at California State and bought a house. Tim operated a deep-sea diving fishing business out of Seattle and the San Juan Islands and traveled to other locations on diving jobs. Eric studied at Arizona State University, changed part-time jobs frequently and was selected for a church mission trip to Lima, Peru. In the evenings I wrote many letters and they enjoyed hearing from us. And we sure enjoyed getting theirs.

Elderly women from nearby villages, who were widows, came to our back kitchen door early in the morning asking for food. We bought one-hundred-pound sacks of rice for the orphanage at the market, so we decided that we would buy an extra sack of rice of our own and give them a cup in their containers that they brought to us. We soon noticed a pretty long line of women every morning and they in return brought special grass and plants for the rabbits to eat. Sarah never had looked for food for the rabbits. Soap was a high premium for the women so we often gave out soap in exchange also. They brought in their rabbits for mating with those in our cages when they needed, and left them overnight. Sarah's rabbit project seemed to be blossoming in all directions. It produced a lot of attention among the people in the villages.

One day I heard Sarah yelling, "Ring gahu nak shuru" at her friends that she played with. I went outside and asked her what the problem was. She said she had put her bar of soap on the window ledge while washing and one of the children had taken it and she wanted it back. She kept good relationships with them but did not let them take things unless she gave them. In the house later, I asked what she was saying since I didn't recognize any of the Swahili words that she used. She smiled and replied that she said

"Get out of here or I will beat you up." Then I knew why I had not recognized the words.

A local potentate in a nearby village returned home and was given a royal welcome. We were invited and got to see how the people greeted the King of Walungu, back to his village from his exile in France. We learned so much about African customs in the time that we were there. We had a very hard time watching a very common sight that greeted us when we first arrived in Zaire. The women were treated like beasts of burden, carrying the very heavy bundles of firewood on their backs climbing the steep hills.

Phillip and Pam made plans to fly into Kinshasa, Zaire with the Air Force to come for a visit sometime, and Chip and Elizabeth hoped to visit Africa next year. Sarah and I would take any company that we could get. Sarah was missing her whole family. She became very homesick and unable to concentrate on her studies. I felt that we were going to have to make alternate arrangements for her schooling. She expressed her feelings about being in Afrika and isolated from kids her age and her family. She was very unhappy.

We went to Bukavu for the weekend so I could talk to the nurse for the mission who had raised her four children here in past years when they worked twenty years in Bukavu. After sixth grade, they sent all their children to boarding school in Nairobi and only saw them twice a year. I knew this was the accepted practice of many missionaries around the world, but I was definitely against Sarah going to Nairobi and our separation. My earlier studies and degree in Family and Child Development made me more aware of the emotional and psychological needs of my children, which only I could meet. I made the decision that we would not be separated before accepting this position as Director of the Orphanage.

After consulting and discussing our situation with the mission, we decided that Sarah should go back to the States for her education. The nurse advised me that she would have done it differently and taken her teenagers back to the States. While in Bukavu we met with others in the mission and made our plans. It was a difficult decision for me to make, but as soon as I told Sarah and saw how happy she was, I knew that it was the right one. Cutting our time in Zaire short, left us three months to finish up all that we wanted to accomplish at the orphanage and packed to return to the States in August. This was the turning point for our work at Kidodobo.

Before we even let our family know of our change in plans, Chip sent us tickets on American Airlines for our return trip. When we received them Sarah knew that God was watching over her and had him send the tickets. In her own mind, she felt that it was best for us to leave Zaire, and not just a problem with her schooling. Chip read articles in the Chicago papers about building unrest in the government and violence in Zaire, and wanted to make sure that we had tickets in hand to get on a plane when we needed. He knew the chaos and confusion that took place if it was a forced evacuation and had remembered watching on television the revolution in Haiti that I landed in during June of 1986. We were very grateful for his foresight and God's guidance for us. He sent us more tickets later since they expired in three months.

When I accepted a position with the mission, I signed papers that no ransom would be paid if we were taken hostage. We were briefed on keeping the gas tank of our truck full and sufficient drinking water on hand, food and papers and passports ready to be able to evacuate in fifteen minutes if necessary. And we always listened to Voice of America and the BBC to keep up on the news. We were aware of the building tensions in Bukavu. Soldiers on the streets had not received any pay for months and were stopping us to beg for bread. There had been shooting on the streets and we had to take cover and hide in buildings and stay in the guesthouse in Bukavu one weekend instead of going back to the mission at Kidodobo. The government of Zaire became increasingly unstable every day with the value of the money dropping to a pittance and a revolution was expected at any time. Having been through these same conditions in Haiti and very frightened for the children in 1984, I was concerned for Sarah's safety and decided that the Lord wanted us out of Zaire. I could read the signs and it did not look promising for missionaries. I felt that their days were numbered.

Sarah and I were taking antimalarials the whole time we were in Afrika, but Sarah got a light case of malaria. I put her immediately on Chloroquine and she recovered quickly. It was a difficult job just to stay well here. She invited three African girls that lived in the village near Kidodobo for a slumber party and they had a wonderful time. Sarah communicated very well with all the children.

Joshua Richard Long, our twelfth grandchild, arrived in Seattle to Tim and Colleen. We called to congratulate them and they were doing well. We wouldn't have to wait another year to see him, but planned to go back to the states in August. We looked forward to seeing all the grandchildren and especially the two born while we were in Zaire.

While I was trying to keep seventy children at the orphanage safe from typhoid, malaria, TB, meningitis, measles and cholera, I had grandchildren who were born, others who had gotten their first new teeth, some learned to walk, others were potty-trained, and some just starting kindergarten. My name had become "Grandma in Afrika" to my grandchildren in America.

I was not making any plans for us after we returned to the States, but concentrating on getting all the work at the orphanage taken care of and in order before we left. Diane was returning in January to resume her duties with the orphanage. The African nurse, Ntabala, would fill in for a few months before she returned.

We received the news of Eric's plans to join us for our last month here and his arrival time in Nairobi, Kenya. We planned to meet him at the Nairobi Airport on July 5th. Sarah was so excited and eager to have Eric visit and show him all her projects the places in Zaire.

We left Kidodobo and drove to Bujumbura, Burundi on July 3rd to get passport extension at the American Embassy, a Burundi visa, and tickets on Kenyan Airlines for Nairobi, Kenya. We stayed at a guesthouse and enjoyed the beautiful white sandy beach on Lake Tanganyika. There were many gigantic hippopotamuses that were grazing around our guesthouse and in the parking lot between the cars. They looked so out-of-place, but acted like they belonged there. Some of the hippos were as big as or bigger than the cars.

After flying by Kenyan Airlines to Nairobi, we took a taxi to the Mayfield Guesthouse where we stayed in January. We felt that we knew our way around Nairobi after our stay there and visit at the hospital. It was good to be back in Nairobi. Aim Air took us to meet Eric's Pan American flight from Frankfurt, Germany that arrived at midnight on July 5th. When we met him at the Nairobi Airport we were so happy to see him and could hardly believe that he was really here. Sarah and I kept hugging and kissing him. It was then that we realized how much we missed all of our family. We had rooms at the Mayfield Guesthouse for three nights and caught up on all the news from the family. We had not seen Eric for over a year.

We decided to take the train to Mombasa so Eric could see Kenya while he was in Africa. It was the night train through the Tsavo National Game Park, the largest in the world. In the early morning we saw herds of zebra, gazelle, impala, and many hippos, wildebeest and giraffe grazing near the train tracks and lift their heads to stare at us as our train made its way to Mombasa. It was a beautiful trip. In Mombasa we stayed on the beach for a couple of nights and enjoyed the off-tourist season prices and relaxed on the fine powder-white beaches. Eric and Sarah wind and body surfed. Sarah rode a camel on the beach looking very high and strange as it loped near the water. We picked out very large lobsters caught in the Indian Ocean and watched the men grill them right on the beach for us. We ate so much lobster that we thought we would never eat again. We all thought that we never wanted to leave. The Indian Ocean was so warm and we swam every day.

We celebrated Eric's birthday early and went to dinner at a lovely restaurant high on a hill overlooking the Mombasa, called the Tamarind. The view from the outside dining rooms with all the lights at night overlooking Mombasa Bay was very beautiful. It was a very special time for Eric, Sarah and I and a real highlight of all our travels together to Haiti, England, and Africa. It made us realize how fortunate we were to have this opportunity to travel and how grateful we were to God for watching over us.

After taking an overnight train ride back to Nairobi we scheduled reservations on Eric's return flight with him to Frankfurt, Germany. We then took Air Kenya back to Kigali and stayed one night at a lovely guesthouse on top of a hill overlooking Kigali. It was a spectacular view of the city and one that we had not seen before on our three dental visits there. They had a small zoo with two enormous boa constrictors in cages that they fed with goats once a month.

From Kigali we flew Air Rwanda to Cyangugu, Rwanda. Eric remembers that we flew so low that he could smell the smoke from the campfires and could see Rwandans in the jungles. We had chickens in a cage on the small plane with us. He was introduced to Rwanda and Zaire on that memorable flight. Sarah and I were so used to Afrika by now that we didn't notice these things. He met many of the missionaries at the guesthouse and Eric delivered some airplane parts and things that he brought in very heavy duffel bags from the missionary office in Illinois for the Mission. We picked up our Toyota truck that we left in Bukavu.

We introduced Eric to many of our friends in Bukavu and he was impressed when he met a young man on a five-year bicycling trip around the world that had just come from China. When we gassed up our Toyota truck, we stopped at locations along the main road in Bukavu where men held jerry cans of gasoline with a rag stuffed in the top opening. With no gas stations, these entrepreneurs sold us our gas and strained it with the rag held across the opening of our gasoline tank. We jokingly called them Muammar el-Qaddafi's gasoline stations. This was our only choice for gasoline and Eric was amazed. The condition of the roads also amazed him as we let him drive to Kidodobo. Sarah gave him her room to use and she slept in with me. We both had double beds. Eric is a coffee drinker so I made coffee for him in one of his socks every morning since I had no coffee pot. While listening to our short-wave radio, he heard English spoken by truckers on their CB's in Oklahoma and couldn't believe it. Howard Crowl told him that it was called a satellite skip, sounds that go out to a satellite and are amplified and skipped around the world. The middle of the Congo was not where he expected to hear Oklahoma truckers on the CB radios.

Packages from home were always an exciting event, especially Christmas packages arriving in July. Grace sent us a twenty-pound-tin of candy and treats that we eagerly opened, shared, and enjoyed our last month at Kidodobo. Eric was able to witness the gratitude and excitement for packages and mail received from America.

We went on a mountain climbing trip to Mount Kahousie in the jungle of Zaire. Eric was in excellent shape but coming from sea level in Phoenix to above 7,000 feet, he was a little light headed and we stopped just short of the top. We went through a bamboo jungle that reminded us of a stack of Tinker Toys that had landed in all directions, and left our names on some bamboo. Our trek with a video camera through a game park with the silverback gorillas was very exciting for us all. Since Sarah and I were residents of Zaire and I had a Zairian driver's license, we were not charged the tourist price of $100 each. We saw two guerilla groups of twenty-five, each warring with each other, swinging from vine to vine and beating their chests. It was amazing! They were crashing around and very loud. The two guides felt that we better leave these groups and after much more hiking through dense jungle we found another more peaceful group and got very close. Our Zairian jungle guides stayed close between us and the eight-hundred-pound gorillas as we took pictures. As Eric snapped the camera, one gorilla lunged at us to scare us, and the Zairians with their machetes jumped in between. We were as close as just two or three feet, so we could see them in detail. One gorilla broke off a bamboo tree stump and picked his teeth while staring at us. A mother in a tree held her baby and looked curiously down at us. It was fantastic getting so close and seeing them in their natural habitat doing these things. We felt very fortunate even though we found out later that the video camera didn't work properly and we had no pictures. That was a disappointment of this once-in-a-life event, but we still have vivid memories of the silver-back gorillas and the jungle.

Eric's six weeks with us went fast and he was able to help us with some projects at Kidodobo. We were putting up swings for the small children in the courtyard of the new orphanage. We all said our goodbyes and left on August 5th from Kidodobo and drove to Bukavu and then Cyangugu, Rwanda where we caught our flight to Nairobi. Sarah and I made many friends, and I had both sad and happy feelings about leaving. Looking forward to seeing our family again, I just trusted the future to the Lord whether I ever came back to Afrika. The Africans at Kidodobo had opened their hearts to us and treated us so kindly.

We arrived at the Nairobi Airport in the afternoon and left about midnight for Frankfurt. Sarah's thirteenth birthday was August 6th, so we traveled all night on the 5th and arrived the next day in Frankfurt, Germany, and then caught our flight to Chicago, and still arrived in Chicago on August 6th. Sarah was on three different continents on her thirteenth birthday. We had split up with Eric in Frankfurt since we were taking different flights and he went on to Phoenix and Sarah and I went to Chicago. Elizabeth met us at the airport since Chip was flying, and Sarah asked to stop at McDonald's for french fries and a hamburger that she had missed for the past year. It sure was good to be back in the States, but quite a culture shock. We had Sarah's request for Pizza Hut pizza for her birthday dinner that night. I think it was more of a shock coming back to the States than going to Afrika.

It was wonderful being with Morgan and Kenny, Chip and Elizabeth in Woodstock, where they had just moved into a new house. We talked to all the children on the phone and made plans for visits. Grace asked us not to make a decision yet on where we planned to live until after we had our last visit with them in Tallahassee. Andrew and

Shawnae planned to come and visit us after we settled somewhere. We sure appreciated Chip and Elizabeth's hospitality, since Sarah and I were homeless since we moved from the farm. We planned to choose a place near one of the children to live but had made no decision. We considered some places around Woodstock, but we were not ready for the very cold weather there yet. Sarah and I were amazed at all the food in the house and being able to drink the water. It took us awhile to get rested up; Sarah had an ear infection and was on antibiotics.

Our family renting the farm moved out and the football coach at Kansas State called to see if we would rent out the farm again with an option to buy. I definitely said no because I really wanted to sell it. We all had a good time catching up on everyone's news of the past year.

We flew next to visit Phillip and Pam and their three boys, Jacob, Dirk and Simon in Phoenix and had a great time. All the grandchildren had grown so much in one year. They were all doing well and enjoyed having Eric in town. They were still in the Air Force and Phillip was thinking about flying with airlines the following year. Amber and Pat and family came to see us and we got to meet Jordan, just six months old. These grandchildren were really getting big, and Alex was five years old. Kelsey and Lance were so much bigger. It was just wonderful seeing all these healthy and happy children. After a year at Kidodobo with many sick children, I had a tremendous appreciation for healthy children like never before. And there were no worries of malnutrition, parasites, malaria, cholera, typhoid or measles with these grandchildren. It was quite a blessing.

We arrived in El Paso to visit with the Theobalds for a few days. Amber had done such a good job as my Forwarding Agent while I was in Africa, and I really appreciated her help. We enjoyed good food, good fun, and a good rest. We were really enjoying all these grandchildren.

Sarah and I adjusted to all the comforts of America again and started thinking about where we wanted to live.

We took our last flight on August 20th to Tallahassee to visit Grace and family, and then we needed to make a decision. We flew into Atlanta, Georgia and Grace picked us up with Jason and Eric. Jason was taller and Eric very shy. A year made such a difference, and the boys had really changed as had all the rest of the grandchildren. Sarah loved all our visits with her brothers and sisters and getting to play with them all.

After visiting for a couple of days, I went to Florida State University to inquire about a Master's Program in Nursing. I met with the head of the Graduate Nursing Program and was invited to apply for a scholarship and attend a Family Nurse Practitioner Program for a Master's Degree in Nursing. I had heard about this program, but didn't know much about it. It was getting very close for Sarah to get into school somewhere and we had to make a decision. I felt pressed to quickly decide on where we would live. I had already lived in the South many times before and was familiar with the climate. The offer at Florida State with the Nurse Practitioner Program was what I wanted, and Sarah and I decided that we would make a decision soon.

On August 24th, we discussed our options and prayed about it. We decided to stay in Tallahassee and look for a house to rent and get Sarah into eighth grade. We found a house to rent and her school in the same area the very same day. It was a relief to have a decision made and plans for us both. Grace helped us find a house to rent and a car to buy while we stayed with them. It was a very busy month with many decisions. In less than a month we had moved out of Kidodobo and found a new place and house to live. We moved into our new house on Yorktown Drive the first day of September.

Chip called and asked us to come to their house for Labor Day Holiday and Tim and Joshua were coming. We looked forward to meeting Joshua for the first time. American Airlines started flying into Tallahassee that year, so Sarah and I flew to Chicago, and Tim and Josh flew in from Seattle. Chip picked us all up and we went to Woodstock. Josh was a big, healthy, handsome grandson and Tim was doing a good job in his role as a very proud dad. He said that it was quite a challenge changing diapers on the plane. Josh looked so much like Tim. He was a very good baby. Morgan and Kenny were fun to be with, and Sarah had a great time with them all. Morgan was starting kindergarten. Now we had seen all 12 grandchildren. It was a great time to be together and we did a lot of visiting and catching up on the last year. We had missed a lot of family news and family gatherings.

We came back to Tallahassee for Sarah's school and stayed in our new house. The school bus picked Sarah up right in front of our house each morning. We settled in quickly, and I wrote the last newsletter to everyone who supported us in Zaire and scheduled a visit to the mission office in Illinois. Sarah made friends at school and enjoyed having Grace and the boys so close to visit with. They lived about thirty minutes from us on the other side of Tallahassee.

While we were in Africa we missed news of the San Francisco earthquake of 1989 and didn't hear about it for days afterwards. Chip wrote in one of his letters about the hijacking of an American Airlines airplane in Port-au-Prince, Haiti. We missed the news of the U.S. military invasion of Panama, and the Berlin Wall coming down reuniting Eastern Europeans with their families. I saw it just a few months after it was built while living in Germany in 1962.

Nightline on September 7, 2001, reported terrible genocide in Rwanda and Zaire. It showed Lake Kivu and said it is polluted with human bodies and sewage, causing hundreds of cases of cholera. Bukavu is destroyed and many refugees still fleeing. All looks so hopeless and sad.

# Chapter 20: Sound the Trumpets

OUR LIFE IN TALLAHASSEE settled into a regular routine, and we once again enjoyed all the comforts of this rich country. Sarah enjoyed all the new challenges and was soon happily occupied with eighth grade activities and becoming acquainted with children in our neighborhood. She found a small orange and white kitten that quickly became her first pet in Tallahassee. Free kittens were always easy to find. She gave it the unusual name of Piglet. I flew to Chicago, and then went to the mission office in Kansas, Oklahoma to officially resign my status as medical missionary nurse in Zaire, and sent out our last newsletter. I received a warm welcome at the mission office and they were glad to have us back, and happy for Sarah to be safely in school in Tallahassee. So was I. They were still receiving support for the mission from many people interested in our work. In one of my newsletters I had requested donations of sweaters for the village people up in the mountains near Kidodobo. They received so many sweaters from all the churches and friends supporting us, that they could not handle any more for shipping. I was thrilled with the outpouring response of love and sweaters. I enjoyed this wonderful picture in my mind of the elderly widows who had been dressed in a few rags as they came to our back door, now receiving nice warm wool sweaters for their cold nights in the mountains. I could just see their smiles as they said "koko" in Mashi, and feel the warmth that these sweaters provided. I was very grateful for all those who had sent sweaters in response to that newsletter.

I visited the Graduate Nursing Department at Florida State University to present all my requirements for entering the graduate nursing program. The head of the department just had a new baby and was nursing it in her

office. I liked that. She wanted to hear about nursing in
Africa and encouraged me to get started in the Family
Nurse Practitioner Program. She pointed out many
advantages to their program. I transferred my nursing
license from Kansas to Florida. I could start courses before
taking my graduate exam, as a special student, and then be
admitted to the program when I passed. In order to get a
scholarship, I needed to go full time and do some teaching
in the nursing program. They were interested in my
nursing experience in other cultures and hoped to have me
put together and teach a seminar in Cross-Cultural Nursing
in their nursing program for undergraduate students.
Florida had a large migrant worker population plus many
Haitian and Cuban immigrants in South Florida.

I knew I could find a place here, and I planned to
complete a master's degree that I could use whenever I
returned to nursing abroad. I met other nurses who had
worked in the past with international organizations abroad,
and we had similar experiences. Some worked with the
Peace Corps in Africa and others with the World Health
Organization in India. We all agreed that the nurses trained
in programs in the U.S. had little or no preparation for the
challenges of nursing abroad. I was given the most recent
published book in Cross-Cultural Nursing to review that I
recommended, and it was ordered for the Florida State
Nursing Library.

We went to Panama City Beach with Grace and her
boys and enjoyed the beaches. Tallahassee garage sales
provided some nice used furniture to add to the few things
we kept from the farm. We also enjoyed going to Grace's
church in Tallahassee. Sarah was able to go skiing in
Gatlinburg, Tennessee with the church youth group. People
in Tallahassee seemed very friendly.

We appreciated our house and nice backyard where
we raked and burned leaves in the fall, one of our favorite

outdoor pastimes, and roasted hot dogs and had picnics. Sarah invited friends for a Halloween party on our outside deck. She had her own room and bath upstairs and enjoyed a variety of music. I think this is when she started liking the African beat. The African singing and drums had definitely made an impression on her. She still had her African drum in her room. We enjoyed living close to family and liked the church we were attending.

Studying for the graduate exam and taking graduate level nursing courses was my main occupation. I planned to start classes full time in January of 1991. The farm was sold in Manhattan, Kansas with Philip's help, and I began thinking about buying a home after renting in Tallahassee for the first year. My graduate program would take two years to complete if I attended full time and longer if I took fewer courses. We enjoyed Grace and her family, and they welcomed another son and grandchild born in November, Matthew Steven. With Phillip and Pam expecting another grandchild due in December, I realized that with many weddings that followed one after the other, babies were the logical sequence of events and grandchildren kept coming.

I traveled around to see all my children and got to spend more time with my grandchildren. There was an extended trip to Chicago, Seattle, Sacramento, El Paso and Phoenix, where I met Jena Marie who was born at Williams Air Force Base in Phoenix in December. Phillip and Pam now enjoyed a little girl and had four children. Everyone was doing well and happy to have us back in America. Sarah stayed with Grace and family when I traveled, and she did well in school and was on the honor roll. She was enthusiastic about memorizing the Declaration of Independence for her history class. I think that it had added meaning for her after a year in Africa. We spent that Christmas with Grace and family and then I went to Kansas in January to visit some churches. My brother, Richard, met me at the Kansas City Airport, and I stayed with them in Rossville. I enjoyed seeing all our friends and family in Manhattan and the church at Zeandale. They were eager to learn more about Africa and our experiences there.

Eric spent the next semester with the Presidential Classroom Program in Washington, D.C., learning about the workings of government and was caught up in the excitement of the capitol. He was responsible for the program's logistics, meeting new students at the airport, and showing them around. He met many high-level government leaders and decided that he wanted to go into the Foreign Service when he graduated. He was able to take a trip with Chip and Elizabeth, Morgan and Kenny to Germany on a ski trip when he finished.

We received a very nice letter in January from all the missionaries in Zaire thanking us for our help. We knew how much they appreciated all the help they could get, and we were glad to be there. We definitely knew the hardships and dangers they still went through. I celebrated my fifty-sixth birthday and was very grateful for my family, children and grandchildren, and the experiences of the past year. Grace and I drove to Alligator Point, and I booked a very large beach house on the Gulf for a family reunion in June. All the children and grandchildren planned to come. The house would be stretched to the limit but could accommodate all of us. Andrew called and said that he needed to have Jesse put to sleep, since she was suffering very much and she was twelve years old. Sarah lost her best friend, and she never forgot all the good times that they had together. She began looking for another Labrador and planned to get one as soon as we moved to our own home.

Phillip left the Air Force and accepted a job with Delta Airlines and started his training in Atlanta. They all came for a visit and began making the adjustment to civilian life. They were stationed in the Air Force in Mississippi earlier. We hoped that we would see them more often.

My first semester of classes went well, and I was admitted to the Family Nurse Practitioner Program after passing the Graduate Record Exam. I decided that I wasn't able to go full time as a graduate student and do my thesis, so had to forgo the scholarship and teaching. It took me longer to finish since I needed forty-five hours for my Master's Degree in Science as a Family Nurse Practitioner. Sarah decided to run on the track team in high school, and I wanted to attend her out of town track meets with other parents. She needed my support. Grace and her boys came with me sometimes and enjoyed watching Sarah run. Grace ran track in high school and one season at Kansas State. She coached Sarah a lot.

Sarah and I looked for a house to buy with some land so that she could raise Labradors and have a horse to ride. She never forgot the farm and all her animals and would settle for horses and dogs again instead of cows. We looked all that semester without finding a house with a small pasture, and finally bought three acres out of Tallahassee and found a builder to start our house. Our family reunion at Alligator Point at the end of May and the first week of June was fun for us all. There were now fourteen grandchildren, and Andrew and Shawnae expected another in September. All of the grandchildren played in the sand together, ate watermelon, swam and had much fun as we all watched them play with their cousins. The moms all entertained them with crafts and the children kept us all busy. The beach house was large and versatile with huge tables in a large kitchen, a pool table, many couches, sofas and beds, many decks, swings and an outside barbecue kitchen with safe places for the children. Phillip was in training with Delta and couldn't come, but Pam and the children came for a visit. It was a good time of eating, swimming and visiting.

In July I went to an Evans reunion in Wichita. It was a large gathering of Evans cousins; it had been many years since I had been to one. Our reunions as children were always greatly anticipated. No one really changes that much. Later in July, a good friend, Marlyn Rademacher and I took a trip to Tokyo and on to Okinawa to visit her daughter, Catherine. Grace and Sarah traveled with Amber back to Texas for a visit. Marilyn and I traveled in Germany together with our children many years ago in the 1960s. It was fun to be traveling together with no children. Her husband Leon, retired from the Army and working with American Airlines, was in a dive club and they did as much travelling as I did. I traveled on passes since Chip was flying with American. We flew on a brand new MD-11, its first flight to Tokyo. We had some funny experiences in Tokyo, and I enjoyed our time with Catherine and her family. Catherine taught for the Department of Defense and her husband Bruce was a Major in the Air Force.

We received news that all the missionaries had to evacuate Zaire and many went to Nairobi, Kenya to work and wait. There was revolution brewing, and Mobutu was losing power. I knew what kind of dangers the missionaries were going through and prayed for their safety. I was just very glad that we hadn't waited to leave until this happened.

We moved out of our house in August and rented another house temporarily while ours was being built. Sarah found a yellow eight-week-old Labrador retriever puppy that she named Babe. She was delighted and a very happy girl with her kitten and puppy. Babe was very sweet and we both fell in love with her. Piglet her kitten ended up at the city pound on one occasion and we had to rescue her.

We drove out to our new property and celebrated Sarah's fourteenth birthday there and cooked hamburgers under our tall pines in the woods on our portable grill. We ate a nice dinner and looked forward in just three months to moving there when our house was finished. Before we could leave our property and without any warning, the rain started pouring down very hard, filling the gully where we were parked. With our car quickly sinking in the mud, we asked our new neighbors to help pull us out. Roy Hancock came over to help us and he must have wondered what kind of wild women from Africa they were getting for neighbors. I knocked down a wooden street sign in front of his house, backing out of our driveway in the rain. My driving skills had become more aggressive after driving the dangerously narrow and muddy roads in the mountains of Zaire in my 4 -wheel drive Toyota truck. The construction of the foundation for our new house on three acres of tall pine trees began in the last part of August. We drove out to our property often to see the progress, but never parked in that gully again.

I started my Family Nurse Practitioner Program at Florida State University and Sarah started high school at Lincoln High in Tallahassee. We attended our first Seminole football game at Florida State University and cheered our team to victory. We realized that there was more tradition and school spirit in Tallahassee for their team than we had seen anywhere. The whole city was behind them. Their first ranking in the nation might have been the reason.

Each time we went out to see our house being built we counted the days until we could move in. It was exciting to think of having a place of our own again. I remarked that I would never build another house after the farm, but here I was again doing just that. I was learning again to "never say never." Since I was occupied with graduate school,

Sarah helped pick out the colors and accessories for our new home. I was glad for the help.

Jenner was born to Andrew and Shawnea arrived on September 30th, a big healthy and handsome baby boy. We found their message waiting on our answering machine when we came home that evening. We called to congratulate them and learned it had been a difficult birth, but they were all doing well. We arrived home late that day because we were rear-ended while stopped for a stoplight. I had picked up Sarah after school from track practice. A young girl "hydroplaned" in the rain into the rear end of our white Honda Civic Wagon as she tried to stop and totaled our car. We were both uninjured, but I suffered a slight whiplash. The young girl driving the car had only minor burns on her face from her airbag. In Manhattan when Sarah was three years old, another teenager hit us while we were stopped at a stoplight in another blue Honda car. We were also fortunate with no injuries at that time.

Our Honda was just repaired with a "lifetime warranty" muffler an hour before the accident, and I picked up all the new glass light fixtures for our new house that were packed in boxes in the back of our wagon. That must have been the shortest-lived new muffler in history with a "lifetime warranty" before it was totaled. When we unpacked all the light fixtures the next day at our new house, I thought it was a miracle and could hardly believe that none were broken.

School was very busy for us both. Our house was finished and we moved into it on Manor House Drive at the end of October. I tried to put up mini blinds on all the windows in the house before we went to bed the first night. I hadn't realized how many windows we had. Since we were farther out of town, it took three weeks for us to have a phone. But we were content with our new place.

Grace and family moved to Pensacola during this time and they came to spend Thanksgiving with us in our new house. Chip and Elizabeth welcomed another baby at the end of November, Adrienne Elizabeth, their third child. Four grandchildren had arrived in the family in 1990 and two in 1991. I made trips to Chicago, Seattle, Sacramento, and El Paso after my semester finished and before Christmas. We were so happy for Eric to arrive at our new house for the Christmas holiday. I hired fences to be constructed to enclose our backwoods, and Sarah got another quarter horse that arrived before Christmas. She was back in the horse business again with a pregnant mare, Annabelle. The foal was expected in April. Annabelle arrived from Kansas with a limp, so Sarah was never able to ride her.

My sister Betty had an appointment at the Scottsdale, Arizona Mayo Clinic, and I met her there at the end of December for a few days. She had not recovered from her surgery in June, and tests were done which did not reveal the source of her weakness. Eric and Sarah spent a few days in Pensacola with Grace and family until Eric flew back to school in Phoenix. Betty and I visited him there one evening before we left.

We were adding to our three acres and I planted thirty-six azalea plants of pink, fuchsia and white in March. We admired our neighbors' yards surrounded by beautiful large azalea bushes and we wanted some of our own. Sarah had ordered some beautiful blue Siberian Iris for my birthday to plant by our front door. We enjoyed working outside in the nice weather and found a lot to do on our three acres. Sarah ran the Springtime Tallahassee Run and came in second place.

Annabelle was bred to a paint horse before we bought her. She was due with a new foal any day now, so Sarah checked her regularly. On the night she thought the foal was due, we both took sleeping bags and slept on our screened-in porch close to the pasture. About two-o'clock in the morning, we heard a thud that woke us up from a sound sleep. Annabelle was standing by the fence near us with a big bundle on the ground beside her. Sarah and I rushed out, and Sarah helped Annabelle get the sack off the new baby foal. It was so tiny with soft hooves, and Sarah sat on the ground in her nightgown holding the foal until it was able to stand. Annabelle was a good mother and the foal took right to nursing. The colt had the flashy reddish-brown and white markings of a paint horse like Sarah's first horse Money at the farm. She named him Sky and enjoyed playing with him every day before and after school.

　　The news from Rwanda, Burundi, and Zaire was so horrible that I was glad not to have television. Just to listen to all the horrible atrocities on the radio was too much for me. The genocide of one million Rwandans was hard to believe. It was more than I could comprehend after being there such a short time ago. Many memories flooded my mind. I couldn't comprehend how this could happen and remembered seeing the President's wives of the countries of Rwanda and Burundi in Bukavu, Zaire. We went to Cyangugu, Rwanda on the border of Zaire often to make phone calls and shop. We just walked across the bridge and showed our passports. We had made two trips to Burundi and had our passports renewed there at the American Embassy and enjoyed the lovely beach at Lake Tanganyika. We enjoyed our many long trips to Kigali, Rwanda through the beautiful rainforest. My dental bridge was put in, and I bought all my Christmas presents for the children at the beautiful craft kiosks. I still had a beautiful colorful batik of the Rwandan people hanging in my living room. All this was such a short time ago! I knew nothing about the tribal rivalry between the Hutus and the Tutsis Tribes. How could we ever imagine that the beautiful rivers of that peaceful countryside were now filled with the bodies and blood of all those people? We grieved for the one million people and families who had been slaughtered. What a world catastrophe in this beautiful country! Many Rwandans fled to refugee camps in Goma, Zaire.

In June, Sarah was invited to go to El Paso to stay with Amber and Pat and family. I stayed in classes and worked nights at a Migrant Health Clinic in order to see patients who worked all day in the fields. Most did not speak English, and we worked through interpreters. We had a suturing class at school, and I bought a package of pigs' feet at Winn Dixie and invited some fellow nurse practitioner students out so that we could practice our suturing. We laughed and sewed and improved our expertise, confident that we might become even better when confronted with a real person in need of stitches. I've been sewing since I was thirteen years old, but this was my first experience with sutures and flesh. The object was a neat and sterile closure, and there were just medical principles to follow and the condition of the wound and patient involved. When we were finished with our pigs' feet and my friends left, I threw them out in the back yard for Sarah's puppy, Babe, to chew on and enjoy. She was very discreet, eating one and hiding the rest in the front and back yard for a rainy day. Many months later she dug up the sutured pig's feet and had a treat.

The American Academy of Nurse Practitioner organization was seeking nurse practitioners with experience abroad to be on a planning committee to form an International Nurse Practitioner Conference that could meet in various countries. This sounded right up my line. I wanted to be a part of the Committee for International Work, to promote nurse practitioners abroad, and I sent in my resume and an endorsement from the dean of our graduate program. I knew that I would be working abroad eventually in my career.

Eric came for a visit in July and helped us plant grass in the front yard. Sarah came back from her visit in El Paso and it sure was good to have Eric there, since it was a bigger job than I thought. It was almost an acre, and we planted patches of grass turf that was a great improvement. With much watering it would take off and cover the entire front yard. We were always fighting the fire ants and had many unpleasant experiences of disturbing their homes. These particular ants are called fire ants because they have teeth, and after they bite you, it burns something fierce. I often thought that the fire ants really owned this property and I was considerably outnumbered. When I worked in the backwoods of pine trees and accidently got them down in my cowboy boots, I ran and danced all the way to the water hose to take off my boots and get them out. Their bites burned like fire! I worked outside constantly but never developed a peaceful coexistence with them in our four years in Tallahassee. When the grass grew and covered the whole front yard, I bought a new riding lawn mower, and Sarah helped with the mowing. Lake Iamonia was close by in our neighborhood, and Sarah took Babe there on her walks. The horses were content in the pasture. And Sarah was content with her animals, but always wanted more.

We drove to Pensacola to spend the 4th of July with Grace and family, and while we were there, Andrew called from Sacramento in the middle of the night with news of Tim's diving accident in Seattle on the afternoon of the 4th. He was in critical condition. When I called the hospital, Colleen said that Tim was in Intensive Care and on a respirator. He spent seven hours in their Hyperbaric Chamber at one hundred and sixty feet. When I got off the phone all of us immediately joined hands in prayer in Grace's kitchen. The prognosis for this kind of injury was not good and the doctors gave Colleen little hope for a normal recovery. We asked God to watch over Tim and restore oxygen to every cell of Tim's body and entrusted him to His care. I called Phillip and got a Delta pass to fly from Pensacola to Seattle and then called all the other children to tell them about the accident and for their prayers for Tim. I left for the airport in a few hours and arrived in Seattle at 1:30 am that morning where Phillip met me at the airport. He drove from Vancouver, Washington and arrived earlier to be with Tim.

You can never be prepared to see a child in ICU and looking as badly as Tim looked. But I prayed the entire flight to Seattle and entrusted him to God's care. Tim was conscious but very upset. I talked to him and promised him a whole "dead cow" in steaks, when he was better. I saw him smile! He was the biggest meat eater of all the children when he was growing up on the farm, and I knew that his favorite was a big steak cooked by his dad on the grill. And protein would be an important part of his recovery. I talked to the doctors and nurses who were taking care of him and asked medical questions. They were very helpful and knew my concern as a nurse for Tim's condition and recovery as well as his mother. He was off the respirator in a few hours. Tim had two collapsed lungs with chest tubes. Andrew started driving from Sacramento as soon as he got the news about Tim's accident and arrived about 7:00 that morning. Along with Colleen and his friends who were very concerned for him, it was so good to have family there for Tim's encouragement and support. Tim really appreciated his two brothers Phillip and Andrew. It was good to see a family response to this terrible accident and know that Tim had the prayers of everyone who could not be there. We called with reports of Tim's progress and they were all very concerned and praying for Tim. Eric worked a previous summer with Tim and knew the seriousness of the accident.

An elderly couple out in their pleasure boat on the 4th of July had entered the diving waters, not seeing their signs, and ran over Tim's air hose while he was out diving. The propeller on their motorboat dragged Tim forty feet before stopping. Tim had resurfaced from too great a depth too quickly, and was yelling when he came up and then his body went limp. A diving friend who was watching him from the boat beside him got Tim out of the water and immediately put him on oxygen that they carry on their boat. It took them twenty-three minutes to get him to the ambulance at Port Ludlow where they had radioed for an ambulance to be waiting. Tim said that the ambulance workers were having a hard time inserting the tube in his trachea for ventilation and a girl walking along the beach, who was a nurse, offered to assist them and accomplished the intubation quickly. Tim said that he experienced numbness and heavy feeling in his body, starting at his toes and progressing up to his chest before he had sufficient oxygen to breathe. He needed oxygen badly. He said that this unidentified nurse saved his life again. The accident happened about 4:00 p.m. on Friday afternoon and they waited at Port Ludlow an hour to stabilize him before a Coast Guard medical-evacuation helicopter came and took him to the downtown Seattle Virginia Mason Hospital. When he was brought in, the doctors all diagnosed him with the worst case of air embolism that they had ever seen. Good decisions had been made at every point after the accident for his recovery.

Phillip, Andrew, and I got a room at the Hospital Inn, and stayed Saturday night, spending as much time with Tim as possible. Phillip stayed until Sunday evening and then drove home to Vancouver. Tim went for three more Hyperbaric Treatments and steadily improved. His coordination improved and he could feed himself. It was touch and go for a while before he could get his spoon from his plate to his mouth, missing it by many inches. He was out of Intensive Care on Sunday and we visited him in his hospital room. He looked so much better. He received excellent nursing care and had a miraculous recovery. He looked so good and wanted more to eat and asked me to get him some real food. Jell-O and liquids were not helping his hunger. He asked for a hamburger, so I brought him one from the hospital cafeteria and he devoured it. Andrew talked with him about making arrangements to pick up his truck and boat at Port Ludlow and get a copy of the Coast Guard report and police report of the accident. Tim and he also talked about a choice of a lawyer. I visited with Tim all that day and prayed with him. The chest tubes came out on Tuesday while I was there. The doctors said that this was the fastest recovery from the worst air embolism diving accident that they had ever seen. And this hospital had seen many and was the best hospital for treatment. They all said that it was a miracle. And we knew that it was. It was a miracle of circumstances and healing. Tim had been swimming ten miles a day in his commercial deep sea diving business, diving for sea cucumbers and sea urchins for the past six years. He was in excellent shape before the accident. Friends and medical personnel who assisted him every step of the way had done their job. And God brought about his healing through all of the prayers of his friends and family.

Andrew stayed with Tim and found the butcher for me to give Tim his "dead cow" and fill his freezer with meat. I flew back to Pensacola on Tuesday as the doctors said that Tim could go home on Wednesday. Everyone was anxious to hear the news of Tim and his recovery in the hospital. We all praised God for his miraculous recovery. Eric, Sarah, and I drove to Tallahassee that evening. Tim amazed all the doctors and set some recovery records that will probably not be surpassed, and walked out of the hospital on Wednesday. The fifth day after the accident. He began a long recovery period at home where he had to learn to do many things over again. When we called him on Wednesday night from Tallahassee he was cooking T-bone steaks out on his grill at home. I knew that he was a tough kid to go through all that he had in his accident and recovery in ICU. He rested on the couch one day before he had to get on with his life. The trauma to his brain gave him long-term memory loss, but he continued to improve. Short term, he couldn't remember where he put things, which was a little depressing. Eventually he decided to sell his boat and get into a safer business. I called him frequently to encourage him since depression was a normal process after his accident and during his recovery at home. I learned that the power and grace and mercy of God through prayer were what had given Tim back his life. I could see God's love for His children more than ever before. And there is nothing beyond His power.

Tim was recovering, and Eric and Sarah wanted to watch the Olympics at our house. Without a television in the house, Eric was bemoaning the fact that we would miss the Olympics. So we rented a television and enjoyed watching them every day, while Eric and Sarah fixed giant submarine sandwiches and cheered on their teams. I was still in school and they enjoyed their vacation time together. Sky, her colt, was weaned and Sarah was looking for a buyer for Annabelle, who wanted a good broodmare. Eric went with a neighbor to get some baled alfalfa hay for the horses. Grace and the boys drove up to help us celebrate Sarah and Eric's birthdays in August before Eric went back to Arizona State University.

Annabelle was a good mother and Sky was growing big. We often took them out of the back pasture and let them eat the grass in the front yard while we were outside watching them, and they never left since there was plenty of grass to eat. Sky stayed right beside his mother and learned to chomp away. They looked so pretty in the front yard in the green grass, Annabelle with her beautiful reddish-brown silky coat and Sky with his flashy reddish-brown and white spots, all gangly legs and very handsome. Heads were turned at the handsome mother and son when cars drove by and stopped to watch them eat. The neighbors saw Sky when he was first born and often commented how pretty he was and watched his growth into a tall, gangly long-legged colt.

I applied for a Migrant Health Fellowship through the National Health Service Corps for the next summer so that I would have more nursing experience in the migrant population. I made the decision to do my thesis on Migrant Health Care. I was happy to finish my summer semester at Florida State, and Dorothy and I decided to take a trip to Alaska before I got back in school.

The last of August, Dorothy and I flew to Sacramento and visited with Andrew and family in their new house, then they drove us to Seattle. They had just moved in. We had a beautiful drive through northern California, Oregon, and Washington and stayed on the lake with Tim and Colleen, enjoying their hospitality a few days before taking the ferry to Alaska. Tim looked really good after his accident in July and cooked dinner out on the grill for us. We were glad to see Josh and how much he had grown. He drove a little battery-operated car around in their yard and looked so cute. He was at the top of the growth charts.

We had a very beautiful relaxing trip on the ferry along the inner coast to Alaska getting off the ferry at Ketchikan. We enjoyed the small frontier town, beautiful flowers, salmon hatcheries, and good food. I visited the Indian Health Clinic to see what possibilities there were for nurse practitioners, since I wasn't sure where I would be working upon graduation. They encouraged me to come and settle there with a very good relocation package and salary. The Native Alaskans needed more patient education with nutrition and alcohol problems. The Anchorage, Juneau, and Ketchikan Airports were closing because of volcanic eruptions near Anchorage. Alaskan Airlines put on extra planes to get us out before the airport closed and we saw the beautiful crystal blue of the glaciers as we flew out of Ketchikan and back to Seattle. I had never seen such a beautiful blue.

Hurricane Andrew had hit South Florida just before we left on our trip. Many of the nurses in Tallahassee went with groups there to assist in the disaster recovery. My next semester was starting and I was rested up and ready to go back to classes.

A new grandchild had arrived! Evan McKenzie Theobald, a healthy and handsome boy arrived on August 28th in El Paso. Amber said that he was born at home five minutes after the midwife arrived. August babies can't come soon enough, and we were happy for them. He was the first grandchild of 1992, and Grace was due in Pensacola with another in December.

In September after school started, Sarah sold her horse Annabelle. She would miss her, but she had Sky to take care of. She had her Labrador Babe bred to another registered Lab and puppies were expected in November. She was fixing up the garage for these. She decided to raise puppies now instead of more horses. She built some rabbit cages and started raising a few rabbits on the side of the house.

My brother Dwight was out of touch with our family for many years since a divorce and alcohol problem, but was now driving around to visit everyone. We were glad to see him again. During the time we hadn't seen him, he lived with his children or on the streets. He decided to rent a place and settle in Tulsa, Oklahoma for a while and I flew out there to see him for the first time in many years. We visited at Dale and Ivy's in Tulsa and welcomed him back into the family after his long absence from our family reunions. He did not look well, and I knew that he probably developed some chronic problems that contributed to his poor health. He drove me to the airport, and I flew to El Paso to meet Evan, my newest grandchild, before I came back to Tallahassee. Evan was just a month old and looked like a very healthy baby. Amber and Pat had a new house and the children enjoyed a small but nice backyard to play in with some fruit trees. A few months later Amber and Evan flew to Pensacola to visit Grace and they had a sister's reunion when Sarah and I drove there. We enjoyed a picnic on the beach and had a great visit together. Amber came back with us to Tallahassee and saw our new house.

Sarah ran cross-country track meets almost every weekend that season. I traveled to all of them to watch her run, and she and her team did very well. It was fun and relaxing to watch the meets and it kept our weekends very busy. Grace and the boys, Jason, Eric and Matt joined us when the meets were in Pensacola or close. Phillip and Pam drove six hours from Georgia and met us with their family, Jake, Dirk, Simon and Jena. Their children had grown so much since I had seen them. They all helped us cheer on Sarah at her last meet. She really appreciated having so much of her family that could attend her races. Grace, very pregnant, enjoyed coaching and watching Sarah. Sarah was one of the youngest on her cross-country team and carried a lot of responsibility. After one of her last track meets in Jacksonville, Sarah and I came home to find that Babe had eleven puppies in the garage while we were gone. She had fixed Babe a birthing place in the hay in the garage and had taken very good care of her. Babe had six healthy black puppies and five blonde puppies, but one blonde puppy died the first night.

For one of my courses, I started a support group for International Student Wives who accompanied their husbands to Tallahassee where they were in doctoral programs. I taught Chinese, Korean and Iranian wives who knew no English or very little. We met together each week for tea and coffee and I helped them communicate and tried to find out what their needs were. It was a social occasion for them to learn more about Tallahassee and the resources available.

At the beginning of the semester, I began working at a medical clinic in Panacea, Florida, about a forty-five minute drive along the coast. I worked with an experienced nurse practitioner from Indiana, who also taught our Pharmacology course, and learned a lot about the nurse practitioner role and diagnosing patients. There were many poor people in the community without any health care. Some were homeless. One patient had an adverse drug reaction to Nubain and quick action averted a serious problem. I was able to use all my new knowledge counseling and seeing my own patients under the supervision of the nurse practitioner.

Sarah and I drove to Pensacola and picked up Jason, Eric and Matt to be with us while Grace welcomed their baby. Grace had their fourth baby, a little girl in Pensacola on December twenty-third. They named her Amber, and Sarah and I drove to Pensacola with the boys to meet her and fix the Christmas dinner. Amber was a sweet, healthy, brownish-red haired beautiful little girl. We brought the boys back to Tallahassee with us to give Grace more rest and took them back home on the thirty-first. They loved seeing and playing with all the puppies and Sky, Sarah's horse. We had a big pile of sand in our front yard below a nice tree with a swing and near a stream. They loved playing there for hours every time they went outside. We bought a used bicycle, and Sarah taught Jason how to ride while he was here. The year just flew by and we were going into a New Year, 1993.

In January Sarah sold three of her puppies and had the others advertised. She started off 1993 with many new animals. She had horses, rabbits, puppies, and a goat. Babe was an excellent mother and the puppies were so big and roly-poly, just adorable. When they ran and played in the grass outside the dining room, I watched them from the window and they looked so comical all sprawled out in different directions. They just fell asleep in whatever position they landed when they were tired. They looked like they had been shot down in flight. She wanted to keep them all, but after a few weeks of them getting out of the garage and roaming around the neighborhood, she changed her mind and was ready for them to leave. Early on a Sunday morning, she found all ten following Babe in a line along our street, so tired that they could hardly get home. A neighbor came to our door before Sarah got out of bed to let us know. Her rabbits also got out on occasion and I think that she was suffering from "animal overload."

After Annabelle left, Sarah thought that Sky would be lonely and bought a goat from some friends to keep him company. The goat and Sky got along very well together, and when I woke up first thing in the morning, the goat was sleeping on top of Sky's back while he was lying on the ground. It sure looked funny, and I didn't know that they would become that friendly. After she finally sold all the puppies, but one that she planned to give to Grace, Sarah bought a five-year-old, silver and white dappled Arabian mare to ride. Sky became very frisky and was more than she could handle by one year. She worked in the pasture with him every weekend and trained him to halter, but could not ride him yet and decided that she would not be able to handle him the bigger and stronger he grew. He was much stronger than she was and usually went wherever he wanted to go. She had waited long enough for a horse to ride and she needed one.

I liked to get up early in the morning, and I started running a few miles in our neighborhood. On my fifty-eighth birthday I ran an eight-minute mile and was feeling very fit. My clinical work the next semester was the best that I had yet, and I really enjoyed it. I liked all of my courses and felt that I was learning what I needed. The doctor that was head of the Department of Health in the small town of Wakulla Springs near my clinic, planned to take a group of nurse practitioner students to Jamaica with him in April to work up in the mountains at Buff Bay Community Hospital. I joined the group and we spent one week in April working. I finished my clinical hours that I needed in Jamaica that semester. We had a good experience of rural community health in Jamaica and visited one day at the beach in Kingston with a chance to go down Dunn River Falls. It was a fun challenge after our work in the mountains.

Eric planned to apply to the Foreign Service for a job upon graduation in the summer with a degree in business and history from Arizona State. After his semester working in Washington D.C., he wanted to work in government with the State Department. But he called and changed his mind, planning to stay in Phoenix and get a job when he finished school. I was very happy to have him graduating and knew that it was his choice as to what kind of work he wanted to do.

When school was finished, I drove Sarah to Pensacola to spend time with Grace and family and I drove to Avon Park, South Florida to work with the National Health Service Corps at Migrant Health Clinics for six weeks. Sarah planned to spend a week with all her brothers and sisters in El Paso, Chicago, Seattle, and Sacramento. I lived in an apartment in Sebring, Florida and drove to Migrant Health Clinics to work in the clinics of interesting places like Frostproof, Wauchula, and Sumterville. The Wauchula Hospital had made national news a few years earlier, when it was found that newborn baby girls were switched at birth and given to the wrong parents. This was not discovered until sixteen years later and there were custody battles in the courts. It was very interesting work and nice people to work with.

The migrant workers were my target population that I had selected for my thesis. I even finished the first three chapters of my thesis and designed a portable OB chart for the migrant maternity patients to carry with them, since they move so often and usually don't finish their maternity visits at one clinic. Their high-risk status combined with inadequate prenatal care resulted in complications and crises for both mother and baby that could be prevented. This was my work project for the National Health Service Corps that summer along with seeing patients in the clinics. I also wrote an article that was published in their newspaper encouraging other medical students to apply for the Scholarship Program. I received letters from Sarah while she flew to each family to visit and enjoyed hearing about her summer. At fifteen, she really enjoyed flying by herself after all the years spent in airports around the world. I had confidence that she could find her way around in America.

I finished up my work in South Florida and drove back to Tallahassee at the end of July. I added a lot of expertise to my clinical skills. The first of August, I flew to Phoenix for Eric's graduation from Arizona State University. Chip, Phillip, Andrew and Tim and their families came for the celebration and we had a great time. Everyone was happy for Eric, and Chip made a sign and held it up for a photo saying, "No Job Yet," teasing Eric. Eric knew he wanted to stay in the Phoenix area and just hadn't decided where he wanted to work. He loved Arizona and had made many friends here in the past five years. After the graduation celebration, we all drove to Bennett Springs, Arkansas where Chip reserved some cabins for us to have a family reunion. The whole family, children and spouses and grandchildren were together for a week of swimming, fishing, cooking out and eating and games together. Andrew gave Sarah his red 1987 Toyota truck while she was visiting them, and she drove it with Eric back to Tallahassee after the family reunion. We celebrated Sarah's sixteenth birthday while we were all together and Eric's twenty-third.

Eric found a job in Phoenix at a new furniture store that was opening and bought a new white double-cab Toyota truck to drive to his new job. He shared a condo with a friend. He wanted to get into management with the company and needed a job to get started. This was a new store expanding from Dallas, but planned to build many more branches that needed managers in the Phoenix area.

Sarah started her junior year at Leon High School and drove her red truck to school each day. These were her first wheels and she loved driving. Now that she had her driver's license, for the first time I was off duty as chauffeur in many years of driving children to school and sports events. I felt that we had arrived at some milestones. She rode her new dappled-silver and white Arabian horse, with Babe following close on her heels, after school and on weekends in the fields around our neighborhood.

I received the news that my older brother, Dwight, died at the age of sixty-five in October. His children lived in California, but they decided to bury him in Madison at the Evans plot in the cemetery with Mom, Pop, Norma Jean, and Charlie. The family all met that could come, and we had graveside services with one of his sons, Mark Evans, who came from California. We were glad to have seen Dwight recently and restored our relationship with him.

The semester went whizzing by for Sarah and me, and we spent Christmas in Chicago and Sacramento. My friends, Leon and Marilyn called with terrible news while we were visiting Andrew and Shawnae in Sacramento. Their home and everything in it burned to the ground on Christmas Eve in Tulsa, Oklahoma where they lived for many years. Leon's elderly father was visiting them, and they all got out of the house, but his father went into a coma from smoke inhalation and never recovered. We had gone through many hard times together over the years, and I grieved with them in their loss. Everything that they had collected and built during nearly thirty years' time in the military was destroyed. Their furniture was antiques from Panama, Japan, Germany and Iran where they were stationed. All pictures and records of their family of six children, grandchildren, personal and professional records were destroyed in the fire. They were in shock. It was going to be a very difficult year for them and I prayed often that God comforted and helped them through.

The next year, 1994, came with a rush. This was the year that I planned to finish my Master's Degree. I bought a new 1994 model Ford Taurus sedan, champagne colored, in February in Tallahassee. I had put many miles on my white Volvo that had replaced my Honda when it was totaled, and needed a dependable car for my drive to work. I had even hit a hundred-and-eighty-pound deer with the grill of my Volvo right after moving into our house. It was repaired and was still running well. I enjoyed driving my new car and we were planning a trip in June.

Sarah went on a two-week trip to Paris in March with her French class. She had a wonderful time and did well in French. During this time while she was in Paris, I went to Caracas, Venezuela with Leon and Marilyn Rademacher. We flew to the small mountain village of Merida, and stayed at a lovely guesthouse. It was still a difficult time for them, but Leon and Marilyn were building a new house and getting on with their lives as I knew they would. We were glad to be together in such a beautiful place and shared many of our times together in the military. I think that this was a good break for them to get away from the disaster of their house fire. Sarah and I both had a wonderful time on our spring break.

I worked many hours to finish up my thesis on Migrant Health Care, interviewing workers from Costa Rica, El Salvador, Honduras and Mexico. I tabulated all my research on my computer with an Ethnograph Program that helped me categorize my interviews noting dominant themes. It was very interesting and challenging work. I found that the biggest factor resulting in inadequate healthcare for migrant workers was lack of access to our health care system. The main factors affecting that were lack of transportation, translators, inflexibility of clinic hours, attitudes, and differing cultural values of the health practitioner. This was quite interesting and not what we expected. It brought out the importance of the role of the health practitioner to communicate effectively and relate appropriately with patients in differing cultures with different values than the expected norm for an American population. Thus emphasizing the need for education in multicultural health care for the health care professional. America was a multicultural population whether we recognize it or not. Basic lifestyle patterns of learned behavior affected everyone's health. The perception of health and differing values of many cultures influenced their health.

I started working part time at Wakulla High School, opening a medical clinic for the 1000 high school students in conjunction with the Wakulla Health Department. I ran the clinic and referred patients to the Wakulla County Health Department or other clinics for treatment. I counseled and advised students in preventative health care practices. Many of the girls came in with headaches asking for Tylenol each day around mid-morning. I always asked them what they had eaten for breakfast and other general questions about their health. Usually, none even drank a glass of juice or ate a piece of fruit for breakfast. I always gave my good nutrition lecture and "an ounce of prevention is worth a pound of cure" lecture that Sarah always heard. I said that was why they experienced headaches each morning about this time and gave them crackers to eat that I kept in my office. The girls got together in the mornings in the lunchroom, eating before class, and called themselves "Phyllis' Breakfast Club." I didn't find out about this until much later. Any school clinic can expect to have all the health problems of any other clinic and more. There were broken arms from basketball games, injuries from ball bat fights, domestic violence among dating partners in the school, alcohol and drug problems, and sexually transmitted diseases. I learned that a nurse practitioner has a broad health focus on health promotion and disease prevention. That includes about everything. I drove to Wakulla at seven each morning and worked until noon, then went to Florida State to attend classes and work on my thesis. It was a strenuous day.

I finished all my schoolwork and thesis and received my Master's Degree in Nursing from Florida State University in April 1994. I was elated and very relieved to finish after three years, the oldest nurse practitioner in the class and a year before I turned sixty.

My major professor for my thesis was a good friend and great help during my last semester when the anxiety for completing my thesis was high. She encouraged me to go on for my doctorate at the University of Miami in Transcultural Nursing. She liked my thesis very much and thought it presented the basis for further doctoral work. She said that if I wanted to do this, she would get me a scholarship and recommend me at the University of Miami. She was from South Florida, having taught and worked there previously. She was a respected faculty member and knew my potential, but these last three years showed me that I was not academic, but more practical in my interests for working with the populations that were under-served in America and abroad in health care. I knew that it was a great opportunity to go on with my Transcultural Nursing preparation, but chose not to. I didn't think that I wanted to teach nursing at the university level as much as teach a broader scope of health care that could be transported to all cultures. It could be that I was tired, lazy, lacking in motivation and confidence in my academic staying ability, and knew my short attention span, or just the wrong timing. Politics were not my thing, but I knew that I enjoyed meeting the intellectual challenges. I was ready to be finished. Sarah was very proud of me as were all my children and family. After graduation, I found out that half my class had not passed their GRE, the Graduate Record Exam. I was amazed. But with the next class doubled in size, there would be stricter requirements.

Our class gathered together to celebrate the end of a very hard graduate program, and I have never seen such a happy group of nurses! The stress and hard work had finally come to an end. The relief was so strong that I could feel the release of anxiety replaced with an overwhelming sense of accomplishment. I wanted to sound the trumpets! I think that I could have run a seven-minute mile on adrenaline! We thought that we had achieved so much in just getting there. My license as an Advanced Registered Nurse Practitioner in Florida came in May, and I signed a contract to continue my job for the next year as a nurse practitioner at Wakulla High School Health Clinic that I had started.

Sarah was photographed for the Leon High School Calendar along with twelve other beauties at school. It was published and sold each year to raise funds. She was the month of April, and it was a very pretty picture of her standing on a train. She won a school letter in track and had it on her red and white letter jacket that she wore. She had her senior year of high school before her and planned to go on to college somewhere to get a Veterinary Degree. She wanted to continue to learn and work with animals.

Grace experienced serious family problems and moved to Nebraska to be near Pat and Amber and their family right after Christmas last year. Phillip and Pam were very helpful and helped her get settled, and Chip provided his old Volvo for her to drive. We prayed that counseling would help and things would work out for her. But in doing research on domestic violence, I didn't find many cases like hers with positive outcomes unless there was in-house treatment. But we prayed. Grace was a very strong, intelligent and capable mother who could do whatever she needed for herself and her children. And she had all the family support that she needed.

Andrew and Shawane were expecting their second baby, and she arrived on May 3rd, a beautiful little girl and my nineteenth grandchild. Sarah Jane had a problem with eating and went on a special soy milk formula right after birth. We were all very concerned for the baby and praying for her. And she did well.

I continued working at the clinic in the mornings until school was out and enjoyed being home in the afternoons. What luxury, no more schoolwork and studying. I could just enjoy reading. A job was so easy compared with all the research and writing of my last year. Life was relaxed and laid back. Sarah and I went to the movies and worked outside. Life had suddenly calmed down a bit.

On Mother's Day, some of our good friends, a Chinese couple, asked us for dinner as they were moving to a new job at Johns Hopkins University in Maryland. Feng Gao was a research chemist, and Ben Lin and their two children were good friends since I met her as part of my support group for International Student Wives the previous year. They ate Thanksgiving dinner with us and we had become good friends. During Christmas break the previous year, they returned to their family home in Beijing, China and invited Sarah and I to go with them for three weeks. But I declined, knowing that I could never finish my thesis by April to graduate if I went to China. I wanted to go with them very much, not wanting to pass up this unique opportunity to see China and stay with their family, and it was such a hard decision to make. I was very disappointed to miss the trip.

Sarah and I planned a trip to Kansas on June 11th to meet Amber and Grace and their families for a camping week at Tuttle Creek Park in Manhattan, Kansas. Sarah wanted to check out the Schools of Veterinary Medicine for college. She wrote letters to Iowa State and Colorado State, inquiring about entrance requirements. I flew to Phoenix to spend a few days with Eric, and we drove to Sedona for lunch in his new truck. He was very happy with his new job. Although Kenny and I lived near Tucson when we were first married, we had never driven to Sedona and I loved the beautiful red rock everywhere. I stopped in Chicago with Chip and Elizabeth for three days and visited with the grandchildren and saw their new house. It was very large and nice in a new area of Woodstock. When I got home, Phillip and Pam came for a few days to visit before we left for Kansas. They were enjoying their home in Georgia and the children were doing well.

After Sarah made arrangements for her horse and Babe, we left on our six-week road trip in our new Ford

Taurus with a car phone and watermelons that I bought in Thomasville, Georgia, just ten miles away from our house near the state border. Camping trips needed all the watermelon we could carry for Sarah and the grandchildren.

We enjoyed a wonderful week of camping with plenty of things for the grandchildren to do. Amber with all her children, Grace and all her children, and Sarah and I slept out under the stars or in tents. Many friends and relatives came out to see us and to visit. The Tran family brought out wontons for lunch one day with a lovely family picture as a gift and to visit. Sleeping outside in the cool breeze and hearing the bullfrogs and the crows was a treat for us all. The grandchildren fished and swam. Eric dropped in for a few days, as did Phillip and Jake on their drive to Washington with their furniture, Dorothy and Bud, Dorcas, Bud's sister, and friends from the church.

At the end of our vacation, Grace left for Chicago to visit Chip, Amber back home to Nebraska, and Sarah and I drove to Colorado Springs to visit with Betty and Pat for a couple of nights. We drove to Fort Collins next to check out the veterinary school and campus for Sarah. She really liked the campus, the veterinarian school, and Fort Collins. We drove to Nebraska and spent a few days with Amber and Pat and Amber drove us to Omaha to catch a plane for Seattle.

Phillip picked us up at the airport and we spent a week with Phillip and Pam and family in Ridgefield, Washington where they rented a farm with an orchard, and we celebrated the 4th of July. Tim and Josh came from Seattle to spend the 4th with us. We had a wonderful time together, and picked lots of blueberries. Sarah flew back to Omaha to Amber's while I flew on to Sacramento for a visit with Andrew and Shawnae and family. Sarah's flight on Delta to Omaha ran into bad weather in Salt Lake, and she didn't get back to Amber's until the next day. She spent the night alone in Salt Lake at a motel.

Grace was living in the small town of Peru near Amber, so Sarah and I drove home from Nebraska with Grace's three boys, Jason, Eric and Matt, so Grace could fly to California for a visit with Andrew and Shawnae. The boys were good on the two-day trip and spent two weeks with us and we had a great time. After two weeks we met Grace in Kentucky for one night and delivered the boys for their trip back home. Eric was afraid of water, but learned to dive in the motel swimming pool for the first time. Sarah and I drove home and realized how many miles we covered that summer in our new car.

While in Nebraska, Sarah and I drove to Ames Iowa to check out the university and vet school. We looked over the campus and checked out the small town of Ames. She liked Iowa State University and Ames. She also liked Colorado State and Fort Collins and it was a tough decision for her to make. Sarah had her senior year of high school to finish in Tallahassee, and I had a job that was expecting me back the middle of August. We arrived back in Tallahassee by July twenty-first and talked about where she wanted to go to college. She said that it was hard to make a decision. She called Ames, Iowa again and asked more questions. After all our travels and looking at possible choices for her college, we prayed and talked a long time in the evenings about what would be best for her. She said that her choice was either Iowa State or Colorado State.

Sarah did not want to leave her friends in Tallahassee, and I told her that was normal. I understood how she felt and said that she could graduate here and then we would move the next year. I did not plan to stay in Tallahassee and knew that I could get a job most anywhere since Family Nurse Practitioners were needed in all states. But I told her that I moved the summer before my senior year and it turned out well for me. Then she thought about that for a few days. She called Iowa State University one more time. Visiting the colleges and talking with people about the courses needed, Sarah looked forward to starting and considered the possibility of getting closer. Finally she decided that she would have to leave Tallahassee sometime, even though she loved our place and her friends here. So she made the decision that it would be good to move to where she wanted to go to college and get acquainted there and finish high school.

We had spent one night with my niece, Melanie, and her family in Fort Collins and my sister Betty lived two hours from there in Colorado Springs. Mike had been diagnosed with an inoperable brain tumor and we were all hoping and praying for healing for him after his treatment. Since we both liked the mountains, Sarah thought she would like to go to Fort Collins for college. She had visited the vet science program and really liked it. She loved hiking and camping and all outdoor sports. But we had to make a decision fast if we wanted to be there by the end of August for her school to start. And I needed to put our house up for sale.

Sarah finally decided that she would choose Colorado State for her college and wanted to finish her last year of high school there. It was July 28th and high school started on August 20th. We had less than a month to do many things. First I notified the Wakulla Health Department that I was moving and couldn't go back to my job. I listed our house for sale with a friend in our church who was a realtor, and she hoped to sell it before we left. I did not plan to buy a house in Fort Collins, but only rent for a year until Sarah moved into the dormitory on campus. We called Melanie in Fort Collins and she started looking for a house for us. We had other friends from Manhattan who lived there and helped us with school information. Having resigned from my job, we began packing immediately. Sarah put her horse up for sale and cleaned our three acres. There was very little to do to get the house ready and it was already being shown. I called Eric and he said that he would drive our U-Haul trailer there for us, and I would drive my car. I called Fort Collins about nurse practitioner jobs and lined up an interview with a migrant clinic in Greeley, a small town very close by. There were plenty of jobs in Denver and the suburbs, but I didn't want to drive in the snow and ice very far to work. We had lived in the tropics and the warm Florida climate for five years, and I was not excited about going back to dangerous icy roads.

Our departure date to move out of the house was set for August 20 or earlier if we could make it. And we needed to be in our house in Fort Collins on the 21st. Melanie had located a two-bedroom home for rent in a good location near the city park, close to the high school and looked at it for us. I thought it sounded fine. I called the owner and asked more questions and decided that we would put down a deposit and take it. We could move in on August 18th and Sarah would enroll and start school on the 20th. I knew that we were cutting it very close, but once we made our decision to move, we found that everything just worked out.

We loaded up our U-Haul with help from some of Sarah's friends and drove out of Tallahassee very early in the morning in a thunderstorm and pouring rain. We got an earlier start than I expected and left before the 20th. I drove the U-Haul pulling Sarah's truck, and she drove my car to Birmingham, Alabama where we picked up Eric at the airport; he drove the U-Haul the rest of the way to Fort Collins. That was far enough for me. We stopped in Kentucky the first night and Nebraska the second night with Amber and Pat and family; Grace and her family joined us.

# Chapter 21: Here Come the Pink Ladies

**WE LEFT TALLAHASSEE** in the dark in pouring rain at six in the morning. Our neighbors, Roy and Mattie Hancock fixed us breakfast and bid us goodbye. They had been wonderful neighbors. There was a lot of road construction, and I could hardly see in the rain. Although we didn't have an accident, we had a very close call after we stopped at a rest stop on I-10 before Birmingham. While we were standing by the roadside park and restaurant walking Babe on a leash, a large semi-trailer tire came rolling down the highway toward us. Although we couldn't see it, passing motorists passed by, frantically honking their horns and waving to us trying to warn us of the coming danger. We thought they were just acting very friendly. In just seconds we saw the huge rolling tire rapidly approaching and career off the interstate and head towards us. We jumped out of its way and it crashed into the concrete picnic table where we had been sitting moments before and broke the concrete table in half! We just stood there stunned. Everyone from the restaurant came out to see if we were hurt. It was a very interesting way to start our two-day trip to Colorado.

We stopped and picked up Eric at the Birmingham Airport after we had gotten lost in a very unsavory part of Birmingham looking for diesel gas for the U-Haul. I told Sarah to keep her door locked. At the airport, Eric got behind the wheel of the U-Haul. I was ready to leave the U-Haul driving to him and Sarah and Babe, and drive my new Ford Taurus the rest of the way alone to settle my nerves. We stopped in Nebraska City to visit Amber and family one night before we drove on to Fort Collins. Grace and family arrived and we had dinner together, a belated 17th birthday celebration for Sarah and early 24th one for Eric. Sarah enjoyed her birthdays with all the grandchildren there the best.

We arrived in Fort Collins on the evening of August 17th and spent three nights with Mike and Melanie and family. Melanie had just broken her toe and was hobbling around. We were very grateful for their hospitality and their help in finding us a house. Eric had to get back to college at Arizona State, so I drove him to the Denver Airport on the 18th for his flight. We appreciated all his help with the driving; we couldn't have made it without him. I knew that I would never get behind the wheel of a U-Haul truck again in my life.

We moved into our house that Melanie had picked out for us in Fort Collins on August 20th and slept on the floor, since we still hadn't unloaded the U-Haul. Sarah was lucky to find clothes and school supplies for school the next morning and went off for her first day at Poudre High School. Friends and family helped us unload the next day and we were soon settled in our house at 201 Columbine Court near Fort Collins City Park.

Sarah had the basement with bedroom, lounge and bath that she shared with Babe. She loved it. We had a nice deck and backyard for Babe. The city park with a lake was very close, and Sarah walked Babe there. It was a good running distance for me around the park each day.

We went to downtown Fort Collins to attend a craft fair on the weekend and joined hundreds of milling people in the streets filled with vendors of crafts and refreshments, a holiday atmosphere. We decided that we had made a good choice and liked this city, but there seemed to be something missing; we couldn't put our finger on it. Fort Collins just seemed rather anemic. Then we realized that there was no visible African American population on the streets of Fort Collins. We had become so accustomed to it in Haiti, Africa, and Tallahassee, that we just missed it. I had forgotten that there were practically all-white cities in the Midwest.

I received an appointment for an interview with a Migrant Health Clinic in Greeley, just thirty minutes away, and waited for more interviews. I felt at home and very comfortable in the Migrant Clinic since it was set up the same way many others were where I had worked in Florida for the past three years. However, I was uncomfortable with the interview with the director. He employed a few physician's assistants and expressed favoritism for their professional preparation over nurse practitioners. And they worked directly under him without the independence the nurse practitioner was trained to practice. He stressed that he was a National Health Service Corps scholar. I don't know what his problem was, but I think it was a gender thing with him. He had just combined the professional and gender bias and was very arrogant.

Meanwhile I studied for a National Certification Exam for Nurse Practitioners in Denver. Instead of waiting to have a couple years of practice before taking it, which I should have, I wanted to take it now and hoped that some additional preparation might help. Many nurse practitioners had to take it more than one time to pass. Since I didn't want to drive out of Fort Collins with the winter snow, I sent professional resumes out to all family practice groups in the city. I received offers for job interviews in Loveland, Aurora, a suburb of Denver, and Boulder, about one and one half-hours away. I was offered a job with a new clinic in Loveland and a job in Fort Collins at the same time. I decided on the job in Fort Collins in a family practice clinic and started in November.

Melanie and I enjoyed many visits and telephone conversations together. Mike came over to help me put our sofa together and fixed a part that had broken in moving. Melanie shared all her good resources for finding things and people in Fort Collins, since she and Mike had both graduated from Colorado State and lived here with their family. We were very happy with the house that she picked out for us. It was just right for Sarah and me.

On my first day at my new position in the family practice clinic, I arrived to find a beautiful flower arrangement on my desk a card congratulating me on my new job.. It from the grandchildren. How nice! My family all enjoyed my success. I enjoyed the doctors that I worked with and started doing the well women checks with PAPs, well-baby checks, and employment exams. I also saw clients with the normal types of throat and ear infections, migraine headaches, rashes and stomach problems. It was a challenging time and I spent a lot of time referencing my notes and books from class, but I enjoyed the professional opportunity. I was doing what I had chosen to prepare for. I taught health promotion and disease prevention to every client and really enjoyed the health education part of my practice. I really believed that an ounce of prevention is better than a pound of cure. I wanted to teach clients to want to take care of themselves and give them the knowledge to do this. My mentor and boss, Dr. Renae Justin, was an excellent teacher and very patient with my new skills. I had my own office space and an LPN to assist me and set up my examining rooms with clients. I liked my job and Sarah liked school.

Sarah decided to join the swim team instead of running track. I thought that was a good change for her too. She became active in a high school Christian Group called Young Life and attended their meetings. She enjoyed taking Babe in the back of her red truck and driving up to Horsetooth Mountain to climb with her. Sarah loved all the opportunities for climbing, hiking and biking in the area. She bought a new mountain bike and rode it with Babe at her side. We both ran a 10K race in the fall in Fort Collins. It was good to get back to more long distance running for me, but I really didn't like running in the mountains. I am sure it was probably the change in altitude. We had gone from sea level in Tallahassee to almost 6000 feet in Fort Collins. I should have waited to adjust to the change. Sarah discovered that she could take advanced placement classes in high school and start some college credit like Eric had done. She took entomology and a science. Sarah found a church that she really liked and started meeting more people. It ministered to many of the college students and she would soon be one. She also volunteered to teach in the Sunday school. I joined a Missions Committee of another Christian church where I attended and also joined Sarah.

My sister Betty came for visits, and we both enjoyed living so close together for the first time. She said that our trip out the previous summer had been my first in sixteen years! I couldn't believe it was that long. We had seen each other often, but I had not driven to Colorado in that long. Colorado Springs was just two hours away. Betty often drove here to see Melanie and Mike and her three grandchildren, Sarah, Amber and Tyler.  Fort Collins reminded us a lot of Tallahassee, in fact the Mayor of Tallahassee had just moved here and been elected by the city of Fort Collins.

Sarah liked to take Babe in her pick-up truck and go to drive-in movies. We put blankets and folding chairs in the back and popped corn and often went on Friday and Saturday nights. It was fun to be out under the stars when it wasn't too cold, and Babe went everywhere with her. They shared her bedroom together. One day Babe saw her image in a floor length mirror in Sarah's bedroom and really got excited. She barked and barked and growled at herself. Sarah and I were doubled over with laughter while she barked and barked, thinking another dog was in her room.

Tim and his son Josh and Eric came to celebrate Christmas with us and we were very happy to have family there. Mike and Melanie and family joined us during the holidays for dinner. Mike, a mountain climber who had climbed most of the 14,000 footers in Colorado, had visited us at our farm in Kansas and knew all of our family. He was courageously fighting his inoperable brain tumor with all our prayers, and still working at his office as a Certified Public Accountant. Tim shared with Mike his own diving accident and near death experience in Seattle the year before. Tim was still recovering and had gone into the pizza business with Andrew in California. Tim and Eric shot off some big fireworks at New Year's while we celebrated.

Chip had called and asked that I come for a visit around my birthday in January, so I planned to fly to Chicago at the end of the month so I could be there on the 28th. When I arrived in Chicago, I was very surprised. Phillip met me at the airport and said that he had decided to visit at this time also. Chip had finished his basement the year before and had a very large house. When I arrived at Chip's house and walked downstairs, all my children but Amber, who was expecting a baby any day, were sitting there waiting for me! I was shocked! I had not suspected anything! On a video, I have this shocked look on my face and am clutching my heart, looking like I'm about to have a heart attack. Seeing all my children in one room when I knew that they were living all over the country vast distances from Chicago was hard for me at first to comprehend. It took a few moments for my brain to sort this out, but after a few moments of adjustment, I accepted this wonderful, unexpected surprise as my birthday present. The children enjoyed the total surprise that they had carried out. It was a very wonderful family time of visiting and being together. I knew how blessed I was. Amber had a little girl, Riley Jean on January 27th in Nebraska, and we all congratulated her, happy that she was at home for the birth. With many hours of work and telephone calls and communication, Chip and Elizabeth had put together all our family photos for a beautiful video of Kenny and me and our family with copies for each one of us. Everyone had contributed their best and funniest pictures. It was a very special gift and much appreciated by us all. Their house stretched to take us all in. Their hospitality was wonderful and everyone had a great time of singing, laughing and dancing. It was wild! We had a Chinese dinner out at a restaurant together and took many photos. There was lots of laughing and storytelling and dancing and eating together. We all treasure the time together as a family and the video. It was a birthday never to forget!

Dr. Justin asked me to do follow–up visits on some of her hospital patients and apply for hospital privileges, since this would help her in her busy clinic. I did and was approved for hospital privileges at Poudre Hospital, making a few visits. I also did her nursing home visits with the elderly. I was getting good experience in all areas for my nurse practitioner practice and had her encouragement. She then revealed to me that she had sold her practice to a national managed healthcare corporation that bought up eight different practices in Fort Collins. She would be moving her office to a larger new complex. I had heard rumors of this when I started my job, but hoped they were not true. There were no nurse practitioners working with the eight doctors in this group. I terminated my position with her in February and started looking for another one with her excellent recommendations.

Riley Jean arrived right before my birthday, so I now had time to drive to Nebraska to spend some time with Amber and help her. Riley was a beautiful baby with dark hair and eyes and Amber was getting along well. It was very cold in Nebraska and they lived on a farm near

Nebraska City where Pat had his chiropractic clinic. Riley was a very healthy baby and joined her five brothers and sisters. The older children went to a country school near their house that they really liked. I stayed for a few days and drove back to be with Sarah in Fort Collins.

During this time I met many other nurse practitioners in Fort Collins, and started an Advanced Practice Nurse Practitioner Group to meet monthly for dinners with speakers. During my master's program in Tallahassee, we had an organized group that was very helpful to the students in networking and locating jobs. There had been a small group in the past in Fort Collins, but it was defunct. Rosie Goetz, a new NP friend that I met in Fort Collins, worked with me and we located and contacted fifty NP's and physician assistants in the area. She wanted an organization like this in this area also. We scheduled meetings and speakers to discuss our practice, job opportunities, pay and benefits, offered continuing education hours, and took the name of Colorado Advanced Practice Nurses Association. We offered professional help to each other and brought in new nurse practitioners when they arrived. Rosie and I shared the responsibilities of leadership.

I interviewed and was asked to start a new position on May first, but decided that I wanted to work abroad again as soon as Sarah started her freshman year at Colorado State. She had to live in the freshman dormitory her first year if I wasn't in town, so I began planning work in another country. The very full nest over almost forty years was finally becoming empty! Sarah was eager to be out on her own and had talked about this for quite some time.

I traveled to Quito, Ecuador and interviewed with a mission group in April to work with another nurse practitioner in the jungle near the Shell Mission Station. We traveled a very dangerous road there where they had a hospital, church, guesthouse and housing for the staff. I knew John and Kathy Beck in Quito and stayed with them while I visited. The nurse practitioner, Miriam, was doing a great job visiting different stations in the jungle and had asked for help. We talked about the work that we could do together, stressing health education and preventive care practices, but the mission was not ready to put another nurse in the field. Five years later I met Miriam at an International Nurse Practitioner Conference in San Diego, and the mission still hadn't found anyone to work with her. Missionaries simply do the best they can with what they have.

Sarah dated and attended dances at Poudre High School. She entertained friends and had pizza parties at our house. The Young Life group also had meetings at our house. They were a very lively group, and Sarah enjoyed their meetings and especially one young leader from Oregon. Sarah had her wisdom teeth pulled in April and soon recovered. She graduated in May with Pat and Amber and family, and Grace coming for her graduation from Nebraska. We enjoyed a good time of celebration, and Sarah received a three-piece set of forest green soft luggage for graduation and other gifts. Amber, Grace, and Sarah climbed Horsetooth Mountain with the grandchildren. Sarah applied for and was accepted at Colorado State. Since I resided and worked in Colorado for a year when she started, she was able to get in-state residence for tuition. After her move into the freshman dormitory, I planned to leave Fort Collins.

Drew planned another family reunion at Bodega Bay on the coast north of San Francisco. He rented enough condos for us all and made the arrangements. I started making plans to go and decided that all the grandchildren needed a beach hat made of denim. I had a great time sewing twenty hats, one for each of the grandchildren. Sarah and I flew to Chicago. We all met at Drew and Shawnae's house and caravanned in minivans, station wagons, and pick-up trucks filled with beach supplies and a trampoline, and a Cadillac, through downtown San Francisco and stopped for pictures at the Golden Gate Bridge. We made it through all the stoplights and no one got lost. It was really a sight! Then we drove on to Bodega Bay for our week stay at the beach. Everyone had a wonderful time and went deep-sea fishing on boats and caught lots of fish. Amber and I watched the small babies while everyone fished. We cooked and cleaned crab and ate and ate seafood. My nephew, Mark Evans, joined us for one night as did friends from Manhattan, Kansas who had moved to Garden Grove, California. It was a great time of visiting and watching the children and the guys even played golf. The children loved the beach and trampoline. All the pictures were good and everyone had a great time. I have a great picture of all the grandchildren scattered around the lounge, sleeping in window seats, on their dad's back, floor, couches, chairs, or watching a cartoon that is hilarious! It reminded me of all the tired Labrador puppies we had in Tallahassee that just dropped where they were in all positions of exhaustion. Children and puppies act about the same. We drove back to Sacramento and some of the kids, not grandchildren, went white water rafting in the American River. I heard stories of wild and dangerous rides from Chip and Elizabeth, Grace and Sarah, and Tim and Drew. I was just glad not to have to witness it. But I think everyone had a great time. We have a group picture with many happy faces.

In July my sisters, Dorothy and Betty, and I decided to have a sister's reunion in Colorado and go to Steamboat Springs. My sister Elaine couldn't come from California and we were disappointed. This was a popular ski resort in the winter and a lovely place to visit in the summer. Betty had

been there but Dorothy and I hadn't. Betty drove from
Colorado Springs and brought Dorothy who had flown in
from Manhattan, Kansas. We went to a local country
western club and tried line dancing. Dorothy brought us all
identical pink cotton sports shirts that we wore before we
took off on our trip, and Sarah took our pictures on our back
deck. We all drove in my car from Fort Collins and it was
only a three-hour drive. We stopped in Steamboat Springs at
a restaurant for cold drinks. When we walked in a waitress
announced, "Here come the pink ladies." We had forgotten
that we were all wearing identical pink shirts and just
looked at each other and wondered what that was all about,
or did they do that to everyone? Since our conversations are
very rapid and hilarious, it took us a while to realize that we
were all wearing identical pink shirts and really laughed at
ourselves. We had a good time of visiting, laughing and
reminiscing of our childhood days, which Betty tried to get
on tape. It was relaxing and fun. We hadn't been together
for quite a while.

I met with a missions group from the First Christian
Church and often talked about going back abroad to work.
We hosted a missionary from Regis, Latvia in the Spring
who worked with Youth For A Mission. We packed up our
furniture at the end of July, without knowing yet exactly
where I would be working, but I had sent out inquiries to
international health organizations. The first of August a
friend called to ask if I could go to the newly independent
former Soviet State of Georgia. Just a couple of years before
while living in Tallahassee, I had listened to the radio and
cheered on the break-away of the Baltic States, Estonia,
Lithuania and Latvia from the U.S.S.R. But I had not
followed the news or heard of the revolution for
independence in Georgia that had taken place in 1992. A
mission group in Loveland, Colorado, Mark IV Harvest, had
accepted the invitation of President Chevranadze to open

Christian schools with the Accelerated Christian Education, ACE Program. Missionaries were going from Loveland and needed others to bring in educational material. I was invited to go.

My first thought was that I had never heard of this country or where it was. Looking on the map it was in a part of the world that I had never traveled, except for my time in Moscow. Actually although I hadn't known it, Sochi on the Black Sea was a former city of Georgia, and I had been only seventy kilometers from Georgia when I was there in 1987. Phillip said that Delta flew into Istanbul, so I decided that this was where I would go for a three-month visit to work with the school and see if the Lord had work for me to do there. The schools were in Tbilisi, the capital of Georgia, a city of one million. I would meet the other missionaries in Denver before our flights to Istanbul. Sarah and I loaded and packed all our furniture, except what she needed for her freshman dormitory room, in a storage unit in Loveland and moved out of our house in Fort Collins the first week of August.

Sarah and I drove to Amber's for a short visit, and I left my car and Sarah asked Amber to keep Babe since she couldn't keep her in the dormitory. I flew back to Denver where I met the other missionaries before flying to New York. Chip had left family pictures for me of my 60th birthday reunion in January, at my gate in Denver with the American Airline attendant when he had a flight there earlier, and I was able to take the most recent pictures with me to Tbilisi, Georgia. It was August 18th when Phillip met me in New York at JFK at my Delta flight for Istanbul, Turkey. He had family pictures for me too, and we were able to visit for a short while before I took off. I really appreciated him meeting me.

It was a long flight, and I arrived in time to meet the other four missionaries and two children who arrived on a different flight to Istanbul. After purchasing our tickets, Earl Treat, the American director traveling with us, decided that he and Dan, another young missionary, would take a bus to Trabizone with all the boxes. Then they could take a bus on to Tbilisi with the boxes of supplies. It would be too expensive for so many boxes to go as airfreight. They left by taxi for the bus station. A chalkboard listed all the flights and we waited for ours to arrive. It was a few hours before we boarded a Georgia Air flight to Istanbul. The Istanbul Airport was very interesting, and I bought some pastries to eat and a coke to drink while we waited. The flight to Tbilisi looked full, and we flew out around midnight, arriving in Tbilisi at 3:00 a.m. It was still August 18th.

# Chapter 22: The Hokey Pokey

**AT 3:00 A.M., AND TIRED** after a long trip on a plane that looked like it had better days many years ago, the airport approaching in the dark night was faintly marked. The pilot did not have much to go by. The antique plane had a bumpy landing on the tarmac, where there were very few landing lights, and rolled to a stop. Like Russia in 1987, we walked down the stairs and walked to the airport building in darkness. It was a very long walk.

Unable to understand anything in Georgian, and very little in Russian, I just waited for the other family to gather and hoped that someone would meet us. We had to fill out forms for a visa before we could go through immigration. The visa form was in Russian and Georgian with no English, so I just guessed at what they wanted on the paper and wrote down my passport number, our flight, and the address of our mission. After standing in a long line at a window and paying $90 for my visa, we went through immigration and customs. That too quite a while but we were able to collect our bags, which were all just dumped in the middle of the room.

We gathered our bags and were crushed in a throng of people headed for the exit. My body was just carried with the flow of people. When we emerged into a larger room, a tall, thin young man with blond hair and friendly smile, his head above the crowd, motioned to us from beyond the exit doors, speaking English. After this very long journey, it was a relief to find someone who expected us.

Batcho was director of the Christian school and had sent Misha, his assistant director accompanied by another dark-haired Georgian, to meet us. Misha greeted us warmly with a broad smile and loaded our bags in a black Russian Lada car. He was very happy to see us and we were very glad to see him. He said that they had a flat waiting for us where we could stay and rest. We had heard of Misha and we knew that we were in good hands. We appreciated his warm welcome to Georgia.

As we entered the old-world city of Tbilisi and drove over the bumpy cobblestone streets, there were hardly any streetlights and very few cars on the streets this early in the morning. We pulled up in front of a battered and scarred gray apartment building that looked like it had been through a war. There were piles of trash on the streets and windows out of buildings. We carried our luggage up a dirty dark stairwell with scarred walls and peeling plaster, to the second floor of the building. With trash everywhere, it looked like there had been no maintenance on the building or in it for many years.

I was curious to see what the inside looked like. It was a pleasant change with lights, hot water, a bathroom, very old furniture, kitchen, living room and bedrooms. My bedroom had an antique bed with French doors that opened onto a balcony. Since I had been awake for what felt like many days, I could have slept anywhere, but the bed was nice. All I wanted to do was to crawl into bed and sleep, which I did until about noon that day. We were all grateful for a safe trip and now an apartment to share until we found a place of our own to live.

I found black tea in the kitchen and boiled water for my morning cup. Rested, Georgia already was looking better. Deciding that bread would be nice, I went out to look for whatever I could find at a bakery and see what else was on our street.

I stepped over a huge dead rat in the pile of garbage on the broken front steps of our building. I was surprised and tried to step carefully to avoid the trash and the rat. At least it was dead! This one was bigger than those I had seen in Haiti running in my rafters above my head at night. The village people in Zaire roasted and ate theirs. I had learned to evaluate the health of a country by the size of the visible rat population and this did not look good.

I changed my money into Georgian rubles, and thought I could follow my nose or see a picture, but could not find a bakery on our street. I returned to our flat after this brief sortie and we had fruit and cheese for lunch.

A Georgian teacher from the Christian school, who spoke excellent English and lived in an apartment nearby on the twelfth floor where the elevators didn't work, came to visit. She gave us directions of where to shop for food and her telephone number if we needed her and said that she would come again tomorrow. Our second floor apartment was looking even better. If the elevators in Tbilisi didn't work, I made a mental note to find an apartment on a low floor.

We didn't have a working telephone yet, but hoped to have one soon. That day I met Tamriko, a girl working as an English translator and had worked for the Russian Intourist Organization in their communist days, and she asked if she could give me lessons in Georgian. I decided to hire her and start tomorrow so that I could learn a few of the basic words for shopping and getting around. The sooner I started the better since I only planned to be here for three months. There weren't any Georgian books available so I had not learned any before leaving the States.

We met another missionary family from Fort Collins, Colorado that had been in Tbilisi for two years and were on their way back to the States. Gene and Mary Fran had two young boys and were teaching at the Christian school, the School of Tomorrow. They asked us to meet them in the main park in Tbilisi called Vake.

They received an email message that day for me from Sarah in Fort Collins and gave it to me. That was great! I was so far from my family, 9000 miles, but already a message from Sarah. I hoped that I could continue to send messages from the school office. We talked about Tbilisi, the school and the mission, and they ordered the favorite Georgian food of kinkgali for us to try. It was little triangular pouches of dough, filled with a spicy meat mixture and boiled in water. Served by the plateful, you stuck a fork in the end of one dough pouch, and ate it while it dangled, sucking up the savory meat juice inside. This was one of their pasta dishes and very good. I was reminded of the bugali that we ate in Zaire, which was a ball of dough dipped in their special meat sauce. I wondered what the significance was of the same ending on the words.

My Swahili was coming back very quickly while I added another language to the left side of my brain. I was beginning to stir up all those brain cells that had functioned so well with French and Swahili. This was interesting, but comparing the languages as I learned a new one would slow me down, as it had when I tried to think of the French word while learning Swahili. I needed to forget Swahili and French and go directly to Georgian. That is much easier said than done.

Gene and Mary Fran were welcoming and helpful and we walked across the park to their flat to visit. With no bottled water to buy and unable to drink the local water, and only coke to drink at the park, we were desperately thirsty when we arrived at their flat on this hot August day. The tall glasses of cold, boiled water from their refrigerator was the most delicious water that I drank in a long time. They had a nicely furnished flat for their family near the school. I gave them a short email message to send back to Sarah and the rest of my family that our trip went well and we had a safe arrival.

I could tell this was a hard language to study when I learned that my English letters were obsolete and I needed to learn a new alphabet. The letters of the alphabet looked totally confusing. Many of the letters looked so much alike with only a tail of difference that was initially hard to distinguish. But the unusual sounds in pronunciation were more difficult than Swahili had been for me. With Swahili, I had to do lip exercises to warm up my mouth, with Georgian I needed to clear my throat and spit to get some of the sounds. A foreign language with a foreign alphabet was a challenge. But I got started on the first day with an hour lesson and learned the words for greetings, yes and no, bread and water, and the value of the money, rubles. Here I was in kindergarten all over again, how humbling.

I started memorizing and writing the thirty-two letters and sounds of the Georgian alphabet. This is the only country where Georgian in spoken. After I learned a few words, I immediately tried to use them on the street greeting people, buying bread and asking for directions. I bought some notebooks and started organizing my vocabulary by subject to memorize. Verbs on one page, adverbs, adjectives, pronouns, names, proper nouns on others, anything to start getting some order to this difficult language. I wrote the words how they sounded in the English alphabet in my notebook. After the first week I had memorized the Georgian alphabet and felt elated that I could now see letters instead of lines and figures and symbols. It was amazing!

I started reading some signs on the streets. A little vocabulary goes a long way when you are desperate! I walked many miles each day exploring the city and trying to find my way around, becoming familiar with the streets and shops. I tried jogging on the streets, but attracted a group of hungry, starving, stray dogs; I decided that wasn't safe. There was a shortage of food here and the dogs were last in line. I thought that some looked so starved, that any reasonable veterinarian would have put them out of their misery.

During my first week, there was a meeting I needed to attend, so I started out walking early in the morning to arrive in time. On the way I saw a lot of activity with armored trucks and tanks with their cannons out patrolling the streets and many armed soldiers. I thought that Tbilisi must have martial law for some reason right now. As I passed the TV station, I saw that it was barricaded with tanks and soldiers with machine guns, and gave them a wide berth. After Haiti and Zaire, I just accepted things like this as normal.

As soon as I made it to school I asked what the problem was in Tbilisi. Batcho just laughed and told me that there was an assassination attempt on the President. A car bomb had gone off late yesterday afternoon behind the Parliament building and people had been killed, but the President escaped. Georgians seemed disappointed. Batcho tried to call the apartment last night to tell us to stay off the streets, but the phone wasn't working. Tamriko and I had been walking in front of the Parliament building just an hour before the car bomb exploded in the back.

Tbilisi was more dangerous than I expected, and anything could happen. Their revolution ended in 1992 with President Shevranadze taking over after their first democratically elected President was assassinated. The buildings in the main part of Tbilisi still showed the bullet holes. Their election for president was just another three months away. Someone evidently decided not to wait for the election.

Tamriko, my Georgian teacher, took me to her flat and said that she would share it with me, but it had no running water inside or bathroom. Her landlord was a doctor working in a clinic and offered to show me her clinic. It was very bare and there were no patients. People had no money for health care. While I was in her home a neighbor ran over to say that her mother had spilled boiling water on herself and could she have some medicine. The doctor gave her some ointment and went to check on her later. Many people had very little or no income and health care looked to be much neglected from what I surmised.

I decided that I would not share a flat with Tamriko and kept looking for a flat with running water and an inside bathroom at a minimum. I had only been here for a week and could stay in my temporary flat until I found another. There was no rush.

After two weeks a Georgian schoolteacher from our Christian school who spoke English, Maia Maisuradze, offered me a furnished flat in her house to rent. I moved from our temporary flat to my own place, where I planned to stay as long as I lived in Tbilisi. Maia was very friendly and helpful and concerned that I was comfortable. She had kept Americans before and seemed to know of our need for luxuries like hot water and electricity, if it was available. I paid $200 a month for my rooms and two meals a day. I ate breakfast and dinner in the kitchen with the Maisuradze family and shared their bathroom at the end of the hall. There was hot water for the shower if the electric heater worked.

Her husband's name was Gia, and their three boys, Sasha, Dato and Giorgi were all school age. George was a common Gerorgian name after their King George; Gia and Giorgi were diminutives of George. Maia's relatives lived in Tbilisi, and Gia's father lived near the Russian border.

The gray granite apartment building had been the Communist Government Headquarters. The building looked very shabby and was need of desperate maintenance and repair and had been divided up into flats. Despite the lack of maintenance, it had huge marble front steps, a large foyer, and wide marble stairway. It was up a steep hill on a very old narrow, winding cobblestone street in the central part of Tbilisi. I got plenty of exercise many times daily climbing the fifty steps up past the metro on the main avenue, Rustaveli, to the Parliament Building to reach Chonkadze Street. So I knew exactly how many steps there were. If I was feeling fit I took them two at a time going up

My address was number twelve Chonkadze Street, close to Freedom Square and Metro, and the Parliament Building. Freedom Square is where a large towering statue of Lenin stood in the middle, and was toppled and destroyed during the 1992 revolution. I learned that there was easy access to the airport only fifteen minutes away. This was definitely a plus if there was another revolution and we needed to leave fast. After living in Haiti and Zaire, I felt that revolutions followed me and I wanted to live close to the airport. I could have been paranoid.

My flat had twenty-foot ceilings. I am sure that it had originally been a grand and beautiful building, but many years ago. I had a large living room with black antique piano, chairs, table, china cupboard and small library, and bedroom that had French doors, with a balcony off the bedroom facing Chonkadze Street and sheltered with trees. In August it was very hot and I didn't need any heat. I kept my windows open.

My first night in my new flat I noticed that a group of men were playing cards at a table in the courtyard below my window. They played and laughed until two in the morning enjoying a rousing game. I wondered how long I could take this and closed my windows. I was told to buy an electric or kerosene heater or I would freeze to death in winter. The electricity and water only functioned erratically and there was only propane for cooking and heating.

When Georgia broke away from the Soviet Union in 1992, Moscow cut off all their links of water, electricity, gas and rail. Tbilisi had been connected to the whole Soviet Union and had never had their own infrastructure for the seventy years that they were part of the U.S.S.R. Being a

Former Soviet State had its drawbacks, the people would
have to suffer. And every winter they did. I started
negotiating trying to find a source of heat before winter
came. After all, I was from Kansas and knew what winter
could be like without heat. I settled into my flat and by
November found an electric heater and installed it in my
living room. It only worked when the electricity went on,
which was very unpredictable. Maia's husband Gia was a
very ingenious man and hot-wired my electric heater
connection to the city lights of Tbilisi. He just smiled and
said that Shevardnadze could pay for my heat. I had heat
when the lights went on at dusk and no heat when they
went off in the morning. That was about as predictable as I
could get in this place. I was not choosy and would take
heat wherever I could get it.

I could not drink the water or buy bottled water so I
boiled it in a small one-cup electric pot and filled up large
empty plastic coke bottles that I kept on hand in my room.
Since no one ever knew when the water would go off or
when it would be turned on, everyone tried to keep enough
water on hand for drinking and cooking. People just
adjusted their living habits and schedules to the availability
of water and electricity. They had to do this to survive. They
left the water faucets turned on at night so they could hear it
come on, and then many people cooked and did their
laundry in the middle of the night when water was most
often available. I would wake up in the middle of the night
and hear the water running and smell all kinds of delicious
cooking odors. But sometimes we went for days or a week
without water. Large used plastic coke bottles had many
uses in Tbilisi, and I gave them to many Georgians. Bottled
coke was my drink of choice and hot tea where the water
was definitely boiled. But I usually had stomach problems
with the food or water.

Batcho, the Georgian Director, asked if I would stay through December and teach in the School of Tomorrow. I decided that there was a definite need for English teachers that I could help fill, with the possibility of school nursing in the future with the students. There were about four hundred students located in three different locations in Tbilisi. But I had no materials for teaching English as a second language and would have to invent my own. The Mission was happy with my presence and whatever I offered. There were very few westerners and missionaries in Georgia. Volunteers were accepted.

The school buildings looked in terrible condition. In America they would have been condemned and closed up, but this was not America. Seventy years under communism and a revolution had made Georgia a very poor country. There were many beggars on the streets. Trash, broken sidewalks, broken streets and signs of neglect were everywhere. Communism had taken their lives and left them with nothing. With broken or no glass in the windows at school, wooden floors had been broken up and used to fuel stoves for heating for the last two years. The Georgians were just very grateful to have any building and a school for their children. The children wore their hats, coats and gloves in the classroom all winter. The fact that the building had no electricity, water or heat was sad, but secondary.

People were grateful for the School of Tomorrow, and the books and supplies offered to their children came at a price some could afford if they had jobs or were rich. Fifty percent of the people in this country were unemployed. Doctors drove taxis, and professors at the University sold their books for food. It was a desperate situation in a country that had enjoyed a favored southern location in the U.S.S.R. for tourism and luxuries under communism. And they were now selling their luxuries for food.

The school office was within walking distance from my flat and I went there to send email after I finished my teaching. Without electricity or water much of the time, it was difficult to send messages, but someone had hooked up the laptop computer to a car battery. We could receive and send mail at least once a week. Whenever the battery ran down, they put it back in the car and recharged it. I wrote my messages in the dark without a screen and often with a candle on the laptop for light. Since it was very cold, I sometimes wore gloves with the windows open for light. It was still communication and that was what was important since no regular surface mail could get through.

With the dangerous traffic in Tbilisi I frequently saw accidents as I walked along the streets. It was almost suicide to try and cross, since there were very few streetlights. I knew to wait for the surge of a crowd of Georgians and cross with them. I preferred the middle. The cars came very close to hitting people on the outer edges even then.

There was a large Mafia presence in Tbilisi and their children came to our schools. Their parents were the richest people in town. They traded in black market goods and made huge profits. Their children had all the things they needed and many luxuries. Their parents wanted them to learn English and attend Universities in America or England. They traveled and vacationed all over the world. The Georgian teachers in our school taught them their regular required Georgian courses. There were Christian education classes taught by Georgian and American teachers from the curriculum brought from the U.S., and also English grammar, conversational English, discipline and the Bible. The Georgian and American sections of the school were integrated, and the Georgian Director and American Director worked together.

As soon as the weather turned cold I was in dire need of warmer clothes. I had brought enough for weather through October, but November was something else. The teachers were all very well dressed in the latest fashion. I bought some black leather fur lined Russian boots and kept my feet warm as I walked everywhere. My feet had really taken a beating on these cobblestone streets and felt very sore. I knew that I had to take better care of them and the boots wrapped them in soft comfort. A missionary friend, Ellen, loaned me a coat and some warm sweaters so that I could stay through December. Ellen invited me to their house for Thanksgiving dinner along with other Americans. It was potluck and wonderful to taste familiar food! They had a lovely home at the top of a hill and four children. I knew how hard Ellen worked to take care of the needs of all her children. I ate and enjoyed all the Georgian food, but I was just never certain about what I was eating.

At the breakfast table before leaving for school, I had left my glasses in my flat while I ate. Thinking I had dropped a crumb of bread on the white cloth, I picked it up and put it in my mouth. The tangy spicy taste immediately alerted me to something that was not bread. When I took it out and looked at it more closely, I realized that it was an ant. I hadn't noticed that it was moving!

My conversational English classes were to help the students increase their vocabulary, to use their English vocabulary that they already knew, and to learn how to speak in sentences. I quickly found that it was not an easy job for either of us. I had helped others learn English, but this was my first attempt directed at a class. Only English could be spoken in the class and many had very limited vocabulary or ability to speak. Just as the Georgian words were so difficult for me, the students had the same difficulty with English. But my classes were small, and I usually had six classes each day with different age groups from seven years to seventeen years. Discipline and keeping the students' interest were the greatest challenges for me. I was learning Georgian and many children had very little English. There was a huge gap.

I found games were a good way to bridge that gap and challenge their interest. We played like we were on the television show, "911 Emergency," which many of them knew. Most watched television and this Russian show was their favorite. I had them pretend to call me on their telephone and report an accident and ask for an ambulance. We talked about what you should do in case of fires and accidents. When they telephoned I asked them questions. They told me the details, their name, location and telephone number, cause of accident, number of people involved, type of injuries and other problems. It was hilarious! Many went into long, gruesome details of shootings, knife fights, fires, auto accidents, brawls, etc. The boys particularly enjoyed this game and became very animated in talking. My goal for them was to use their English vocabulary and be able to talk in sentences, so their use of words was interesting. The older students enjoyed this the most, but it was a good way to get in some preventive health education also.

Another game called "Upset the Fruit Basket" started out fine, but soon became riotous and dangerous when they switched chairs. First we put our chairs in a circle in the classroom. Then each student chose the English word for a piece of fruit that they would be, each different. Then one student standing in the middle of the circle and with no seat, called out the name of two pieces of fruit that they wanted to exchange chairs, and tried to steal a chair for themselves, leaving another student in the middle without a seat. And this went on and on, students exchanging seats and learning the right words for fruit. The student in the middle might say apple and orange, change chairs. The children choosing those names jumped to exchange chairs across the circle.

This went well until someone in the middle shouted, "Upset the Fruit Basket," and everyone made a mad dash to find a new chair. I just watched and laughed, reminding them to always use the English words. This was utter chaos and became very loud with children diving for chairs and pushing people off their chairs. They became so excited and intense about finding a new chair that it got reckless. They enjoyed it very much, and I think it was the favorite of the younger students, but I had to quit after a short while since they became too loud and rowdy. They learned the names of many fruits, cuts of meat, and vegetables this way. They had only known to describe meat in English as cow, pig, and chicken. They learned, ham, fried chicken, hamburger, hot dog, pork chops, roast beef, steak, etc.

I asked them to put their new English words to use by ordering food in a restaurant. Some stuck to the cow, pig, and chicken, but many liked the sound of the new words and used them. I couldn't really tell if they liked learning English at times, or if it was just a required course, but I tried to give them variety and show them how useful and practical that it was for them. We listed the number of English speaking countries in the world and I think that they got my point. Georgian is only spoken in Georgia.

Since many of them traveled to other countries, I asked them to tell me in English the steps to get where they were going. It is amazing how much English you can teach in playing games. My favorite was "Opposites." We divided the class into two teams and they selected a name for their team. I wrote these on the chalkboard and drew columns and kept score for each team. I called out an English word and they had to say the opposite in English. Each team had a turn. If one team could not come up with the correct opposite word in one minute, then the other team got a chance. This was a quieter game and really taught them to think. I started out with simple words for the younger students like hot and cold, up and down, and fast and slow. Then progressed to more difficult ones for the older students like freedom and slavery, hope and despair, honest and dishonest, and liberty and tyranny. I added new words each day to my notebook and enjoyed the challenge myself. They learned prefixes and suffixes for opposites and enjoyed the team competition.

I taught songs for the younger students and the "The Hokey Pokey" with actions, which they loved. The left and right hand, arm, leg, foot, shoulder and hip, in and out and turn around was a challenge for them to get correct, but they all had a good time. Georgians love to sing. They wanted to sing it every day. Even the older students liked "The Hokey Pokey." The authoritarian rule of the teachers was the norm for Georgians, and I don't think they expected teachers to interact with them on that level. They enjoyed watching me do the Hokey Pokey along with them.

I walked down Chonkadze Street each morning to Rustaveli Avenue and caught an old school bus to the school where I taught. There were usually thirty-five students and teachers who rode the bus. In the afternoons, I rode the bus back and walked to my flat. There was a portrait of Stalin inside the door on the right side as I got on the bus. I wondered why they kept that there. It irritated me even if he was still a hero to the Georgians. The buses were so old and rickety that I wasn't sure they would make it to school each day. I sometimes stayed after school and didn't ride the bus back home.

A teacher called me late in the afternoon one day and told me that the bus had caught on fire after it left the school and burned completely. All the children and parents had escaped, but some were badly burned and at the hospital. I could hardly believe that was the bus I rode that morning. I had no television in my flat, but Maia came to get me to watch the report and pictures of the bus fire on the evening news. My school bus was just a blackened charred shell pictured on the nightly news. It was horrible to watch and think about the children who had been on it that day.

I went to the hospital to visit them. One teacher, who was the last person off the bus, had second and third degree burns and was on an IV. Her whole face and arms were wrapped in bandages. One child was in shock and the others treated for burns and discharged by the time I got there. The lack of supplies at the hospital was a shock in itself.

The back doors of the old yellow school bus didn't open and the fire started in the engine up front. Many of the children broke the bus windows and jumped out. When the fire started, the bus had stopped in front of a church and a priest came out when he saw the bus on fire and the black smoke and flames billowing out. The priest broke out the back windows and many children escaped. The parent who was severely burned was the last one off the bus. She stayed on the bus until she could see through the dense black smoke that all the children were out. Then she jumped through the front door that was engulfed in flames. It was truly a miracle that all the children were safe. All recovered, some sooner than others, and came back to school. I visited the homes of all the children who suffered burns. They all wanted to tell me their story. One of the boys who had kicked out the side windows of the bus, was one of my pupils who had enjoyed our game of "911 Emergency" in my conversational English class. He definitely took action when the emergency came.

They all recovered and eventually returned to school. I visited Nana, the parent who was the heroine, often in the hospital until she was sent home. She recovered with very few scars. We were very grateful that God had spared all the children and those who were on the bus. It was a very sober time for us all knowing what could have happened. It was just too terrible to think about. We now rode a newer replacement bus leased by the school.

I was invited by the President of the "English Teachers of Georgia," called ETAG at the University of Tbilisi, to teach a class on "Teaching Conversational English" at one of their monthly meetings at the University on Saturday morning. I shared all my newly invented concepts and taught the teachers "The Hokey Pokey." They loved it, too, and took it back to their English classes. I was amazed! The conjunctions and how to use them are the hardest to teach it to Georgians, and this song helped them understand.

Most of our Georgian school teachers also had private students to supplement their income. Parents wanted their children to have more English instruction than they could have in school classes. The teachers taught Georgian adults and children English. Everyone wanted to learn English. Two of the teachers asked me if I would have a conversational class with high school students studying for their Toefl Exam from different Georgian High Schools. This was an English Equivalency Exam given to foreign students who applied for exchange programs in the United States. They wanted me to teach for two or three hours each Saturday morning.

I thought I needed my Saturdays off, but hated to say no when there was no one else to teach the students. So I met a group of six students each Saturday morning and we just talked. I had them tell stories, describe pictures and discuss subjects that they were interested in like music, slang and fashion. They just wanted to speak English with an American. Georgia had been so closed off to Western influence for seventy years that they were hungry for anything that they could learn of the West. It was an interesting time but exhausting for me. I had to take a bus and walk a long distance and then hope the elevator worked to the sixth floor, which it seldom did, to get to the classroom. Everyone wanted a piece of an American, and I was invited to their homes for tea because their families had never known or entertained any Americans. I kept a very heavy social schedule, ate many celebration dinners and was accepted into their homes like royalty and family. The Georgians are the most hospitable people that I had ever met. They are so generous and giving to strangers. I felt like the mother and grandmother of many Georgians.

I was invited to a birthday celebration at the home of a Georgian friend. The father sat at the head of the table and welcomed me with a toast. The Georgians make some of the best wine in the world and always have a large supply in bottles and pitchers on their tables. I started out with coke and finally joined them, sipping a glass all evening. But they are not content with sippers. You never get to the bottom of your glass. The father asked me to drink a toast to Stalin, Churchill and Roosevelt. I said that I would not drink to Stalin and didn't elaborate. Stalin had been their most famous Georgian and was from the town of Guri near Tbilisi. Americans all knew him as an evil and murderous man who had more of his own people killed when he was in power than Hitler during World War II. He asked me why I came to Georgia, and I said that God had sent me. They all cheered and toasted me.

Much later I found out that I had just confirmed a Georgian belief that all strangers are sent to them by God. Hence, the basis for their most generous hospitality. That evening, the father told me that they loved Americans and that I would always be welcomed in their home. I think President Regan was their hero who had helped liberate them from the Communists. As the evening wore on and the father as the "Tamada," designated toastmaster who always leads the toast for the whole evening, and the pitchers of wine were refilled many times, he became more and more generous. The welcoming into their home became always welcome to come again soon, then come often, then they would pick me up anytime, then, why don't I just move in with them. I became a little uncomfortable with this and decided that I should soon leave. The food was continually replaced on the table when the dishes became empty and I could see no end in sight. This was my first birthday dinner in Georgia and I didn't want to be rude, so I stayed on until I was almost asleep. My friend took a taxi with me and I got home safely.

The first week of November was a presidential election and American Embassy personnel were asked to be present and monitor the polling stations. One of the polling stations was down the street from my flat. Everyone was cautious and concerned whether there would be any violence. It was a quiet time and President Chevranadze won again. The peaceful event was considered an important step toward democracy for Georgia. The ruble had been changed to the Lari after I arrived, and had become a stable currency for this country, which was very important for their international standing. The exchange rate was now at nearly two lari to the dollar. This was much easier for us foreigners than their ruble. I changed my dollars at a cash window at Freedom Square and kept note of the slight fluctuation of value each day.

On Sunday mornings, I invited the Georgian teachers from the school where I taught and other Georgians that I met, to my flat for tea and Bible study. I borrowed extra chairs, cups, and saucers from Maia. I served tea and cakes that I bought at the bakery, we sang as Maia Maisuradze played the piano, and studied the Bible together. I'm sure that I learned more than they did. When discussing the account in Matthew of the wedding in Cana where Jesus turned the water into wine, they gave me wonderful insights into the middle-eastern culture where

Jesus lived. The story came alive to me as it never had before as I listened to these women discuss the value and importance of wine in their culture for weddings. What a tragedy it was to run out of wine at a wedding, this would never happen in Georgia! And I believed that. We talked and prayed together and had wonderful fellowship.

Their Georgian Orthodox Church was so much a part of their culture that there was a blending of their beliefs and their traditions and practices. I had visited their Historical Museums and they had a 12th century Christian Queen Tamara, who had been martyred for her faith. Christianity had come to Georgia in the fourth century with Saint Nino, and their first church still stood outside Tbilisi at Misketti that was still being used. All the churches in Georgia were built like impenetrable forts to defend them from the invading Turks and Muslims. There was a high tower at the top where a lookout could survey the countryside and give warning of approaching armies. They would build a fire on the top floor of the tower and let the smoke curl up through the sky for the country people to see as a warning. Everyone came to the church to defend their faith and their land behind the fortress from the invading armies. I visited many of these churches in the countryside. It was easy to imagine their defensive wars from those walls, many feet thick. Georgia as a country never in all its history started a war, but it had lost land to many countries. They spent five hundred years under the invading Turks that conquered them, but never lost their faith. I was amazed!

Tiniko Peradze also taught at my school and we became friends. She came to my flat on Sunday mornings, and she invited me to her house to meet her family. Tiniko's mother was a doctor and had just died of cancer only one year before. We had a wonderful dinner there, and I met her grandmother, father, and brother and family and some neighbors. They made a fabulous feast of Gerorgian dishes with many toasts to Georgian-American friendship, and we had music and dancing. They made me feel very welcome.

Lela Abdushvili was one of our youngest Georgian teachers at my school and still studying at the University of Tbilisi. She came to my flat on Sunday mornings and often brought a friend, Nino, who soon planned to study in Germany. She invited me to dinner at her home and I met her mother, father, and brother and friends. Her parents were about my age and the Georgian food was delicious and their hospitality was wonderful.

An American received a message from the States saying that the San Francisco newspaper had carried an article stating that the downtown market in the city of Tbilisi, Georgia kept the bread dough in the city morgue before it was cooked and sold on the streets. We knew the Back Market in downtown Tbilisi had several unique features, but weren't aware of this. We knew that it was very believable in this country where there were shortages everywhere. I never bought bread there again.

I was really surprised to receive a call from Sarah, who had turned eighteen the week before I left Colorado, and a freshman at Colorado State University. The phone line, which didn't always work, was very clear and we visited about her college. Although I emailed her, it was great to hear her voice. She didn't like the dormitory living and was hoping that I would send her a letter saying that she was free to break her one-year contract and move into an apartment with a girlfriend off campus. She had met someone who needed a roommate. I needed to send her a letter with power of attorney given to Chip so he could give her permission. I went to the American consulate and filled out the form and sent it to Chip with someone returning to the States.

It was exhausting being the recipient of so much hospitality. These Georgians were wearing me out! Their hospitality over the centuries was legendary throughout the world. What was lacking in basic necessities was made up for by the Georgians warm hospitality.

I had made the decision to stay through December, but as the Christmas holidays approached, I knew it would be difficult to get an available seat on my stand by status if I waited too late. With only one week of classes left, I flew out of Tbilisi to Istanbul in the second week of December 1995 and stayed overnight in Istanbul before flying on Delta to New York. I stayed in a lovely Turkish hotel near the American Embassy and shopped for Christmas gifts for the children and grandchildren in an antique shop across the street from the hotel. I enjoyed browsing through all the ornamental antique swords, daggers, scimitars, samovars, beautiful Persian rugs, wall hangings, brass and wooden souvenirs and decided that I needed to come back when I had more time. It was getting dark, and I wanted to get back to my hotel for an early dinner and good night's rest. I bought a few Christmas gifts, including a beautiful silver and gold antique sword for Phillip, and then worried about how I would take it back. I ended up packing it in my carryon luggage and checking it through. Early the next morning I took a taxi from my hotel and arrived at the Istanbul Airport early enough to catch my Delta flight to New York.

I was not sure about returning to Tbilisi, but I knew that I needed a rest. Batcho had left for the U.S. to learn more about the mission, and Misha as the Director asked me to return to Tbilisi to teach English in the school in January. When Misha took me to the Tbilisi Airport, Maia Maisuradze rode with us to tell me goodbye. They weren't sure that I would return and neither was I. They asked me to "please come back."

After a restful and wonderful Christmas vacation visiting with children and grandchildren, I felt more positive about my work in Tbilisi and decided that was where the Lord needed me. Evaluating my past four months of work in Tbilisi, I knew that there were many opportunities to share the Gospel. I made plans to return and finish the school year. After Christmas I visited Earl Treat, the American Missions Director in Loveland, Colorado, and picked up more boxes of school materials to take back to Georgia. I drove to Chicago and visited at Chip's house and left my Ford Taurus with him before leaving for Georgia. Elizabeth helped me to find a medical clinic that would donate medicines for Georgia. Morgan and Adrienne helped me pack it before I left. I also purchased some English books to use for my classes.

Before I returned to Tbilisi in January, another young couple from our church in Fort Collins came to Georgia to teach in the Christian school. Right out of College at Colorado State University, they stayed a while with the Maisuradzes in my old flat until they found their own apartment. Having rested for a month, I was ready to return to Tbilisi and finish out the school year in my classes.

I flew American Airlines this time from Chicago to Paris into Orly, and then took a bus to Terminal Three at Charles de Gaulle. I was transporting more boxes of school materials for the Christian school and had a difficult time changing airports. A bit of my French proved successful. I had a long wait before I bought my round trip ticket on Georgian Air to Tbilisi. Although flying a different airline and a different route to Georgia, I felt more assured knowing where I was going and my flat and job that awaited me. And I had made many Georgian friends who had urged me to return.

Starting the New Year in 1996 in Tbilisi was more relaxing than when I had arrived last August. I brought back with me a few more comforts from home. A coat and winter wardrobe helped a lot. Phillip had given me some chemical heat packs that I could put in my bed for warmth when the electricity went off. Each of these lasted eighteen hours and I saved them for an extreme emergency. I visited with Phillip and Pam and family after Christmas and also spoke to a group from the American Bible Society who wanted to know about Russia. They had been sending Russian Bibles there since the collapse of the Soviet Union. They asked a lot of questions, and I gave them the recent news of the Georgian Christians and the work of missionaries there.

I taught in a different school this trip, and walked to Vake School each day from my flat with Maia Maisuradze since she taught there also. It was a smaller school with better facilities. The children asked many questions, and I had a Bible study after school for students wanting to attend. Teachers attended also. They were eager to learn and had many questions about the Bible. Students who really wanted to know what the Bible says were a missionary's dream. It was a challenging but very exciting time. They were asking questions about the Bible that no one had ever asked me before.

Maia and Gia had tickets for the Opera and we saw *Macbeth*. It was a very old and beautiful building and I enjoyed it very much. A group of singing comedians in tuxedos and tall black top hats were hilarious. Tbilisi had once been a beautiful city with tall trees along Rustaveli, the main street. It reminded me of Paris.

Linda and Ron were officers in the Salvation Army in charge of their mission in Georgia. I met Linda who lived near me, and asked about their work. Upon learning that I was a family nurse practitioner, she asked if I would like to give medical care with some Georgian doctors who came to their feeding station at the Moscow Café. They were receiving donated medical supplies from an organization in America. They could get the room adjacent to the Moscow Café and open a clinic. She knew that I was in Tbilisi teaching with another mission. I told her that I finished my teaching at two in the afternoon and could help, but I needed an interpreter. I only knew the basic words in Georgian.

The Salvation Army fed about 5,000 people each day in Georgia at different locations. They were given U.S. Department of Agriculture food surpluses sent as food aid to Georgia. Linda also purchased local fruits and vegetables for their kitchens. Linda picked me up on Tuesdays and Fridays in Vake after I finished with my teaching at school, and we went to the Moscow Café on Tuesdays. It was in a very poor section of Tbilisi called the African section, where some of the houses had dirt floors. The room we used beside the café was very bare, with a table, a heating stove, and a few chairs. The elderly people came there when they finished eating to sit and visit and get warm. Many of the elderly were on government pensions of just a few dollars each month, and sometimes didn't even receive that. They could not subsist on their meager pensions.

There was not much to work with in the small room that we used. Two Georgian doctors came with medical supplies and medicines and I had my own stethoscope. I saw all the patients and took blood pressures and histories and symptoms, then referred them to one of the doctors. They people came each day for food. Some brought containers to take the soup home with them. Some were younger, but disabled. I met another American friend, Angie, who was a licensed practical nurse and wanted to help us. Her husband was a pilot with the World Food Program. We worked together and shared one interpreter. I also diagnosed health problems and prescribed medications with the doctor's assistance. It was a very crowded room and not very clean, but the best they could find. On Fridays, we went to another location where the Salvation Army fixed meals for the elderly. We had a nicer room there with more supplies. I was glad to be able to help. I assisted with these two clinics for the elderly until I left Tbilisi.

The grandmother of one of our students, a Georgian pediatrician, had volunteered to be in the school for emergencies with the children. Because of the broken glass in the windows, there was always the danger of cuts from glass.

Shortly after I began my nursing work with the Salvation Army, I learned that the nurse practitioner at the American Embassy had been air evacuated to England with uncontrollable high blood pressure and wasn't coming back. I knew that it was a terribly stressful job and was very sorry for my friend, Beverly. As the nurse practitioner position was now vacant, I was asked by the Embassy if I was interested in the job. I declined the offer since I had already begun my work with the Salvation Army. My first priority in coming to Georgia was to work with missions. I was not interested in a full time nurse practitioner position or the amount of paperwork involved in filling out government reports.

My friend Angie invited me to her low impact aerobics class that met in an old gymnasium behind our school. I started exercising with a small group with a Georgian teacher, Nino. Since I hadn't been running, it felt very good to get in some regular exercise each week. The music we used was very old but had the right beat. We had a good time. Before my aerobics class, I watched many young girls and boys doing gymnastics and training for competition with their coaches. The coaches were very demanding in their training and the gymnasts very good and hard working. It was a pleasure to watch these children on the bars, but the equipment and facilities were very sad.

Angie homeschooled their two boys and did a lot of walking around the city with them. She asked me to stay in their apartment when they left for a week and that was a real treat, with all the American comforts that they brought with them to Georgia. With her husband flying to different cities, he shopped for things that were not available in Tbilisi. Craig was head of the group of two pilots and a mechanic that worked in Tbilisi.

I met many different teachers in this new school where I taught and some of them came to my flat on Sunday mornings for Bible studies. They all had families and private students and were very busy along with their teaching jobs with the Christian school. Women worked very hard in Tbilisi just to care for their families. The lack of water and electricity was an increased burden on their time. Extended family members lived with them and helped. There were not enough apartments, but they couldn't afford them either. Three generations often lived in the same flat, and there were only one or two children in their families. Three children were a large family.

The Maisuradze family with three boys, were happy to have me back and renting their flat. It added money to their family income that they needed. Maia's mother often came over to help her daughter on weekends. She was about my age, but knew no English, and I could barely communicate in Georgian. Maia and her mother taught me to make khinkali, their traditional food and chocolate butter. Working in the kitchen brings its own camaraderie and you don't need a lot of words. Her mother told me how she and her husband had lived in Cuba, working for the Communists, and she smuggled a beautiful parrot back to Georgia in the inside of a radio. Whenever the parrot squawked, they just pointed to the radio. With my very little Georgian and Maia to interpret for us, we enjoyed visiting.

I experienced some very cold nights in my flat and was grateful for the chemical heat packs to warm my bed. When there was no electricity for a few days, I just never took off my coat. I bought candles and used them for light for reading in the evenings. I had a candle on my table for reading and roasting chestnuts on a needle in the flame. I read and ate roasted chestnuts until the cold got to me and then jumped into bed. The heat packs really lasted for eighteen hours. The warmth was wonderful! I wore my jeans only on weekends and remember going three months that winter before washing them. I thought that jeans could go a long time before they looked that dirty. I washed everything by hand and hung it on my balcony, but because of the cold it took them a long time to dry. I bought some local wool fabric and hand sewed a long wool skirt that came to my boots and was very warm.

Sarah, a freshman at Colorado State, decided to come in May for a visit before I went back to the States. When her classes finished, she planned to come and stay in my flat with me for two weeks and we made plans to travel together around Georgia by train. I looked forward to her coming and decided on some places to visit.

I received an email from Chip that Tim had what was thought to be a heart attack but was released and was home. Adhesions had formed from the chest tubes that were inserted after his diving accident. These had produced severe chest pain and he went to the hospital but was soon released. All this had taken place over two or three days and by the time I got the news, it was almost a week. I felt the 9,000 miles of separation from all my children were too far. I wanted to be closer. Email was great, but the time difference and distance was still too long.

The American Embassy had a pizza night and allowed Americans living in Tbilisi to come and enjoy movies in their cafeteria. It was a good time to meet other missionaries and families working in Tbilisi. It was still a very small group. The cooks had no experience in making pizza, but we enjoyed the pizza and time together. I gave the cooks a few tips about putting on more sauce. One movie night they showed a modern version of *The Return of the Lone Ranger and Tonto*. I had watched the original movies of the Lone Ranger as a child and thought it was really funny to see these in Tbilisi fifty years later. It was deja vu. I enjoyed every bit of it as it brought back so many memories of Madison and my childhood there. Life is full of surprises!

Two other young teachers from the Christian school, Lela and ZaZa, took me to the Hotel Ajira that had a jazz club in the basement. They thought that I would like to hear some American jazz. I really enjoyed it and saw huge pictures of Louis Armstrong blown up and painted on the walls. I recognized "Satchmo" immediately blowing on his trumpet. I mentioned to my friends that my husband and I had seen Louis at a concert on our honeymoon and had danced to his music. They were amazed! One of their friends was the lead female singer and they told her. She announced the fact to the entire audience in Georgian. They were a Louis Armstrong fan club. It was an interesting evening, but the smoke was so thick you could cut it with a knife. It had been forty years ago in 1956 when Kenny and I danced to "Satchmo."

Refugees from the war in Abkhazia now lived permanently in hotels in Tbilisi. The Russians had forcefully taken over that part of Georgia with guns and all the people left their homes and land and fled or were killed. They were not able to go back. It had been a very wealthy part of the country on the Black Sea where most of the tropical fruit was grown. I visited some of the refugees and their stories were very sad; they had no place to go. Without land and homes they were still living in hotels after many years.

The first part of May, I joined crowds of Georgians to watch the May Day Military Parade come down Rustaveli. The wide tree-lined main avenue had six-eight tanks with mounted guns spreading the breadth of the cobble-stoned street, reminding me of the first week that I had arrived. Many vehicles and lines of marching soldiers came towards us as I took pictures of the Georgian display of their military. I didn't last long. I knew that they had few in comparison to the former Soviet Military, but I knew that I was watching history being made as they celebrated their independence in May 1996.

I wore my black leather fur lined boots until it started to get warm in May. School was coming to a close and Sarah arrived. She flew to Frankfurt, Germany and then got a Georgian Air flight to Tbilisi. I was worried about her flying alone, but she made it just fine. I met her at the airport and was elated to see her. She looked so young! She had no problems on her flight and was very glad to be in Georgia. She thought my flat was very nice, and I had put up signs saying "WELCOME TO GEORGIA SARAH." She met the Maisuradze family, and I had her bring some gifts. We talked and talked as she told me about her last semester at college. She attended some of my classes with me and enjoyed meeting the students. We walked a lot, even more than she did on campus.

We shared my flat and were in bed one night reading and heard a loud chirping bird very close. I had my balcony doors open and told her it was probably on the balcony. She said no, it was much closer and in the room, but I didn't believe her. She looked under the bed. Sure enough we had a bird under my bed. She tried to catch it and it ran to my side. I tried to reach under and catch it and it ran her way. Finally I asked her to get a broom from Maia, and we finally scooped it out from under my bed with the broom. Trees hung over my balcony, so I thought it had just flown in by mistake. I took it to the balcony and tossed it into the air. It was a baby bird and couldn't fly, so it just fluttered to the ground and ran down the cobblestone street, looking very funny. A small child came along and tried to catch it, but it sprouted its wings and took off on a low flight. Sarah and I laughed and laughed. We couldn't imagine how it got under the bed without us seeing it. She had a hard time convincing me that it was in my room, and we didn't know that it couldn't fly. She remembers that incident as one of the funniest of her trip there. We still laugh about the bird under my bed in Tbilisi.

When my school was out, we went to the railway station in Tbilisi and bought tickets to Batumi on the Black Sea. Sarah said that she saw huge rats as large as dogs running along the concrete by the station. I didn't even want to look. We had been told that the trains were not very nice, but we had no idea. It was supposed to be a seven-hour train ride and we had a small compartment to ourselves with two bunks. The train stopped at every town and village along the way, so it never got up much in speed. Some of the train windows had broken glass or no glass. When we tried the restroom, the smell of ammonia almost knocked us out. They were filthy. We wanted off just as soon as we could and finally came to a small town of Lobinsk, where people told us would be nice to stay. We went walking to find a hotel and walked into a large nice one, but there seemed to be no guests. Men sitting in the lounge were wearing shoulder holsters with guns. We asked to look at a room and checked to see that we could lock the door and took it. It was a strange place, but we spent the night. I didn't sleep very well that night and we saw no more guests, it was empty. Sarah and I went out for breakfast the next morning and caught another train to Batumi on the coast. We stayed at a large Intourist Hotel there and they were very friendly, but had few guests. The receptionist wanted to keep my passport and I argued with him. I had a copy of the first page with my picture and number so I gave that to him instead. He was not happy, but I wasn't leaving him my passport. After arriving we had lunch in a small bar, the only guests. They asked me in Georgian if Sarah was my daughter. I said yes, but I had eight children and many grandchildren and they were all excited and smiling. They were very surprised that Americans had so many children. They asked many questions about Chicago, New York, and the large cities. You could tell that they had not ever spoken to an American. They watched us constantly, but there were no armed men in the lobby.

After checking out the streets around the hotel, we rested in a park near the beach. It was a little chilly yet for swimming. For dinner we sat in a huge ornate dining room with an orchestra and just a sprinkling of guests. Batumi is the closest city to the Russian border and we must have hit the off tourist season, or no one was traveling. But I knew that many people from Tbilisi came here for vacations. We walked along the beach and then the narrow streets of houses and shops near the hotel. After we had walked a block someone called, "Mrs. Long, Mrs. Long." I didn't know anyone in Batumi and was surprised to hear English and my name coming from one of the houses. We stopped and looked back and a little girl was holding a rabbit and calling my name. We turned around and came back to see her and I recognized her as one of my students from our school in Tbilisi. She explained that she was visiting her grandmother in Batumi for the summer. She visited us for a while and showed us her pet rabbit and then we continued our walk. I told Sarah that you never knew when or where you might run into someone you knew in this world. It happened to me so many times. We took pictures along the docks in Batumi, watching the ships come into port and go out. We entered one restaurant along the docks to order a drink and realized that there were no women.

Our first night there was very interesting. I heard a crinkling noise coming from Sarah's backpack sitting on the floor. She emptied it out and saw signs of a mouse having eaten some crackers in her backpack. We were wary about who else we might be sharing our room with us that night. We got ready for bed and went to sleep, and I woke up thinking something was on my shoulder. Sure enough it was a mouse! I jumped out of bed and didn't sleep much. Early the next morning I heard someone in the hall corridor outside our door that sounded like an old man coughing. I was half asleep and wondered why he didn't just find his room and go to bed. The noise was very irritating and just kept on. When Sarah woke up I told her about the mouse on my shoulder and the noise all night from some old man wandering around in the hall corridor. She looked out our windows and saw a herd of cows below eating grass. Then I heard that noise again. The cows had been mooing and making that noise. We both laughed so hard and often tell that story. Before we checked out we checked our luggage and backpacks for mice and made sure that we didn't take any with us.

We were not really excited about getting back on the same train that we took to Batumi, so we found out about a van that we could ride. We knew that we couldn't get on that train again. It was a faster, but wilder ride down narrow, mountain, winding roads with heavy truck traffic. The van was very crowded and the young driver very aggressive and gutsy about taking his share of the road. We were both in the front seat and had a panoramic view of the mountains and all the narrow mishaps and dangerous corners. My feet were constantly braced on the floor. We were pretty tired when we arrived in Tbilisi six hours later and glad to be back in our flat. I did not recommend the train to Batumi to anyone who asked.

Sarah's two weeks went too fast and she had to leave a couple of days before I did. We went to the Tbilisi airport and I kissed her goodbye and saw her off with a little anxiety. She was still just eighteen years old and looked awfully young to be traveling so far by herself. I was concerned about her making her connections in Frankfurt, Germany on the way back. Later when she told me about her flight, I had reason to be. Her seat companion on her Georgia Air flight from Tbilisi to Frankfurt suggested a flight to Paris and a vacation with him. In Frankfurt their American flight was cancelled and American Airlines put them in a hotel for the night and she went out the next morning. She emailed me, and I was relieved when she arrived safely back in the States.

I had last minute farewell parties and friends took me to the Tbilisi Airport. It was a sad goodbye, knowing that I probably would not see them again. At that time I had no plans for returning. I flew Georgia Air to Paris and found a small hotel for the night near Orly Airport. I noticed a McDonald's within a short walk and couldn't resist. By this time I thought McDonald's was gourmet food! A hamburger and milkshake tasted absolutely delicious. I went for a walk in the neighborhood and decided this place would go into my address book for a good place to stay if I ever get stranded at Orly again. After a good night's rest I flew American Airlines out the next day to Chicago.

My experience and memories of Tbilisi with so many friends and students to teach there was sweet, and I knew that there was a real need for missionaries and teachers. But 9000 miles was too far to live away from so many children and grandchildren. I wanted to find medical mission work that was closer and easier to keep in touch with my family. My friend Linda in Tbilisi had advised me to fill out an application with the Salvation Army in the Chicago area for medical work abroad. After arriving for a visit with Chip and Liz, Morgan, Kenny and Adrienne, I met with the Salvation Army Office in Des Plaines, Illinois near Chicago and waited.

Chip had suggested that I call an inner city Rescue Mission in Rockford, Illinois that needed help. I met the director, Nadine and appreciated the work they were doing with women and children. She asked me to fill in for two weeks. I worked as a nurse with them for two weeks. The mission provided housing and meals and supervision for mothers and children who had been placed there by the courts. They were locked down in one building for medical and drug treatment and counseling. It was a closely supervised, but loving and caring environment with daycare facilities for the children. I lived in an apartment on the top floor and helped in their care. Many of the mothers came from downtown Chicago. After rehabilitation and progress, they graduated and moved to their own apartments.

My sisters, Dorothy and Betty, had planned our sisters' reunion in Minneapolis-Saint Paul, Minnesota and asked if I could join them in the middle of August. I drove there in my Ford Taurus that I had left with Chip and picked them up at the Minneapolis Airport. Betty arranged hotel rooms downtown for a few days in one of the malls. We shopped and saw a play and then drove to the largest mall in the country, Mall of America. We stayed overnight at a Fairfield Inn right next door so that we could drop when we finished shopping. And we did. I had never seen such a gigantic mall. After shopping all morning, we saw a movie in the afternoon to rest our feet. I bought a pair of very nice black leather pumps and wore them for all my travels for the next five years.

# Chapter 23: A World of Language, One Eternal Message

I VISITED ALL THE CHILDREN while I waited to hear about my work with the Salvation Army. While I was visiting with Sarah in Fort Collins in September, the Salvation Army called and offered me a choice of medical work in Jamaica or Cochabamba, Bolivia. I worked only a short time in Jamaica at a rural community hospital during my graduate school and never worked in South America. Since my main interest was in transcultural nursing, I knew that I wanted to work in Bolivia. I had worked with two black populations in Haiti and Zaire, and now I wanted to experience community health work in Cochabamba, Bolivia, the poorest nation in South America. Bolivia is South America's most impoverished country and had been plagued by economic decline and social discontent. The war on cocaine production was in progress, and anti-American feeling was high after years of fighting the Drug War. I didn't know, but soon found out just how anti-American it really was.

Grace met me in Sacramento in August while I was visiting with Andrew and Shawnae. She just finished her teaching degree and was interviewing for a job. She scheduled an interview in San Bernardino, California, so we rented a car and drove there together for her interview. It was a seven-hour drive from Sacramento. Her interview went well and she was assured of a teaching job in an elementary school in San Bernardino. Her grades were excellent in her education courses and she had outstanding references from her professors. I was very proud of her. She went through a difficult time as a single parent getting her teaching degree and caring for her four children and had survived. She now had her new future before her. I was very happy for her. We looked at apartments in San Bernardino and she found one for her family. She planned to move from Nebraska the first of September, in time for the beginning school year. She was so excited and happy with her new location in California and her first teaching job. We drove back to Sacramento celebrating and then she flew home to Nebraska to get ready to pack and move with her children to California.

When I visited with Sarah in Fort Collins, I left my Ford Taurus for her to drive while I was in Cochabamba. She planned to sell her red Toyota truck and drive my car. Most of our household things were still in storage in Loveland, and I only needed to take my clothes with me when I left for South America. I spent the month of October with Eric in his new house in Chandler, Arizona. This was his first house. Friends had helped him move in and get settled. We landscaped with colored red rock in his front yard and it looked very nice. He worked a business of his own in balloon advertising with his office in his home. I visited Grace and the grandchildren in San Bernardino at Christmas. Little Amber was preschool, and I kept her while Grace taught fourth grade at Davidson School. She had a nice condo in a gated community and a swimming pool. I enjoyed taking the children to the pool and swimming laps. It was still very warm weather. I worked at getting my finances ready so that I could be out of the country for an extended period of time.

My week of orientation the first of February with the Salvation Army in Des Plaines, Illinois. I met many nice and warm Christians and they printed a biography and resume for their publications. Kathleen, in charge of overseas projects was especially kind and helpful. In just a week, we became good friends and I wrote to her from Bolivia to let her know how things were going. It was good to have this personal contact with her and know of her concern for a difficult job. They provided generous funds and a new Toshiba laptop computer for my work with the International Community Health Project in Cochabamba.

They let me know that any funds and resources were for my own personal use as I worked for this project, and they were not intended to be thrown into a general fund under the Project Director. They trusted my judgement. I'm sure that they were very wise and had learned this many times in developing countries over the years. Corruption occurs everywhere, but when working in the most corrupt government in the world, it is a sure thing. Bolivia was at the top of the list for corruption, inventing new schemes daily. I heard their message loud and clear and knew also from my own experience. I just didn't know how difficult this part of my job would be. They were entrusting me with funds and resources for a specific job.

Kathleen advised me on household and personal things to buy. I made my once-per-year trip to Walmart to purchase the items I needed. This was my tradition, my last stop before getting on the plane for the Third World, and I enjoyed shopping to prepare for my work. I have always made my last stop there before getting on the plane for the Third World. Ziploc bags are always high on my list; they must be the greatest invention of the 20th century. I also bought a television with VCR and extra clothing and supplies that I needed for my stay in Bolivia. This included sturdy hiking boots, cotton khaki pants with leather belt, white short sleeved cotton shirts, sun glasses, and sun lotion for my job in Alto Cochabamba. My job was in a rural community with steep hills and dirt roads. The elevation was 8,000 feet, and I was going higher. I planned to purchase a straw hat when I arrived to complete my working outfit.

Chip and family met me at my flat in Des Plaines and we enjoyed going out for pizza together before I left.

Now that I had bought, packed, and shipped everything, I was getting excited about this new job and going to Cochabamba. Chip drove me to the airport and helped me tag all my bags for Cochabamba. He and friends from the Salvation Army office saw me off. He appreciated my first class equipment that I took with me. I flew out of Chicago on February 11th, 1997, for Miami where I caught my flight for Bolivia.

I flew American Airlines into La Paz, Bolivia at 12,000 feet, the highest altitude of any capital in the world, with a few hours layover in the home of a Salvation Army family. I remember carrying my luggage up one flight of stairs at the airport and becoming short of breath with the sudden change to high altitude. After lunch and a short rest I caught the domestic airliner, Lloyd Air of Bolivia, for the one-hour flight from La Paz to Cochabamba. We flew over some very tall mountains and into a valley of many farms and trees with tropical vegetation surrounded by mountains. It was very beautiful.

The Director of the health project, a Chilean Salvation Army officer and an American nurse, Darlene Ayers, met me and welcomed me to Cochabamba. I had corresponded with Darlene by email before leaving the States. Darlene worked for two years with the project and was leaving in two months. She now worked as an administrator with the hospital until she left Cochabamba in April and returned to her home in Portland, Maine.

I moved into the fourth floor of an apartment building that housed our office, my flat, and the flat of a Chilean Salvation Army Officer, Martha, and her two sons. It was quite spacious with two bathrooms, five bedrooms, project office, kitchen, dining room, living room and lounge. The rooms were very large and it had been newly completed. The whole staff met here for meetings every morning to plan our activities before we went out into the community. The staff included the Chilean Director, Bolivian driver, cook, secretary, nurse, doctor, social worker, and myself. A friendly camaraderie developed between us as we discussed the work of The Project.

The area that we covered included a population of eighteen thousand people in a densely packed impoverished area outside the city called Alto Cochabamba. There were primitive adobe block-houses with no electricity, water, sewers or bathrooms, along very steep hills. Many narrow dirt paths led to small one-room houses high upon the hillsides. Dusty roads that turned dangerously muddy in the wet season limited access to some areas. The Project had a four-wheel-drive vehicle that took us to all our community meetings and home visits. My job was to learn Spanish first and to plan and direct the health promotion and disease prevention activities for The Project. I visited in homes and assessed the tragic environmental and community health problems that we encountered, making referrals to the doctor and hospitals for very sick patients. Most of the people in Alto Cochabamba spoke Quechua, a local Indian language, and our Bolivian nurse also spoke Quechua and served as an interpreter.

We had another computer in addition to mine, plus a telephone-fax-copy machine in our office with the secretary in charge. I was in charge of all medical supplies and medicines with additional boxes of oral rehydration packets. There were large cans of powdered milk donated by the Swiss.

We went to a different location each day and mixed the milk to distribute to the children and babies. I enjoyed the contact with the mothers and children in Alto Cochabamba, and I was glad that I didn't have to spend all my days in meetings, as did the Director. It was enjoyable to be part of a team working to improve the health of this very poor group of people. We usually went out in the mornings to one location and came back to The Project for lunch together. The team had a good sense of humor and we often stopped for drinks or Cokes in the neighborhood and visited. After lunch we had some free time, and I brought Uno cards with me and taught the team the game. They caught on very easy and really enjoyed playing. It was a relaxing time.

I shopped in supermarkets near my flat and did my own cooking in the evenings after work. I ate typical Bolivian food at lunch with the team, which was very good, and liked to cook a hamburger in the evenings. We had lunch at about two and the Bolivians started their dinner hour in the evening about nine. I was getting ready for bed by then. In riding taxis and shopping, I sensed a definite anti-Americanism that was so different from Tbilisi.

The long war on drugs and other problems preceded me here. I felt like I had inherited plenty of animosity. I had really been welcomed by the people in Tbilisi, but did not find a welcome in Bolivia. Politically, I felt that I had gone from one extreme to the other. While I read the local paper after lunch I noticed the headlines in bold print saying "The U.S. sends $10 Million in Aid to Bolivia." I commented on this to our driver in The Project, and he replied "not enough."

Looking back now with a few years of perspective, I think Bolivians were always comparing their losses in coca production to everything else, and it would never be enough. While I was in Bolivia through 1997 and 1998, the success of coca eradication devastated the economy. Farmers took to the streets in protests. When I started language school I found and watched a 60 Minutes Special video by Peter Jennings titled "How the War on Cocaine Was Lost in Bolivia" that had been made the previous year. It was very interesting and understood the situation now that I was in Cochabamba. Americans can't even begin to understand the culture and ways of thinking. Later in May, I did have a chance to visit Chapare, the coca growing jungle area of Bolivia.

I started an eight-week course at the language school in Cochabamba that met in the mornings. Before my first week of classes, I had fallen in Cochabamba and suffered a third degree sprain of my right ankle. Standing on a hill with small rocks, I started down and my feet slid on the rocks faster than my body, with my right foot buckled underneath me. I saw a doctor and kept it wrapped in a soft cast. I found crutches and went to classes each day, walking down and back up four flights of stairs to my flat. The cobblestone streets were not easy with crutches. My right ankle was terribly swollen with a lovely color of black, blue, purple and yellow the first week— very painful. I bought a bicycle when I first arrived and rode it all over Cochabamba for exercise, but with my sprained my ankle, I had to quit until I threw away my crutches. Once I was able to ride again, cycling was good exercise for my ankle. I remember riding it for the whole day and returning with my ankle feeling better and stronger than when I left. I needed those hours of bicycle-pedaling.

I learned Spanish quickly since I had already listened to tapes and studied it some on my own, but my pronunciation left a lot to be desired when I spoke. I could read it somewhat better than I could speak. It seemed to me a mixture of English and French and Spanish. I could recognize many words from Latin also, but there was nothing similar to Georgian. After studying so many languages, I knew that I could learn the basics. I now knew how to say, "I don't know" in five languages, which I considered quite an accomplishment.

Learning some Spanish helped me write plans and goals for The Project, but I still depended on the Bolivian nurse for keeping records. She was a recent nursing graduate and loved to do this. This was her first nursing job, and I thought this would probably be my last nursing job in a rural area like Alto Cochabamba. We made a good team and became good friends. The doctor I worked with was very good and we concurred on most of our decisions, plans and goals. He was very similar to many of the doctors in the Third World that I had met in London in Tropical Medicine, and others I worked with in Haiti and Africa.

Health education and community health all looked very much the same in the most impoverished areas of the poorest countries. And the Lord had led me here. I learned to just start at the bottom and work with what I had, not expecting gigantic steps in education or health. I was happy with any accomplishment and celebrated the small accomplishments. It's a lot like working with children, and I had enough experience in that area. Sometimes being effective means just being there. I felt compassion for mothers that had to raise their children and take care of their families in such horrible conditions.

I finished my language classes and my six weeks on crutches about the same time. I couldn't have timed it better. I had enough Spanish to get started, and I would just have to learn the rest as I went. My ankle had healed, but I was careful with sliding rocks when I climbed the steep hillsides for home visits in Alto Cochabamba. It did pass through my mind that a sixty-two year old grandmother of many, might consider easier work in the future. Life can be risky.

In May, I was asked to go to Chapare, the jungle area in the south of Bolivia, with a group for a health clinic in the small village of Paris. We gathered medical supplies and medicines for a week of clinics in this jungle area. I took antimalarials and insect repellent and mosquito netting to sleep under at night. The Bolivian nurse and I would be working with two Bolivian doctors from our hospital seeing patients. It was a six-hour drive through beautiful country, but dangerous roads. We were in a caravan of cars and trucks and we crossed six rivers by ferry or driving through in four-wheel-drive vehicles. It was a major project just to get there, but we arrived and set up tents and tables for our clinic. The next morning, the people came. Hundreds of people lined up to be seen. I managed the triage station and funneled patients to the doctors after I took blood pressures and temperatures and decided what kind of medical problems there were. Abdominal pain opened all kinds of possible diagnoses, depending on the age and gender. Fanny kept the pharmacy along with another helper. We had another station for dispensing worm medicine and delousing. It went smoothly, and we saw as many people as we could, quitting at about six in the evening. It was an exhausting day, and we did this clinic for a week. We saw over five hundred patients by the end of the week.

Sarah called and said that my brother Dale in Tulsa, Oklahoma had been diagnosed with lung cancer. He was in treatment. Since I knew the prognosis for lung cancer I knew this was very serious. It was very sad news to hear and I prayed for him daily.

My eight children and spouses and twenty-one grandchildren were meeting in Chicago and going to Squaw Lake in Wisconsin for a family reunion the first of August, but I had not planned to be there. Chip had found a large lodge to accommodate all thirty-five of us and made all the arrangements. I was sad to have to miss it, but I received a call from Eric in Phoenix and he said that he had met a girl, shortly before I left, and they were planning an August wedding if I could be there. I was so surprised! But I knew that at twenty-six years, Eric had waited to marry longer than all his four brothers. They wanted to get married earlier, but would wait on me. I was very happy for him and started making plans to fly back for the family reunion and wedding. I did not plan to miss Eric's wedding. Bolivia was just a seven-hour flight from Miami. I was glad that I was working in South America and so close. Everyone would meet Mayra Gonzalez from Vera Cruz, Mexico at the family reunion. She had moved to Phoenix to be with her mother. She ran her own business and was teaching dance classes in the Phoenix public schools and performing with "Ballet Folklorico," a professional dance group. I was very excited to meet her. I had not seen pictures yet, but Eric told me she was a beautiful girl and I believed him.

On the weekends I usually enjoyed walking around Cochabamba and checking my post office box at the "correo" downtown. There was only one post office and no delivered mail. Someone from The Project usually checked our box each day. The lovely blue jacaranda trees lined the streets of Cochabamba and certain sections had a narrow park down the middle with many trees with benches underneath to sit. I enjoyed wearing sandals instead of hiking boots I was wearing each day in The Project. The Cochabamba Hotel was lovely and I occasionally had dinner there.

Saturday was my only free day. I attended the Salvation Army church on Sundays with the whole Bolivian group, and then I usually read or wrote letters in the afternoon. Our Project driver was off on weekends and I was asked to fill in, but declined to be The Project driver on my days off. No one else drove, but I needed time to myself. That is not easily explained or understood in Bolivia. I think that a person desiring privacy is highly suspect. I was beginning to feel like I was living in a glass fishbowl.

I had many interesting discussions with the Chilean Director of The Project. Her experience had only been in South America. She confided to me that the bank had stolen $30,000 from the general fund of a children's organization. The Salvation Army had long experience in Bolivia. I remembered their emphasis on trusting their resources to people that they knew and trusted. I had brought cash with me and didn't use the banks.

Marta's circumstances were especially sad. Her mother, father and husband had died, and she claimed no close relatives. But later I met her brother-in-law and mother-in-law when they came to visit. She said that she had no friends and was very hardworking, but psychologically disturbed. She proudly wore her uniform but abandoned herself to her work at the cost of her own health and her children. She had grown up in the Salvation Army Organization that proclaims God's love in kind and caring actions throughout the world, but could not take that love that was offered to others for herself and her children. She was a workaholic and a very unhappy person. There was no balance in her life and her children were neglected.

I thought that every American who stepped into Bolivia was seen by the Bolivians as having the word "Money" tattooed on their forehead. We are expected to pick up the tab and share all our resources with no complaints. If you loan your only pen to be used, they are offended if you ask to have it back. Loan is not a word that has any meaning. I think everyone there must have nice collections of pens and pencils at home, because they get a new one every day. I think it must be a game. They just assume that you have unlimited resources. Friendship is defined by how willing you are to be used for their purposes. It was a hard lesson to learn, but the reality is also liberating. There were no disappointments when you realize that you can't change your passport and identity. Trust was never given because they can't give it to one another. You are no exception.

Sarah planned to take a semester off college and backpack throughout South America with a friend. They talked about it before I left the States and planned to arrive in Bolivia in August after our family reunion. She wanted to spend some of her time with me in Cochabamba. The Project headquarters had many people coming and going and my flat was not large enough. I knew that I needed to find another place to live if she stayed for a month and I wanted the privacy. Both living and working with The Project was more company than I wanted.

So I considered renting my own flat and started checking the ads in the local paper. I found one listed and called the realtor number and she was able to show it to me after lunch the next day. I liked it immediately, location, price and size, but we looked at three more flats. The first one was a small casita within walking distance of a nice supermarket, downtown, and many places. It had one large bedroom with two beds, two baths, a nice eat-in kitchen and living room. There was even a small office that I could use for an extra bedroom if I wanted. It had a lovely outside enclosed garden and rock patio in the front, with an outside grill and space to park a car when I got one.

I decided it was perfect just for me and had room for Sarah and her friend to visit and for Sarah to stay longer if she wanted. I knew that I would enjoy my privacy from The Project. I checked with the landlord who was from Argentina, and she said this was possible. I signed the papers and put down a deposit. The realtor was very nice and said that I could move in at the first of the month. I was very happy to have my own place, privacy and be able to entertain family and friends if they came for a visit.

I moved into my new furnished casita the first of July with a young neighbor's pick-up truck. I didn't have much, but my computer, television and bicycle went with me. I loved it! The Salvation Army had stipulated that any funds or supplies provided by them were for my own personal use and went wherever I went. It was nice and comfortable, with a lovely garden in front and lots of windows and light in the house. The location was good and the outside patio secure and private. It was an attractive casita and the landlord next door was quite amiable. They had foreigners for former renters. I would start looking for a car soon.

I had decided the Brazilian-made Volkswagen, called a Peta, was just right for me. It was very common to see many on the streets of Cochabamba when sitting at sidewalk cafes. I had driven Volkswagens while living at our farm and really liked them. My realtor, Martha Izquerida from Uruguay, drove a white Peta and she said that she would help me find one like hers. We went to a section of Cochabamba where used cars were parked and she negotiated a good price for me. I bought a 1987 white Volkswagen Peta and really enjoyed driving it. Martha and I became very good friends.

I had told the Bolivian Captain of the Salvation Army of my plans to move and they were fine with that as long as it didn't cost them anything. They wanted to check that I wasn't charged too much and understood my need for more space and privacy. The Salvation Army provided room and board with a small stipend at The Project headquarters. The added cost to me of my casita was well worth it in my judgement. I had not planned on being available twenty-four hours a day for duties that might come up. They understood and I drove to the office each morning in my new car. At six in the evening or later, I drove to my little casita and enjoyed reading or a movie. I found a video store very close to my casita and watched *Les Miserable* in French with Spanish subtitles. That was an exercise in translation!

At the end of July, I flew to Santa Cruz and caught my American Airlines flight to Miami and then Chicago. Sarah and her friend drove my car to Chicago. Grace and her children drove to Phoenix and picked up Eric and

Mayra, then they all drove to Chicago. Grace and I set up camping with her children in a nice camping park near Chip's house. It was great to see everyone. We were all happy to meet Mayra for the first time. When I grabbed Mayra and hugged her, I saw a short, petite young girl with long dark hair, very pretty, quiet, and vivacious. Eric hadn't had a chance! So this girl was his choice! I could see why their romance and marriage plans went fast. I thought he had done well. She was prepared for the occasion as Eric had gone through all his pictures of our family and she had been memorizing names of children that belonged to each family. Mayra came from a large extended family of grandparents, aunts, uncles, and cousins in Vera Cruz, Mexico, so she had much experience with large family gatherings. Mayra also brought her professional camera and tripod to record the event and show her family photos when she returned. Later I saw beautiful pictures of the grandchildren that she took. She was the photographer for her dance groups and had lots of experience. She was definitely a professional and just what our family needed with all those darling grandchildren to photograph. I think Mayra had a great time with her camera.

Chip and Elizabeth and family extended their hospitality to all of us. Elizabeth had a framed picture in her kitchen that said it best for our family reunions: "Sit long, talk much, laugh often." Chip built a beautiful deck overlooking the woods on the back of his house, and we had a wonderful gathering and cook out. He had a house full of family and seemed to be enjoying it! The whole family joined together at Chip and Elizabeth's church and then met at the Woodstock Park for family pictures and a picnic. The children ran and played nonstop. We had no serious accidents, plenty of food, and laughing and visiting, and I was excited and happy to be there. The girls put together a shower for Mayra. We had a wonderful time welcoming her to our family. Eric was very proud of her. They planned their wedding the first of August in Tempe, Arizona.

Eric and Mayra had to get back to their work and plans in Phoenix. Chip had rented a large lodge on Squaw Lake and the rest of us all drove there to spend a week of vacation. It was a beautiful location in Wisconsin about four hours from Chip's house. The lodge had private rooms for all of us with room to spare. A wonderful choice of breakfast was served at any morning hour we chose until eleven. Everyone enjoyed eating a big breakfast with plenty of choices and no complaints. The moms all loved it. The moms fixed sandwiches for lunch and the guys grilled out for dinner. Everyone had a lot of fun fishing, hiking, golfing, camping out on an island, canoeing, paddle-boating, swimming, and playing games.

Lilia Theobald was the youngest grandchild at six months and there were twenty more of all ages. Everyone took lots of pictures. I had my picture taken with all the grandchildren and it is one of my favorite pictures. I sent it out to friends and my family the next Christmas. The grandchildren formed cousin liaisons among the different age groups of children. Adult gatherings with no hurry or schedules provided plenty of time for this very active family to get to know one another better. Enough space for everyone to have their own whether they wanted quiet or activities. After reading the Bible and prayer, Chip baptized Grace's oldest son Jason Brentano in the lake. The adults decided upon ground rules for the safety of the children and they were strictly adhered and ministered. We wanted no accidents. There were plenty of discussions, but no obvious irreconcilable arguments.

I lay on a reclining beach chair near the lake and did nothing. I praised God for my family and just watched it all, grateful for so many emergency medically trained kids to be on duty. I was very glad to be there. Bolivia was out of my thoughts. It was a wonderfully relaxing time for us all and we all remember the time fondly.

When it was time to pack up and leave Squaw Lake and all the children had been accounted for and all the photos taken, we were a tired but happy crew. Everyone drove back to Chip's house in Woodstock and started their trip home. Someone took me to the airport, and I flew American to Eric and Mayra's wedding in Phoenix, arriving just in time.

Eric's friend Steve picked me up at the airport, and I had time to buy a dress and get to the wedding in Tempe. We took pictures outside before the wedding. Eric looked very handsome in his tux, and Mayra was beautiful in her long, white wedding dress. She had decorated the room and tables with beautiful candles and flowers everywhere. It was very lovely. A friend of Eric's, assistant pastor from his church, had the wedding ceremony. I met Mayra's mother, Maria, and her brothers and sisters. It was a happy time for us all. The next morning I had breakfast with Eric and Mayra, and they were very happy that I could be at their wedding. My flight from Phoenix to Miami, then La Paz and Cochabamba was uneventful. There had been so many activities with so much visiting with children and grandchildren that I think I was in recovery on the plane.

My little casita in Cochabamba was now home, and Sarah planned to arrive in just a few days. I received a call at The Project office from Sarah and she was at the Cochabamba Airport. It was only a ten-minute drive there, and I quickly hopped into my Peta and found Sarah and her friend sitting on their duffel bags waiting for me in front of the airport. They had spent the night in La Paz and the high altitude had made them sick. This was their first stop on their backpacking trip around South America. We chatted and I took them to my casita to rest and get settled and went back to work.

They sure appreciated my place. Sarah just loved it. I had found it and moved in just in time and was glad to have the space for them. I worked each day, so they relaxed and found their way around Cochabamba, and we cooked dinner together in the evenings. I gave them storage places for their duffel bags and they reorganized their camping and backpacking gear for their trip. I took them out to a very nice restaurant on the top floor of the Sofer Tower and Mall for Sarah's twentieth birthday and we celebrated. They were excited about their plans for backpacking around South America. Sarah enjoyed driving me to work in my Peta and had the car until she needed to pick me up after work. We had a health fair in one of the poorer areas of Cochabamba and the girls helped in the dental clinic shortly after they arrived. It was quite an experience for them.

While Sarah was with me she fixed my flower-beds on the patio and helped me get my goals and objectives for the Health Project for the coming year on my computer. She had more computer experience and I appreciated her help. I enjoyed the girls' company, but they were anxious to get on with their backpacking to see Chile and Peru. They planned a trip to Machu Picchu in Cuzco, Peru, and then fly into Santiago and backpack the length of Chile. Depending on how their money lasted, they had the whole semester off college. Sarah had bought a South American Lonely Planet Guide and was planning their trip. They packed up and I drove them to the airport.

The Health Project was hearing rumors that funding may not come for the next year. They were running out of money. Since I had nothing to do with the accounting and we spent few dollars on supplies, I really didn't know the entire story. But I could guess that a mismanagement of funds was being checked. A Salvation Army Officer from the South American Office in Chile came to check things out. He was from Scotland and I really enjoyed meeting him. There were many meetings within the organization to assess the progress and future of The Project. I didn't learn of any definite decision or outcome for the future of the Health Project. Many countries were involved.

I began making alternate plans for work in Cochabamba so that I could stay and work if there was no more funding. I did not want to leave if The Project finished and I was reassigned to another country with the Salvation Army. I was settled here and knew many internationals working with mission projects. I met an Australian woman who was working to get a domestic violence program started with the Cochabamba Police Department. There was a brigada of policewomen officers who wanted to start a program. Her husband was Bolivian and he had helped me get my Peta registered. Phoebe and Tim were involved with the Anglican Church. This was something that I could help with and she asked if I was interested. Yes I was. I told them that if I left the Health Project, I would work with them on a temporary volunteer basis.

By the end of September things started happening. I could see that The Project was going nowhere without sufficient funds, and I gave my notice of retirement for the beginning of October. I had finished up the goals and objectives of the Health Project for 1998 and submitted them to The Project office. I had done the best that I could and felt that I was no longer needed. The Chilean Director was under pressure and did not want to lose their only American and called me at my home to ask if I would take over as Director. She said that I was the only one who knew what was really going on with the Health Project. I knew that was right and it was tempting to step in and take over and do things the way that I thought they should be done. Since I was in Alto Cochabamba every day and worked with the mothers and children and the Project Team, I was the closest to knowing what was needed. I had trained the

Bolivian nurse and the doctor was quite capable, and I thought it was time for me to step out. I wanted the Bolivians to do it for themselves. As a professional I was not needed. My expertise was Nursing and Health Education. I said no. I knew that the director's job was one meeting after another with no nursing or patients and not much accomplished. The job was more involved with politics and funding. I felt that I would be spinning my wheels in the bureaucracy and paperwork. I had finished my job with the Health Project. I wrote a letter of termination to my friends in the Chicago office expressing these feelings and let them know what was going on. Looking back, at that time I was not so sure that I was doing the right thing, but now understand the Lord's guidance in my decision.

Meanwhile Sarah called from Chile and said that her friend was out of funds and homesick and planned to go back to Colorado. They had been backpacking with various backpackers from Australia, England, South Africa, and New Zealand along the way. Did I want to go to the tip of Chile with her backpacking? I thought the timing was great and told her that I would love to go. I had already planned to fly to Cusco, Peru, so I told her that I would fly to Santiago on my return from Cusco and meet her in Chile. We made plans to meet at a bed and breakfast in Pucon.

I decided to go traveling in October and be back in my flat in November. I told my friends at The Project goodbye and left for Cusco. A travel agent that I had booked with in Cochabamba arranged for someone to meet me at the airport who spoke English and took me to a very nice German bed and breakfast. I made all my bus and trip arrangements through Francisca, a lovely young Peruvian girl in Cusco. We went out for dinner on the main square my first night there. I enjoyed the restaurants and shops in Cusco. I didn't buy much, but it was fun to be a part of the crowd and look at the interesting Inca relics and crafts. I found a coffee shop with recent English newspapers and enjoyed tea and lunches there. I took a bus around the city to see museums and historical Cathedrals, the main tourist attractions. The amazing architecture of the Incas in building the walls was astounding. They were like that of the pyramids in Egypt. Each large stone was chiseled to a perfect fit. One bus went out into the countryside for the day and we stopped at a lovely restaurant for lunch. It was a very poor country as I could see.

Finding the train station I bought my ticket to Machu Picchu. I boarded with many backpackers who planned to get off at a certain stop. When the backpackers laden with heavy packs and camping gear all got off to continue their ascent on Machu Picchu, I rode to the end of the line dressed comfortable in sandals and jeans. At this location we could shop at many kiosks and enjoy the mountain views. After a cup of tea a bus took us the rest of the climb to the top of the mountain. It was very beautiful. The ancient Inca city that had mysteriously been abandoned in the fourteen hundreds was amazingly still very evident in the ruins. The tour guide described a well-organized and functioning city with canals for water and children's play area. The Incas had chosen a mountain-view that was magnificent. And then just left it in the 14th Century for an unknown reason. Everything was speculation. I watched as backpackers ending their climb came into the old city ruins, tired and thirsty from their long hike. I was glad that I took the bus. I had read a lot about Machu Picchu, but was more impressed when I saw the ruins of that ancient civilization. I liked the music of the Incas and it reminded me of Bolivian music. At the airport before I left, I bought a tape to remind me of the haunting flutes and melodies of the Inca Indians of Peru.

I needed to get more cash and my tour agent took me to one of the downtown banks to use my Mastercard. I had never seen so many heavily armed soldiers around a bank before. There was no way anyone could rob it. They had a small army and arsenal in the lobby. I quietly went to the cash window not wanting to draw any attention to myself and left with my cash. I bought my ticket to Santiago and left the next day on Peruvian Airlines. It was a good flight over the Andes Mountains; very beautiful as I had remembered them in Quito, Ecuador when I visited.

In Santiago I took a taxi to the bus station and bought my ticket for Pucon, where I would meet Sarah and her friend. It was a short wait and I saw that Chile was a very rich country compared to Bolivia. The streets were not lined with beggars and the people looked prosperous and nicely dressed at the bus station.

Everyone seemed to be wearing leather shoes. Not so in Bolivia. When my bus left Sarah had told me that it would be a long ride and it was. But I enjoyed seeing the countryside. I don't think I looked at a map of Chile in Cochabamba to see how long the country is as it proceeds down the western side of Chile to the tip of South America. Sarah and her friend met me at the bus station in Pucon and took me to their bed and breakfast. It was nicely furnished and comfortable and they had bunks in a back-packers dormitory. I had a private room on the second floor and we talked about their travels and her friend's trip back in a couple of days to Cochabamba. Sarah and I made plans to go on to Punta Arenas at the southern tip of Chile. I gave her friend the key to my casita so she could stay until she left for the States. We saw her off on a bus to Santiago where she would fly back to Bolivia. Sarah and I bought our tickets to Punta Arenas. Sarah had her backpack and hiking boots and I had my roll-on carry-on flight bag that I had taken to Cusco. We looked forward to our adventure. This mother-daughter trip should be interesting.

It was a thirty-six hour bus ride, and I think we went in and out of Argentina twice. In the middle of the night, we stopped at a restaurant and I felt like I had to keep track of Sarah. She would have none of it. She had invited me to come with her, but only as a fellow traveler, not a mother protector. I got the message. The amazing diversity of Patagonia's vast plains, gorgeous mountains, pristine lands, volcanoes, and glaciers seemed untouched by human inhabitants. The hot sun revealed startling contrast in this vast land. Patagonia had its own distinct beauty with much barren landscape. There were many lakes as we got closer to Punta Arenas and roadside signs saying that we were coming to the end of the world. It felt like that at times as the bus ride went on and on. I had not taken this long of a bus trip since I was fifteen years old from Georgia to Kansas.

We looked in Sarah's travel book and found a bed and breakfast to stay downtown within walking distance of the main square, park, and shops in Punta Arenas. This usually included the post office, banks and ATMs, restaurants, tourist information offices, buses, and travel agencies. We checked into our bed and breakfast and I fixed us a cup of tea after we got settled into our separate bedrooms. We took off in different directions to explore the city. This was a method used by backpackers, and then they met up in the park and shared their discoveries. They could cover much more area in a shorter time and find the cheapest buys on items that they usually needed. Sounded like a good idea to me. I thought I was traveling cheap when I bought a hamburger, but Sarah informed me that I was spending too much on food and we could just buy bread, cheese, and fruit. And I was addicted to Coke. Sarah only drank water.

After a few days, we had seen everything in Punta Arenas that interested us, and we started thinking about other places to go. I especially liked the Magellan Maritime Museum with all of Magellan's ships and discoveries. I wrote in the guest book at the museum my name, address, country and impressions of the museum. I remembered Magellan's name from grade school history books and it was fascinating. I imagined him sailing here with his crew. We took a bus to a shopping mall and bought waterproof windbreakers that we decided we needed for the rest of our trip.

It took me a while to relax and forget about a schedule, but I was beginning to enjoy this laid-back backpacker's life, just deciding where to go next. I could get used to this. We looked at a map and wished that we could go to the continent of Antarctica. While it always seemed like it was at the end of the world, it was only a short boat ride from Punta Arenas. This sounded like a great idea to me also. We checked into the tour ships going there but they didn't start until December and this was October. We visited with a young girl who was a translator working on the ships and it sounded like a great trip. We were very disappointed not to see this continent and we had wanted to see a lot of penguins. Here we were at the end of the world and no place to go but up. We started discussing plans for a possible alternate trip to the Falkland Islands and read all we could find. It was just a small dot in the ocean.

After making our decision we bought our tickets on LanChile to Port Stanley in the Falkland Islands. I had never heard of this place before. It was a British colony and had a war in the 80s when Argentina tried to reclaim it. We had a good flight, but in landing could not believe how small it was and so very windy! We found a nice bed and breakfast for the night. The next day we booked on the Falkland Airlines to Carcass Island for three nights where we were advised that we would see the most wildlife, especially unusual birds and penguins. It was too small for even a dot on the map! We enjoyed our visits in Stanley and heard about the British War with Argentina in great detail. The

Argentinans had sailed into Port Stanley Harbor by night and surprised their small military guard. The war was only won when the British came in to defend them.

This had been a terrifically frightening time for the Islanders, but there was only one elderly woman killed by a bomb in her bed. Everyone else had evacuated their houses. There were still land mines to be avoided in certain areas.

We met an English author of bird books, Robin Wood, at our bed and breakfast who was going on our flight to Carcass Island to count the bird population for his next book. He and a friend had booked the cottage next to us. Sarah and I had miscalculated our money with the English pound and I called Andrew and had him send us additional funds from my account to the bank in Stanley. These arrived while we were on Carcass Island.

We flew very low over the Pacific with strong winds for about an hour. When we landed at Carcass Island, which was a very small strip of land, the lone male human inhabitant driving a jeep with a windsock flying from the back met us on a grassy strip close to the water. It was a very small island with only sheep and one family tending the ship with three cottages. He welcomed us to Carcass Island with a cheery smile and his enthusiasm for visitors was quite evident. We had a short ride in his jeep to one of the cottages and he checked us in explaining how everything worked and what was available. He invited us to come to his house for tea sometime before we left the island. Sarah and I talked about what hikes we wanted to take in order to see the most penguins and other unique birds that summered here. Sarah was happy to see that there was also a horse to ride if we were so inclined. The main bird population group that was here was the Caracara bird. Robin and his friend planned to hike around the entire island and count all the Caracara adult birds as well as eggs inside the nests they discovered.

These Caracara birds looked like large vultures and they make their home on Carcass Island to breed each year. There were carcasses of large Canadian geese scattered and lying around in the grass on the island, which must have been the favorite food of the Caracaras. It was definitely not a sanctuary for the geese. The Canadian geese moved slowly compared to the large Caracara birds, with no trees on the island and no place to hide. It was easy for the Caracara to swoop down and catch them. I really hope that I wouldn't see this death struggle. After we moved into our cottage, we decided to take a walk to the top of the hill to catch the view from Carcass Island.

The birds followed us in a sortie of four over-head, then landed closely and walked boldly toward us. They were very curious of our presence, not being used to people. They often hovered close above our heads in the wind looking very threatening with their long beaks and cawing loudly. We didn't want them landing on our heads with their sharp claws, so we carried a garden rake to scatter them when they got too close. We were told that they were juveniles and would not hurt us. I couldn't imagine how that was supposed to give us any peace of mind. They were very intimidating, and they would not go away. Sarah and I decided that we really didn't need to see the island from the top of the hill anyway. It was their island. These birds were too close for our comfort and we cowardly ran back to our cottage, the birds following and swooping low over our heads all the way.

I found an interesting paperback to read in the cottage and went outside to sit on the back steps and read in the sunshine. Sarah thought the book looked interesting, so I wanted to finish it so she could have a chance to read it before we left Carcass. The large birds perched on the top roof gable outside our cottage door and stared at me. I had seen Alfred Hitchcock's movie *Birds* many years ago and wondered why he didn't do it here; it would have been even more terrifying. We were just interesting objects that had entered their existence on this island. They acted like they wanted to be friendly, but didn't know how. Meanwhile we kept our garden rake close at hand, and I was ready to close the back door quickly if they decided to fly into the house. That would have been an ugly scene with me screaming and thrashing the air with my garden rake, and chasing birds around our quiet cottage. Sarah would have been doubled over rolling on the floor with laughter and no help. That would not have been fun!

We took long walks along the Pacific Ocean beach and found many penguins. I kept a stick that I found with a rope on the end of it to scare away the Caracaras if they followed us and they did. I thought that this was ridiculous, and I was tired of their intimidation. There were penguins of all varieties basking in the sun, or holed up in their homes along the tall grassy mounds near the beach. There were four varieties of penguins here, King, Jackass, Emperor and Gentoo. The black and white penguins were much smaller than I imagined. They had a funny way of sticking their heads up and throwing them back like they were laughing at us. These were called jackass penguins. We lay on our stomachs on the ground and quietly inched our way up as close as we could get to a large group. Sarah said that they had fleas and took some good pictures. We were amazed that there were hundreds of penguins here. It was fun to see them walking back and forth into the ocean and swimming and waddling back up the hill. We also saw sea lions frolicking out in the ocean. We must have walked close to a nest of the Caracaras because they descended on us, coming very close. Large beautiful birds of many kinds I've never seen before, swooped down and ran along the beach. We were definitely in a bird paradise.

Sarah decided to take a ride on the horse, and I got some good pictures of her riding, showing the tiny island and the vastness of the Pacific Ocean in the background. But she couldn't get the horse to run very fast and didn't ride very long. We found food to cook in the kitchen and just relaxed and enjoyed knowing that we were on this bird sanctuary in the middle of the Pacific. We could not get any closer to Antarctica.

We had tea in the house of the only human permanent inhabitant of Carcass Island and he said that he entertained cruise ships a few times each year. That was probably enough company to last him for the rest of the year. They landed and took boats in to see the penguins and birds, but stayed nights on their ships in the bay. He must have had a lonely life, but they had raised two children on Carcass Island, now grown and living in England. His only son was a pilot and flew for British Airways.

On the third day we flew back to Stanley, and what had looked like such a tiny island before, now looked very large. I picked up my money at the bank and shopped for some penguin glasses for the grandchildren in a gift shop. We ate a nice dinner at the only hotel, ready to tell Port Stanley goodbye the next day. We enjoyed our last night at the bed and breakfast. We asked questions and listened to some interesting stories about the local inhabitants. We had seen it all and were ready to go back to Chile. Our flight back to Punta Arenas was good and we enjoyed flying on LanChile.

It was the end of October and Sarah and I parted company in Punta Arenas. I flew back to Santiago, Chile to catch a flight to Cochababma. She planned to meet up with other backpackers and go to the park at Torres del Paine in Tierra Del Fuego as her next stop. I received calls and postcards from her as she traveled.

Free of all job constraints, I enjoyed visiting with other missionaries in Cochabamba to find out what they were doing. An English girl invited me to a luncheon and Bible study of women from the Women's Club of Cochabamba. Later I was asked to teach this Bible study group, and we met in different homes of the women attending. I had additional meetings to plan the Program of Domestic Violence with the police brigada. We made plans to open a childcare center where the children of abused women could stay temporarily. My friend, Phoebe, was working on the funding and political end of the project since she knew many influential people in town. I supported her efforts and gave my time to writing teaching materials for the Cochabamba policewomen officers. We were given a building in the police headquarters and got it ready for the childcare center. I spoke to a monthly meeting of the Cochabamba Women's Club about the project and also to the American high school teachers who were looking for Christmas projects for their students to sponsor. That was my contribution for the funding efforts.

I had missed running and more physical exercise while working. I found a tennis club in Cochabamba and started taking lessons with the pro there named Oscar. The club had clay courts, and I really liked the challenge of getting back to tennis since I hadn't played since school in Columbus, Georgia such a long time ago. It was good to be able to hit the ball again, and I had a lot to learn since I had never taken lessons. I drove to the tennis club early before my lesson to be able to practice. I also started running on one of the bicycle paths near my casita.

Sarah surprised me one day and arrived at my casita while I was at work. She didn't have a key to my street entrance, but had no trouble getting over the wall. She had a key to my casita, and I was so glad to see her when I got home from work. She had been gone over a month and enjoyed her camping in the park at Torres del Paine in Tierra del Fuego at the bottom of Chile. Along with other backpackers she had a wonderful time camping and seeing the beautiful sights. She was ready to spend some time with me in Cochabamba before she went back to the States. She had been writing another friend in Colorado and was expecting Bob to arrive and planned to meet him in La Paz for Christmas.

Sarah and I drove to a nearby small town of Quillacollo so that I could introduce her to some of my friends. Jane Duran and her Bolivian husband, Jorge, and two children were building on to their house. Jane and I had become good friends and met each other in town, or Jane dropped by my house when she shopped in Cochabamba. Jane and Jorge worked with the Christian Church and School in Quillacollo. Jane had arrived in Cochabamba with a mission group from Virginia many years before and met and married Jorge. Jane and Jorge ministered to the street people in Quillacollo. They were a lovely couple with their kids, John and Jessica. Jane's mother often visited from Virginia and Ruth and I became friends when she came. Sarah and I had Thanksgiving dinner with the Durans and enjoyed their hospitality.

Sarah enjoyed her time in Cochabamba and made plans for her last trip to La Paz and Cororico, a small village in the mountains. We visited a new church that I had found closer my flat. She liked to shop and cook for me while she was there. After her trip to Cororico and Christmas in Bolivia, she planned to return to Colorado. While she checked the mail for me each day, she discovered a small Bolivian craft and sweater shop downtown near the "Correo" and bought some warm alpaca sweaters for Christmas presents. The alpaca sweaters were very pretty colors and the shop owners also sold to shops in Colorado. She took many back for college friends and family. I received warm alpaca gloves from her that I appreciated later when I lived in the mountains of Arizona.

Eric and Mayra called with the news of a new granddaughter, Naomi Giselle, born on December 19th. Mayra and Naomi were healthy and doing well in the hospital. We were happy to have the news. I was so anxious to see my new grandchild. They asked me to visit them in Phoenix after Christmas and before I flew back to Bolivia. Sarah packed up all her camping gear and planned to come back to my flat to pick it up before leaving Bolivia.

We flew to La Paz the day before Christmas and found a nice hotel where we had dinner Christmas Eve together. We exchanged presents and decided to leave for the airport early the next morning to meet Bob. Christmas Day we met Bob at the La Paz Airport, and I flew out on his plane's returning flight to Miami. We had just a few minutes to visit before I left. They took a bus to Cororico and went on to Cusco, Peru backpacking.

Christmas with my family was great, and I also visited my brother Dale and his family in Tulsa. He was not doing well, but still having treatment for his lung cancer. I flew to Phoenix and Eric met me at the airport with Mayra and Naomi. What a sweet and beautiful dark haired, dark eyed little baby girl, my twenty-second grandchild! Eric was a very proud father! I had a few days visit with them before I flew to Miami and back to Bolivia.

Sarah came to Phoenix to visit me before I left for Bolivia. She had not been able to get her in-state residence back in Colorado and decided to go to college in California and establish residency for finishing school. I was sorry that she wouldn't be able to get back in school in January.

Returning to Cochabamba, I met my neighbor Carmen and her family next door to my casita. She was from La Paz, but she had grown up in Golden, Colorado where her father was a professor at the Colorado School of

Mines. Carmen spoke fluent English and German and worked for a German company that manufactured and sold medical equipment. She was the distributor in Cochabamba and had her office in her home. She was a very pretty, talented and lovely person. We visited often and we became good friends along with her two girls who came over to visit me. I made them pretty colors of play dough to use when they came to my house. They loved it. Carmen wanted to know what I was doing, and I told her about the domestic violence program and the effects on families. She wanted to hear more and came to me for counseling; I referred her to her doctor.

Carmen donated children's clothing and toys to the childcare center. We talked about what her options were in her own home since she had read the literature I wrote on domestic violence because wrote the Spanish translation for me on her computer. She wrote an excellent translation with personal experience that gave it a very urgent emphasis. She was very intelligent and wanted help with her family. She received more counseling from her doctor and made some very hard decisions on her own about what was best for her family. Her husband was a very influential man in Cochabamba managing a bank. She was determined to take action. I supported her and helped her through this difficult time.

In South American cultures, domestic violence is expected and accepted as a part of marriage. Her mother and father from La Paz visited often and I met them. Carlos and Lydia were a lovely couple about my age and we spoke English together. Their time with Americans and living and working in American culture gave them a broader understanding of the social problems in Bolivia. They wanted help for their daughter. They often thanked me for helping Carmen and invited me to visit their farm and home in Coroico. Sarah had told me that this was the prettiest place in Bolivia, and that I should visit. I looked forward to visiting their home before I left Cochabamba in the summer.

This time was not easy for Carmen, but she decided to divorce her husband since she felt very responsible for her two girls. She could not let them suffer. I stayed with her while she was afraid to stay alone in her house. Her husband was very angry and threatened more violence. The Cochabamba Police Brigada Domestic Violence Program offered her assistance if she needed it. She had reported the violence in her home and had the program's telephone number to call and they would come. I lived right next door and offered her help when she needed me. She made plans to move back to La Paz to be near her family and manage her business there. In La Paz, she would have the help of all her relatives.

In February I flew to Trinidad, Bolivia in the jungle and near the border of Peru. This was a small village built on a central-park and square with a climate similar to Chapare. While sitting at a restaurant across from the park, I watched a sloth perched at the top of a street light close to a tree. He had mistaken the streetlight for a tree branch and now found himself at the top of the pole with no place to go. Young boys gathered around him curiously watching his shy and slow movements. I had never seen one before and walked over to the park to get a closer look. Looking like a monkey, but moving so slowly, he was a very interesting creature. The adjective "sloth" or adverb "slothful" took on new meaning for me. The boys finally left him alone and the sloth eventually crawled back to his tree home.

I knew the best way to see the jungle and river was to schedule a tour, so I signed up for a small group the next morning. The three of us with our Bolivian guide motored slowly four hours down the river, with the jungle on both sides watching groups of small yellow monkeys jumping from tree to tree. They chattered and talked to their friends across the river, but could never cross the wide muddy brown expanse of water. Baby crocodiles were nesting on the sunny banks in the sunshine with their mothers, looking so bright green and clean and sweet. Only twelve inches long, slithering in piles, they looked harmless, but sweet and harmless they were not. The two-year-old, two-foot long juvenile crocodiles, looked at us with their small beady eyes considering us for lunch. I remembered that song I used to sing to the children "Never Smile at a Crocodile." The white storks had their nests in the tops of trees, and we could always tell them from afar. The Bolivian guide identified many different varieties of birds and pointed them out for us or we would have missed them in the trees. Fish occasionally jumped into the air in front of our boat as we lazily went down river. Other boats came back up the river with their catches of fish and the boat drivers talked back and forth. A school of pink dolphins surrounded our boat and gave us their own special show! We were so glad they picked us for their fantastic performance. It was amazing! Then they just swam away. What a treat! There was so much to see on this river.

We stopped for our own lunch after we had come near the fork where the river joins a larger one that leads to the Amazon. The guide had brought along food and fixed salad and bread and cheese that we hungrily devoured. We all had bottled water and a nice lunch break, sitting in the sun and enjoying all the frogs, insects and bird sounds. On our way back up the river, we found a nice sand bar and took a hike in the jungle single-file behind our seasoned Bolivian river-guide who carried a machete. We came upon a small anaconda, camouflaged so well against the leaves and sticks in the jungle. We would have stepped on it if the guide hadn't told us it was there. The guide took a stick and nudged it along from a distance and we watched cautiously.

No one wanted to get very close, but it had very pretty markings.

We arrived safely back to port and had a taxi to town. In my hotel lobby, there was a large multi-colored parrot that spoke English and was very loud and noisy. I tried to teach him "Garmajoba," which is hello in Georgian, and a few other Georgian words. I'll bet that he had never heard those words before and he never forgot them. After three days in Trinidad I flew back to Cochabamba.

Back in Cochabamba, I received information in the mail that the 1998 International Nurse Practitioner Conference was meeting in Australia in February, and I very much wanted to go. I followed the last meeting, which had met in Dublin, Ireland, but was not able to attend. I had never been to Australia and thought that this was a good opportunity. Flying from Bolivia to Sydney, Australia would take more time than I could afford right now, and decided maybe next year. I decided to attend the 1998 American Academy Nurse Practitioner Conference in Phoenix, Arizona in the summer instead. Eric and Mayra lived close to the South Pointe Hilton where the conference was meeting, and I sent in my registration for the conference. I planned to leave Cochabamba and move back to the States in July. I asked Eric to send me some information on Arizona, because I wanted to retire and had not chosen the state of where I wanted to live.

My friend Fiona, a young girl from England, and I wrote up a study of scriptures for the Bible Study group to pursue after I left in the summer. We met at my house and enjoyed sharing our ideas and finishing a study on terminal illness and death that she planned to teach. I shared my nursing resources with her. Many of the women had lost husbands or friends to cancer and wanted guidance in visiting the sick. Many of the women felt lost in knowing how to comfort their families. Fiona was a missionary with

Latin Links from England and was very busy with her student programs. There were students arriving for six-week work programs with their mission. She was also responsible for oversight of a kindergarten that they supported near my casita. She traveled around Bolivia and located and set up work programs for her students. She met them in Cochabamba on arrival and gave them a short orientation before they started their work. I helped orient one group to downtown Cochabamba.

I planned a trip to Iguazu Falls on the borders of Brazil, Argentina and Paraguay and left a few days before Easter. The Falls were a famous and beautiful area where many people came to enjoy the rainforest of Brazil and the beautiful Iguazu Falls larger than Niagara Falls in America. I flew Lloyd Air of Bolivia, LAB, from Cochabamba to Asuncion, Paraguay and planned to be in Brazil at Easter. LAB lost my luggage and I had to go on to the Hotel in Asuncion without it. After spending one night there, I rode a bus to Ferazo, Brazil where I stayed at the Hotel. Still without luggage, I bought a swimming suit, dresses and shorts at the gift shop. I spoke Spanish and could understand a lot of Portuguese. I swam in the large pool and enjoyed my Easter weekend. I went to a church across the street for Easter service and was grateful for the Risen Lord and being able to worship there. No matter what the language, the eternal message is our hope in the Risen Lord.

My trip to the rainforest and Iguazu Falls was just wonderful. The Falls extend for what seems like a mile long with platforms reaching out to them where you could walk very close. So close that you could enjoy the mist and spray while feeling the cool breeze. There were walks beside the water the entire distance of the Falls. I took a small boat with others, wearing a life jacket, up under the falls that was quite exhilarating. We came back drenched but it was well worth it. I was amazed that so much water cascading down the Falls just keeps going day and night for thousands of years, never ending. What power! I loved my trip through the rainforest and the thousands of beautiful butterflies landing everywhere. There were amazing numbers of tiny red frogs along the paths. The beautiful colored toucan birds were up in the trees and looked so pretty. I could look across the gorge to Argentina's rainforest.

I left Brazil and took the bus back to the Asuncion Airport. American Airlines flies in there, and I saw many Americans coming in for the holidays. My luggage was waiting for me when I checked in for my flight. LAB gave me a claim form to fill out, which I did, and I received $70 in reimbursement for the clothing I had to purchase at the Brazilian hotel for my vacation. I felt very fortunate to have any reimbursement. My luggage went with me to Cochabamba this time and I arrived home with everything.

As my time of departure was drawing near and summer in America was approaching, I made plans for just one more trip before I departed South America. Since I had other previous trips to Quito, Ecuador and Merida, Venezuela, I decided to consider my travels of South America sufficient. The year and a half I had lived in Bolivia, I had seen Peru, Chile, Argentina, Paraguay and Brazil. Carlos and Lydia asked me to come for a week and visit them in La Paz and they would drive me to their coffee farm in Coroico.

Carmen told me many stories about their farm and how much she had loved going there as a child to see her grandfather. They had held many family reunions there. Her grandfather now lived in La Paz. She told me that I had to make a visit and how much I would love it. I had not seen the Alto Plano but we would pass through it as we climbed the mountains to Coroico, Bolivia.

I flew to La Paz and took a taxi downtown to Carlos and Lydia's address that they had given me. They had a very spacious and lovely flat on the sixth floor of a large building with shops on the street. I spent that night with them, then we drove to Coroico in their Toyota four-wheel drive vehicle. Sarah had told me that this was the most dangerous road in the world and that kept me on the edge of my seat. Carlos had driven it two or three times a year for many years, so I had confidence in his driving. But the narrow road and large trucks coming and going were rather hazardous. It was only one lane. It was a four or five-hour ascending drive and we stopped about half way up at a small waterfall that cleaned the car and cooled us off as we drove by. The Alto Plano was never ending and the mountains looked taller the higher we climbed.

When we arrived into Coroico, we left the gravel road and turned right into the jungle. Carlos opened a gate and we drove through and onto a path to their coffee farm, with huge beautiful tropical plants and flowers lining the path. Only a caretaker kept the farm and no one lived in the house. Lydia and I swept and cleaned the kitchen to get food fixed for dinner. She had brought bread and cheese and tea from La Paz. It was a very beautiful setting surrounded by gorgeous flowers everywhere. There was no electricity, so we made up our beds before it got dark and used candles in the kitchen.

I no longer had my mosquito netting that I had used in Chapare, but brought insect repellant and thought that was enough. It wasn't. The next morning I was covered with mosquito bites all over my neck, face and arms, with not much space between bites. I was pretty miserable.

The main square in the small village of Coroico had all the shops around it. Descendants of African slaves who were brought here by the Spanish still lived in Cororico and were the darkest of the Bolivians. A drug inspection was in progress near the main part of the town where coca was spread out on the grass. I visited a bed and breakfast called Esmerelda situated on top of a hill and looking down into the valley. Sarah mentioned that she had stayed here. The view was gorgeous and the facilities run by a Dutch and American. Internet access, restaurant and swimming pool made it a very lovely location.

Carlos, Lydia, and I packed up and they brought some of their freshly ground coffee beans for me to take back to the States for my coffee-drinking sons. It smelled delicious. They pick, grind, and roast it in large ovens right there at the house. We carried sacks of fruit back to their family and relatives in La Paz. Carlos had told me on our way up the mountain that cars coming down the mountain have the right of way. It is just accepted. On our way down, a large truck came toward us in the middle of the road and expected us to back up to a side sot so he could pass us. Carlos refused to give way. They sat facing each other in the middle of the road, each refusing to budge. Carlos honked his horn and shouted, and the driver of the truck sat looking at us. Finally the truck driver backed down and let us pass. Experience is what counts on this road. Later we came across a tree that had fallen across the road, and Carlos got out and moved the end off the road enough so we could pass. We were still very close to the side of the road that fell precipitously straight down, what looked like miles. I came to the conclusion on the ride down that this was the most dangerous road in the world.

Arriving safely in La Paz, I spent that night with Carlos and Lydia in their flat and took the flight back to Cochabamba the next afternoon. My last night in La Paz, there was an earthquake and our building was evacuated in the middle of the night. Carlos, Lydia and I were not aware of this until the next morning. I sleep soundly, and I did remember hearing a loud crash in the middle of the night, thinking that Carlos must have fallen out of bed, and went right back to sleep. I must have been dead tired. On the front page of the La Paz newspaper that morning, we saw pictures of the tremor of tall downtown buildings and people all in the streets. There had been much damage in La Paz, but a village closer to Cochabamba had been devastated and completely destroyed with many deaths. I thanked Carlos and Lydia for the wonderful visit, and Carlos drove me to the airport.

Arriving on my LAB flight in Cochabamba, I took a taxi to my casita and was exhausted and very glad to get home. I had forgotten my key and landlord's doorbell. He opened his door very excited telling me about an earthquake that had just struck that moment and his wife was hysterical. While I was in the taxi, going over the rough cobblestone streets, I hadn't even noticed. I went into my casita grateful to be home safely and found no damage. Cochabamba received several strong aftershocks from the earthquake, but no damage either.

It was time to start getting rid of my household purchases and pack my bags for Arizona. Eric had sent me some library books of the cities and locations in Arizona that made Arizona a favorite retirement spot for many people around the United States. I remembered the time much earlier when Kenny and I lived there. We remarked then that we would like to come back and retire in Arizona someday. I got out my Rand and McNally Atlas and checked the mileage to other locations where the children all lived. Arizona looked like a good spot to be, but I no longer liked the extremely hot climate of Phoenix and Tucson areas. Retirement would have to be farther north.

I had sent in a registration for my American Academy of Nurse Practitioners National Conference in Phoenix, and looked forward to attending and staying with Eric and Mayra. This would be my first National Conference of Nurse Practitioners. I was scheduled to arrive in Phoenix the day before. After the conference, I wanted to visit places north of Phoenix and look for a condo to rent for a year.

Jane had expressed interest in buying my household things since they were adding on to their house. So I packed my Peta and drove to her house in Quillacollo so I could finish up my packing. My friend Martha Izquerida wanted to buy my Peta since it was a few years newer than hers. We made arrangements for her to buy it just a few days before I left and she took me to the airport. Jane met me at the airport to tell me goodbye, and I knew that I was leaving very good friends in Cochabamba. But I was excited about getting on with my life in the States and seeing all the children and grandchildren again.

I flew to Santa Cruz, spent the night at a nice hotel, and flew out for La Paz the next morning on American Airlines and then to Miami. I called Eric and waited a few hours for my flight to Phoenix. He met me at the airport and welcomed me to Arizona. He was very excited that I had decided to find a place to retire. After my Conference, Mayra and I would drive north to Prescott and Flagstaff to look.

My conference went well. Since I was living in Cochabamba at the time of my registration that was on my nametag as my home. In introducing ourselves, it provided many opportunities for interesting conversations for jobs abroad for nurse practitioners. The quality and presentation of the American Academy of Nurse Practitioners was excellent, but on the last day I wrote on my evaluation that I was very disappointed that there was not one presentation on multicultural care or methods of working in countries abroad. I felt that it was neglected in the continuing education of nurse practitioners as it had been in my graduate program. I enjoyed the conference very much and felt professionally stimulated by all the excellent presentations. Professionally refreshed and challenged, I left the conference with suggestions by fellow participants to present something on multicultural care next year at the Academy National Conference. That went along with my mother's admonition, "If you want something done, do it yourself." I had heard this many times as a child.

I enjoyed my visit with Eric, Mayra and Naomi. Naomi was six months and a loveable sweet little girl. Mayra had furnished their house so nicely and they were very happy. Eric cooked on the grill, and I enjoyed their hospitality. It was good to be back in the States with no further plans to work abroad. I told Eric how much the books he sent had helped me to make the decision on Arizona to live.

Mayra and I with baby Naomi drove to Flagstaff the next day and looked for condos for me to rent. I wanted to get an idea of prices, locations, and what was offered. July was a good time to look, but I didn't plan to move in until August. Furniture that I had was still in a storage unit in Loveland, Colorado and my car was with Amber in Marshfield, Missouri. I wanted to visit with all the children before moving. Mayra was very helpful and we looked at condos in East Flagstaff off Country Club Road. We were only in Flagstaff a couple of hours, but it looked fine to me. I took numbers and names of real estate agents and we drove around seeing Flagstaff and had lunch, then left town. I considered stopping in Prescott, closer to Phoenix, but it was getting late and we were all pretty tired. We arrived back in Chandler at their house, and I with Eric about what we had found. He told me more about Flagstaff since that was my first trip there. It was two and a half-hours to Sky Harbor Airport in Phoenix and that was fine with me.

I made the decision on one of the condos that we had looked at and called the real estate agent in Flagstaff. She advised me to send a deposit to hold the condo for August, so I did. Eric said that he would help me move, and we could meet in Loveland, Colorado on August 15 with his pick-up truck and get my furniture from storage. That would be a great help and I appreciated his offer. He had helped us move so many times. With my decision made to live in Flagstaff, I was free to enjoy the rest of the summer.

# Chapter 24: "Retirement"

**GRACE AND HER FAMILY** drove in her new white Dodge minivan to Phoenix for a visit, and I rode back to Running Springs, California with them. Their school in San Bernardino was scheduled year-round. While I visited with Grace I had time to think more about the American Academy of Nurse Practitioner Conference I had just attended in Phoenix, and consider whether I was really interested in presenting something on multicultural care for the next year. The subject was sadly lacking at the conference and did not seem a high priority for anyone, but was I the one to make the effort. Surely many nurse practitioners worked abroad and had the same if not more experience than I did.

In an informal discussion with conference participants that week in Phoenix, I voiced my disappointment at the lack of multicultural education in the conference. A nurse practitioner sitting at our table just replied, "Write something and put it together for next year." My immediate thought was that it would be a lot of work getting a presentation ready. I knew the deadline for acceptance of the original abstract to the 1999 American Academy of Nurse Practitioners National Conference was in October and the notification of acceptance in December. The 1999 conference next year was in June in Atlanta, Georgia.

I visited the library at California State University at San Bernardino and researched articles while Grace was in school teaching. I used her home computer to put together my research. I was beginning to form a plan on what should be covered. It wasn't all that difficult. Since I had so recently returned from the trenches abroad in Bolivia and before that Tbilisi, Georgia, the topic was fresh in my mind. It was obviously clear that there was education to be done for nurse practitioners, and what better place than the national conference level. When I was settled, I knew that I had a lot of articles and research in my home files that I had done on multicultural health care while working on my thesis that I could use. It just seemed the thing for me to do.

After travelling and visiting all the children and grandchildren in the summer of 1998, I realized that I would soon need to move into my new condo in Flagstaff. It was time to establish residency in the States and have all my belongings in one place. It had been three years without roots in the States.

In August I drove in my Ford Taurus to Loveland, Colorado and rented a U-Haul trailer for Eric to load with my furniture from our storage unit. I drove from Missouri arriving early to make the arrangements, and Eric drove from Phoenix. Eric met me in his red Chevrolet truck at the U-Haul rental place and we hooked up the trailer. After loading everything in his truck that night, the trailer and my car, and closing out the storage unit, we spent the night in Loveland at the Starlight Motel leaving early the next morning, August 15th. It was a fifteen-hour drive for us on I-25 changing to I-40 at Albuquerque, and we arrived in Flagstaff about nine in the evening.

Since I had only been to Flagstaff and the condo one time, I wasn't sure of what exit to take for Flagstaff or if I could find my condo. But the sign for Country Club Road sounded familiar and we exited. I got lost from Eric, who was pulling the trailer, after we exited I-40, and it took a while for us to find each other and the real estate office in the dark. Since it was after business hours the real estate office was closed, there were no keys left or anyone around when we finally found it. It had been afternoon when Mayra and I left Flagstaff in the first week of July and it sure looked different now. Eric and I were both pretty tired after our long drive. I inquired in a bar next to the office and found the telephone number for the realtor. I called the realtor at home to see if she could meet us at my condo with my keys, apologizing for being so late. She was not really happy about the late hour, even though I had called her earlier that day and asked her to leave the keys for me. She did consent to meet us at the condo and Eric and I waited for her.

We could not find the main electrical switch box to turn on my lights, and unloaded the U-Haul by flashlight carrying everything into my dark condo. Since I didn't have much it went quickly. In our hurry to get to Flagstaff we didn't stop for dinner, but I had picked up a large supreme pizza at Pizza Hut in Flagstaff before we met at my condo. We ate pizza in my living room sitting on the fireplace hearth by flashlight and talked about how nice it was to be living so close together again. He had left the farm in Kansas for college in 1988, ten years ago. I was extremely grateful for Eric's help with my move and being in my own place with furniture. He offered to bring me a nice new comfortable bed from his furniture store later when he came for a visit. Eric had to leave for Phoenix early in the morning and go back to work. We got a good night's sleep and returned the U-Haul the next morning, and Eric drove the two-and-a-half hour drive to Phoenix.

It was wonderful to be in my new condo, and I enjoyed a lovely view of the mountains from my deck that I had forgotten about. In fact, I looked at this place and quite a few more so quickly in July when Mayra and I were there, it was completely new to me. I had a combined living room and kitchen with vaulted ceiling and fireplace, one bedroom and bath, with a circular stairs to a large loft, and a nice deck off the living room. It was just right for me, and I had signed a one-year rental contract with Dallas Real Estate. I soon had electricity and gas and water. My first day in my new condo, I got my Arizona driver's license and tags for my car and registered to vote. The U.S. West Telephone Company was on strike and it took a couple of weeks to get a telephone. I went from the Motor Vehicle Department to the bank to open a bank account with my new Arizona driver's license. They couldn't open my bank account because an error had been made on the date of my birth, stating that I was twenty-six years old. I went back to the Motor Vehicle Department had it corrected and was able to open my bank account. It was many months later that I realized that my birth date had been corrected, but not the expiration date. So my license was good until 2033, when I would be ninety-six years old!

Since I had decided to retire I did not look for a full time job and leisurely settled into my condo and enjoyed the mountains and my new location. I made many trips to Walmart for household items. On one of my numerous trips, the checkout girl was about five foot eleven inches tall, skinny, and friendly, with curly haired blond and blue eyes. As I visited with her, I noticed an unusual body tremor within her that I knew was not normal. I diagnosed a medical problem, but wasn't sure which, and when I left the store I prayed that she would get help.

My condo had swimming, golf, and tennis available, which I looked forward to enjoying. I enjoyed learning to play tennis again in Cochabamba and was eager to continue. I didn't know one person in Flagstaff, but started attending a church. I ran the five kilometer Flagstaff Family Fun Run in September at Thorpe Park, and thought I would have a heart attack going up the steep hill, but I finished in good time for my age group. Males and females ran together or I would have won the trophy for the first woman to finish. I knew that it was 7,000 feet elevation here in Flagstaff and Cochabamba had been higher, but I was totally out of shape. I played tennis three times a week and ran a frequently in Cochabamba, but not enough. I hadn't felt so exhausted running since Heartbreak Hill in Kansas City many years before. I needed to start a regular running schedule, and I preferred no hills!

Flagstaff has millions of tourists coming through each year on their way to the Grand Canyon. Amtrak also stopped here to deposit more tourists. The streets were crowded with motor homes, campers, bicycle riders, motorcyclists, back-packers, with people coming and going to the Grand Canyon. For a city of sixty thousand, there was an overabundance of hotels and motels. The famous Route 66 ran right through the city.

I worked on my abstract and presentation for the 1999 American Academy of Nurse Practitioner Conference and submitted it in October. I had pulled all my research together from graduate school and added my new research and experiences in Russia and Bolivia to stress the importance of multicultural care in nurse practitioner clinical practice and the importance of nursing education. I was convinced that this had never been adequately addressed at the conference level. I was pleased with the results and waited to hear from the planning committee.

My sister Dorothy planned a trip to Bangkok, Thailand in October, accompanying her daughter who was teaching a graduate course at the University of Siam. We had talked about taking more trips together, so I joined them on this trip. We met in Tokyo and stayed one night before flying to Bangkok.

We had two weeks in Bangkok shopping, visiting, and seeing the sights. Dorothy and I took a boat down the river each day to a shopping mall with restaurants and shops while Adrienne worked hard with her graduate students at the university. We had a good time, and I was glad to be there so Dorothy had company. We had dinner at the home of one of the Thai students and enjoyed all the delicacies of Thai food. A special evening with a five-course dinner and Thai dancing was especially beautiful. The gorgeous and ornate costumes were elegant as the professional dancers performed all the traditional Thai dances.

A student served as our tour guide taking us to many beautiful temples with enormous golden statues of Buddha. The largest golden statue was a 150-foot Buddha reclining. Many hundreds of golden statues of all sizes banked both sides of the largest statues. As people took off their shoes and bowed down to worship these statues, I couldn't help but think about the scriptures in the Bible and how sad it was. The truth had not come here. Christ is alive and Buddha is dead! Lovely gardens and buildings with ancient oriental architecture at the Grand Palace were very impressive. I also noticed the barefoot, orange-robed Buddhist young men in training walking and begging in the streets. The elephant parade and show was fantastic. We were amazed at the young men wrestling with the enormous crocodiles in one of the performances.

It was a wonderful trip. At the end of our stay, I left a day early for Honolulu where we planned to stop for a few days on our way back to the States. My United flight was booked the day we planned to leave, and I would rather leave earlier than stay late in Bangkok trying to get out on a flight.

A customs official was waiting for me when my flight arrived in Honolulu and asked me many questions. He wanted to know why I was in Bangkok, my work was, why I had worked in Bolivia, and now why I was in Honolulu. I could not understand his interest and had never received such detailed questioning before in any of my travels. I had done all my Christmas shopping for the children and grandchildren in Bangkok, and was loaded down with presents. I told him that I was a missionary nurse and had shopped for all my twenty-three grandchildren and had worked in many places. My passport looked like an unusually suspicious well-traveled document. Haiti, England, many African countries, Japan, Turkey, Europe, Russia, many South American countries, and now Tokyo, Bangkok and here I was in Honolulu.

The custom official examined all my packages. These included many items such as large baskets, traditionally dressed Thai china dolls, wooden boxes with pounded tin elephants on the tops, blue and white china fish dishes, fresh-water pearl necklaces, small jars of Tiger Balm, pastel silk picture frames, malachite necklaces, silk blouses, and oriental silk paintings. He then let me through, satisfied with my answers. I don't think he thought that anyone would make up such an incredible unbelievable story. This was my first trip to Hawaii, and I did not know that it was so hard for a citizen of the U.S. to get through customs. I was puzzled with my customs interrogation, but just forgot about it and found a bus to a hotel. Much later I was told that Bolivia-Bangkok-Honolulu was a well-established drug smuggling triangle.

Dorothy and Adrienne arrived the next day, and I met them at the Hale Koa Waikiki Hotel where we stayed. The beaches were beautiful and we were glad to be back to the States. Dorothy and I took a walk along the beach the next morning enjoying the wonderful smells of the salt air and the beautiful hotel complex of swimming pools, restaurants and shopping. We looked forward to a relaxing stay. While walking on the sidewalk, I called Dorothy's attention to some gorgeous multicolored parrots that were on the beach with a photographer taking pictures of people with the parrots. We were distracted looking at the parrots, and both stumbled at the end of the sidewalk where there was a step. Neither one of us had seen the end of the sidewalk and the step. When our feet hit the front of the step I caught myself, but Dorothy fell on the sidewalk and couldn't get up. She was in pain and just wanted to sit there a while. I was afraid that she had seriously injured herself and waited. She asked me to take her hand and try to lift her up, but it was too painful for her. She couldn't move. I suspected that she had broken her hip, but was praying that it wasn't broken. If she couldn't move, it was a very bad sign. Another lady came by and asked if she could help, and I ran to the closest phone and called the main desk asking for assistance. The Hale Koa staff sent a golf cart, but Dorothy couldn't be moved. I asked them to call an ambulance and they did.

Dorothy sat on the sidewalk quietly and patiently waiting for the ambulance. A woman sat behind her, her back pressing on Dorothy's to relieve her pressure on her hip. I ran to find Adrienne and met her coming towards the beach and told her that her mother had fallen. Adrienne got there about the same time as the ambulance and they put Dorothy on a stretcher and Adrienne rode in the back of the ambulance with her while I sat up front with the driver. I knew this was very serious and possibly a broken hip. She was in excellent physical condition and walked every day at home and on the trip. All I could think about was the past two weeks that we had spent in Bangkok. We walked over uneven and dangerous streets worrying about being hit by traffic, walking the gangplanks on and off the river-boats every day, shopping and sightseeing. Dorothy had not fallen and we were so grateful since the hospitals and health care would have been sadly lacking. I had brought a sterile pack with intravenous set up just for emergencies. And now to have stumbled and fallen on the sidewalk by the beach seemed too terrible to grasp. I had distracted her and asked her to look at the parrots. I just felt terrible, praying that her hip was not broken.

Dorothy lay in the hospital emergency room on a table with no pain medication until the doctor examined her. Her pain and immobility indicated that her hip was broken. They took x-rays that confirmed her right hip was fractured and scheduled surgery. Adrienne called her dad in Manhattan, Kansas, and Bud made plans to fly to Honolulu immediately.

We met Bud at the airport the next night and he said that he brought his gun to shoot those parrots on the beach that had distracted us and caused Dorothy to stumble and fall. He said that he told others that I pushed her; he tried to lighten my load of guilt. Bud talked to the doctors and took charge of the situation. As a retired full colonel in the military he had plenty of experience. He said that I was free to leave since he and Adrienne were there, and we had planned to fly back the next day. I wanted to stay and help Dorothy home when she could go, but he said that he would see her home safely. I stayed until after Dorothy had her surgery and it was successful. Then I flew back to Phoenix. Adrienne left the next day for Oklahoma, and Bud stayed with Dorothy at the hospital until she went home. They took her by ambulance to the plane and she was given special medication for the trip. Our trip to Bangkok had been a fun trip, but ended sadly for us all.

Dorothy started physical therapy in Manhattan at the hospital when she returned and slowly recovered. Her excellent physical condition and positive attitude helped her recover. She started walking little by little to get the use of her hip back to function at the highest level possible. I called her often. She said that she had received excellent care in the Honolulu hospital. We both talked about what a good time that we had in Bangkok, but what a freak accident it had been on Waikiki Beach. She had always walked every morning at the Manhattan Mall and wanted to get back to walking again as soon as she could. She would not plan any more trips for a long time.

Back home in November, I looked in the telephone directory and found a listing for nurse practitioners working in Flagstaff. I met Chris, another family nurse practitioner, and she encouraged me to submit my resume for part time work at Northern Arizona University. I filled out an application for the Student Health Clinic. I was invited to a monthly nurse practitioner dinner and meeting at one of the local hotels and met many other nurse practitioners working in Flagstaff. Graduate nursing students from Northern Arizona University also attended.

I heard back that the position I applied for at the university had been filled, but I received a call from Marge Conger in the nursing department asking if I would be interested in piloting a new project as a parish nurse. I met with her to find out more information and prayed about this. I only wanted part time work and the job was thirty hours a week working with two churches. Knowing the number of meetings involved, I could see that this could easily end up to more hours than I wanted. But working as a parish nurse sounded interesting, and I wanted to learn more about it. I didn't know any parish nurses but had read articles on the concept in graduate school. Nurse practitioners held positions in large urban city churches working with the poor providing spiritual counseling and health care. I had already been doing this in Haiti, Africa, Russia and Bolivia.

I considered working as a parish nurse was an expanded role of the nurse practitioner. It seemed to me to be community health nursing with spirituality and wholeness concepts added, and that interested me. Plus, I would be under the direction of the pastors of two churches. Most of my nursing experience was with community health and Christian medical mission groups abroad with other cultures. The Parish Nurse Project had been funded, but no nurse had yet been found who wanted to do the job. I had pioneered other projects so this was something I could do.

As a family nurse practitioner, I knew the importance and dynamics of the family unit and family health care.

I received a fax from the American Academy National Office informing me that my abstract on Multicultural Health Care had been accepted for presentation at the June 1999 American Academy of Nurse Practitioners National Conference in Atlanta, Georgia. I could hardly believe it! I was very happy and excited about this opportunity. I needed to have the complete presentation finished by December so the conference brochures with topics, schedules, and presenters could be mailed in January to all nurse practitioners in the U.S. and abroad. I really had to get busy. My presentation on Multicultural Health Care was scheduled for a thirty-minute podium presentation, and my conference registration was paid. I booked my hotel room for June 28 – 30, 1999.

I interviewed with the Caregiving Coalition of Flagstaff and the Parish Nursing Board, and both pastors of the churches involved for the position of Parish Nurse. I informed them that I needed to be absent in June for the American Academy of Nurse Practitioner Conference, but was approved for the position and accepted to start in January. The grant for the pilot project was given by the Flagstaff Medical Center. I had tests and paperwork to complete at the hospital and after Christmas I'd begin my new position.

Christmas with Grace and family in Running Springs was fun, and Sarah came from San Diego where she had moved and was working with South Pacific Bell Telephone Company. Sarah and Lata were planning on getting married after Christmas, and she didn't want a big wedding. Sarah and Lata were married in San Diego on New Year's Eve, and we had a family reception and party for them in Running Springs at Grace's house. We were all very happy for them and celebrated the New Year. Sarah and Lata both worked in San Diego and were going to San Diego City College. They had an upstairs flat right across the street one half block from the university and close to the gaslight district of San Diego. Sarah and I talked about a reception in the summer for the family in Arizona or Missouri where Amber and Pat lived. Grace and I bought Sarah many things that she needed for her flat.

Lata, Asaike Efalata Paea, and his family lived in Sacramento and they were from the Island of Tonga in the South Pacific. Sarah and Lata had met each other while they were both working for Andrew at Red Runner Pizza in Sacramento. They knew each other almost a year when they were married. Sarah moved to San Diego, and I helped her get an apartment there in November. She found a job and was living with Babe, her yellow Labrador. It was just a short two-hour drive from Grace's house to Sarah's. They visited often.

I started my work as a parish nurse in January and met both pastors of the Shepherd of the Hills Lutheran church and the Episcopal Church. My office was in the Lutheran Church. After just one week of work, I had an attack of pancreatitis, thinking it was a heart attack. I had gone to Phoenix with a nurse practitioner friend, Chris, and we stopped to visit Eric and Mayra and Naomi before going to the play, *Miss Saigon*. On our drive back to Flagstaff, I told Chris that I wasn't feeling well, and we tried diagnosing my problem on our trip home. We got home late and about five pm the next evening I called Chris to come over and take me to the hospital. I was having severe chest pains, but before she could get there, I was afraid that I would pass out and called the ambulance. The ambulance arrived right before Chris, and I was taken to the hospital. I was put in the Intensive Care Unit and Chris came to the hospital and called Eric in Phoenix. Eric called the other children Chip, Phillip, Amber, Grace, Andrew, Tim, and

Sarah. It was very much a shock to them as they all knew how much I ran and had been in good shape. Grace in Running Springs and Sarah in San Diego started for Flagstaff as soon as they could. When they received the news all the children called the hospital, and Chris stayed with me and talked to them. Eric and Mayra came to the hospital to see me as soon as they could get here. Phillip was on a flight and flew in first to Phoenix and then drove to Flagstaff.

Tests revealed that it was not a heart attack and the pancreas was the guilty culprit. I was diagnosed with acute pancreatitis. Chris and I were both disappointed in our diagnostic skills for my case. No medication except morphine for pain was given, and I left the hospital on a totally liquid diet to allow the inflamed pancreas to heal itself with rest. I was weak and recovering from the trauma of the attack on my system. Some of the children were there with me all the time that I was in the hospital. I appreciated having them there, all the telephone calls and love and concern. I was grateful to be in America and not in Russia or Bolivia or Africa.

I was discharged from the hospital on January twenty-eighth, my birthday, in time to have my birthday cake and see all the children before they left. We have a picture with me on the couch and Phillip, Eric, Mayra and Naomi, Sarah, Lata, Grace, and her children when I got home. The children teased me that I had faked a heart attack just to get them there for my birthday party. I rested for a week and went back to work on a special liquid diet. Chip came to Flagstaff to see me before I went back to work, and I was still feeling very weak. I was just eating Jell-O and soup and looked very tired.

I soon attended a Parish Nursing Conference in Phoenix with many parish nurses attending from the Phoenix area. The Phoenix Parish Nurse Organization provided resources and education for those in Arizona. It was great to meet other parish nurse, and I learned more about the role of the parish nurse in the church and community. Since I was the first in Flagstaff, I invented my job as I went and explained the concept to many groups and organizations. I networked with many resources within the community. I found a welcoming spirit of camaraderie within the medical community of Flagstaff. The pastors of both churches gave me direction and their whole-hearted support to reach the elderly and sick within their congregations. They needed the help. I soon discovered there were more needs than I could meet in my thirty hours each week, but I set my own office hours and made home visits and attended meetings. I kept monthly records for further grant support and to substantiate the parish nurse in the project.

My position of parish nurse was a quick way to become introduced into a new community and meet a large number of people. The Episcopal and Lutheran churches were both large and well established in Flagstaff community. Their congregations welcomed me and accepted me as a part of their church family. Since I served as a member of their staff, I met with them each week for Bible study and to coordinate my new ministry with theirs and report my activities. I enjoyed all the staff and learned how our ministries complimented each other. I wrote monthly articles for the church newsletters.

I also received referrals from organizations within the community. The Health Department called to see if I would make a home visit. An employee from Walmart had called them with a fellow employee friend in need of a doctor's referral. Her friend had a serious health problem but had not seen a doctor and had no contacts within the community. I accepted the referral and called the client, making a doctor's appointment for an evaluation including a neurological assessment. A few weeks later I called again to confirm the client's ability to keep the appointment and giving her my office number for further health needs. Later the Health Department called me saying the same client needed transportation to the Mayo Clinic in Scottsdale for a second opinion with the neurologist there. I was given permission by the Caregiving Coalition to accept this client as part of my caseload and made plans to pick her up.

Imagine my surprise when I stopped and picked up Anne Hula to find that she was the same tall, blue eyed blonde that I had seen at Walmart on one of my trips there when I first moved to Flagstaff. Anne had checked me out at the cash register, and I recognized her symptoms and her need for medical care. And now we were together to find out her needs. We talked on our trip to the Mayo Clinic in Scottsdale, and I found out more about her history and health problems. In Scottsdale I checked her into the clinic and we both went in together for her appointment with a neurologist. Her records and tests had been sent earlier from the neurologist in Flagstaff.

We had about an hour appointment with the neurologist and after reviewing her records and asking her questions, he confirmed her diagnosis of Huntington's Chorea that she had received from her neurologist in Flagstaff. We went over her recommended treatment. Anne had suspected the diagnosis to be right since her mother and grandmother had died of the same disease at an early age. Anne was thirty-two years old, a single mom and still happily working at Walmart where she had been for three years. She loved her job and had many friends there. She had problems with her balance and fell at work alerting a friend to call the Health Department. She did not intend to quit her job. She had a hopeful and optimistic outlook on her condition although she had watched her mother die in a State Hospital in Tennessee at fifty years of age.

This began my long association with Anne and her health needs. I worked with every resource in Flagstaff and many kind and efficient people to get her the medical and community assistance that she needed. Anne was always positive and strong in her desire to beat this disease and function as normally as possible. We became good friends, and I visited her often in her apartment and at work often and met her little two-year old girl, Danny, the love and light of her life. Although Anne was not a member of any church, she was a client in need of considerable medical and community assistance and counseling that I was glad to help provide. The parish nurse could fulfill a role to bring health and resources to her urgent and needy situation. I learned a lot and became a part of her support group of friends and family. I began to understand how important my position was in the church and in the community.

With the preparations for my presentation at the Academy Conference finished the night before I was to leave Flagstaff, I drove to Phoenix and flew to Atlanta, Georgia, somewhat nervous about speaking before a large group of my peers. I had been out of the professional circle of working nurse practitioners for four years since I had left Colorado. Although my position as a parish nurse did not allow clinical practice as a nurse practitioner, it fully challenged my family counseling and diagnostic skills of psychosocial problems within the community, with additional opportunities for addressing spiritual needs.

I arrived in Atlanta the night before my presentation and prepared my materials for the next day. I enjoyed the displays and other excellent presentations and met family nurse practitioners from my Florida State Nurse Practitioner Program in Tallahassee. My presentation was well received, and I was relieved to have it finished in the afternoon. After I concluded, an editor with the national magazine *ADVANCE For Nurse Practitioners* asked me to write an article for the following May magazine on Multicultural Health Care. I took her card, but I was not much interested in writing anything else at the moment. I gained a lot from the conference, and I was glad that I had contributed to the awareness for meeting the health needs of the increasing numbers of clients from many cultures that nurse practitioners meet every day in their practices.

I made good friends in Flagstaff within the medical community and in both churches I worked with and another that I also attended. I felt a vital and accepted part of the caring community of professionals. My retirement would have to wait. The Episcopal Church was sending a medical and construction team to their church in Tegucigalpa, Honduras in July, and I volunteered to go with the group. As much as I enjoyed my work in Flagstaff, I enjoyed the challenges of working in missions abroad.

We flew to Miami and then on American Airlines to Tegucigalpa, Honduras. Hurricane Mitch hit this city and area the year before leaving hundreds of miles of devastation. Already a poor country, Honduras was much in need of construction, rebuilding, and medical assistance in the villages. The Episcopal Church responded with help for their churches in Tegucigalpa. We met for prayer and devotions each morning in our hotel before we went to our jobs. I worked in a village clinic each day seeing many patients, both adults and children. We had doctors, nurses, and a pharmacist on our team. The Hondurans were grateful for the assistance.

Chip and Elizabeth made plans with their friends from church in Woodstock, Illinois to raft the Colorado River through the Grand Canyon in July. Chip had to get their reservations a year in advance for them to go. They stayed in my condo for a couple of days while I was in Honduras, and I saw them when I returned. They had a wonderful and adventurous trip on the river and told me about their exciting time. It sounded like great fun.

Later in July, my friend Marilyn Rademacher and I met in Dallas and flew to Honolulu together for a few days' vacation. We stayed at the Hale Koa Hotel, since they had retired from the military. We caught up on all the news of our families and enjoyed the excellent food and lovely beach.

The first week of August Amber and I had planned a family reception for Sarah and Lata at the Theobalds in Marshfield. Amber, Grace, and I had decided that was a central location for my family. Amber worked hard planting flowers and arranging everything for the reception. Lata and Sarah and Bella, Lata's mother, drove to my house from San Diego, then on to Missouri. I was glad to meet Bella and happy that she could come to the reception. They only stayed a few hours in Flagstaff before they left about midnight. I drove to Phoenix and flew to Springfield a couple of days later.

It was a great time of celebration and visiting, welcoming Lata into our family. Everyone was happy to meet Bella also. Lata did traditional Tongan dances and taught my grandsons. They were all in hula skirts and did Tongan dances to the island music. Bella tried to teach all the girls the hula. She did it so easy and beautifully, and we tried. Lata and Bella made a special Tongan celebration drink of coconut, pineapple, watermelon and cream with ice. It was delicious. Everyone wore lavalavas, a beautiful wrap-around cotton floral print cloth. Bella gave me an exquisitely made shell lei to wear. Elizabeth, Morgan, Kenny and Adrienne came, and Elizabeth provided the wedding cake. Lata and Pat cooked a roasted pig on the spit for the reception.

Amber had a green and white plastic gazebo set up in the front yard and many beautiful plants and flowers

596                                    PHYLLIS EVANS LONG

growing in tubs, pots, flower beds and hanging planters. We all enjoyed great food and island music and entertainment; it was a wonderful and happy time. My brother Richard and his family came, Rick and Saundra and their children, Allison and the twin boys, Michelle and Brendon, and Ivy, Brooke and Rachel. Leon and Marlyn Rademacher from Tulsa, and Deltan and Jean Washburn from Kansas City came. A few days later, Lata and Sarah drove back to San Diego, thoroughly welcomed into our constantly growing family.

Phillip was flying Delta Airlines International this year and had his flight to Milan, Italy coming up in August. He had flown there before and this time it was a back-to-back flight from JFK in New York to Milan, Italy, back to JFK and to Milan again and back. He asked me to go with him and stay for a few days, and he would pick me up on his second flight and he would fly us home. We would have a couple of nights in Milan together. I had never flown with him and wanted to. I said yes, I wanted to go.

Drew and Shawnae were expecting their third baby anytime. On August 24th, I flew to Atlanta and met Phillip and then we flew together on to JFK in New York, where he got ready for his Milan, Italy flight. Hayden Andrew Long was born to Drew and Shawnae that night, but we didn't find out until a few days later. My twenty-third grandchild arrived handsome and healthy in Sacramento.

The flight to Milan went well, and I was given the red carpet treatment in first class after Phillip introduced me to the crew. They gave me red roses and special attention. The flight seemed faster when I had the crew to visit with. In Milan, I joined Phillip and the crew at the hotel where they usually stayed. We arrived in the morning and had the day for sightseeing. Phillip and I walked downtown, and he showed me a park and places where he had visited on his trips there. He took off for the airport early the next morning, and I considered buying a ticket at the railway station to Venice for the day. It was a short train trip, and I could spend the night and be back the next day. At breakfast I considered my options. I wanted to buy a black cashmere cardigan and had seen some in the Milan shop windows. I decided to stay in Milan and go shopping after I finished breakfast.

While drinking a cup of tea in the dining room, I suddenly had extreme pain in my lower right side of my abdomen. I had never had pain like this before and knew it was very unusual. Phillip and I had walked a long time the day before, and I felt my normal self. I decided that I should get to my room and lay down and see if this was just temporary. I left the dining room and took the elevator to our room and laid down on the bed. The pain in my right side became acute, and I started vomiting. Making it to the bathroom, I stayed and vomited many times. The first thing I could diagnose for myself was acute appendicitis. I waited for about thirty minutes, but the pain and vomiting did not quit. Weakly I dialed the hotel desk and asked for a doctor to be contacted and sent to my room. I explained that I was acutely ill and needed a doctor right away. In short time someone was knocking on my door. The desk had called an ambulance, and I went out of my room and down the elevator carried on a stretcher. I was in so much pain that I really didn't care about anything.

I didn't speak Italian, but tried Spanish and English to explain that I thought I was having appendicitis to the emergency room physician. They could give me nothing for pain, but I was becoming extremely insistent that they do. I was placed on a gurney in the hallway while they did blood work and scheduled a cat scan. I was almost screaming with pain and became irrational, but could get nothing. A young man with a mop walked by, the closest within my reach, and I grabbed his arm and begged him for pain medication.

Finally, a nurse gave me an injection and I went to sleep. What a relief to be out of pain! The ultra sound of my right side showed a kidney stone. I had known kidney stones to be very, very painful and now believed it. I was admitted and taken on a gurney to a floor in the hospital. I remember asking for more pain medication and an IV drip was put in my arm. I finally went to sleep. I lost the whole day in the hospital and slept well that night.

When I woke up the next morning, I was sharing a room with two other Italian women. Neither woman spoke English, but I tried Spanish. One woman was Peruvian and married to an Italian and could understand me. When the doctor came in she interpreted for me. I received excellent care, and the only problem in my admittance and explaining my problem was the language barrier. I spent the whole day in the hospital and the Peruvian woman and I conversed. She had a deck of cards, and I taught her how to play gin rummy. She helped me to find the bathroom, towels, and my personal things that I had when I was brought in. I had remembered to grab my fanny pack with my passport, cards, and money before the ambulance had come to my hotel and whisked me off to the hospital. I was extremely grateful for the hospital and most of all to be out of the terrible pain.

Phillip arrived that evening from his flight back to Milan, and visited me at the hospital. The hotel desk had called Delta in New York who had contacted his home and when Phillip called Pam, she told him that I was in the hospital in Milan. He just wanted to know what I was doing there, and if I had checked out of our hotel. By this time, I was feeling weak but fine and wanted to leave. He had to fly back to JFK the next day and wanted me to go with him. I sure wanted to go also. We made an appointment to talk to the doctor who spoke English to see if I could be discharged that evening.

The doctor explained the location of the kidney stone in the ureter that leads to the bladder and said that I should stay for another day in the hospital. I explained that I was a nurse and if I could get some pain pills, I would see a doctor as soon as I got back to the States. He was hesitant, but released me with a prescription for pain. I offered to pay my bill with my credit card, but he said that Italy has National Health Service and there would be no bill. He took down the name of my insurance company and said that he would submit it to the American Consulate. I would hear from them if there was a bill. Phillip and I thanked the doctor and we walked out of the hospital.

I needed to have my prescription filled, so we walked to a pharmacy at the train station. After having my prescription filled, we stopped at a restaurant to eat, then went back to the hotel to get to bed early for Phillip's next morning flight to New York. Weak, but armed with pain medication, I was sure that I could make the trip. I slept all the way to New York and was monitored by the flight crew. Phillip landed in New York and had a smooth landing; I was proud of him. He helped me to get my flight to Phoenix and caught his flight to Atlanta. Eric met me at Sky Harbor Airport, and I was really glad to get my car and drive back to Flagstaff. I had no further pain and didn't take any pain medication.

I went back to work and considered what needed to be done for my kidney stone. I made an appointment with the urologist in Flagstaff who recommended laser surgery for the kidney stone. I had this done in September as an outpatient. It was successful and I had no other problems.

My presentation was accepted again for the 2000 American Academy of Nurse Practitioner Conference in Washington D.C. at the Hilton Hotel next June.

Sarah and Lata made plans to move to Missouri at Christmas. They planned to drive to Grace's, then all drive to my house and have Christmas with me. Eric and Mayra and Naomi would join us for the holidays. Sarah and Lata had decided that San Diego was an expensive place to live and they wanted to find a place in the country. After Christmas, they would drive to Missouri where Amber and Max and Carol had found a house for them to rent in the country. Sarah was so excited about having animals again. She had Babe, her Labrador, and two cats in their San Diego apartment. We had a great time together after they all arrived and stretched my condo to the limit. Grace needed to get back to Running Springs, and I drove with Sarah in their Honda with Babe and their car packed, while Lata drove their new Toyota truck loaded with all their household goods and clothes. Sarah and I took turns driving, and Lata had the cats and parakeet. It was twenty-two hours of driving, and we stopped for a dinner break in Amarillo, Texas for pizza. By the time we got to Missouri, Sarah and I were both dead tired at the wheel. She finished the last few miles to Amber's house. Their house was ready for them to move in and I helped them to get settled. I was happy that they had their place in the country. I celebrated the New Year and their anniversary with them in their new home.

I decided that I would retire from nursing in June of 2000 and go back to Tbilisi, Georgia for three months to visit and work. I wrote an article for the Nurse Practitioner magazine *ADVANCE* and sent it in March. After I had been the recipient of health care in a foreign country while in Milan, Italy, I had experienced multicultural care from the patient's viewpoint. This unwanted experience with kidney stones in a foreign country made me doubly compassionate of the needs of foreigners in our country. It added authenticity to my article. It appeared in their May magazine, and I was pleased with it.

I had submitted my abstract on Multicultural Health Care for the International Conference for Nurse Practitioners to be held in San Diego, California, and it was accepted for the 2000 conference at the end of September. I had always intended to attend an International Conference and now was my opportunity.

I looked forward to meeting many nurse practitioners working abroad with the same concerns that I had in the past twenty years. My friend, Miriam, in Quito, Ecuador planned to meet me at the conference. We would get to visit again after many years since I had been there and seen her work. I made plans to visit a friend in Cape Town, South Africa after the conference for a month.

By March I submitted my request for termination of my job with the Community Caregiving Coalition of Flagstaff as parish nurse. I started interviewing and training two nurses to replace me, one for each church. I had met many parish nurses in Arizona and respected their dedication, creative nursing practice, and holistic approach to parish nursing. They were wonderful caring nurses. We started a support group in Flagstaff for parish nurses that were in Northern Arizona and met each month to encourage and help each other. I spoke to other churches in Flagstaff about starting parish nurse programs for their congregation. The Catholic Church was actively pursuing the idea for a parish nurse program.

Naomi came to Flagstaff to spend a week with me in June before I left for Russia. We had a wonderful time feeding the ducks, having picnics, and playing at the park. She enjoyed cats and we visited a friend of mine with two. Naomi loved to hold them and was fascinated with their tails and watching them eat. I decided when I got back to Flagstaff that I would buy her one for her birthday in December and Christmas. She would be three years old.

\* \* \*

## PARISH NURSING: A LINK TO THE PAST & A WAVE OF THE FUTURE

There is a new aspect of health ministry within the church. Parish Nurses are discovering that churches are a very fertile ground for establishing health prevention and health education programs. As part of the healthcare system, churches provide a wealth of care and concern for their parishes. History is resplendent with the religious foundation of hospitals and medical schools born out of Christ's commandment to care for the poor and the sick in this world. The gospel includes the caring component that Christ introduced through the parable of The Good Samaritan, His commandment that we should love one another as He has loved us, and the admonition of Paul in his letters to bear one another's burdens, and so fulfil the law of Christ.

The historical roots for parish nursing are found in many sisterhoods and deaconess movements throughout the world. It is only a logical step to bring this care and concern in the form of: home and hospital visits, health prevention and promotion with health education classes, blood pressure screenings, flu immunization programs, healthy relationship programs, personal health counseling and outreach to the elderly, disabled, poor and sick in the community. The integrity of the pastoral care component of the church takes on renewed and deepened understanding of what it is to minister to the whole person, as we understand that spiritual health impacts all areas of life. Ownership of holistic health needs to be returned to the church that follows the Great Physician who healed and promised a life that centers on a relationship with God and the empowerment of the Holy Spirit. We are not left without direction or purpose, hope or comfort. Quality of life is not found without considering and coming to terms with what gives lives joy, purpose and meaning.

As the family of God, the household of faith, the body of Christ, and the place where we grow, practice, and pass on our faith to future generations, the Church must continue to bring fresh meaning to the culture of health and healing as it is found in the scriptures. Integration of faith and health is the job of the Parish Nurse who works within the congregations. Health is a concern that congregations are well suited to integrate into their spiritual care for their people, and is well understood and accepted as part of the Christian life-style. Parish Nurses have the education and preparation to empower the Church as they minister on the leading edge and bleeding edge of congregations.

## PARISH NURSE ASSESSMENT

- Courage
- Hope
- Engagement with life
- Loneliness
- Fears
- Joy
- Flexibility
- Quality of Relationships
- Ability to ask for help when needed
- Enjoyment of the present
- Awareness and receptivity towards you
- Attitude of gratitude
- Curiosity
- Knowledge of their weaknesses and strengths
- Acceptance of self
- Adventurous attitude toward life
- Non-patronizing
- Expectations

The outcomes were measured in the Parish Nursing Program by numbers in my monthly reports. But I considered other outcomes that I thought were important.

## OUTCOMES FOR PARISH NURSING PROGRAM

1. Certain numbers are being seen, referred and thinking about ways to improve their health.
2. Conscious raising or sensitivity of ways to improve their health with early interventions.
3. Increased commitment to programs and involvement in services of the church: Ex: More attending prayer and healing services, more requests for prayer during surgery and sickness.

4.  Closer parish community that would recognize and identify the needs of the church family - children, youth, adults, elderly and disabled.

5.  Increased prayer life as members find a cause and effect relationship in faith and health.

6.  More interconnectedness within all ministries of the church.

7.  Increased number of volunteers and teachers to help others.

8.  More members contacting the Parish Nurse for potential or present health problems.

9.  Increased quality of life for the homebound and disabled. Ex: Sharing church news and activities - young to older members.

10. Deeper involvement and loyalty to the mission of the church.

11. Growth and understanding and accountability for how faith impacts health.

12. Increased accountability for health in the broader community.

13. To enable the congregation to see their possibilities and strengths for health.

14. Individuals take more responsibility for behavioral changes and their destiny.

15. Forgiveness and reconciliation is a high priority in relationships and part of the healing process. - The way people relate with each other is as important as the level of pollution, and as important as access to medical care. Spirituality is as fundamental as physical and psychological health.

Parish Nursing is intended to help members accept accountability for their own health, see opportunities for growth, and become motivated for behavioral changes.

## 1999 STATISTICS OF PARISH NURSING

## COMMUNITY CAREGIVING COALITION OF
## GREATER FLAGSTAFF
### Parish Nurse Statistical Report: January - November 1999

Initial Contacts ------------------------------------------------- 286
Follow-up Contacts ------------------------------------------ 1041
Male ------------------------------------------------------------- 300
Female ---------------------------------------------------------- 943
Member --------------------------------------------------------- 831
Nonmember ---------------------------------------------------- 332

LOCATION:
Nurses Office -------------------------------------------------- 220
Hospital -------------------------------------------------------- 122
Home Visits --------------------------------------------------- 172
Phone Visits -------------------------------------------------- 671
Other ----------------------------------------------------------- 160

AGE GROUPS
18 - 30 --------------------------------------------------------- 45
31 - 50 --------------------------------------------------------- 348
51 - 65 --------------------------------------------------------- 172
66 - 80 --------------------------------------------------------- 278
Over 80 -------------------------------------------------------- 173

CONCERNS:
Psychosocial / Spiritual ----------------------------------- 504
Health / Wellness ------------------------------------------- 393
Physiological ------------------------------------------------- 505
Environmental ----------------------------------------------- 298

# Chapter 25: Empowering Nurse Practitioners

AS A GRADUATE family nurse practitioner student at Florida State University, I first learned of this professional organization for nurse practitioners in 1992. I joined as a graduate nursing student and realized that it represented the concerns of all nurse practitioners across the country, and I received the monthly *Journal of the American Academy of Nurse Practitioners*. The mission of the academy was to:

- Serve as a resource for nurse practitioners, their patients and other health care consumers
- Promote excellence in practice, education and research
- Provide legislative leadership
- Advance health policy
- Establish health care standards
- Advocate for access to quality, cost-effective health care
- Offer representation in all Nurse Practitioner professional groups
- Academy Continuing Education Credentialing Program
- Consultation for practice and legislative issues
- Representation on Capitol Hill
- Academy Update
- Home Study

Although I was not able to attend National Conferences each year, I followed the organization through my student membership. While working in a clinic on the Gulf Coast in Florida, I discovered that my family nurse practitioner mentor who I practiced with was a Florida delegate to the organization. Linda attended National

Conferences each year and encouraged me to become active in the academy. I thought this was a good idea to keep current on all the new legislation affecting our practice and educational opportunities. While I was just beginning to understand what nurse practitioners were trained to do, I looked forward to accomplishing all my requirements and finishing my thesis in two or three years. All through graduate school while working on my master's degree, I eagerly read each monthly journal to see what other nurse practitioners were doing and what jobs were offered upon graduation. The journal advertised a variety of positions for nurse practitioners in the country and abroad.

A new focus and camaraderie of experiences developed among the graduate nursing students as we learned new skills and encouraged each other. Where we wanted to work as family nurse practitioners was the topic of most our conversations when we met informally to talk about our program. We were confident that nurse practitioners were unique in practice, important and on the cutting edge of the healthcare system. We knew that this program was a challenge for our new nursing skills and were excited about our prospects. We were empowered as nurse practitioners to practice at our highest level of training, and it was encouraging to know that we were needed and could work anywhere. There were many jobs available in Florida for nurse practitioners and it was just a matter of transferring our license from Florida to any other state we chose to work.

After graduation and moving to Colorado, I met with nurse practitioners in Fort Collins, Colorado, and helped start an advanced practice group with a colleague in Fort Collins in 1995. I enjoyed being a part of this group for the short time I was there. The exchange of information concerning our practice and camaraderie was part of the fun of being a nurse practitioner. We all had similar problems and concerns. Leaving the States in August 1995, a year after graduation, I didn't attend any conferences until I returned in 1998. But I had ordered tapes of the 1997 American Academy Conference sessions on presentations that I was interested in, and I took these with me to Bolivia. I listened to these tapes and used some of the material for my educational presentation on Domestic Violence to groups in Cochabamba, Bolivia. I registered in April while living in Cochabamba for the July 1998 Academy National Conference in Phoenix, Arizona, and left just in time to get there the night before. I had missed the ongoing camaraderie of nurse practitioners in my work, even though I knew that few had the problems that I had encountered abroad in Russia or Bolivia. After three years working abroad without any peers, I looked forward to attending my first National Conference of Nurse Practitioners in Phoenix.

* * *

## 1998 National American Academy of Nurse Practitioner Conference--Phoenix, Arizona

Arriving the night before in Phoenix, Eric picked me up at the airport and I stayed with them in their house in Chandler. It was such a delight to hold my twenty-second grandchild. Naomi was a sweet, curly haired baby girl with dark eyes and six months old. What fun to hold and love her! The first day of my conference, Mayra drove me to the South Pointe Hilton Conference Center. We stopped at Arizona Mills on the way, and I quickly bought some new black leather sandals to wear in this hot climate. She and Naomi dropped me off and I registered for the 1998 American Academy National Conference.

It was a gorgeous hotel with conference facilities, and there were about 2,000 nurse practitioners registered.

This was a drastic change from the poorest country in South America. I picked up my registration packet with a name tag prepared with my name and location, Cochabamba, Bolivia. It was a great conference with excellent presentations and good food. I went to all the presentations that I had marked on my registration and appreciated the variety and depth of the program. A large number of pharmaceutical companies had displays and new products with samples to give out.

Since this was my first conference, this was all new to me. Coming from Bolivia, it all looked so expensive, lavish, and enormously rich. I was impressed with the facilities and abundance of food! The five days of meetings were filled with interesting and challenging sessions and opportunities to catch up on nurse practitioner practice in the States. I thought it was wonderful! It was here that I noticed a lack of emphasis on multicultural health care and was challenged by other nurse practitioners to contribute what I had learned from practicing abroad.

* * *

## 1999 American Academy of Nurse Practitioner National Conference--Atlanta, Georgia

I drove from my home in Flagstaff to Phoenix and spent the night with Eric, Mayra and Naomi. Eric took me to Sky Harbor Airport, and I flew Delta Airlines, compliments of my son Phillip, from Phoenix to Atlanta with trepidation and anxiety, thinking about my first presentation to this large body of peers. Eric had given me a copier-fax machine, and I had stayed up late the night before I left Flagstaff copying a large number of information packets that I planned to have available for nurse practitioners attending my presentation. I was extremely nervous about getting everything right and having enough material to present for my thirty minutes. I had overheads made instead of using PowerPoint on my laptop computer because I didn't feel comfortable with that.

In Atlanta, I took the airport shuttle to the downtown Hilton Hotel and unpacked and settled in my room. It was a beautiful hotel with hundreds of nurse practitioners milling about the lobby and registering. I picked up my registration packet with my nametag marked with a special white ribbon identifying me as part of the faculty for the 1999 American Academy of Nurse Practitioner National Conference. That sounded a little more prestigious than I felt.

I had tried to look through my presentation papers on Multicultural Health Care on the plane, but didn't feel prepared yet. After checking in, I went through my presentation again in my room and organized my overheads and copies. I bought a new soft, foam-green traveling suit with pants and jacket in Flagstaff to wear at the conference. It was comfortable and a good color for me. Now all I needed was a good night's sleep and a clear mind in the morning for my podium presentation before a large group of my peers. When I went to bed that night I wondered why I had sent in my abstract and regretted putting myself through this anxiety. I felt entirely inadequate for this new professional challenge.

I felt renewed and eager to the next morning. I dressed and went down to the main floor of the Hilton where our conference rooms were located. It covered a large area with many rooms reserved for scheduled presentations each hour throughout the morning and afternoon. I was scheduled on the brochure for afternoon and could attend many other sessions before and after my own. I scoped out my presentation room and examined all the equipment that I planned to use to see if it was working properly. It was all well prepared for each nurse practitioner or doctor scheduled to present.

I was especially glad that no one was taking my blood pressure while I waited to begin. A nurse practitioner that was a member of the Academy Executive Committee, introduced me to those attending my session and gave a short introduction of my education, personal qualifications, and work experiences, then took a seat at the back of the room to evaluate my performance. As the conference room filled, there were two familiar faces from my graduate program in Tallahassee, Florida and they had huge smiles of encouragement for me. I knew the session was being taped and the tapes were made available throughout the conference and could be ordered through the academy's monthly journal in the future.

The presentation went well, but I started before the tape recorder was set. There was adequate time for questions at the conclusion which I had planned for. I visited with my friends from Tallahassee and we exchanged news on others who had been in our graduate program. Many of the family nurse practitioners were still practicing in Tallahassee or other cities on the Florida Coast. The editor with *ADVANCE for Nurse Practitioners* magazine, Michelle Perron Pronsati, stopped to visit with me and gave me her card. She asked if I would write an article on the subject of Multicultural Health Care for the 2000 May issue of their magazine. She was friendly and interested in my subject, but I thought at the time that I was so glad to get through this, I was not going to commit myself to do this again. I put her card in my briefcase and forgot about it for a long time. Later in the mail, I received an excellent evaluation of my first presentation at a National Nurse Practitioner Conference.

* * *

## Article Invitation for May 2000 *ADVANCE for Nurse Practitioners Magazine*

I received an email from Michelle asking me about an article for the magazine and decided that I would try my hand at writing an article for publication. I had published an article for *Nurse Practitioner News* when I was in Graduate School. My first professional presentation at the Academy Conference had built up my confidence. After my trip to Milan, Italy with Philip in August and my recovery from kidney stones, I wrote the article the editor wanted. I sent this in to the *ADVANCE for Nurse Practitioners* magazine. It was published and came out in their May 2000 issue. The published article was well presented with pictures and graphs and looked good to me.

\* \* \*

## 2000 American Academy of Nurse Practitioner National Conference--Washington D.C.

I was encouraged to send in another abstract for the 2000 conference to present in Washington, D.C., and it was accepted. I already had my presentation from last year, so the stress of preparation and the podium presentation was minimal. I had been there before and knew what to expect at the Academy National Conference. It is amazing how just taking away the fear of the unknown can boost your confidence. I also made the decision to retire from parish nursing in Flagstaff where I had worked for the past year and a half. I planned to attend the special July 4th, 2000, American Academy of Nurse Practitioner National Conference in Washington. Then I would fly to Tbilisi, Georgia, in the former Soviet Union and work three months with the Christian schools where I had worked in 1995 and 1996.

After driving from my home in Flagstaff to Phoenix, I stayed with Eric and Mayra and Naomi, and Eric drove me to Sky Harbor Airport again. I flew Delta Airlines, compliments of my son Phillip, to Washington, D.C., in June for the National Conference. I met other nurse practitioners on the airport shuttle to the Hilton Hotel. It was a beautiful hotel, and I received my registration packet with my special white ribbon Conference Faculty name tag as I had last year. I was a seasoned member now. I enjoyed the other presentations that day, and the poster presentations were especially well presented. There were posters on Transcultural Education and Nursing that were well planned and challenging. I was delighted to see other presentations on Cross Cultural Nursing. It was beginning to take an important place at the national conference.

I was scheduled to present at the first session in my conference room the next morning. I arrived early and found everything ready. Hotel waiters asked me if there was anything else that I needed. I was wearing a small microphone and the chairs, tables, drinks, podium, overhead, screen, and projector were all ready if I needed them. This was the first time that I had been the first presenter scheduled for the first day in the conference room, and I felt confident. I had brought copies of my materials and my published article in *ADVANCE* magazine to hand out. I also left one copy at the business and copying center at the Hilton if I ran out and other participants wanted to make their own copies.

My presentation went well and the room was full. In the beginning I forgot to talk into the microphone but realized my mistake and corrected it quickly. I ran out of copies to hand out and informed others to check the Business Center if they wanted to make their own. The question and answer time went well, but we ran out of time. There were still raised hands with nurse practitioners who had questions. I was thrilled to see so much interest. After it ended, several nurse practitioners came to me with questions. Some questions were about working abroad and some questions were on the role of the parish nurse. There were other nurse practitioners interested in becoming parish nurses. I realized that parish nursing was a whole different presentation. Later, I received my evaluation in the mail and was very pleased with this second presentation at our National Conference.

I had always wanted to attend an International Conference of Nurse Practitioners, and Sarah and Lata were living in San Diego where the next conference was to be held in September of 2000. I thought this was a good time to go and that I could stay with them and have a chance to visit. I submitted my abstract on Multicultural Healthcare for the 2000 International Conference in October 1999. It was accepted for presentation in San Diego, California at the end of September and first few days of October 2000. Sarah and Lata had since moved from San Diego to Missouri at Christmas in 1999, so I would not be able to stay with them. I was happy for their move, but disappointed that I wouldn't see them in San Diego. A nurse practitioner friend of mine working in Quito, Ecuador, where I had visited her jungle site in 1995, planned to meet me in San Diego at this conference. I planned my return from Tbilisi, Georgia in the former Soviet Union the night before the conference started. I didn't want to take my briefcase and all my papers with me to Tbilisi, so I left them with Grace who lived just two hours from San Diego in Running Springs, California. She planned to send them to me at the Princess Hotel Resort and Conference Center or meet me there for the International Conference.

* * *

618                           PHYLLIS EVANS LONG

## Article for May 2001 *ADVANCE for Nurse Practitioners* Magazine

I checked with the editor of *ADVANCE for Nurse Practitioners* who I had met at the 1999 Academy conference in Atlanta, and she was interested in another article. I had met other nurse practitioners in the military at the 2000 Academy Conference in Washington, and thought the position as Medical Officer in the American Embassy in Tbilisi, Georgia, was unique and extremely interesting for nurse practitioner readers. Finished with my parish nursing position and no professional commitments until the end of September for the International Conference in San Diego, I had time to do more writing. I knew the medical officer at the American Embassy was a nurse practitioner as it had been in 1995 while I was living in Tbilisi. I had met with the family nurse practitioner at the Embassy during that time and knew a little about the demanding work that she did.

I arrived in Tbilisi, Georgia, during the school vacation in July 2000. I called the Embassy to introduce myself and set up an appointment to meet the current family nurse practitioner, Susan Summers. I admired her hard work and tenacity in her position. She asked if I could meet her at a healthcare meeting at Metechi Hotel. I had never been to this beautiful and expensive hotel, but took a taxi.

After the meeting we visited about Tbilisi and arranged for a time when I could interview her for an article for the magazine *ADVANCE for Nurse Practitioners*. Susan received the nursing magazine at her office and was familiar with it also. I asked if I could write up an interview with her on the Nurse Practitioner position in the Foreign Service. Although extremely busy, Susan consented and we scheduled another meeting in her office at the American Embassy. Susan and I shared many experiences and I wrote up the article for the magazine. The editor said she liked my article and wanted to use it for their May 2001 issue of the *ADVANCE* nursing magazine. It was titled "The Path Less Traveled" as a career option for nurse practitioners. Susan and I met for lunch and talked about health care work in Tbilisi. I became busy with my English teaching and Bible studies at the Christian School and Susan traveled to other countries out of Tbilisi many times for meetings and conferences.

\* \* \*

## ABSTRACT ON MULTICULTURAL HEALTH CARE FOR ACADEMY NATIONAL CONFERENCE PRESENTATION JUNE 1999 AND JUNE 2000

### MULTICULTURAL HEALTHCARE

Phyllis E. Long, RN, MSN, ARNP

**Purpose:** To encourage nurse practitioners to develop cultural insight and have a deeper appreciation and respect for the rights of culturally diverse individuals in order to provide optimal care for all clients.

Are all cultures equal? We as health care providers know that the population and culture of the United States is becoming more diverse. We may have already faced the challenge in our practice and felt a little uncomfortable or inadequate. All cultures are equal and communication is the key to quality of care. Miscommunication and cultural insensitivity can result in providing inferior health care, low patient satisfaction, and stressed and inflexible health care providers. Culture is a very important determinant in the United States that significantly impacts a consumer's health care decision-making process. Cultural awareness and good communication by nurse practitioners allows delivery of holistic client care that emphasizes the interrelationships among person, environment (culture) and health.

**Implications for Nurse Practitioners:** An individual's interpretation or perception of health and illness is most often determined by culture and ethnicity. The implication for nurse practitioners working with a multicultural population is to use culturally safe practices. Possibilities for miscommunication, misinterpretation of non-verbal behaviors, misdiagnosis, danger signals being overlooked, and inaccurate assessments are real. If we consider the cultural challenge, nurse practitioners can develop cultural insight, have a deeper appreciation and respect for the rights of culturally diverse individuals, and have increased client satisfaction.

\* \* \*

## ADVANCE NEWS MAGAZINE ARTICLE PUBLISHED
## MAY 2000
## MULTICULTURAL CARE
### Meeting the Challenge

The population and the culture of the United States are becoming more diverse. We as health care providers realize that in order to provide optimal care for all clients, we must develop cultural insight and have a deeper appreciation and respect for the rights of culturally diverse individuals. How we approach this challenge of cross-cultural or multicultural care can affect our bottom line.

In what ways is the U. S. population changing?
- In the year 2000, ethnic minorities will represent 25 percent of the population. Depending on where we practice, it could be much higher.
- 14 percent of the U.S. population today speak a language other than English.
- Increased worldwide travel can bring clients from Moscow or Bangkok any day.
- Global business produces global clients from local corporations in our cities.
- 40 - 50 million tourists visit the U.S. each year.
- Five million came to the Grand Canyon in 1998

Our goal is to provide health care that is culturally acceptable, as well as effective and economical. In order to accomplish this cultural sensitivity is an important priority. What is cultural sensitivity?
1. Possessing a self-understanding and awareness of one's own culture
2. Having skills to identify and appreciate cultural differences
3. Having empathy and tolerance for differing cultural values
4. Interacting with perception and insight with a culture other than one's own
5. Having a worldview of culture
6. Perceiving a shared human experience with those of another culture
7. Having an inside view of culture

What are the main strategies in helping Nurse Practitioners in becoming more culturally sensitive?
1. Recognize that all cultures are equal and deserve equal quality of care that can only be achieved by

good communication. Place of birth, length of stay in the U.S., and first language should be included in a cultural assessment.

2. Good communication can mean getting a good translator, winning consensus in a family or group, being open minded, being flexible, and explaining clearly. It is our responsibility to communicate clearly in order to achieve optimal care for the client.

3. Recognize the difference between generalizations and stereotyping. You are treating individuals within different cultures that will not fit your general conceptions. Recognize that there is cultural diversity within ethnic groups.

4. Realize that culture and ethnicity often determines the clients' perception of health and illness. Be aware of and value the cultural diversity in your own background.

5. Use culturally safe practices: be sensitive and aware of non-verbal behaviors. Misdiagnosis resulting from inaccurate assessments or danger signals being overlooked, are real possibilities.

What are the qualities of an effective cross-cultural communicator? Respect, friendliness, patience, sincerity, acceptance, appreciation, personal flexibility, sense of humor, tolerance for ambiguity, and the ability to recognize your similarities, are a basis for developing communication.

Working in many countries, I was accustomed to the need for cultural sensitivity for other populations. In August of this year, I found myself in a situation where I was the recipient of medical care in a foreign country, alone with no translator, and very ill. I was taken by ambulance to a hospital near my hotel in Milan, Italy, with acute right lower quadrant pain, sweating, nausea and vomiting. Not speaking Italian, I could not adequately explain my problem. An interpreter in ER was found, x-rays diagnosed kidney stones, and I was put on IV pain medication, and taken to a room. I shared my room with two other Italian women. No one on the floor spoke English, so I asked in Spanish if one of my roommates spoke Spanish. One women turned out to be Peruvian and responded, so I was able to communicate in Spanish with her and she spoke to the nurses and urologist for me. I felt so powerless and isolated until I could communicate my needs. I realized how foreigners feel in our healthcare system without English. But through the Peruvian interpreter, I received excellent care and even found where they had put my clothes, located the bathroom, towels and soap, and the coke machine. She had a deck of cards and I taught her how to play gin rummy and we became friends. Until we suffer cultural isolation, we can only guess at the extent that our clients do. But becoming aware can be learned and cultural sensitivity is needed in our practice.

If we can face this challenge with courage and cultural insight, we can develop deeper appreciation and respect for those for whom we see in our practice. An increased client satisfaction, better relationships in the community, increased job satisfaction, and a broader scope of practice, are benefits that demonstrate the skills that reflect our training as Nurse Practitioners. Other considerations include quality of care, holding clients in a competitive marketplace, and positioning our office in the community as a friendly and welcome practice. We can accept the challenge, which is within our control, by becoming culturally aware and stay on the cutting edge as health care providers.

* * *

## INTERNATIONAL NURSE PRACTITIONER
## CONFERENCE PRESENTATION SEPTEMBER 2000

## MULTICULTURAL CARE
## INTRODUCTION AND OPENING IN SWAHILI

Jambo, habari gani? Muzuri sana, ndo? Jin a langu ni Phyllis Long. Nitasema kiswahili kidogo sasa hivi. Unahitajinini? Unahitaji kwenda kukipimo. Naupande kulala kumeza, tafazali. Na inalazima kutia mufiniko huyu kufumia kati kati ya. Kuenda kukipimo labdo ba do. Nitakupima sasa hivi. Unamimba? Bei gani watu watoto wangu? Ungali unakamata dawa? Gani kinini? Unasika kizungu zungu? Are you having diarrhea? Unamizuwa wapi? Una uma ndani. Bei gani kinini? Utapima amu leo? Silazima kupata sindano. Sikuenda jkusema tena labda tunahitaji kuvumil ana. Unasema kingreza labda hapana kiswahili. Ninasema kidogo kiswahili. Kumbe. Iko tabu! Musisahau! Na kwaheri.

Now, how do you feel? Lost. Confused. Powerless. Stupid. Angry. Resentful?

Possibly intimidated and inferior, because you didn't understand? If everyone else spoke this language, but you, you probably would feel this way. This was a normal conversation that you might hear with a patient in the clinic or hospital in the Congo in Africa.

What would you do or say if there was no one to tell you in your language?

I think that you get the picture of what possibilities there are for miscommunication and misunderstandings within the health care system for ethnic minorities that have no understanding or very little understanding of the language and culture in which they now live.

Last August I was in Italy. Going on a vacation to Milan I didn't expect to end up going to the Emergency Room by ambulance, with acute, right lower quadrant pain, sweating, nausea and vomiting. I was alone, knew no one, and knew no Italian and desperately tried, but just could not communicate how very ill I was. An English-speaking interpreter in the ER assisted me in communicating with the health care team, and x-rays led to a diagnosis of kidney stones. I felt lost, confused, and angry. I was not an easy patient. It was definitely an education in knowing what non-English speaking patients in our hospitals experience.

Since we all speak English here, let's create two different groups and make them feel different. Would the blue-eyed people please stand?

I will address all my questions to you, and you need to be prepared to answer them respectfully.

What would you say if a health care provider said to you --- "Your appointment was at 1:00 p.m. and it is now 2:00 p.m. Do you expect to be seen?

How would you feel? Stupid? Resentful?

Or if someone in the hospital or clinic makes the remark : "Why are you blue-eyed people always shaking your heads yes and never do what we say here?"

How would you feel? Intimidated, powerless?

(You may sit down)

Or a health care provider says: "Don't tell me that another family member has died. When you make an appointment, you are expected to keep it."

How would you feel? Resentful, hurt?

What about this scenario: You've just had a morning appt. and are waiting for paperwork or test results. And a nurse says to you: "The clinic is closed over the lunch hour, come back before 5:00 p.m. If we don't get to you, come back in the morning."

How would you feel about making another trip from 80 miles or so without a car on public transportation? This might be the situation in another healthcare setting.

**"All you blue eyed people have a health problem, and because you are different, you have to find someone else to speak for you.

Males need to find a female.

Females need to find a male.

How would you feel about being powerless to speak for yourself?

This is how people feel who cannot speak the same language and explain their health problems.

The issues here are:

- Language
- Time
- Noncompliance
- Transportation and Resources

These are just some of the areas where differences exist as the basis for miscommunication.

My interest and twenty years' experience in multicultural health care comes from being a health care provider in over eight countries where I have lived or visited and worked.

Connecting with your client and with people on a very basic level of health care for them and their families is very rewarding, challenging, and you know when you have been culturally competent.

\* \* \*

## ADVANCE NEWS MAGAZINE ARTICLE PUBLISHED
## MAY 2001

## "THE PATH LESS TRAVELED"

## FROM ABROAD - THE PATH LESS TRAVELLED

Short, blonde, vivacious, conversant in Russian, dressed in a bright orange Moroccan outfit; at home in Moscow, Tokyo, Morocco or Tbilisi, Georgia in the Caucasus, Susan Summers, MN, ARNP, CNP, and I made instant rapport when we first met at the Metechi Sheraton Hotel overlooking Tbilisi, then walked along the streets of Tbilisi, Georgia, from her American Embassy office, where she is Medical Attaché for the Embassy Community. We walked to her tailor in this Old World City of one million, situated between the Black Sea and the Caspian Sea, along what is known as the Silk Road. She explained that she had purchased a travelling suit in Tokyo for $1,000 at a very good price, and now had her tailor here make a copy of it for her. Warmly greeted in Russian by the local shopkeepers, she explained her tailoring needs in Russian and tried on and examined the work that had been done for her. As we sipped on cups of Coca Cola together, she made jokes with all the seamstresses and had the approving eye of the gentlemen who were happy to do business with her. The women in the shop were sewing on foot operated treadmill Singers, vintage 1935. Susan and I exchanged information on Family Nurse Practitioner Graduate Programs, work experience and how she got here to this former Soviet country as a Foreign Service Nurse Practitioner.

The special camaraderie we experienced is typical of many Nurse Practitioners who work abroad. My arrival in Tbilisi, Georgia, straight from the American Academy National Conference in Washington, D.C., in June, reminded me of the divers and challenging roles of the Nurse Practitioner. Susan and I swapped stories of the special challenges of working in foreign countries. Since my own background and work experience is in Multicultural Health Care, I found that we had much in common. We both realized the cultural challenges of working abroad in healthcare and the need to keep perspective and professionally current, often in professionally isolated situations in foreign countries. Although Susan communicated very well in Russian, she had felt professionally isolated until a fellow nurse had arrived with USAID.

Around 1978, there were Community Health Nurses, BSN's working in the Foreign Service who were asked to return to the university to do a Nurse Practitioner Certificate course at California State College at San Diego, in order to keep their jobs. Later in the '80s, Nurse Practitioners became masters prepared and some Physician Assistants were accepted into the Foreign Service. They are all referred to as Health Practitioners. Susan states that Foreign Service Nurse Practitioners are the only federally funded noncommissioned Health Professionals. Susan reports to an administrative officer here and to a Medical Officer in Frankfurt, Germany. She also clears some protocol issues with the Director of Health Care Practitioners in Washington, D.C.

Before coming to the Foreign Service, Susan had a varied background as an FNP working with a medium security male population in the State Prison System, a Drug Addiction Center and five years with the homeless population in Seattle, Washington. Susan is an undergraduate of the University of New Mexico and graduate of the University of Washington Nurse Practitioner Graduate Program. Now 12 years in the Foreign Service, she has found her niche and loves her job.

Susan arrived in Tbilisi, Georgia, in August 1999, from Morocco, where she had the Regional Office for Algeria, Tunisia and Malta, which required her to visit these areas regularly. She also enjoyed a visit from the First Lady while she was in Morocco. She had arrived in Africa just seven days before the Embassy bombings in Nairobi, Kenya, where she lost a good friend. Before Morocco, she was based in Tokyo and the Regional Office for all of Japan and Vladivostok, an East Russian Seaport. In Tokyo, coming upon a friend in cardiac arrest on the squash court unable to be revived with CPR , was a great loss for her there. While based in Moscow in 1989, her Region was Moscow and Leningrad. Now based in Tbilisi, she travels to Baku, Azerbaijan and Yerevan, Armenia. She states that 20 percent of her job involves travel and much more is administrative work.

Since her job is the healthcare of the American Embassy personnel, she doesn't see a lot of patients in her clinical setting. The demands of her position requires her to be on call seven days a week, 24 hours a day, and she will take patients into her house after hours or on weekends when necessary. She keeps a small infirmary in her home, as do most Nurse Practitioners in the Foreign Service. Although having patients in her home may be rare, Susan states that she would rather have them in her home than go to her office. She keeps a bag packed with basic medical supplies including a trauma kit with sterile IV set up, suturing supplies, and medicines. She practices telemedicine with the U.S. Military in Germany, using her digital camera to send pictures and also x-rays.

When asked "What are the greatest challenges for you as a Foreign Service Nurse Practitioner?" Susan states, "The hardest to face are the lack of adequate medical equipment in the local medical facilities for trauma crises and injury, and the different perspective of a more fatalistic outlook versus crises interventions that exist with the Health Care Professionals in developing countries. Also to maintain boundaries - they are not possible here. Your patients are your friends, so you manipulate boundaries in order to be professional and friendly at the same time. Honesty and integrity is the key in relationships."

In her medical practice, she sees the usual common problems and does a lot of health education. She likes most the variety and independence of her profession. Living in a small country, sixty miles from the Chechnya border, with the Caucasus Mountain passes open, and no barriers from outside invasion, plus the economic collapse that Georgia is now experiencing, fear and anxiety are common symptoms among patients. As a friend and Healthcare Professional, she must meet the needs that accompany these conditions. Susan also states that professional isolation is the biggest problem for her personally.

In Tbilisi with her family, a husband and 6-year-old daughter, she networks with many international and U. S. organizations, and is a natural health leader and negotiator for this developing country. As a Family Nurse Practitioner, along with her Embassy position, she has the knowledge and professional perspective needed to bring improved healthcare for those lacking resources and neglected by their government, working with USAID and Counterpart International, a Humanitarian Assistance Program. She is an invaluable part of a team seeking to improve access to medicines and healthcare services in Tbilisi. With only an American community of 300, Tbilisi has a fast growing consumer population for western commodities and ideas, though the average Georgian makes very little. Tourism is coming, McDonalds and Baskin Robbins have arrived and the Marriott is building on Rustaveli, the main avenue of Tbilisi. There is one English bookstore and an English daily newspaper. There are no nursing schools, but the Georgian

Nurses Association has a plan to start one and is looking for interested persons, states Susan.

But Tbilisi is not an easy place to live. Georgian and Russian are the main languages spoken and both very difficult to learn. English is taught in the schools and the city has many more English speakers than in 1995 when I first lived and worked here. Water and electricity services can be sporadic, traffic dangerous and the mosquitoes treacherous in July. Bottled water has arrived and some western style public bathrooms. A gracious and friendly people are not provided for by their highly corrupt and slow to change old style communist government. A recent Wall Street Journal quotes Georgia as having an average cost of 8 percent of the annual revenue of their economy paid out in bribes. The people do not look for any better living conditions to happen very soon or changes in government.

The Foreign Service Nurse Practitioner can readily practice all the disease prevention, health promotion, and basic health care for which she has been quite adequately trained in this very needy country. Susan reports that there were 39 cases of reported malaria in 1999 in Tbilisi. The Director of the National Center for Disease Control states that there were 47 cases of malaria as of July 2000 this year. Although she delivers healthcare to Americans, she has been active in volunteer work in the communities where she has lived and won two Volunteer Awards for both Asia and North Africa. The American Embassy Community is happy to have a knowledgeable health care professional that can diagnose and treat their health problems, or refer them to specialists. In a strange and unfamiliar environment, they trust her judgement and experience in the American healthcare system, while she serves as a bridge to living and adapting to a new culture. And she can serve as mentor and teacher to Georgian health professionals.

When asked what advice she would give anyone interested in the Foreign Service, Susan stated, "You really need some experience. There is no one out here as mentor or peer."

Interested applicants should call Rita Torchia, Human Resources Officer, and Office of Medical Services, Department of State. 202 -663 - 1746.

PHYLLIS E. LONG, RN, BSN, MSN, FNP from Tbilisi, Georgia, in the Caucasus

A shortened version of this article appeared in the *ADVANCE for Nurse Practitioner Magazine*.

# EPILOGUE

**SINCE LEAVING MY JOB** as parish nurse and profession as family nurse practitioner, life has been filled with more travel, writing, and visiting children and grandchildren. Family reunions are a regular function whether we gather in Arizona, California, Illinois, Kansas, Oklahoma, or Missouri. I keep in closer touch with brothers and sisters, children and grandchildren, and friends around the world. Reading and writing, swimming, jogging, tennis, and golf compete for my attention when I'm at home, which isn't often.

There are continuing wars and conflicts in places where I have lived and worked, with life growing more desperate for the poor, which I did not think was possible. It has occurred to me that at one time I have lived in countries that fed, housed, and reared the most evil men in our 20th Century: Germany the home of Hitler, and Georgia in the former Soviet Union, the home of Stalin. I also lived in Baby Doc's Haiti and Mobutu's Zaire, minor players on the world stage of evil men. Millions have been killed in Rwanda, Zaire, (now the Republic of Congo) and Haiti. I know that our only hope is in Christ, who is our peace.

Inauguration Day of 2001 was a privilege for me to witness on television. I was happy to be in this country and proud to be a part of this nation. After living under the dictatorial regimes of Haiti and Africa and literally fleeing with the children, and living in the former communist regime of Georgia, I don't take my freedom for granted. I know the value of my passport and citizenship and the privileges they entail. I remember the feelings of relief when I entered customs at Miami Airport, Chicago, or JFK. I have returned to law and order, safe from unpredictable, tyrannical governments enforced with machine guns. With all the weakness and failures of our government, I am so grateful to be an American. Courage and compassion are valued, the majority vote is accepted, and open discussion and criticism is our birthright as citizens. Praise God for those who designed its basic structure that still works.

Our country and our family survived the horrifying events of September 11, 2001. With two sons as commercial pilots, one with American Airlines and one with Delta Airlines closely involved that day, I experienced the horror and fear, grief and devastation of terrorism and war with all Americans firsthand in our own country. No one will forget; we are forever changed.

The world is not permanent, ever changing, and full of human suffering. But God's grace and mercy and love never changes, continuing steadfast and sure and available for each of us. The mystery of our physical birth into this world sets the stage for our choosing. Our lives show the goodness of God through human suffering. God has never failed me through all the events and wars of history during my lifetime, or my own personal struggles with sorrow and suffering, and He will be with me through death until I am with Him forever. Only by His grace have I found the sure knowledge of Jesus Christ, which nothing can shake. Redeeming love triumphs through adversity and loss, even in death.

Long Family Reunion

# A Special Thanks

We would like to record our deepest gratitude to the three individuals of our "85th birthday book project team" who helped create this book from a rough 200,000 word manuscript in less than 90 days. In late October the floppy discs containing the manuscript were discovered, and by late January the book was completed, just in time for the 85th birthday celebration.

- Thank you to Wendy Garfinkle who suddenly dedicated a week between Thanksgiving and Christmas 2019 to formatting this entire project for upload to the Amazon KDP platform.
- Thank you to Aaron Smith, aka Cultural Savage, who not only designed and created the book cover art, but also handled every detail of uploading files to the KDP platform shepherding creation of the actual printed books.
- Thank you above all to Leanne Sype, the very kind and capable editor who dropped everything as the holiday season rapidly approached to embrace the gargantuan task of editing the entire manuscript (often from before dawn to well after dusk) during four intense weeks, while constantly engaging with the content, solving manuscript issues, and creating the chapter breaks with chapter titles from meaningful "found phrases" she discovered within the text. Additionally, her experience and expertise in publishing has eagerly embraced guiding many other aspects of this project. Appreciation overflows.

The eager effort and capable enthusiasm each of these individuals have given to this project is what transformed this sudden wild impulse of a project into something very special for our family.

Made in the USA
Middletown, DE
17 October 2021

50469045R00356